285

THE
CIVILIZATION
OF THE
RENAISSANCE
IN ITALY

VOLUME I

TEMPLA DOMVM EXPOSITIS.VICOS.FORA MOENIA PONTES:
VIRGINEAM TRIVII QVOD REPARARIS AQVAM.
PRISCA LICET NAVTIS STATVAS DARE COMMODA PORTVS:
ET VATICANVM CINGERE SIXTE IVGVM.
PLVS TAMEN VRBS DEBET:NAM QVAE SQVALORE LATEBAT:
CERNITVR IN CELEBRI BIBLIOTHECA LOCO.

RECEPTION OF THE HUMANIST PLATINA BY SIXTUS IV
By Melozzo da Forli
Vatican, Rome

THE CIVILIZATION OF THE RENAISSANCE IN ITALY

VOLUME I

JACOB BURCKHARDT

INTRODUCTION BY
BENJAMIN NELSON AND CHARLES TRINKAUS

HARPER COLOPHON BOOKS
Harper & Row, Publishers
New York, Hagerstown, San Francisco, London

This edition of *The Civilization of the Renaissance* was
first published in the United States by Harper & Row,
Publishers, Incorporated in 1929.

First HARPER TORCHBOOK edition published 1958

Translator's Note

This translation is made from the fifteenth edition of the German original,
with slight additions to the text and large additions to the notes by Dr. Ludwig
Geiger and Professor Walther Götz.

In a few cases where Dr. Geiger's and Professor Götz's views differ from
those taken by Dr. Burckhardt I have called attention to the fact by bracket-
ing their opinions and adding their initials.

The illustrations in the present edition appear for the first time in an
English translation of this work. Previous English editions have not been
illustrated. It is hoped that the illustrations will be found to be a valuable
adjunct to the text.

S. G. C. MIDDLEMORE

Library of Congress catalog card number: 58-10149 - Vol. I

83 84   30 29 28 27 26 25

CONTENTS

CONTENTS

ILLUSTRATIONS

ILLUSTRATIONS

ILLUSTRATIONS

ILLUSTRATIONS

ILLUSTRATIONS

THE CIVILIZATION OF THE RENAISSANCE IN ITALY

VOLUME I

INTRODUCTION TO
THE TORCHBOOK EDITION

We are not . . . privy to the purposes of eternal wisdom: they are beyond our ken. This [Hegel's] bold assumption of a world plan leads to fallacies because it starts out from false premises. . . .

We, however, shall start out from the one point accessible to us, the one eternal center of all things—man suffering, striving, doing, as he is and was and ever shall be.

—Jacob Burckhardt, Introduction to
Reflections on History

I

When, nearly a century ago, Jacob Burckhardt first published his *The Civilization of the Renaissance in Italy*,[1] he could hardly have foreseen that this study, which he introduced so modestly and called an essay, would become the decisive interpretation of a great period in history. Even less could he have guessed that every important future historian of the Renaissance would attempt either to sharpen or to obliterate the image that Burckhardt had created. Rarely has an historical work had so persistent an influence. Indeed, the very notion that a new and unique civilization called "The Renaissance" existed in Italy in the fourteenth, fifteenth, and sixteenth centuries seems to stand or fall with one's acceptance or rejection of the Burckhardtian image. To be sure, this conception of the period did not emerge full-fledged from the head of Burckhardt unconnected with and unaffected by earlier interpretations. Nor is it without certain omissions and weaknesses that must be taken into account.

Burckhardt would not have been offended by latter-day suggestions that he had not done full justice to the many-faceted civilization which he had studied

<hr>

[1] *The notes to this introduction follow p. 278.*

with such affection and care, for he viewed his own efforts as essentially tentative:

> In the wide ocean upon which we venture, the possible ways and directions are many; and the same studies which have served for this work might easily, in other hands, not only receive a wholly different treatment and application, but lead also to essentially different conclusions. Such, indeed, is the importance of the subject that it still calls for fresh investigation, and may be studied with advantage from the most varied points of view.[2]

In the light of this statement, one may well ask why this book has occasioned so much controversy among its large and notable company of scholarly readers. Some of them have even contended that Burckhardt's Renaissance is more truly a reflection of the ideas and ideals of the author and his age than of the reality he sought to portray. But though it may be granted that many features of mid-nineteenth century civilization still retain their vitality, so many new concerns have since arisen that the continued potency of this great book cannot be explained wholly by the emotional and cultural demands of the 1850's. Whatever the contemporary involvements of historians, these seldom entirely becloud the reality of a period under study. Sometimes, indeed, such involvements may actually help clarify the past.

In the view of the present writers, the central insights in Burckhardt's vision of the Renaissance remain essentially unimpaired. Despite his oversights and errors, his deep cultural and moral commitments, his book exhibits a reality that subsequent scholarship, however reluctantly, has been compelled to affirm.[3] And where the onslaught against the Burckhardtian conception was intended to be total—in the sense of denying that there was a period in the history of European civilization, bounded in time and place, which may fittingly be called the Italian Renaissance—it is demonstrable that what is being repudiated is not so much the historical reality that Burckhardt described as the value he put upon it.[4] Leaving aside those moral and intellectual attempts to revise the Burckhardtian image that have collapsed under the weight of their own exaggerations,[5] the many endeavors to show the presence of Renaissance qualities in the Middle Ages or of medieval qualities in the Renaissance by seizing upon particular details of Burckhardt's canvass have failed as a rule to consider the design of the whole.[6]

For what concerned Burckhardt was not the parts but the totality of Renaissance civilization. His earlier writings had dealt with medieval art and literature,[7] and he was by no means ignorant of medieval culture or insensitive to its values. A careful reading of *The Civilization of the Renaissance* will show how clearly he recognized the persistence of medieval outlooks and practices in the very period about which he was writing.[8] Nor did he share the naïve belief that the intensified study of classical literature and philosophy in a given age could of itself bring about a new civilization. Rather, he saw the "Revival of Antiquity" as combining with other indigenous elements of Italian culture whose roots were medieval to form the Renaissance:

> With this tendency [to admire antiquity], other elements—the popular character which time had now greatly modified, the political institutions imported by the Lombards from Germany, chivalry and other northern forms of civilization, and the influence of religion and the Church—combined to produce the modern Italian spirit.[9]

Indeed, Burckhardt was so mindful of the continuity of the classical tradition in medieval Europe, and of its special vitality at particular times, that he came close to putting forth the concept of a Carolingian Renaissance, and of a later twelfth-century one:[10]

> The civilization of Greece and Rome . . . had long been exerting a partial influence on medieval Europe, even beyond the boundaries of Italy. The culture of which Charles the Great was a representative was, in face of the barbarism of the seventh and eighth centuries, essentially a Renaissance, and could appear under no other form. Just as in the Romanesque architecture of the North, beside the general outlines inherited from antiquity, remarkable direct imitations of the antique also occur, so too monastic scholarship had not only gradually absorbed an immense mass of materials from the Roman writers, but the style of it, from the days of Eginhard onward, shows traces of conscious imitation.[11]

Burckhardt was, to be sure, unaware of many of the details of both medieval and Renaissance accomplishment in classical studies that have been elaborated and emphasized since the days of Georg Voigt.[12] But what mattered to him—and what matters to us—was how such a single element of the culture entered into the general world-view of the men of the time.

The fact is that Burckhardt presupposed a far greater knowledge of medieval and early modern political, social, and cultural history on the part of the readers of his "essay" than they, or at least some of them, have been willing to concede to him. On hindsight it appears that he was imprudent to make this assumption. He was over-generous, too, in estimating the empathy of his learned readers. Above all, he did not foresee the enormous popularity of his work, which would place it in the hands of so many who could not have known what a learned professor of the University of Basel had to know. He surely sensed, however, that it would have been aesthetically ruinous to preface his interpretation of the Renaissance with an detailed recital of historical facts. Had he done so, his work might have shared the undeserved oblivion that has overtaken many a solid and factually informative production. For English readers, the volumes of Henry Hallam are cases in point.

Burckhardt was attempting to create a portrait of something which he called "national spirit"—and that in a particular, self-contained age. What he achieved was not only a pioneer work of its genre, but a unique example of the study of a historical culture that has rarely, if ever, been surpassed.[13]

The difficulties that have long beset scholars in arriving at a just appraisal of Burckhardt's intention and achievement are largely due to the impatience of historians with what they regard as his flights of imagination and his dubious philosophical commitments. As is often the case in such matters, the positions ascribed to Burckhardt involved little or no reference to the subtle modulations of his book or to the evidence concerning his outlook to be derived from other of his writings. Instead, he was held responsible for every excess committed in his name by vulgarizers of his thought and work.

It is now evident that Burckhardt was far less a Hegelian than some of his interpreters have maintained. But his use of certain Hegelian terms and concepts, though common enough among Europeans of varied philosophical persuasions, has proved uncongenial to many English and American scholars[14] who have strong empirical and even anti-philosophical notions of the proper historian. Ironically, on the other hand, many of the more romantic and mystical of Burckhardt's continental critics have found his usage far too rational and matter-of-fact for their tastes.

As was intimated at the outset, the key to what Burckhardt was trying to get at is in the title of his book—*Die Cultur der Renaissance in Italien*. The translation of *Cultur* into the more inclusive *Civilization* was a response to the fact that Burckhardt's concept of *Geist* and *Cultur* clearly meant something more than the traditionally narrow connotation of the English word "culture," that is, education combined with refinement and acceptable taste in aesthetic matters. At the time the translation was made, British and American historical thought and usage lagged regrettably behind Burckhardt's.

Today the situation is changed. Thanks to recent developments in the study of man, in which, as it happens, British and American scholars have taken the lead, the old barriers to the understanding of Burckhardt's intentions and methods no longer exist. Social scientists and the educated public now regularly use the term "culture" in a different sense. Under the impact of the writings of leading anthropologists and sociologists, "culture" has come to designate the generally shared outlook on life and characteristic modes of responding to situations on the part of a given socially related group of people. The group's institutions, implements, techniques, norms, social and political organizations, its mental and emotional attitudes—all of its so-called "designs for living"—are now expected on close study to reveal a "complex *whole*," as Sir Edward Tyler long ago noted.[15] Or to use the language of Ruth Benedict, more familiar to our ears, these culture elements may be said to exhibit "patterns." To see into the heart of a culture and the personalities who embody and express it, contemporary social scientists deem it necessary, above all, to grasp the basic ways in which most individuals think, feel, and relate to whatever—whether objects, occasions, or persons—they chance to confront. The root patterns of orientation and motivation—what philosophers and psychologists, respectively, like to call the characteristic *subjectivity* and *affectivity* of a given social unit—define the ways in which existing objective factors are approached and adapted.

It was culture in this sense—the sense current among anthropologists today—with which Burckhardt was primarily concerned. If this has not always been apparent, and until recently has escaped the notice of anthropologists, it is because he applied the concept to an urbanized people rather than to a primitive society.[16] Indeed, if long and familiar tradition were not behind the word "civilization," it would be to the point to reissue Burckhardt's work as *The Culture of the Renaissance in Italy*.

With this clarification of Burckhardt's purpose, it is now possible to regard the arrangement and content of his book in a fresh light. Once it is recognized that his primary aim was to depict the characteristic states of mind and underlying motivational patterns of the Italian people during the fourteenth, fifteenth, and sixteenth centuries, he cannot be charged with omitting an adequate account of elements that might properly be included under the term "civilization," but which his own conception of "culture" excluded. Among the chief elements he excluded were an outline of major political events in a chronological and causally connected order; a study of the evolution of economic, political, and ecclesiastic institutions; and an orderly description of intellectual, scientific, professional, and artistic activities and production. All historians require and value such narratives and analyses. Burckhardt drew upon his extensive knowledge of these matters but had no intention of including anything of this sort in his study of the "spirit" and "culture" of the Renaissance.

In his later history of Italian Renaissance architecture, his *Geschichte der Renaissance in Italien*,[17] he produced just such a systematic and "objective" study which even today continues to serve as a handbook. The fundamental strength of the present work, however, lies in the fact that he was not distracted into narrative detail but concentrated on exploring culture as manifested in action, writing, and art. As a consequence, later attempts to create an image of the subjectivity of the Renaissance have been largely unable to break free from his influence.

II

The heart of the Burckhardtian image of the consciousness of the Renaissance is to be found in the opening pages of Part Two, "The Development of the Individual." Whereas the men of the Middle Ages had beyond doubt been "individuals," to Burckhardt's mind they were not particularly conscious of this fact about themselves, nor did they especially value it. "Man was conscious of himself only as a member of a race, people, party, family, or corporation—only through some general category." In Italy, on the other hand, "man became a spiritual *individual* and recognized himself as such." Indissolubly linked with this emergence of a recognition and high evaluation of the individuality of one's self went, according to Burckhardt, a heightened awareness of the separateness of self from the rest of reality so that "an *objective* treatment and consideration of the State and of all things of this world became possible." No such conscious division of experience into subjective and objective existed in the Middle Ages. Then "both sides of human consciousness—that which was turned within as that which was turned without —lay dreaming or half awake beneath a common veil. The veil was woven of faith, illusion, and childish prepossession, through which the world and history were seen clad in strange hues."[18] "The psychological fact itself"[19] that Italians from the time of Dante possessed a double consciousness of themselves as subjective individuals and of the world as something objective and external made them, in Burckhardt's view, "the first-born among the sons of modern Europe."

Burckhardt, it should be noted, does not write "the *only* sons of modern Europe" or "the sires of the European family." The failure to perceive the subtlety of his argument at this point has dogged scholarship since his day. For he was not so much bent on showing that the cultures of modern Europe were to be derived from the Renaissance as on demonstrating that the Renaissance in Italy was itself the first—not the only instance or type—of modern European cultures. It is for this reason, we believe, that he seems to neglect the connections and traditions linking the Renaissance to a medieval past and to offer little to relate Italy to the future of other European nationalities and politics. Historians have, in fact, encountered fundamental difficulties in attempting to develop either a unified conception of a Renaissance period in other European countries or the idea of a European Renaissance itself. The subsequent influence of the Italian Renaissance on the rest of Europe was, perhaps, a piecemeal one—modifying, shaping, but never basically transforming the pre-existing historical lines of development. The "European Renaissance" has thus come to be in effect a rather loose designation for the total history of Europe from 1300 to 1600.[20] The Renaissance in Italy, on the other hand, was to Burckhardt a distinctive culture to be studied and depicted in its actions and its literary and artistic productions as exhibiting this psychological fact of a cherished "all-sided" individuality together with an illusionless objectivity. Nothing concerning the history of Italy in all its phases during the period was to be considered in Burckhardt's book except as illustrations of this fundamental theme, or as explanations or important modifications of it.

This self-contained culture of Renaissance Italy had a beginning and an end, and Burckhardt was as seriously concerned with establishing these temporal boundaries and exploring the distinctive states of soul as he was seemingly indifferent to recording chronological developments in between. It was only in setting forth the conditions that led to the prevalence of a new Italian consciousness and those which account for its demise that Burckhardt assumed the more conventional role of the historian as the student of the problem of change. Even here he is remarkably sparing in his contribution to the problem of historical causation. He is content to emphasize what many, historians would today regard as the "immediate" rather than the "fundamental" cause of the cultural attitudes and social behavior of Italians between 1300 and 1530. The cause which made the Renaissance possible was to Burckhardt the political conditions in Italy at the end of the thirteenth century, conditions which by and large continued until the suppression and domination of the Italian city states and their vigorous civic life by the Spanish Habsburgs during the first half of the sixteenth century. "In the character of these states, whether republics or despotisms, lies not the only, but the chief reason for the early development of the Italian."[21]

Even if a historian were content to minimize economic and social factors and with Burckhardt regard political conditions as the primary cause of Renaissance culture, he would find that here, too, very much is taken for granted. In Part I of his book, "The State as a Work of Art," Burckhardt offers no description or explanation of the constitutional history of the Italian cities. He speaks rather of the bold but calculated pursuit of power by individuals who sought to gain their private ends through the possession of public office, which he sees as unchecked by moral restraint because of the "illegitimacy" of all government. The long struggle between Pope and Emperor which prevented the development of a central power in Italy but allowed innumerable urban authorities to exist by playing the one against the other was followed by the drastic decline of the Emperor's power and the removal of the papal court to Avignon early in the fourteenth century. Spain remained disunited and involved in its long struggle with the Moors; France speedily became engaged in the Hundred Years' War with England, and internally divided as well. The outcome for Italy approximated what today would be called a political vacuum. In this situation of "illegitimacy" the Italian states flourished, fought with one another and were fought over by aspiring tyrants, factions, parties, and social classes. Thus in the briefest fashion Burckhardt provides only what many would consider an obviously partial explanation, and a negative one at best. The freeing of Italy for roughly two centuries from either a native sovereign or any significant interference from without is given as the cause for the remarkable energy that was invested in inner political struggles and individual development.

What Burckhardt is primarily concerned with, of course, are the psychological conditions arising from this political situation, particularly the personal character of the despots and rulers. When he refers to the State as "a Work of Art," he is using the term not in the aesthetic sense of detached love of pure form but to designate that which is deliberately contrived and wrought by individuals as opposed to any unconscious process or "natural" evolution of institutions or styles of life.[22]

> The deliberate adaptation of means to ends, of which no prince out of Italy had at that time a conception, joined to almost absolute power within the limits of the State, produced among the despots both men and modes of life of a peculiar character. . . . The illegitimacy of his rule isolated the tyrant and surrounded him with constant danger; the most honorable alliance which he could form was with intellectual merit, without regard to its origin. The liberality of the northern princes of the thirteenth century was confined to the knights, to the nobility which served and sang. It was otherwise with the Italian despot. With his thirst for fame and his passion for monumental works, it was talent not birth which he needed. In the company of the poet and the scholar he felt himself in a new position—almost, indeed, in possession of a new legitimacy.[23]

Beyond this, Burckhardt offers no explanation, and for most of this section of his book presents a startling array of anecdotes and examples of rulers, great and small, who stopped at nothing in their pursuit of power, of the various provocations to unbridled egotism in both despotisms and republics. It is in this atmosphere of the ever-present struggle for political power that "The Development of the Individual" occurs.

INTRODUCTION

The unrelenting search for "fundamental" causes has led many twentieth-century historians to fix their gaze on economic conditions and forces. Generally accepting Burckhardt's conception of the nature of the Renaissance, they have argued in the main that the spirit of individualism grew out of the practice of economic enterprise by prominent merchants, bankers, and businessmen encouraged by the precocious evolution of "capitalistic" institutions in medieval Italy.[24] It is an interesting historical coincidence that the man whose ideas contributed most to this view of the Renaissance as a "burgher" civilization—Karl Marx—was born in the same year (1818) as Jacob Burckhardt. Although Burckhardt did not regard economic institutions of the same decisive importance in producing the Renaissance, he was by no means unaware of how great a part they played in developing the attitudes and practices of rational calculation, of a quantitative and statistical handling of affairs, of a generally objective treatment of things, especially in the great republics of Florence and Venice.

Twentieth-century researches in the economic developments of Renaissance Italy have profoundly enriched the picture Burckhardt has bequeathed to us and greatly deepened our understanding of the period.[25] Yet we cannot feel that Burckhardt was wrong in placing as much emphasis as he did on the formative political experiences, or in his seeing economic life as only one of the elements conditioning the mode of objective thought, or most importantly in seeing it as the great source of wealth of the Italian cities which enabled their citizens to lavish so much on art, letters, and the amenities of living.[26]

The weight that Burckhardt placed on the social experience of the upper classes of the Italian cities—a conception which moves freely from the necessary political and economic conditions to the essential cultural needs of the population—may be seen when he explains the motivations for "The Revival of Antiquity" and the unprecedented cult of anything classical.

But the great and general enthusiasm of the Italians for classical antiquity did not display itself before the fourteenth century. For this a development of civic life was required, which took place only in Italy, and there not till then. It was needful that noble and burgher should first learn to dwell together on equal terms, and that a social world should arise which felt the want of culture, and had the leisure and the means to obtain it. But culture, as soon as it freed itself from the fantastic bonds of the Middle Ages, could not at once and without help find its way to the understanding of the physical and intellectual world. It needed a guide, and found one in the ancient civilization, with its wealth of truth and knowledge in every spiritual interest. Both the form and substance of this civilization were adopted with admiring gratitude; it became the chief part of the culture of the age.[27]

III

With this observation Burckhardt enters upon an exposition of the revival of antiquity, which was important to him not primarily as a disinterested intellectual achievement but rather as a way by which a certain form was given to the consciousness that the Italians of the Renaissance had of themselves and their period. In thus again emphasizing the underlying state of mind, Burckhardt regards such manifestations of the classical revival as the avid interest in the archaeological remains of Rome and the search for manuscripts of the classics in a fashion that has proved consistent with modern scholarship.

Three points of view have dominated twentieth-century discussions of this issue:

One school has tended to minimize the novelty of the classical studies of the Renaissance in the history of learning, rightly pointing out that medieval scholars (as Burckhardt himself knew) anticipated, and in some ways even excelled, the Italian humanists, and also indicating that the genuinely sound scholarship on which modern philology is based did not come until later.[28] With this view Burckhardt would have had little quarrel since he was not essentially concerned with annals of classical learning:

> The growth of textual criticism which accompanied the advancing study of languages and antiquity belongs as little to the subject of this book as the history of scholarship in general. We are here occupied, not with the learning of the Italians in itself, but with the reproduction of antiquity in literature and life.[29]

A second group of Renaissance scholars has adopted a perspective more in accord with the humanists' enthusiasm concerning themselves. They have gone beyond Burckhardt in stressing the philosophical importance of the humanists as rivals of medieval scholasticism (paradoxically both from contemporary clerical and anti-clerical points of view).[30] A third group, critical of the exaggerations of the second, has produced carefully documented corrective studies emphasizing the professional character of the humanists as continuators—in a period of more complex economic and political organization—of the functions of the medieval scribe.[31] They see humanism as a revival of the ancient Latin rhetorical tradition of the humanities which had also predominated in medieval culture until overshadowed by the rise of the scholastic interest in Graeco-Arabic science and philosophy.[32] Their approach accords well with that of Burckhardt, who stressed the role of the humanists in the life of the time as not only collectors of manuscripts and antiquities and translators from Greek (Part III, ch. ii and iii), but as teachers, epistolographers, public orators and ambassadors, writers of moral treatises, historians, and poets (Part III, ch. v, vii, viii, x)—all in a classical Latin style or mode of thought and directly in the service of princes, aristocrats, burghers, popes, and republics (Part III, ch. vi and ix).[33]

What seems to have concerned Burckhardt most of all was the generation of a new psychological attitude out of the interrelationship of scholar and patron. He speaks of "the natural alliance between the despot and the scholar, each relying solely on his personal talent."[34] In the freer situation of Florence before the domination of the Medici, Burckhardt sees humanists rising to power and influence and prominent citizens devoting their lives to the cultivation of antiquity. In these relationships he sees the humanist developing the same boundless egotism with its values and dangers that he found in the man of position and power:

> Of all men who ever formed a class, they [the humanists] had the least sense of their common interests and least respected what there was of this sense. All means were held lawful, if one of them saw a chance of supplanting another. . . . Not satisfied with refuting, they sought to annihilate an opponent. Something of this must be put to the account of their position and circumstances; we have seen how fiercely the age, whose loudest spokesmen they were, was borne to and fro by the passion for glory and the passion for satire. Their position, too, in practical life was one they had continually to fight for.[35]

The predicament of the precocious and ambitious young man who wished to become a humanist was visualized with extraordinary insight:

> He was thus led to plunge into a life of excitement and vicissitude, in which exhausting studies, tutorships, secretaryships, professorships, offices in princely households, mortal enmities and perils, luxury and beggary, boundless admiration and boundless contempt, followed confusedly one upon the other, and in which the most solid worth and learning were often pushed aside by superficial impudence. But the worst of all was that the position of the humanist was almost incompatible with a fixed home, since it either made frequent changes of dwelling necessary for a

livelihood, or so affected the mind of the individual that he could never be happy for long in one place. . . . Such men can hardly be conceived to exist without an inordinate pride. . . . They are the most striking examples and victims of an unbridled subjectivity.[36]

One of the main reasons why certain modern scholars have been hostile to the Burckhardtian concept of the Renaissance—and even sometimes to the idea that there was an Italian Renaissance at all—is that there exists so little evidence of any direct contribution by the humanists to the development of modern science.[37] It is now clear that the major innovations in science prior to the great advances of the sixteenth and seventeenth centuries occurred within the context of the surviving medieval universities and scholastic studies.[38] Scholasticism developed later in Italy than in the French and English universities, so that its period of significance coincided in time with that of humanism. As humanists gradually were given posts in the universities, they became interdepartmental rivals of the theologians, philosophers, law and medical professors.[39] The important work in medicine, natural philosophy, logic, and metaphysics of the Italian scholastic or university tradition[40] may not, however, be attributed to humanism or to the Renaissance spirit of individualism.

Burckhardt did not concern himself with the universities except to indicate the beginnings of humanistic chairs, a development which he minimized. He was not only aware that the humanists made little contribution to science but he even added that humanistic study attracted to itself the best strength of the nation and thereby no doubt did injury to the inductive investigation of nature.[41] He was also quite aware of his own inadequacies in the history of science.[42] Although he made "The Discovery of the World" a major item in the Renaissance approach to existence, he contented himself with but a few illustrations of his theme: the diffusion through the population of a readiness to view the external world accurately, objectively, and autonomously. He recounted the Italian's interest in geography, journeys, landscapes, plants, animals, and human ethnic types. What concerned him, therefore, was an attitude toward nature, one of broad cultural significance, rather than specific scientific achievements.

Where the humanists encroached more genuinely on the sphere of scholastic philosophy was in the area of ethics and the conception of man's role in life. Many of the humanists set themselves up in opposition to their scholastic rivals on the grounds that the latter were technically and disinterestedly concerned with logic and truth, whereas as students and practitioners of the art of speaking well, the humanists were concerned with persuading and inspiring men to a life of virtue. In this they followed the lead of Petrarch, who at one time said in criticism of Aristotle's *Ethics*, "It is better to will the good than to know the truth."[43] By this stand they supplied themselves with a justification of their classical studies as conducing to a better Christian life.

In their conception of a virtuous life the humanists reflected their own life situation to a high degree and in this respect bear out Burckhardt's emphasis on their subjective individuality. Professionally employed by princes and republics, some of them regarded a life of civic duty as most truly Christian, and were able to draw support for this view from the same *Ethics* of Aristotle, as well as from the *De officiis* of Cicero.[44] But being also in a state of precarious dependence on employment, other humanists emphasized the superior value of a life of literary retirement and inward repose. For this they could find support not only in the monastic tradition but in ancient writers such as the Stoic Seneca.[45] In this realm of moral philosophy they cannot be said to have made systematic contributions of originality or importance, but they again remained true to their rhetorical or ethical emphasis. And what they taught in this sphere does have the significance given them by Burckhardt as revealing and shaping prevailing cultural attitudes and states of mind.

One important phase of the history of philosophy during the Renaissance to which Burckhardt attached exceptional significance was the development by Marsilio Ficino, with encouragement and a subsidy from Cosimo de'Medici, of a Christian theology built upon and reconciled with the writings of Plato and assorted ancient Neoplatonic and mystical texts. Renaissance Neoplatonism unquestionably had a wide and powerful impact on princes, courtiers, scholars, poets, artists, architects, and citizens.[46] Although elaborating a view of the world comprehending both religious and secular activities remarkably parallel to the great syntheses of thirteenth-century scholasticism,[47] it was based primarily on Plato rather than on Aristotle.

Burckhardt saw Italian Neoplatonism as a fusion, essentially modern in outcome, of ancient, medieval, and Renaissance spirituality:

> Echoes of medieval mysticism here flow into one current with Platonic doctrines and with a characteristically modern spirit. One of the most precious fruits of the knowledge of the world and of man here comes to maturity, on whose account alone the Italian Renaissance must be called the leader of modern ages.[48]

He well knew the extent of religious concern in this very worldly period and how the humanists and others sought to reconcile Christianity and the pagan classics. It was his view, however, that in some respects humanism was pagan, and became more and more so as its sphere widened in the fifteenth century. Its representatives, who were already described as the advance guard of an unbridled individualism, display as a rule such a character that even their religion, which is sometimes professed very definitely, becomes a matter of indifference to us.[49]

Burckhardt's suggestion of a Renaissance "paganism" has become a widespread and much exaggerated notion. It has in turn given rise to an opposing school which with equal exaggeration chooses to consider the humanism of the Renaissance as an essentially religious movement.

IV

Despite the distorted views that his too loosely-stated suggestion has engendered, Burckhardt himself suggests the key to understanding in his recognition of the close relationship of "paganism" to individualism. It was the advance of worldly activities themselves and the subjective enthusiasm with which they were pursued, rather than the new religious beliefs, that presented the greatest challenge to the old medieval culture.

Like the great philosopher Hegel, whose views, as he makes clear in the Introduction to *Reflections on History*,[50] he both repudiated and incorporated into his own, Burckhardt saw that every unified historical culture had in its most basic features the seeds of its own destruction. Rare is the scholar who has done justice to Burckhardt's rendering of this part of his story! Italy in the sixteenth century was over-run by foreign armies and lost not only its freedom but the Renaissance culture that it had achieved. But this ruin Burckhardt believes was prepared by the Italians themselves. "It cannot be denied," he writes, "that Italy at the beginning of the sixteenth century found itself in the midst of a grave moral crisis, out of which the best men saw hardly any escape."[51] This crisis was caused by excess of that very individualism he so admired and felt to be the key to Renaissance culture. It should, however, be pointed out that unlike Stendhal or Nietzsche, with whom he had much in common, his admiration for individualism was not unbounded:

If we now attempt to sum up the principle features in the Italian character of that time, as we know it from a study of the life of the upper classes, we shall obtain something like the following result. The fundamental vice of this character was at the same time a condition of its greatness, namely, excessive individualism. The individual first inwardly casts off the authority of a State which, as a fact, is in most cases tyrannical and illegitimate. . . . The sight of victorious egotism in others drives him to defend his own by his own right arm. And while thinking to restore his inward equilibrium, he falls, through the vengeance which he executes, into the hands of the powers of darkness. . . . If, therefore, egotism in its wider as well as narrower sense is the root and fountain of all evil, the more highly developed Italian was for this reason more inclined to wickedness than the members of other nations of that time.[52]

It may be recalled that Burckhardt's indictment included not only the rulers and upper classes of Italy but the humanists and scholars who had been driven by the vicissitudes of life to similar outrages of egotism, corruption, and licentiousness, and that it was this condition which led to the downfall and repudiation of humanism in the sixteenth century presented as the climax of "The Revival of Antiquity." In similar fashion in "The State as a Work of Art" Burckhardt reserves to the end the exposure of corruption in the citadel of holiness: the conditions of the papacy under Alexander VI, Julius II, Leo X, and Clement VII.

It should not be overlooked, however, that Burckhardt did not regard the outcome of the Renaissance, shocking though it was to him, as totally evil. Of the humanists he wrote:

Yet a clear and unmistakable tendency to strictness in matters of religion and morality was alive in many of the philologists, and it is a proof of small knowledge of the period, if the whole class is condemned.[53]

Out of the individualism of the Renaissance there would grow a sense of moral responsibility in modern man:

But this individual development did not come upon him through any fault of his own, but rather through an historical necessity. It did not come upon him alone, but also, and chiefly by means of Italian culture, upon the other nations of Europe, and has constituted since then the higher atmosphere which they breathe. In itself it is neither good nor bad, but necessary; within it has grown up a modern standard of good and evil— a sense of moral responsibility—which is essentially different from that which was familiar to the Middle Ages.[54]

With this utterance Burckhardt's drama of Renaissance man and culture reaches its *dénouement*. The legacy which the Renaissance was to leave to the future was not without ambiguity: it was more a summons to responsibility than a release from restraints. In the end, as Burckhardt conceives it, what the Renaissance bequeathed to man was a burden by the bearing of which alone would come whatever creative renewals and rebirths—whatever

Renaissances—might henceforth issue from the unregenerate mass of men of the looming Age of Iron and Steel which was his own and ours.

V

Jacob Burckhardt must be seen as one of the master philosopher-historians of the nineteenth century. He deserves to be ranked with the company of "earthshakers"—Schopenhauer, Marx, Kierkegaard, and Nietzsche—who turned from the abstractions of Absolute Idealism to the inescapable actualities of existence.[55] It is no wonder, therefore, that Burckhardt is so often mentioned nowadays among the forerunners of contemporary existentialism. Not for him the hollow victories and ultimate reconciliations so easily and inevitably managed by the encompassing dialectic of Hegel. Each individual existence was too vital, each historical contingency too imperious, to be harmonized in a gossamer web of categories. His horror of theodicy masquerading as history was utter, his distaste for apocalyptic politics unalterable, even when the prophet of the faith was so close a friend as Nietzsche. To make of him, as some do, an apostle of pagan indulgence of self or of illimitable progress to perfection is to distort his teachings shamefully.

His whole life through, Burckhardt brooded over the predicaments of self and society, of Western man and culture. If throughout his historical writing he seems disinclined to arrange the facts he knew so well into enchanting stories of human deliverance, it was because he understood that his was a tale not exactly suited to speed the slumber of children as night falls. Remaining ever humble before the fact, he would not so magnify the evidence of design as to obscure the towering importance of lawless will and sheer drift in historical change.

The twentieth-century historians and philosophers of culture with whom Burckhardt may most fittingly be associated are Johan Huizinga and Max Weber. It is of no moment that Huizinga and Weber found flaws in details of Burckhardt's account of the Renaissance. Burckhardt, Huizinga, and Weber are one in their fundamental insights and commitments. Beneath their surfaces, *The Civilization of the Renaissance in Italy*, *The Waning of the Middle Ages*, and *The Protestant Ethic and the Spirit of Capitalism* are variant versions of a common theme:

Western man has irrevocably been cast out—has cast himself out—of a childlike world of enchantment and undividedness. Since the days of his exile (or was it withdrawal?) he has been wandering the world. Wherever he goes he is readily recognized since he bears a burden for everyone to see—

the burden of selfhood. The ego is at once his sign of Cain and his crown of glory.

To seek to put off this burden by whatever device is to wish to reverse the irreversible. Everyman must stumble forward through unending labyrinths without ever finding a quiet haven or journey's end. So to devise as not to be convulsed from within or from without by the fateful heritage of selfhood; so to invest the ambiguous legacy as not to engender spiritual chaos or "mechanical petrification"—these are the grim mandates which were once laid upon the men of the Renaissance and which are now laid upon us who are their heirs.

To read Burckhardt's pages is to look into a mirror.

BENJAMIN NELSON
Hofstra College
CHARLES TRINKAUS
Sarah Lawrence College

New York City
March, 1958

NOTE: The above paper was read to the Columbia University Seminar on The Renaissance on May 6, 1958.

PART I

THE STATE AS A WORK OF ART

CHAPTER I

INTRODUCTION

THIS work bears the title of an essay in the strictest sense of the word. No one is more conscious than the writer with what limited means and strength he has addressed himself to a task so arduous. And even if he could look with greater confidence upon his own researches he would hardly thereby feel more assured of the approval of competent judges. To each eye, perhaps, the outlines of a given civilization present a different picture; and in treating of a civilization which is the mother of our own, and whose influence is still at work among us, it is unavoidable that individual judgment and feeling should tell every moment both on the writer and on the reader. In the wide ocean upon which we venture the possible ways and directions are many; and the same studies which have served for this work might easily, in other hands, not only receive a wholly different treatment and application, but lead also to essentially different conclusions. Such, indeed, is the importance of the subject that it still calls for fresh investigation, and may be studied with advantage from the most varied points of view. Meanwhile we are content if a patient hearing be granted us, and if this book be taken and judged as a whole. It is the most serious difficulty of the history of civilization that a great intellectual process must be broken up into single, and often into what seem arbitrary, categories in order to be in any way intelligible. It was formerly our intention to fill up the gaps in this book by a special work on the art of the Renaissance—an intention, however, which we have been able only to fulfil in part.[1]

The struggle between the Popes and the Hohenstaufen left Italy in a political condition which differed essentially from that of other countries of the West. While in France, Spain, and England the feudal system was so organized that at the close of its existence it was naturally transformed into

---

[1] *History of Architecture*, by Franz Kugler. The first half of the fourth volume, which treats of the architecture and decoration of the Italian Renaissance under the title *History of the Renaissance* (Leipzig, 1868).

a unified monarchy, and while in Germany it helped to maintain, at least outwardly, the unity of the Empire, Italy had shaken it off almost entirely. The Emperors of the fourteenth century, even in the most favourable case, were no longer received and respected as feudal lords, but as possible leaders and supporters of powers already in existence ; while the Papacy,[1] with its creatures and allies, was strong enough to hinder national unity in the future, not strong enough itself to bring about that unity. Between the two lay a multitude of political units—republics and despots—in part of long standing,

FIG. I. THE CASTEL DEL MONTE: STRONGHOLD OF THE HOUSE OF HOHENSTAUFEN

in part of recent origin, whose existence was founded simply on their power to maintain it.[2] In them for the first time we detect the modern political spirit of Europe, surrendered freely to its own instincts, often displaying the worst features of an unbridled egoism, outraging every right, and killing every germ of a healthier culture. But wherever this vicious tendency is overcome or in any way compensated a new fact appears in history—the State as the outcome of reflection and calculation, the State as a work of art. This new life displays itself in a hundred forms, both in the republican and in the despotic states, and determines their inward constitution no less than their foreign policy. We shall limit ourselves to the consideration of the completer and more clearly defined type, which is offered by the despotic states.

[1] Machiavelli, *Discorsi*, lib. i, c. 12 : "E la cagione, che la Italia non sia in quel medesimo termine, ne habbia anch' ella ò una republica ò un prencipe che la governi, è solamente la Chiesa ; perchè havendovi habitato e tenuto imperio temporale non è stata si potente ne di tal virtù, che l' habbia potuto occupare il restante d' Italia e farsene prencipe."

[2] The rulers and their dependents were together called *lo stato*, and this name afterward acquired the meaning of the collective existence of a territory.

FIG. 2. STRONGHOLD OF THE HOHENSTAUFEN AT LUCERA

THE RENAISSANCE IN ITALY

The internal condition of the despotically governed states had a memorable counterpart in the Norman empire of Lower Italy and Sicily after its transformation by the Emperor Frederick II.[1] Bred amid treason and peril in the neighbourhood of the Saracens, Frederick, the first ruler of the modern type who sat upon a throne, had early accustomed himself, both in criticism and action, to a thoroughly objective treatment of affairs. His acquaintance with the internal condition and administration of the Saracenic states was close and intimate; and the mortal struggle in which he was engaged with the Papacy compelled him, no less than his adversaries, to bring into the field all the resources at his command. Frederick's measures (especially after 1231) are aimed at the complete destruction of the feudal state, at the transformation of the people into a multitude destitute of will and of the means of resistance, but profitable in the utmost degree to the exchequer. He centralized, in a manner hitherto unknown in the West, the whole judicial and political administration by establishing the right of appeal from the feudal courts, which he did not, however, abolish, to the imperial judges. No office was henceforth to be filled by popular election, under penalty of the devastation of the offending district and of the enslavement of its inhabitants. Excise duties were introduced; the taxes, based on a comprehensive assessment, and distributed in accordance with Mohammedan usages, were collected by those cruel and vexatious methods without which, it is true, it is impossible to obtain any money from Orientals. Here, in short, we find not a people, but simply a disciplined multitude of subjects; who were forbidden, for example, to marry out of the country without special permission, and under no circumstances were allowed to study abroad. The University of Naples was the first we know of to restrict the freedom of study, while the East, in these respects at all events, left its youth unfettered. It was after the example of Mohammedan rulers that Frederick traded on his own account in all parts of the Mediterranean, reserving to himself the monopoly of many commodities, and restricting in various ways the commerce of his subjects. The Fatimite caliphs, with all their esoteric unbelief, were, at least in their earlier history, tolerant of the differences in the religious faith of their people; Frederick, on the other hand, crowned his system of government by a religious inquisition, which will seem the more reprehensible when we remember that in the persons of the heretics he was persecuting the representatives of a free municipal life. Lastly the internal police, and the kernel of the army for foreign service, was composed of Saracens, who had been brought over from Sicily to Nocera and Lucera—men who were deaf to the cry of misery and careless of the ban of the Church. At a later period the subjects, by whom the use of weapons had long been forgotten, were passive witnesses of the fall of Manfred and of the seizure of the government by Charles of Anjou; the latter continued to use the system which he found already at work.

[1] C. Winckelmann, *De Regni Siculi Administratione qualis fuerit regnante Frederico II* (Berlin, 1859); A. del Vecchio, *La Legislazione di Federico II Imperatore* (Turin, 1874). Frederick II has been fully and thoroughly discussed by Winckelmann, Schirrmacher, and Hampe. *Cf.* especially Hampe, *Kaiser Friedrich II, Hist. Ztschr.*, 83.

INTRODUCTION

At the side of the centralizing Emperor appeared a usurper of the most peculiar kind : his vicar and son-in-law, Ezzelino da Romano. He stands as the representative of no system of government or administration, for all his activity was wasted in struggles for supremacy in the eastern part of Upper Italy ; but as a political type he was a figure of no less importance for the future than his Imperial protector Frederick. The conquests and usurpations which had hitherto taken place in the Middle Ages rested on real or pretended inheritance and other such claims, or else were effected against unbelievers and excommunicated persons. Here for the first time the attempt was openly made to found a throne by wholesale murder and endless barbarities, by the adoption, in short, of any means with a view to nothing but the end pursued. None of his successors, not even Cesare Borgia, rivalled the colossal guilt of Ezzelino ; but the example once set was not forgotten, and his fall led to no return of justice among the nations, and served as no warning to future transgressors.

It was in vain at such a time that St Thomas Aquinas, a born subject of Frederick, set up the theory of a constitutional monarchy, in which the prince was to be supported by an upper house named by himself, and a representative body elected by the people; in vain did he concede to the people the right of revolution.[1] Such theories found no echo outside the lecture-room, and Frederick and Ezzelino were and remain for Italy the great political pheno-mena of the thirteenth century.

FIG. 3. COIN OF THE REIGN OF FREDERICK II

Their personality, already half legendary, forms the most important subject of *The Hundred Old Tales*, whose original com-position falls certainly within this century.[2] In them Frederick is already represented as possessing the right to do as he pleased with the property of his subjects, and exercises on all, even on criminals, a profound influence by the force of his personality; Ezzelino is spoken of with the awe which all mighty impres-sions leave behind them. His person became the centre of a whole literature, from the chronicle of eye-witnesses to the half-mythical tragedy[3] of later poets.

Immediately after the fall of Frederick and Ezzelino a crowd of tyrants appeared upon the scene. The struggle between Guelph and Ghibelline was their opportunity. They came forward in general as Ghibelline leaders, but at times and under conditions so various that it is impossible not to recognize in the fact a law of supreme and universal necessity. The means which they used were those already familiar in the party struggles of the past—the banish-ment or destruction of their adversaries and of their adversaries' households.

[1] Johann Julius Baumann, *Staatslehre des Thomas von Aquino*, especially pp. 136 *sqq.* (Leipzig, 1873).
[2] *Cento Novelle Antiche* (ed. 1525). For Frederick, *Nov.* 2, 21, 22, 23, 24, 30, 53, 59, 90, 100 ; for Ezzelino, *Nov.* 31, and especially 84.
[3] Scardeonius, *De Urbis Patav. Antiqu.*, in J. G. Grævius, *Thes. Antiqu. et Hist. Italicæ*, vi, 3, p. 259.

CHAPTER II

The Tyranny of the Fourteenth Century

THE tyrannies, great and small, of the fourteenth century afford constant proof that examples such as these were not thrown away. Their misdeeds cried forth loudly, and have been circumstantially told by historians. As states depending for existence on themselves alone, and scientifically organized with a view to this object, they present to us a higher interest than that of mere narrative.

The deliberate adaptation of means to ends, of which no prince out of Italy had at that time a conception, joined to almost absolute power within the

FIG. 4. TOWN SCENE OF THE FOURTEENTH CENTURY
By Ambrogio Lorenzetti
Siena, Palazzo Pubblico
Photo Alinari

limits of the state, produced among the despots both men and modes of life of a peculiar character.[1] The chief secret of government in the hands of the prudent ruler lay in leaving the incidence of taxation so far as possible where he found it, or as he had first arranged it. The chief sources of income were a land-tax, based on a valuation; definite taxes on articles of consumption and duties on exported and imported goods; together with the private fortune of the ruling house. The only possible increase was derived from the growth of business and of general prosperity. Loans, such as we find in the

---

[1] Sismondi, *Hist. des Rép. Italiennes*, iv, p. 420; viii, pp. 1 *sqq.*

free cities, were here unknown; a well-planned confiscation was held a preferable means of raising money, provided only that it left public credit unshaken—an end attained, for example, by the truly Oriental practice of deposing and plundering the director of finances.[1]

Out of this income the expenses of the little Court, of the bodyguard, of

FIG. 5. EQUESTRIAN STATUE OF CAN GRANDE DELLA SCALA
From the tombs of the Scaligeri, Verona

the mercenary troops, and of the public buildings were met, as well as of the buffoons and men of talent who belonged to the personal attendants of the prince. The illegitimacy of his rule isolated the tyrant and surrounded him with constant danger; the most honourable alliance which he could form was with intellectual merit, without regard to its origin. The liberality of the Northern princes of the thirteenth century was confined to the knights, to the nobility which served and sang. It was otherwise with the Italian despot. With his thirst for fame and his passion for monumental works

[1] Franco Sacchetti, *Nov.* 61 and 62.

it was talent, not birth, which he needed. In the company of the poet and the scholar he felt himself in a new position—almost, indeed, in possession of a new legitimacy.

No prince was more famous in this respect than the ruler of Verona, Can Grande della Scala, who numbered among the illustrious exiles whom he entertained at his Court representatives of the whole of Italy.[1] The men of letters were not ungrateful. Petrarch, whose visits at the Courts of such men have been so severely censured, sketched an ideal picture of a prince of the fourteenth century.[2] He demands great things from his patron, the lord of Padua, but in a manner which shows that he holds him capable of them.

> Thou must not be the master, but the father of thy subjects, and must love them as thy children ; yea, as members of thy body.[3] Weapons, guards, and soldiers thou mayest employ against the enemy—with thy subjects goodwill is sufficient. By citizens, of course, I mean those who love the existing order ; for those who daily desire change are rebels and traitors, and against such a stern justice may take its course.

Here follows, worked out in detail, the purely modern fiction of the omnipotence of the State. The prince is to be independent of his courtiers, but at the same time to govern with simplicity and modesty ; he is to take everything into his charge, to maintain and restore churohes and public buildings, to keep up the municipal police,[4] to drain the marshes, to look after the supply of wine and corn ; he is to exercise a strict justice, so to distribute the taxes that the people can recognize their necessity and the regret of the ruler to be compelled to put his hands in the pockets of others ; he is to support the sick and the helpless, and to give his protection and society to distinguished scholars, on whom his fame in after ages will depend.

But whatever might be the brighter sides of the system, and the merits of individual rulers, yet the men of the fourteenth century were not without a more or less distinct consciousness of the brief and uncertain tenure of most of these despotisms. Inasmuch as political institutions like these are naturally secure in proportion to the size of the territory in which they exist, the larger principalities were constantly tempted to swallow up the smaller. Whole hecatombs of petty rulers were sacrificed at this time to the Visconti alone. As a result of this outward danger an inward ferment was in ceaseless activity ; and the effect of the situation on the character of the ruler was generally of the most sinister kind. Absolute power, with its temptations to luxury and unbridled selfishness, and the perils to which he was exposed from enemies

[1] Dante, it is true, is said to have lost the favour of this prince, which impostors knew how to keep. See the important account in Petrarch, *De Rerum Memorandarum*, lib. ii, 3, 46.

[2] Petrarch, *Epistolæ Seniles*, lib. xiv, 1, to Francesco di Carrara (November 28, 1373). The letter is sometimes printed separately, with the title *De Republica Optime Administranda*—for example, Bern, 1602.

[3] It is not till a hundred years later that the princess is spoken of as the mother of the people. *Cf.* Hieron. Crivelli's funeral oration oħ Bianca Maria Visconti, in Muratori, *Scriptores Rerum Italicarum*, xxv, col. 429. It was by way of parody of this phrase that a sister of Sixtus IV is called in Jac. Volaterranus (Murat., xxiii, col. 109) *mater ecclesiæ*.

[4] With the parenthetical request, in reference to a previous conversation, that the prince would again forbid the keeping of pigs in the streets of Padua, as the sight of them was unpleasing, especially for strangers, and apt to frighten the horses.

and conspirators, turned him almost inevitably into a tyrant in the worst sense of the word.   Well for him if he could trust his nearest relations !   But where all was illegitimate there could be no regular law of inheritance, either with regard to succession or to the division of the ruler's property ;   and consequently the heir, if incompetent or a minor, was liable in the interest of the family itself to be supplanted by an uncle or cousin of more resolute character. The acknowledgment or exclusion of the bastards was a fruitful source of

FIG. 6. GUIDORICCIO FOGLIANI
By Simone Martini
Siena, Palazzo Pubblico
Photo Seemann, Leipzig

contest ;   and most of these families in consequence were plagued with a crowd of discontented and vindictive kinsmen.   This circumstance gave rise to continual outbreaks of treason and to frightful scenes of domestic bloodshed. Sometimes the pretenders lived abroad in exile, and, like the Visconti who practised the fisherman's craft on the Lake of Garda,[1] viewed the situation with patient indifference.   When asked by a messenger of his rival when and how he thought of returning to Milan he gave the reply : " By the same means as those by which I was expelled, but not till his crimes have outweighed my own." Sometimes, too, with the view of saving the family, the despot was sacrificed by his relations to the public conscience which he had too grossly outraged.[2]

[1] Petrarch, *De Rerum Memorandarum*, lib. iii, 2, 66.   Matteo I Visconti and his adversary, Guido della Torre, then ruling in Milan, are the persons referred to.
[2] Matteo Villani, v, 81 : the secret murder of Matteo II (Maffiolo) Visconti by his brothers.

In a few cases the government was in the hands of the whole family, or at least the ruler was bound to take their advice ; and here too the distribution of property and influence often led to bitter disputes.

FIG. 7. BOAR-HUNT
Miniature from the treatise on hunting written for Francesco Sforza
Chantilly, Musée Condé

The whole of this system excited the deep and persistent hatred of the Florentine writers of that epoch. Even the pomp and display with which the despot was perhaps less anxious to gratify his own vanity than to impress the popular imagination awakened their keenest sarcasm. Woe to an adventurer if he fell into their hands, like the upstart Doge Aguello of Pisa

(1364), who used to ride out with a golden sceptre, and show himself at the window of his house, "as relics are shown," reclining on embroidered drapery and cushions, served like a Pope or emperor by kneeling attendants.[1] More often, however, the old Florentines speak on this subject in a tone of lofty seriousness. Dante saw and characterized well the vulgarity and commonplace which mark the ambition of the new princes.[2] "What mean their trumpets and their bells, their horns and their flutes, but 'Come, hangman— come, vultures'?" The castle of the tyrant, as pictured by the popular mind, is a lofty and solitary building, full of dungeons and listening-tubes,[3] the home of cruelty and misery. Misfortune is foretold to all who enter the service of the despot,[4] who even becomes at last himself an object of pity : he must needs be the enemy of all good and honest men ; he can trust no one, and can read in the faces of his subjects the expectation of his fall. "As despotisms rise, grow, and are consolidated, so grows in their midst the hidden element which must produce their dissolution and ruin."[5] But the deepest ground of dislike has not been stated ; Florence was then the scene of the richest development of human individuality, while for the despots no other individuality could be suffered to live and thrive but their own and that of their nearest dependents. The control of the individual was rigorously carried out, even down to the establishment of a system of passports.[6]

The astrological superstitions and the religious unbelief of many of the tyrants gave, in the minds of their contemporaries, a peculiar colour to this awful and God-forsaken existence. When the last Carrara could no longer defend the walls and gates of the plague-stricken Padua, hemmed in on all sides by the Venetians (1405), the soldiers of the guard heard him cry to the devil "to come and kill him."

The most complete and instructive type of the tyranny of the fourteenth century is to be found unquestionably among the Visconti of Milan, from the death of the Archbishop Giovanni onward (1354). The family likeness which shows itself between Bernabò and the worst of the Roman Emperors is unmistakable ;[7] the most important public object was the prince's boarhunting ; whoever interfered with it was put to death with torture ; the terrified people were forced to maintain five thousand boar-hounds, with strict responsibility for their health and safety. The taxes were extorted by every

---

[1] Filippo Villani, *Istorie*, xi, 101. Petrarch speaks in the same tone of the tyrants dressed out "like altars at a festival." The triumphal procession of Castracane at Lucca is described minutely in his life by Tegrimo, in Murat., xi, col. 1340.

[2] *De Vulgari Eloquentia*, i, c. 12 : ". . . qui non heroico more, sed plebeo sequuntur superbiam."

[3] This we find first in the fifteenth century, but their representations are certainly based on the beliefs of earlier times : L. B. Alberti, *De Re Ædif.*, v, 3 ; Franc. di Giorgio, *Trattato*, in Della Valle, *Lettere Sanesi*, iii, 121.

[4] Franco Sacchetti, *Nov.* 61.   [5] Matteo Villani, vi, 1.

[6] The Paduan passport office about the middle of the fourteenth century is referred to by Franco Sacchetti, *Nov.* 117, in the words "quelli delle bullette." In the last ten years of the reign of Frederick II, when the strictest control was exercised on the personal conduct of his subjects, this system must have been very highly developed.

[7] Corio, *Storia di Milano*, fol. 247 *sqq.* Recent Italian writers have observed that the Visconti have still to find a historian who, keeping the just mean between the exaggerated praises of contemporaries—for example, Petrarch—and the violent denunciations of later political (Guelph) opponents, will pronounce a final judgment upon them.

conceivable sort of compulsion ; seven daughters of the prince received a dowry of 100,000 gold florins apiece ; and an enormous treasure was collected. On the death of his wife (1384) an order was issued "to the subjects" to share his grief, as once they had shared his joy, and to wear mourning for a year. The *coup de main* (1385) by which his nephew Giangaleazzo got him into his power—one of those brilliant plots which make the heart of even late historians beat more quickly [1]—was strikingly characteristic of the man. Giangaleazzo, despised by his relations on account of his religion and his

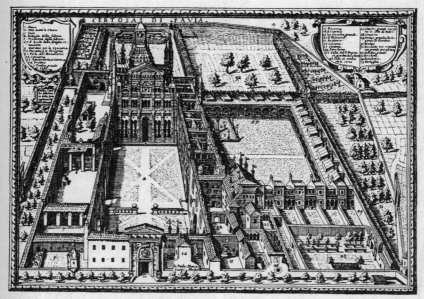

FIG. 8. THE CERTOSA, NEAR PAVIA : GENERAL PLAN

love of science, resolved on vengeance, and, leaving the city under pretext of a pilgrimage, fell upon his unsuspecting uncle, took him prisoner, forced his way back into the city at the head of an armed band, seized on the government, and gave up the palace of Bernabò to general plunder.

In Giangaleazzo that passion for the colossal which was common to most of the despots shows itself on the largest scale. He undertook, at the cost of 300,000 golden florins, the construction of gigantic dikes, to divert in case of need the Mincio from Mantua and the Brenta from Padua, and thus to render these cities defenceless.[2] It is not impossible, indeed, that he thought

---

[1] For example, of Paolo Giovio, *Elogia. Virorum Bellica Virtute Illustrium*, p. 85 (Basel, 1575), in the life of Giangaleazzo (*Vita*, pp. 86 *sqq.*), who is for Giovio "post Theodoricum omnium præstantissimus." *Cf.* also Paul. Jovius, *Vitæ XII Vicecomitum Mediolani Principum*, pp. 165 *sqq.* (Paris, 1549).

[2] Corio, fol. 272, 285.

of draining away the lagoons of Venice. He founded that most wonderful of all convents, the Certosa of Pavia,[1] and the cathedral of Milan, "which exceeds in size and splendour all the churches of Christendom." The palace in Pavia, which his father Galeazzo began, and which he himself finished, was probably by far the most magnificent of the princely dwellings of Europe. There he transferred his famous library and the great collection of relics of the saints, in which he placed a peculiar faith. King Winceslaus made him Duke (1395); he was hoping for nothing less than the kingdom of Italy [2] or the Imperial crown, when (1402) he fell ill and died. His whole territories are said to have paid him in a single year, besides the regular contribution of 1,200,000 gold florins, no less than 800,000 more in extraordinary subsidies. After his death the dominions which he had brought together by every sort of violence fell to pieces ; and for a time even the original nucleus could with difficulty be maintained by his successors. What might have become of his sons Giovanni Maria (d. 1412) and Filippo Maria (d. 1417), had they lived in a different country and among other traditions, cannot be said. But as heirs of their house they inherited that monstrous capital of cruelty and cowardice which had been accumulated from generation to generation.

Giovanni Maria, too, is famed for his dogs, which were no longer, however, used for hunting, but for tearing human bodies. Tradition has preserved their names, like those of the bears of the Emperor Valentinian I.[3] In May 1409, when war was going on, and the starving populace cried to him in the streets, "*Pace ! Pace !* " he let loose his mercenaries upon them, and two hundred lives were sacrificed ; under penalty of the gallows it was forbidden to utter the words *pace* and *guerra*, and the priests were ordered, instead of *dona nobis pacem*, to say *tranquillitatem* ! At last a band of conspirators took advantage of the moment when Facino Cane, the chief *condottiere* of the insane ruler, lay ill at Pavia, and cut down Giovanni Maria in the church of S. Gottardo at Milan ; the dying Facino on the same day made his officers swear to stand by the heir Filippo Maria, whom he himself urged his wife [4] to take for a second husband. His wife, Beatrice di Tenda, followed his advice. We shall have occasion to speak of Filippo Maria later on.

And in times like these Cola di Rienzi was dreaming of founding on the rickety enthusiasm of the corrupt population of Rome a new state which was to comprise all Italy. By the side of rulers such as those whom we have described he seems no better than a poor deluded fool.

[1] Cagnola, in the *Archiv. Stor.*, iii, p. 23.
[2] So Corio, fol. 286, and Poggio, *Hist. Florent.*, lib. iv, in Murat., xx, col. 290. Cagnola (*loc. cit.*) speaks of his designs on the Imperial crown. See too the sonnet in Trucchi, *Poesie Ital. Ined.*, ii, p. 118 :

> " Stan le città lombarde con le chiave
>   In man per darle a voi . . . *etc.*
>   Roma vi chiama : Cesar mio novello
>   Io sono ignuda, e l' anima pur vive :
>   Or mi coprite col vostro mantello," *etc.*

[3] Corio, fol. 301 *sqq. Cf.* Ammian. Marcellin., xxix, 3.
[4] So Paul. Jovius, *Elogia*, pp. 88-92 ; Jo. Maria Philippus ; and *Vitæ XII Vicecomitum*, pp. 175-189.

CHAPTER III

The Tyranny of the Fifteenth Century

THE despotisms of the fifteenth century show an altered character. Many of the less important tyrants, and some of the greater, like the Scala and the Carrara, had disappeared, while the more powerful ones, aggrandized by conquest, had given to their systems each its characteristic development. Naples, for example, received a fresh and stronger impulse from the new Aragonese dynasty. A striking feature of this epoch is the attempt of the *condottieri* to found independent dynasties of their own. Facts and the actual relations of things, apart from traditional estimates, are alone regarded; talent and audacity win the great prizes. The petty despots, to secure a trustworthy support, begin to enter the service of the larger states, and become themselves *condottieri*, receiving in return for their services money and impunity for their misdeeds, if not an increase of territory. All, whether small or great, must exert themselves more, must act with greater caution and calculation, and must learn to refrain from too wholesale barbarities; only so much wrong is permitted by public opinion as is necessary for the end in view, and this the impartial bystander certainly finds no fault with. No trace is here visible of that half-religious loyalty by which the legitimate princes of the West were supported; personal popularity is the nearest approach we can find to it. Talent and calculation are the only means of advancement. A character like that of Charles the Bold, which wore itself out in the passionate pursuit of impracticable ends, was a riddle to the Italian.

> The Swiss were only peasants, and if they were all killed that would be no satisfaction for the Burgundian nobles who might fall in the war. If the Duke got possession of all Switzerland without a struggle his income would not be five thousand ducats the greater.[1]

The medieval features in the character of Charles, his chivalrous aspirations and ideals, had long become unintelligible to the Italian. The diplomatists of the South, when they saw him strike his officers and yet keep them in his service, when he maltreated his troops to punish them for a defeat, and then threw the blame on his counsellors in the presence of the same troops, gave him up for lost.[2] Louis XI, on the other hand, whose policy surpasses that of the Italian princes in their own style, and who was an avowed admirer of

---

[1] De Gingins, *Dépêches des Ambassadeurs Milanais* (Paris and Geneva, 1858), ii, pp. 200 *sqq.* (N. 213). *Cf.* ii, p. 3 (N. 144), and ii, pp. 212 *sqq.* (N. 218).
[2] Paul. Jovius, *Elogia*, pp. 156 *sqq.*

34

Francesco Sforza, must be placed in all that regards culture and refinement far below these rulers.

FIG. 9. THE CROWNING OF AN EMPEROR
By Luca della Robbia (?)
Florence, Museo Nazionale

Good and evil lie strangely mixed together in the Italian states of the fifteenth century. The personality of the ruler is so highly developed, often of such deep significance, and so characteristic of the conditions and needs of the time that to form an adequate moral judgment on it is no easy task.[1]

The foundation of the system was and remained illegitimate, and nothing could remove the curse which rested upon it. The Imperial approval or investiture made no change in the matter, since the people attached little weight to the fact that the despot had bought a piece of parchment somewhere in foreign countries, or from some stranger passing through his territory.[2] If the Emperor had been good for anything—so ran the logic of uncritical common sense—he would never have let the tyrant rise at all. Since the Roman expedition of Charles IV the Emperors had done nothing more in Italy than sanction a tyranny which had arisen without their help; they could give it no other practical authority than what might flow from an Imperial charter. The whole conduct of Charles in Italy was a scandalous political comedy. Matteo Villani[3] relates how the Visconti escorted him round their territory, and at last out of it; how he went about like a hawker selling his wares (privileges, etc.) for money; what a mean appearance he made in Rome, and how at the end, without even drawing the sword, he returned with replenished coffers across the Alps. Nevertheless, patriotic enthusiasts and poets, full of the greatness of the past, conceived high hopes at his coming, which were afterward dissipated by his pitiful conduct. Petrarch, who had written frequent letters exhorting the Emperor to cross the Alps, to give back to Rome its departed greatness, and to set up a new universal empire, now, when the Emperor, careless of these high-flying projects, had come at last, still hoped to see his dreams realized, strove unweariedly, by speech and writing, to impress the Emperor with them, but was at length driven away from him with disgust when he saw the Imperial authority dishonoured by the submission of Charles to the Pope.[4] Sigismund came, on the first occasion at least (1414), with the good intention of persuading John XXIII to take part in his council; it was on that journey, when Pope and Emperor were gazing from the lofty tower of Cremona on the panorama of Lombardy, that their host, the tyrant Gabino Fondolo, was seized with the desire to throw them both over. On his

---

[1] This compound of force and intellect is called by Machiavelli *virtù*, and is quite compatible with *scelleratezza*. For example, *Discorsi*, i, 10, in speaking of Sep. Severus.

[2] On this point Franc. Vettori, *Archiv. Stor.*, vi, pp. 293 *sqq.*: "The investiture at the hands of a man who lives in Germany, and has nothing of the Roman Emperor about him but the empty name, cannot turn a scoundrel into the real lord of a city."

[3] M. Villani, iv, 38, 39, 44, 56, 74, 76, 92; v, 1, 2, 14–16, 21, 22, 36, 51, 54. It is only fair to consider that dislike of the Visconti may have led to worse representations than the facts justified. Charles IV is once (iv, 74) highly praised by Villani.

[4] It was an Italian, Fazio degli Uberti (*Dittamondo*, lib. vi, cap. 5—about 1360), who recommended to Charles IV a crusade to the Holy Land. The passage is one of the best in this poem, and in other respects characteristic. The poet is dismissed from the Holy Sepulchre by an insolent Turk:

> "Coi passi lunghi e con la testa bassa
> Oltre passai e dissi: ecco vergogna
> Del cristian che'l saracin qui lassa!
> Poscia al Pastor [the Pope] mi volsi per rampogna
> E tu ti stai, che sei vicar di Cristo,
> Co' frati tuoi a ingrassar la carogna?
> Similimente dissi a quel sofisto [Charles IV]

second visit Sigismund came as a mere adventurer, giving no proof whatever of his Imperial prerogative, except by crowning Beccadelli as a poet; for more than half a year he remained shut up in Siena, like a debtor in gaol, and only with difficulty, and at a later period, succeeded in being crowned in Rome. And what can be thought of Frederick III? His journeys to Italy have the air of holiday-trips or pleasure-tours made at the expense of those who wanted him to confirm their prerogatives, or whose vanity it flattered to entertain an emperor. The latter was the case with Alfonso of Naples, who paid a hundred and fifty thousand florins for the honour of an Imperial visit.[1] At Ferrara,[2] on his second return from Rome (1469), Frederick spent a whole day without leaving his chamber, distributing no fewer than eighty titles; he created knights, counts, doctors, notaries—counts, indeed, of different degrees, as, for instance, counts palatine, counts with the right to create doctors up to the number of five, counts with the right to legitimatize bastards, to appoint notaries and so forth. The Chancellor, however, expected in return for the patents in question a gratuity which was thought excessive at Ferrara.[3] The opinion of Borso, himself created Duke of Modena and Reggio in return for an annual payment of four thousand gold florins, when his Imperial patron was distributing titles and diplomas to all the little Court, is not mentioned. The humanists, then the chief spokesmen of the age, were divided in opinion according to their personal interests, while the Emperor was greeted by some[4] of them with the conventional acclamations of the poets of Imperial Rome. Poggio[5] confessed that he no longer knew what the coronation meant; in the old times only the victorious Imperator was crowned, and then he was crowned with laurel.[6]

With Maximilian I begins not only the general intervention of foreign nations, but a new Imperial policy with regard to Italy. The first step—the

> Che sta in Buemme [Bohemia] a piantar vigne e fichi
> E che non cura di si caro acquisto:
> Che fai? Perchè non segui i primi antichi
> Cesari Romani, e che non segui,
> Dico, gli Otti, i Corradi, i Federichi?
> E che pur tieni questo imperio in tregui?
> E se non hai lo cuor d' esser Augusto,
> Che no'l rifiuti? o che non ti dilegui?" etc.

Some eight years earlier, about 1352, Petrarch had written (to Charles IV, *Epist. Fam.*, lib. xii, *Ep.* 1, ed. Fracassetti, vol. ii, p. 160): "Simpliciter igitur et aperte . . . pro maturando negotio terræ sanctæ . . . oro tuo egentem auxilio quam primum invisere velis Ausoniam."

[1] See for details Vespas. Fiorent., ed. Mai, *Spicilegium Romanum*, vol. i, p. 54. *Cf.* 160 and Panormita, *De Dictis et Factis Alfonsi*, lib. iv, No. 4.

[2] *Diario Ferrarese*, in Murat., xxiv, col. 217 *sqq.*

[3] "Haveria voluto scortigare la brigata." Giov. Maria Filelfo, then staying at Bergamo, wrote a violent satire "in vulgus equitum auro notatorum." See his biography in Favre, *Mélanges d'Histoire Littéraire*, i, p. 10 (1856).

[4] *Annales Estenses*, in Murat., xx, col. 41.

[5] Poggio, *Hist. Florent. Pop.*, lib. vii., in Murat., xx, col. 381. This view is in accordance with the anti-monarchical sentiments of many of the humanists of that day. *Cf.* the evidence given by Bezold, *Lehre von der Volkssouveränität während des Mittelalters*, *Hist. Ztschr.*, Bd. xxxvi, p. 365.

[6] Some years later the Venetian Leonardo Giustiniani blames the word 'imperator' as unclassical, and therefore unbecoming the German Emperor, and calls the Germans barbarians on account of their ignorance of the language and manners of antiquity. The cause of the Germans was defended by the humanist H. Bebel. See L. Geiger, in the *Allgem. Deutsche Biogr.*, ii, 196.

investiture of Lodovico il Moro with the duchy of Milan and the exclusion of his unhappy nephew—was not of a kind to bear good fruits. According to the modern theory of intervention, when two parties are tearing a country to pieces a third may step in and take its share, and on this principle the Empire acted. But right and justice were appealed to no longer. When Louis XII was expected in Genoa (1502), and the Imperial eagle was removed from the hall of the ducal palace and replaced by painted lilies, the historian Senarega [1] asked what after all was the meaning of the eagle which so many revolutions had spared, and what claims the Empire had upon Genoa. No one knew more about the matter than the old phrase that Genoa was a *camera imperii*. In fact, nobody in Italy could give a clear answer to any such questions. At length, when Charles V held Spain and the Empire together, he was able by means of Spanish forces to make good Imperial claims ; but it is notorious that what he thereby gained turned to the profit not of the Empire, but of the Spanish monarchy.

Closely connected with the political illegitimacy of the dynasties of the fifteenth century was the public indifference to legitimate birth, which to foreigners—for example, to Comines—appeared so remarkable. The two things went naturally together. In Northern countries, as in Burgundy, the illegitimate offspring were provided for by a distinct class of appanages, such as bishoprics and the like; in Portugal an illegitimate line maintained itself on the throne only by constant effort; in Italy, on the contrary, there no longer existed a princely house where, even in the direct line of descent, bastards were not patiently tolerated. The Aragonese monarchs of Naples belonged to the illegitimate line, Aragon itself falling to the lot of the brother of Alfonso I. The great Federigo of Urbino was, perhaps, no Montefeltro at all. When Pius II was on his way to the Congress of Mantua (1459) eight bastards of the house of Este rode to meet him at Ferrara, among them the reigning Duke Borso himself and two illegitimate sons of his illegitimate brother and pre-decessor Leonello.[2] The latter had also had a lawful wife, herself an illegitimate daughter of Alfonso I of Naples by an African woman.[3] The bastards were often admitted to the succession where the lawful children were minors and the dangers of the situation were pressing; and a rule of seniority became recognized which took no account of pure or impure birth. The fitness of the individual, his worth and his capacity, were of more weight than all the laws and usages which prevailed elsewhere in the West. It was the age, indeed, in which the sons of the Popes were founding dynasties. In the sixteenth century, through the influence of foreign ideas and of the Counter-Reformation, which then began, the whole question was judged more strictly: Varchi discovers that the succession of the legitimate children "is ordered by reason, and is the will of heaven from eternity." [4] Cardinal Ippolito de' Medici

[1] Senarega, *De Reb. Genuens.*, in Murat., xxiv, col. 575.

[2] Enumerated in the *Diario Ferrarese*, in Murat., xxiv, col. 203. Cf. *Pii II Comment.*, ii, p. 102 (ed. Rome, 1584).

[3] Marin Sanudo, *Vita dei Duchi di Venezia*, in Murat., xxii, col. 1113.

[4] Varchi, *Stor. Fiorent.*, i, p. 8.

FIG. 10. EQUESTRIAN MONUMENT OF THE CONDOTTIERE BARTOLOMMEO COLLEONI
By Andrea del Verrocchio
Venice
Photo Propyläen-Verlag, Berlin

founded his claim to the lordship of Florence on the fact that he was perhaps the fruit of a lawful marriage, and at all events son of a gentlewoman, and not, like Duke Alessandro, of a servant-girl.[1]   At this time began those morganatic marriages of affection which in the fifteenth century, on grounds either of policy or morality, would have had no meaning at all.

But the highest and the most admired form of illegitimacy in the fifteenth century was presented by the *condottiere*, who, whatever may have been his origin, raised himself to the position of an independent ruler.   At bottom, the occupation of Lower Italy by the Normans in the eleventh century was of this character.   Such attempts now began to keep the peninsula in a constant ferment.

It was possible for a *condottiere* to obtain the lordship of a district even without usurpation, in the case where his employer, through want of money or troops, provided for him in this way;[2] under any circumstances the *condottiere*, even when he dismissed for the time the greater part of his forces, needed a safe place where he could establish his winter quarters and lay up his stores and provisions.   The first example of a captain thus portioned is John Hawkwood, who was invested by Gregory XI with the lordship of Bagnacavallo and Cotignola.[3]   When with Alberigo da Barbiano Italian armies and leaders appeared upon the scene the chances of founding a principality, or of increasing one already acquired, became more frequent.   The first great bacchanalian outbreak of military ambition took place in the duchy of Milan after the death of Giangaleazzo (1402).   The policy of his two sons was chiefly aimed at the destruction of the new despotisms founded by the *condottieri*; and from the greatest of them, Facino Cane, the house of Visconti inherited, together with his widow, a long list of cities, and 400,000 golden florins, not to speak of the soldiers of her first husband whom Beatrice di Tenda brought with her.[4] From henceforth that thoroughly immoral relation between the Governments and their *condottieri* which is characteristic of the fifteenth century became more and more common.   An old story[5]—one of those which are true and not true, everywhere and nowhere—describes it as follows.   The citizens of a certain town (Siena seems to be meant) had once an officer in their service who had freed them from foreign aggression; daily they took counsel how to recompense him, and concluded that no reward in their power was great enough, not even if they made him lord of the city.   At last one of them rose and said, " Let us kill him and then worship him as our patron saint."   And so they did, following the example set by the Roman Senate with Romulus.

¹ Soriano, *Relazione di Roma*, 1533, in Tommaso Gar, *Relaz. della Corte di Roma* (in Alberi, *Relaz. degli Ambasc. Veneti*, ii, ser. iii, p. 281).

² For what follows see Canestrini, in the Introduction to vol. xv of the *Archiv. Stor.*

³ For him see Shepherd-Tonelli, *Vita di Poggio*, App., pp. viii-xvi.

⁴ Cagnola, *Archiv. Stor.*, iii, p. 28: " Et [Filippo Maria] da lei [Beatrice] ebbe molto texoro e denari, e tutte le giente d' arme del dicto Facino, che obedivano a lei."

⁵ Infessura, in Eccard, *Scriptores*, ii, col. 1911.   For the alternatives which Machiavelli puts before the victorious *condottiere* see *Discorsi*, i, 30.   After the victory he is either to hand over the army to his employer and wait quietly for his reward, or else to win the soldiers to his own side to occupy the fortresses and to punish the prince " di quella ingratitudine che esso gli userebbe."

In fact, the *condottieri* had reason to fear none so much as their employers; if they were successful they became dangerous, and were put out of the way like Roberto Malatesta just after the victory he had won for Sixtus IV[1] (1482); if

FIG. 11. THE CONDOTTIERE ROBERTO MALATESTA
Part of Cosimo Rosselli's *Passage of the Red Sea*
Rome, Sixtine Chapel
Photo Anderson, Rome

they failed the vengeance of the Venetians on Carmagnola[2] showed to what risks they were exposed (1432). It is characteristic of the moral aspect of the situation that the *condottieri* had often to give their wives and children as hostages, and, notwithstanding this, neither felt nor inspired confidence. They

[1] This view of Burckhardt's is mistaken. Pastor (*Hist. of the Popes*, Bk. II) has proved conclusively that Roberto Malatesta died of a fever.—W. G.]

[2] *Cf.* Barth. Facius, *De Vir. Ill.*, p. 64, who tells us that Carmagnola commanded an army of 60,000 men. It is uncertain whether the Venetians did not poison Alviano in 1516, because he, as Prato says in *Archiv. Stor.*, iii, p. 348, aided the French too zealously in the battle of S. Donato. The republic made itself Colleoni's heir and after his death in 1475 formally confiscated his property. *Cf.* Malipiero, *Annali Veneti*, in *Archiv. Stor.*, vii, i, 244. It was liked when the *condottieri* invested their money in Venice, *ibid.*, p. 351.

must have been heroes of abnegation, natures like Belisarius himself, not to be cankered by hatred and bitterness; only the most perfect goodness could save them from the most monstrous iniquity. No wonder then if we find them full of contempt for all sacred things, cruel and treacherous to their fellows—men who cared nothing whether or no they died under the ban of the Church. At the same time, and through the force of the same conditions, the genius and capacity of many among them attained the highest conceivable development, and won for them the admiring devotion of their followers; their armies are the first in modern history in which the personal credit of the leader is the one moving power. A brilliant example is shown in the life of Francesco Sforza; [1] no prejudice of birth could prevent him from winning and turning to account when he needed it a boundless devotion from each individual with whom he had to deal; it happened more than once that his enemies laid down their arms at the sight of him, greeting him reverently with uncovered heads, each honouring in him " the common father of the men-at-arms." The race of Sforza has this special interest, that from the very beginning of its history we seem able to trace its endeavours after the crown.[2] The foundation of its fortune lay in the remarkable fruitfulness of the family; Francesco's father, Jacopo, himself a celebrated man, had twenty brothers and sisters, all brought up roughly at Cotignola, near Faenza, amid the perils of one of the endless Romagnole *vendette* between their own house and that of the Pasolini. The family dwelling was a mere arsenal and fortress; the mother and daughters were as warlike as their kinsmen. In his thirteenth year Jacopo ran away and fled to Panicale to the Papal *condottiere* Boldrino—the man who even in death continued to lead his troops, the word of order being given from the bannered tent in which the embalmed body lay, till at last a fit leader was found to succeed him. Jacopo, when he had at length made himself a name in the service of different *condottieri*, sent for his relations, and obtained through them the same advantages that a prince derives from a numerous dynasty. It was these relations who kept the army together when he lay a captive in the Castel dell' Uovo at Naples; his sister took the royal envoys prisoners with her own hands, and saved him by this reprisal from death. It was an indication of the breadth and the range of his plans that in monetary affairs Jacopo was thoroughly trustworthy; even in his defeats he consequently found credit with the bankers. He habitually protected the peasants against the licence of his troops, and reluctantly destroyed or injured a conquered city. He gave his well-known mistress, Lucia, the mother of Francesco, in marriage to another in order to be free from a princely alliance. Even the marriages of his relations were arranged on a definite plan. He kept clear of the impious and profligate life of his contemporaries, and brought up his son Francesco to the three rules: " Let other men's wives alone; strike none of your followers, or, if you do, send the injured man far away; don't ride a hard-mouthed horse, or one that

---

[1] Cagnola, in *Archiv. Stor.*, iii, pp. 121 *sqq.*

[2] At all events in Paul. Jovius, *Vita Magni Sfortiæ (Viri Illustres)*, Rome, 1539 (dedicated to the Cardinal Ascanio Sforza), one of the most attractive of his biographies.

drops his shoe." But his chief source of influence lay in the qualities, if not of a great general, at least of a great soldier. His frame was powerful, and developed by every kind of exercise; his peasant's face and frank manners won general popularity; his memory was marvellous, and after the lapse of years could recall the names of his followers, the number of their horses, and the amount of their pay. His education was purely Italian: he devoted his leisure to the study of history, and had Greek and Latin authors translated for his use. Francesco, his still more famous son, set his mind from the first on founding a powerful state, and through brilliant generalship and a faithlessness which hesitated at nothing got possession of the great city of Milan (1447-50).

His example was contagious. Æneas Sylvius wrote about this time:[1] "In our change-loving Italy, where nothing stands firm, and where no ancient dynasty exists, a servant can easily become a king." One man in particular, who styled himself "the man of fortune," filled the imagination of the whole country: Jacopo Piccinino, the son of Niccolò. It was a burning question of the day if he too would succeed in founding a princely house. The greater states had an obvious interest in hindering it, and even Francesco Sforza thought it would be all the better if the list of self-made sovereigns were not enlarged. But the troops and captains sent against him, at the time, for instance, when he was aiming at the lordship of Siena, recognized their interest in supporting him:[2] "If it were all over with him, we should have to go back and plough our fields." Even while besieging him at Orbetello they supplied him with provisions; and he got out of his straits with honour. But at last Fate overtook him. All Italy was betting on the result, when (1465), after a visit to Sforza at Milan, he went to King Ferrante at Naples. In spite of the pledges given, and of his high connexions, he was murdered in the Castel dell' Uovo.[3] Even the *condottieri* who had obtained their dominions by inheritance never felt themselves safe. When Roberto Malatesta and Federigo of Urbino died on the same day (1482), the one at Rome, the other at Bologna, it was found[4] that each had recommended his state to the care of the other. Against a class of men who themselves stuck at nothing everything was held to be permissible. Francesco Sforza, when quite young, had married a rich Calabrian heiress, Polissena Russa, Countess of Montalto, who bore him a daughter; an aunt poisoned both mother and child, and seized the inheritance.[5]

From the death of Piccinino onward the foundations of new states by the *condottieri* became a scandal not to be tolerated. The four great Powers, Naples, Milan, the Papacy, and Venice, formed among themselves a political

---

[1] Æneas Sylvius, *Comment. de Dictis et Factis Alfonsi*, p. 251, *Opera*, ed. 1538: "Novitate gaudens Italia nihil habet stabile, nullum in ea vetus regnum, facile hic ex servis reges videmus."

[2] *Pii II Comment.*, i, 46; *cf.* 69.

[3] Sismondi, x, 258; Corio, fol. 412, where Sforza is accused of complicity, as he feared danger to his own sons from Piccinino's popularity. This complicity on the part of Sforza, despite recent denials, has been proved by D. Gianpietro in *Archiv. Stor. delle Prov. Napol.*, vii. *Storia Bresciana*, in Murat., xxi, col. 902. How the Venetian *condottiere* Colleoni was tempted in 1466 is told by Malipiero, *Ann. Venet.*, *Archiv. Stor.*, vii, i, p. 210. The Florentine exiles offered to make him Duke of Milan if he would expel from Florence their enemy Piero de' Medici.

[4] Allegretto, *Diari Sanesi*, in Murat., xxiii, p. 811.

[5] *Orationes Philelphi*, fol. 9 (ed. Venet., 1492), in the funeral oration on Francesco.

equilibrium which refused to allow of any disturbance. In the States of the Church, which swarmed with petty tyrants, who in part were, or had been, *condottieri*, the nephews of the Popes, since the time of Sixtus IV, monopolized the right to all such undertakings. But at the first sign of a political crisis the soldiers of fortune appeared again upon the scene. Under the wretched administration of Innocent VIII it was near happening that a certain Boccalino, who had formerly served in the Burgundian army, gave himself and the town of Osimo, of which he was master, up to the Turkish forces;[1] fortunately, through the intervention of Lorenzo the Magnificent, he proved willing to be paid off, and took himself away. In 1495, when the wars of Charles VIII had turned Italy upside-down, the *condottiere* Vidovero, of Brescia, made trial of his strength:[2] he had already seized the town of Cesena and murdered many of the nobles and the burghers; but the citadel held out, and he was forced to withdraw. He then, at the head of a band lent him by another scoundrel, Pandolfo Malatesta of Rimini, son of the Roberto already spoken of, and Venetian *condottiere*, wrested the town of Castelnuovo from the Archbishop of Ravenna. The Venetians, fearing that worse would follow, and urged also by the Pope, ordered Pandolfo, "with the kindest intentions," to take an opportunity of arresting his good friend: the arrest was made, though "with great regret," whereupon the order came to bring the prisoner to the gallows. Pandolfo was considerate enough to strangle him in prison, and then show his corpse to the people. The last notable example of such usurpers is the famous Castellan of Musso, who, during the confusion in the Milanese territory which followed the battle of Pavia (1525), improvised a sovereignty on the Lake of Como.

[1] Marin Sanudo, *Vita dei Duchi di Venezia*, in Murat., xxii, col. 1241. See Reumont, *Lorenzo dei Medici*, ii, pp. 324–327 (Leipzig, 1874), and the authorities there quoted.
[2] Malipiero, *Ann. Venet.*, *Archiv. Stor.*, vii, i, p. 407.

CHAPTER IV

THE PETTY TYRANNIES

T may be said in general of the despotisms of the fifteenth century that the greatest crimes are most frequent in the smallest states. In these, where the family was numerous and all the members wished to live in a manner befitting their rank, disputes respecting the inheritance were unavoidable. Bernardo Varano of Camerino put (1434) two of his brothers to death,[1] wishing to divide their property among his sons. Where the ruler of a single town was distinguished by a wise, moderate, and humane government, and by zeal for intellectual culture, he was generally a member of some great family, or politically dependent on it. This was the case, for example, with Alessandro Sforza,[2] Prince of Pesaro, brother of the great Francesco, and stepfather of Federigo of Urbino (d. 1473). Prudent in administration, just and affable in his rule, he enjoyed, after years of warfare, a tranquil reign, collected a noble library, and passed his leisure in learned or religious conversation. A man of the same class was Giovanni II Bentivoglio of Bologna (1462–1506), whose policy was determined by that of the Este and the Sforza. What ferocity and bloodthirstiness are found, on the other hand, among the Varani of Camerino, the Malatesta of Rimini, the Manfreddi of Faenza, and above all among the Baglioni of Perugia! We find a striking picture of the events in the last-named family toward the close of the fifteenth century in the admirable historical narratives of Graziani and Materazzo.[3]

The Baglioni were one of those families whose rule never took the shape of an avowed despotism. It was rather a leadership exercised by means of their vast wealth and of their practical influence in the choice of public officers. Within the family one man was recognized as head; but deep and secret jealousy prevailed among the members of the different branches. Opposed to the Baglioni stood another aristocratic party, led by the family of the Oddi. In 1487 Perugia was turned into a camp, and the houses of the leading citizens swarmed with bravoes; scenes of violence were of daily occurrence. At the burial of a German student, who had been assassinated, two colleges took arms against one another; sometimes the bravoes of the different houses even joined battle in the public square. The complaints of the merchants and artisans were vain; the Papal Governors and *nipoti* held their tongues, or took themselves off on the first opportunity. At last the Oddi were forced to abandon

[1] *Chron. Eugubinum,* in Murat., xxi, col. 972. *Cf.* Feliciangel in *Giorn. Stor.,* 13, 1 *sqq.*
[2] Vespas. Fiorent., p. 148.
[3] *Archiv. Stor.,* xvi, Parte I and II (ed. Bonaini, Fabretti, Polidori).

Perugia, and the city became a beleaguered fortress under the absolute despotism of the Baglioni, who used even the cathedral as barracks. Plots and surprises were met with cruel vengeance; in 1491, after a hundred and thirty conspirators who had forced their way into the city were killed and hung up at the Palazzo Communale, thirty-five altars were erected in the square, and for three days Mass was performed and processions held to take away the curse which rested on the spot. A nephew of Innocent VIII was in open day run through in the street. A nephew of Alexander VI, who was sent to smooth matters over, was dismissed with public contempt. All the while the two

FIG. 12. THE PALAZZO COMMUNALE, PERUGIA

leaders of the ruling house, Guido and Ridolfo, were holding frequent interviews with Suor Colomba of Rieti, a Dominican nun of saintly reputation and miraculous powers, who under penalty of some great disaster ordered them to make peace—naturally in vain. Nevertheless the chronicle takes the opportunity to point out the devotion and piety of the better men in Perugia during this reign of terror. When in 1494 Charles VIII approached the Baglioni from Perugia and the exiles encamped in and near Assisi conducted the war with such ferocity that every house in the valley was levelled to the ground. The fields lay untilled, the peasants were turned into plundering and murdering savages, the fresh-grown bushes were filled with stags and wolves, and the beasts grew fat on the bodies of the slain, on so-called " Christian flesh." When Alexander VI withdrew (1495) into Umbria before Charles VIII, then returning from Naples, it occurred to him, when at Perugia, that he might now rid himself of the Baglioni once for all; he proposed to Guido a festival or tournament, or something else of the same kind, which would bring the whole family together. Guido, however, was of opinion " that the most impressive

46

spectacle of all would be to see the whole military force of Perugia collected in a body," whereupon the Pope abandoned his project. Soon after the exiles made another attack, in which nothing but the personal heroism of the Baglioni won them the victory. It was then that Simonetto Baglione, a lad of scarcely eighteen, fought in the square with a handful of followers against hundreds of the enemy: he fell at last with more than twenty wounds, but recovered himself when Astorre Baglione came to his help, and, mounting on horseback in

FIG. 13. THE CELESTIAL RIDER FROM "THE EXPULSION OF HELIODORUS FROM THE TEMPLE"
By Raphael
Rome, Vatican

gilded armour with a falcon on his helmet, " like Mars in bearing and in deeds, plunged into the struggle."

At that time Raphael, a boy of twelve years of age, was at school under Pietro Perugino. The impressions of these days are perhaps immortalized in the small early pictures of St Michael and St George: something of them, it may be, lives eternally in the great painting of St Michael; and if Astorre Baglione has anywhere found his apotheosis it is in the figure of the heavenly horseman in the *Heliodorus*.

The opponents of the Baglioni were partly destroyed, partly scattered in terror, and were henceforth incapable of another enterprise of the kind. After a time a partial reconciliation took place, and some of the exiles were allowed to return. But Perugia became none the safer or more tranquil: the inward

47

discord of the ruling family broke out in frightful excesses. An opposition was formed against Guido and Ridolfo and their sons Gianpaolo, Simonetto, Astorre, Gismondo, Gentile, Marcantonio, and others by two great-nephews, Grifone and Carlo Barciglia; the latter of the two was also nephew of Varano, Prince of Camerino, and brother of one of the former exiles, Ieronimo della Penna. In vain did Simonetto, warned by sinister presentiment, entreat his uncle on his knees to allow him to put Penna to death; Guido refused. The plot ripened suddenly on the occasion of the marriage of Astorre with Lavinia Colonna, at midsummer 1500. The festival began and lasted several days amid gloomy forebodings, whose deepening effect is admirably described by Matarazzo. Varano fed and encouraged them with devilish ingenuity: he worked upon Grifone by the prospect of undivided authority, and by stories of an imaginary intrigue of his wife Zenobia with Gianpaolo. Finally each conspirator was provided with a victim. (The Baglioni lived all of them in separate houses, mostly on the site of the present castle.) Each received fifteen of the bravoes at hand; the remainder were set on the watch. In the night of July 15 the doors were forced, and Guido, Astorre, Simonetto, and Gismondo were murdered; the others succeeded in escaping.

As the corpse of Astorre lay by that of Simonetto in the street the spectators, "and especially the foreign students," compared him to an ancient Roman, so great and imposing did he seem. In the features of Simonetto could still be traced the audacity and defiance which death itself had not tamed. The victors went round among the friends of the family, and did their best to recommend themselves; they found all in tears and preparing to leave for the country. Meantime the escaped Baglioni collected forces without the city, and on the following day forced their way in, Gianpaolo at their head, and speedily found adherents among others whom Barciglia had been threatening with death. When Grifone fell into their hands near S. Ercolono Gianpaolo handed him over for execution to his followers. Barciglia and Penna fled to Varano, the chief author of the tragedy, at Camerino; and in a moment, almost without loss, Gianpaolo became master of the city.

Atalanta, the still young and beautiful mother of Grifone, who the day before had withdrawn to a country house with the latter's wife Zenobia and two children of Gianpaolo, and more than once had repulsed her son with a mother's curse, now returned with her stepdaughter in search of the dying man. All stood aside as the two women approached, each man shrinking from being recognized as the slayer of Grifone, and dreading the malediction of the mother. But they were deceived: she herself besought her son to pardon him who had dealt the fatal blow, and he died with her blessing. The eyes of the crowd followed the two women reverently as they crossed the square with bloodstained garments. It was Atalanta for whom Raphael afterward painted the world-famed *Deposition*, with which she laid her own maternal sorrows at the feet of a yet higher and holier suffering.

The cathedral, in the immediate neighbourhood of which the greater part of this tragedy had been enacted, was washed with wine and consecrated afresh.

The triumphal arch, erected for the wedding, still remained standing, painted with the deeds of Astorre and with the laudatory verses of the narrator of these events, the worthy Matarazzo.

A legendary history, which is simply the reflection of these atrocities, arose out of the early days of the Baglioni.   All the members of this family from the beginning were reported to have died an evil death—twenty-seven on one occasion together; their houses were said to have been once before levelled to

FIG. 14. SIGISMONDO MALATESTA
Rimini, Cathedral
Photo Alinari

the ground, and the streets of Perugia paved with the bricks—and more of the same kind.   Under Paul III the destruction of their palaces really took place.[1]

For a time they seem to have formed good resolutions, to have brought their own party into order, and to have protected the public officials against the arbitrary acts of the nobility.   But the old curse broke out again, like a smouldering fire.   Gianpaolo was enticed to Rome under Leo X, and there beheaded; one of his sons, Orazio, who ruled in Perugia for a short time only, and by the most violent means, as the partisan of the Duke of Urbino (himself threatened by the Pope), once more repeated in his own family the horrors of

---

[1] Julius II conquered Perugia with ease in 1506, and compelled Gianpaolo Baglione to submit.   The latter, as Machiavelli (*Discorsi*, i, 27) tells us, missed the chance of immortality by not murdering the Pope.

the past. His uncle and three cousins were murdered, whereupon the Duke sent him word that enough had been done.[1] His brother, Malatesta Baglione, the Florentine general, has made himself immortal by the treason of 1530; and Malatesta's son Ridolfo, the last of the house, attained, by the murder of the legate and the public officers in 1534, a brief but sanguinary authority.

Here and there we meet with the names of the rulers of Rimini. Unscrupulousness, impiety, military skill, and high culture have been seldom so combined in one individual as in Sigismondo Malatesta (d. 1467).[2] But the accumulated crimes of such a family must at last outweigh all talent, however great, and drag the tyrant into the abyss. Pandolfo, Sigismondo's nephew, who has been mentioned already, succeeded in holding his ground for the sole reason that the Venetians refused to abandon their *condottiere*, whatever guilt he might be chargeable with; when his subjects (1497), after ample provocation,[3] bombarded him in his castle at Rimini, and afterward allowed him to escape, a Venetian commissioner brought him back, stained as he was with fratricide and every other abomination. Thirty years later the Malatesta were penniless exiles. In 1527, as in the time of Cesare Borgia, a sort of epidemic fell on the petty tyrants; few of them outlived this date, and none to their own good. At Mirandola, which was governed by insignificant princes of the house of Pico, lived in 1533 a poor scholar, Lilio Gregorio Giraldi, who had fled from the sack of Rome to the hospitable hearth of the aged Giovanni Francesco Pico, nephew of the famous Giovanni; the discussions as to the sepulchral monument which the Prince was constructing for himself gave rise to a treatise, the dedication of which bears the date of April in this year. The postscript is a sad one.[4] "In October of the same year the unhappy Prince was attacked in the night and robbed of life and throne by his brother's son; and I myself escaped narrowly, and am now in the deepest misery."

A pseudo-despotism without characteristic features, such as Pandolfo Petrucci exercised from 1490 in Siena, then torn by faction, is hardly worth a closer consideration. Insignificant and malicious, he governed with the help of a professor of jurisprudence and of an astrologer, and frightened his people by an occasional murder. His pastime in the summer months was to roll blocks of stone from the top of Monte Amiata, without caring what or whom they hit. After succeeding, where the most prudent failed, in escaping from the devices of Cesare Borgia, he died at last forsaken and despised.[5] His sons maintained a qualified supremacy for many years afterward.

---

[1] Varchi, *Stor. Fiorent.*, i, pp. 242 *sqq.*

[2] *Cf.* (*inter al.*) Jov. Pontan., *De Immanitate*, cap. 17.

[3] Malipiero, *Ann. Venet., Archiv. Stor.*, vii, i, pp. 498 *sqq.* After vainly searching for his beloved, whose father had shut her up in a monastery, he threatened the father, burnt the monastery and other buildings, and committed many acts of violence.

[4] Lil. Greg. Giraldus, *De Sepulchris ac Vario Sepeliendi Ritu*, i, pp. 640 *sqq.* (*Opera*, ed. Bas., 1580). Later edition by J. Faes (Helmstädt, 1676). Dedication and postscript of Gir., "ad Carolum Miltz Germanum," in these editions without date; neither contains the passage given in the text. In 1470 a catastrophe in miniature had already occurred in the same family (Galeotto had had his brother Antonio Maria thrown into prison). Cf. *Diario Ferrarese*, in Murat., xxiv, col. 225.

[5] See, in contrast to the above, the defence of Petrucci by C. Falletti-Fossati, *Atti d. Acc. dei Fisiocritici*, vol. x, p. 92 (1883).—L. G.]

CHAPTER V

THE GREATER DYNASTIES

IN treating of the chief dynasties of Italy it is convenient to discuss the Aragonese, on account of its special character, apart from the rest. The feudal system, which from the days of the Normans had survived in the form of a territorial supremacy of the barons, gave a distinctive colour to the political constitution of Naples; while elsewhere in Italy, excepting only in the southern part of the ecclesiastical dominion, and in a few other districts, a direct tenure of land prevailed, and no hereditary powers were permitted by the law. The great Alfonso, who reigned in Naples from 1435 onward (d. 1458), was a man of another kind than his real or alleged descendants. Brilliant in his whole existence, fearless in mixing with his people, mild and generous toward his enemies, dignified and affable in intercourse, modest notwithstanding his legitimate royal descent, admired rather than blamed even for his old man's passion for Lucrezia d'Alagna, he had the one bad quality of extravagance,[1] from which, however, the natural consequence followed. Unscrupulous financiers were long omnipotent at Court, till the bankrupt King robbed them of their spoils; a crusade was preached, as a pretext for taxing the clergy; the Jews were forced to save themselves from conversion and other oppressive measures by presents and the payment of regular taxes; when a great earthquake happened in the Abruzzi the survivors were compelled to make good the contributions of the dead. On the other hand, he abolished unreasonable taxes, like that on dice, and aimed at relieving his poorer subjects from the imposts which pressed most heavily upon them. By such means Alfonso was able to entertain distinguished guests with unrivalled splendour; he found pleasure in ceaseless expense, even for the benefit of his enemies, and in rewarding literary work knew absolutely no measure. Poggio received five hundred pieces of gold for translating Xenophon's *Cyropædia*.

Ferrante,[2] who succeeded him, passed as his illegitimate son by a Spanish

[1] Jov. Pontan., *Opp.*, ed. Basileæ, 1538, t. i, *De Liberalitate*, cap. 19, 29, and *De Obedientia*, lib. 4. *Cf.* Sismondi, x, p. 78, and Panormita, *De Dictis et Factis Alfonsi*, lib. i, No. 61; iv, No. 42.

[2] Tristano Caracciolo, *De Fernando qui postea Rex Aragonum fuit ejusque Posteris*, in Murat., xxii, col. 113–120; Jov. Pontan., *De Prudentia*, lib. iv; *De Magnanimitate*, lib. i; *De Liberalitate*, cap. 29, 36; *De Immanitate*, cap. 8; Cam. Porzio, *Congiura dei Baroni del Regno di Napoli contro il Re Ferdinando I* (Pisa, 1818), cap. 29, 36, *passim* (new ed., Naples, 1859); [Porzio's reliability is called in question by Fr. Torraca, *Scritti Critici*, p. 466 (Naples, 1907).—L. G.] Comines, *Charles VIII*, Chapter 17, with the general characteristics of the Aragonese. See for further information as to Ferrante's works for his people, the *Regis Ferdinandi Primi Instructionum Liber*, 1486–87, edited by Scipione Volpicella (Naples, 1861), which would dispose us to moderate to some extent the harsh judgment which has been passed upon him. Also Trinchera, *Codice Aragonese* (2 vols., Naples, 1868–70).

lady, but was not improbably the son of a half-caste Moor of Valencia. Whether it was his blood or the plots formed against his life by the barons which embittered and darkened his nature, it is certain that he was equalled in ferocity by none among the princes of his time. Restlessly active, recognized as one of the most powerful political minds of the day, and free from the vices of the profligate, he concentrated all his powers, among which must be reckoned profound dissimulation and an irreconcilable spirit of vengeance, on the destruction of his opponents. He had been wounded in every point in which a ruler is open to offence; for the leaders of the barons, though related to him by marriage, were yet the allies of his foreign enemies. Extreme measures became part of his daily policy. The means for this struggle with his barons, and for his external wars, were exacted in the same Mohammedan fashion which Frederick II had introduced: the Government alone dealt in oil and wine; the whole commerce of the country was put by Ferrante into the hands of a wealthy merchant, Francesco Coppola, who had entire control of the anchorage on the coast, and shared the profits with the King. Deficits were made up by forced loans, by executions and confiscations, by open simony, and by contributions levied on the ecclesiastical corporations. Besides hunting, which he practised regardless of all rights of property, his pleasures were of two kinds: he liked to have his opponents near him, either alive in well-guarded prisons, or dead and embalmed, dressed in the costume which they wore in their lifetime.[1] He would chuckle in talking of the captives with his friends, and made no secret whatever of the museum of mummies. His victims were mostly men whom he had got into his power by treachery; some were even seized while guests at the royal table. His conduct to his first minister, Antonello Petrucci, who had grown sick and grey in his service, and from whose increasing fear of death he extorted present after present, was literally devilish. At length the suspicion of complicity with the last conspiracy of the barons gave the pretext for his arrest and execution. With him died Coppola. The way in which all this is narrated in Caracciolo and Porzio makes one's hair stand on end. The elder of the King's sons, Alfonso, Duke of Calabria, enjoyed in later years a kind of coregency with his father. He was a savage, brutal profligate—described by Comines as "the cruellest, worst, most vicious, and basest man ever seen"—who in point of frankness alone had the advantage of Ferrante, and who openly avowed his contempt for religion and its usages.[2] The better and nobler features of the Italian despotisms are not to be found among the princes of this line; all that they possessed of the art and culture of their time served the purposes of luxury or display.[3] Even the genuine Spaniards seem to have almost always degenerated in Italy; but

[1] Paul. Jovius, *Histor.*, i, p. 14, in the speech of a Milanese ambassador; *Diario Ferrarese*, in Murat., xxiv, col. 294. Gothein, *Kulturentwicklung Süditaliens*, p. 525, note 1, explains that this habit of dressing the corpses was not due to any special lack of humanity in Ferrante, but to a custom which the Neapolitans of to-day still approve.

[2] He lived in the closest intimacy with Jews—for example, Isaac Abranavel, who fled with him to Messina. Cf. Zunz, *Zur. Gesch. und Lit.*, p. 529 (Berlin, 1845).

[3] Müntz, *Hist. de l'Art pend. la Renaissance*, declares that under the influence of Lorenzo de' Medici they became great patrons of art.

the end of this cross-bred house (1494 and 1503) gives clear proof of a want of blood. Ferrante died of mental care and trouble; Alfonso accused his brother Federigo, the only honest member of the family, of treason, and insulted him in the vilest manner. At length, though he had hitherto passed for one of the ablest generals in Italy, he lost his head and fled to Sicily, leaving his son, the younger Ferrante, a prey to the French and to domestic treason. A dynasty which had ruled as this had done must at least have sold its life dear, if its children were ever to hope for a restoration. But, as Comines one-sidedly, and yet on the whole rightly, observes on this occasion, " Jamais homme cruel ne fut hardi."

The despotism of the Dukes of Milan, whose government from the time of Giangaleazzo onward was an absolute monarchy of the most thoroughgoing sort, shows the genuine Italian character of the fifteenth century. The last of the Visconti, Filippo Maria (1412–47), is a character of peculiar interest, and of which fortunately an admirable description [1] has been left us. What a

FIG. 15. FILIPPO MARIA VISCONTI

man of uncommon gifts and high position can be made by the passion of fear is here shown with what may be called a mathematical completeness. All the resources of the State were devoted to the one end of securing his personal safety, though happily his cruel egoism did not degenerate into a purposeless thirst for blood. He lived in the citadel of Milan, surrounded by magnificent gardens, arbours, and lawns. For years he never set foot in the city, making his excursions only in the country, where lay several of his splendid castles; the flotilla which, drawn by the swiftest horses, conducted him to them along canals constructed for the purpose was so arranged as to allow of the application of the most rigorous etiquette. Whoever entered the citadel was watched by a hundred eyes; it was forbidden even to stand at the window, lest signs should be given to those without. All who were admitted among the personal

[1] *Petri Candidi Decembrii Vita Philippi Mariæ Vicecomitis*, in Murat., xx, of which, however, Jovius (*Vitæ XII Vicecomitum*, p. 186) says not without reason: "Quum omissis laudibus quæ in Philippo celebrandæ fuerant, vitia notaret." Guarino praises this prince highly. Rosmini, *Guarino*, ii, p. 75. Jovius, in the above-mentioned work (p. 186), and Jov. Pontan., *De Liberalitate*, ii, cap. 28 and 31, take special notice of his generous conduct to the captive Alfonso.

followers of the Prince were subjected to a series of the strictest examinations; then, once accepted, were charged with the highest diplomatic commissions, as well as with the humblest personal services—both in this Court being alike honourable. And this was the man who conducted long and difficult wars, who dealt habitually with political affairs of the first importance, and every day sent his plenipotentiaries to all parts of Italy. His safety lay in the fact that none of his servants trusted the others, that his *condottieri* were watched and

misled by spies, and that the ambassadors and higher officials were baffled and kept apart by artificially nourished jealousies, and in particular by the device of coupling an honest man with a knave. His inward faith too rested upon opposed and contradictory systems; he believed in blind necessity, and in the influence of the stars, and offering prayers at one and the same time to helpers of every sort;[1] he was a student of the ancient authors, as well as of French tales of chivalry. And yet the same man, who would never suffer death to be mentioned in his presence,[2] and caused his dying favourites to be removed from the castle, that no shadow might fall on the abode

FIG. 16. THE CITADEL OF MILAN IN THE FIFTEENTH CENTURY

From the edition of Vitruvius published in 1548

of happiness, deliberately hastened his own death by closing up a wound, and, refusing to be bled, died at last with dignity and grace.

His stepson and successor, the fortunate *condottiere* Francesco Sforza (1450–66, see p. 42), was perhaps of all the Italians of the fifteenth century the man most after the heart of his age. Never was the triumph of genius and individual power more brilliantly displayed than in him; and those who would not recognize his merit were at least forced to wonder at him as the spoilt child of fortune. The Milanese claimed it openly as an honour to be governed by so distinguished a master; when he entered the city the thronging populace bore him on horseback into the cathedral, without giving him the chance to dismount.[3] Let us listen to

---

[1] Were the fourteen marble statues of the saints in the citadel of Milan executed by him? See *History of the Frundsbergs*, fol. 27.

[2] It troubled him: " quod aliquando ' non esse ' necesse esset."

[3] Corio, fol. 400; Cagnola, in *Archiv. Stor.*, iii, p. 125.

the balance-sheet of his life, in the estimate of Pope Pius II, a judge in such matters: [1]

In 1459, when the Duke came to the congress at Mantua, he was sixty [really fifty-eight] years old; on horseback he looked like a young man; of a lofty and imposing

FIG. 17. FRANCESCO SFORZA
Florence, Bargello

figure, with serious features, calm and affable in conversation, princely in his whole bearing, with a combination of bodily and intellectual gifts unrivalled in our time,

[1] *Pii II Comment.*, iii, p. 130. *Cf.* ii, 87, 106. Another and rather darker estimate of Sforza's fortune is given by Caracciolo, *De Varietate Fortunæ*, in Murat., xxii, col. 74. See for the opposite view the praises of Sforza's luck in the *Oratio Parentalis de Divi Francesci Sphortiæ Felicitate*, by Filelfo (the ready eulogist of any master who paid him), who sang, without publishing, the exploits of Francesco in the *Sforziad.* Even Decembrio, the moral and literary opponent of Filelfo, celebrates Sforza's fortune in his biography (*Vita Franc. Sphortiæ*, in Murat., xx). The astrologers said: "Francesco Sforza's star brings good luck to a man, but ruin to his descendants." Arluni, *De Bello Veneto*, lib. vi, in J. G. Grævius, *Thes. Antiqu. et Hist. Italicæ*, v, Pars III. *Cf.* also Barth. Facius, *De Vir. Ill.*, p. 67.

unconquered on the field of battle—such was the man who raised himself from a humble position to the control of an empire. His wife was beautiful and virtuous, his children were like the angels of heaven; he was seldom ill, and all his chief wishes were fulfilled. And yet he was not without misfortune. His wife, out of jealousy, killed his mistress; his old comrades and friends, Troilo and Brunoro, abandoned him and went over to King Alfonso; another, Ciarpollone, he was forced to hang for treason; he had to suffer it that his brother Alessandro set the French upon him; one of his sons formed intrigues against him, and was imprisoned; the March of Ancona, which he had won in war, he lost again in the same way. No man enjoys so unclouded a fortune that he has not somewhere to struggle with adversity. He is happy who has but few troubles.

With this negative definition of happiness the learned Pope dismisses the reader. Had he been able to see into the future, or been willing to stop and discuss the consequences of an uncontrolled despotism, one pervading fact would not have escaped his notice—the absence of all guarantee for the future. Those children, beautiful as angels, carefully and thoroughly educated as they were, fell victims when they grew up to the corruption of a measureless egoism. Galeazzo Maria (1466–76), solicitous only of outward effect, took pride in the beauty of his hands, in the high salaries he paid, in the financial credit he enjoyed, in his treasure of two million pieces of gold, in the distinguished people who surrounded him, and in the army and birds of chase which he maintained.

FIG. 18. GALEAZZO MARIA SFORZA
By Antonio del Pollaiuolo
Florence, Uffizi
Photo Alinari

He was fond of the sound of his own voice, and spoke well, most fluently, perhaps, when he had the chance of insulting a Venetian ambassador.[1]   He

FIG. 19. LODOVICO IL MORO
Part of the Pala Sforzesca (Sforza altar-piece)
Milan, Brera
Photo Alinari

was subject to caprices, such as having a room painted with figures in a single night; and, what was worse, to fits of senseless debauchery and of revolting cruelty to his nearest friends.   To a handful of enthusiasts, at whose head stood Giov. Andrea di Lampugnano, he seemed a tyrant too bad to live;

[1] Malipiero, *Ann. Venet., Archiv. Stor.*, vii, i, pp. 216 *sqq.*, 221–224.

they murdered him,[1] and thereby delivered the state into the power of his brothers, one of whom, Lodovico il Moro, threw his nephew into prison, and took the government into his own hands. From this usurpation followed the French intervention and the disasters which befell the whole of Italy.

The Moor is the most perfect type of the despot of that age, and, as a kind of natural product, almost disarms our moral judgment. Notwithstanding the profound immorality of the means he employed, he used them with perfect

FIG. 20. THE CITADEL OF MILAN: NORTH-WEST FRONT
Photo Seemann, Leipzig

ingenuousness; no one would probably have been more astonished than himself to learn that for the choice of means as well as of ends a human being is morally responsible; he would rather have reckoned it as a singular virtue that, so far as possible, he had abstained from too free a use of the punishment of death. He accepted as no more than his due the almost fabulous respect of the Italians for his political genius.[2] In 1496 he boasted that the Pope Alexander was his chaplain, the Emperor Maximilian his *condottiere*, Venice his chamberlain, and the King of France his courier, who must come and go at his

---

[1] Important documents as to the murder of Galeazzo Maria Sforza are published by G. D'Adda in the *Archivio Storico Lombardo; Giornale della Società Lombarda*, vol. ii, pp. 284–294 (1875): (1) a Latin epitaph on the murderer Lampugnano, who lost his life in the attempt, and whom the writer represents as saying: "Hic lubens quiesco, æternum inquam facinus monumentumque ducibus, principibus, regibus, qui modo sunt quique mox futura trahantur ne quid adversus justitiam faciant dicantve"; (2) a Latin letter of Domenico de' Belli, who, when eleven years old, was present at the murder; (3) the *lamento* of Galeazzo Maria, in which, after calling upon the Virgin Mary and relating the outrage committed upon him, he summons his wife and children, his servants and the Italian cities which obeyed him, to bewail his fate, and sends forth his entreaty to all the nations of the earth, to the nine Muses and the gods of antiquity, to set up a universal cry of grief.

[2] *Chron. Venetum*, in Murat., xxiv, col. 65.

bidding.[1] With marvellous presence of mind he weighed, even in his last extremity, all possible means of escape, and at length decided, to his honour, to trust to the goodness of human nature; he rejected the proposal of his brother, Cardinal Ascanio, who wished to remain in the citadel of Milan, on the ground of a former quarrel: "Monsignore, take it not ill, but I trust you not, brother though you be"; and appointed to the command of the castle, "that pledge of his return," a man to whom he had always done good, but who nevertheless betrayed him.[2] At home the Moor was a good and useful ruler, and to the last he reckoned on his popularity both in Milan and in Como. In former years (after 1496) he had overstrained the resources of his state, and at Cremona had ordered, out of pure expediency, a respectable citizen who had spoken against the new taxes to be quietly strangled. Since that time, in holding audiences, he kept his visitors away from his person by means of a bar, so that in conversing with him they were compelled to speak at the top of their voices.[3] At his Court, the most brilliant in Europe since that of Burgundy had ceased to exist, immorality of the worst kind was prevalent: the daughter was sold by the father, the wife by the husband, the sister by the brother.[4] The Prince himself was incessantly active, and, as son of his own deeds, claimed relationship with all who, like himself, stood on their personal merits—with scholars, poets, artists, and musicians. The academy which he founded[5] served rather for his own purposes than for the instruction of scholars; nor was it the fame of the distinguished men who surrounded him which he heeded, so much as their society and their services. It is certain that Bramante was scantily paid at first;[6] Leonardo, on the other hand, was up to 1496 suitably remunerated—and besides, what kept him at the Court, if not his own free will? The world lay open to him, as perhaps to no other mortal man of that day; and if proof were wanting of the loftier element in the nature of Lodovico il Moro, it is found in the long stay of the enigmatic master at his Court. That afterward Leonardo entered the service of Cesare Borgia and Francis I was probably due to the interest he felt in the unusual and striking character of the two men.

After the fall of the Moor—he was captured in April 1500 by the French, after his return from his flight to Germany—his sons were badly brought up among strangers, and showed no capacity for carrying out his political testament. The elder, Massimiliano, had no resemblance to him; the younger, Francesco, was at all events not without spirit. Milan, which in those years

---

[1] Malipiero, *Ann. Venet.*, *Archiv. Stor.*, vii, i, p. 492. *Cf.* 482, 562.

[2] His last words to the same man, Bernardino da Corte, are to be found, certainly with oratorical decorations, but perhaps agreeing in the main with the thoughts of the Moor, in Senarega, Murat., xxiv, col. 567.

[3] *Diario Ferrarese*, in Murat., xxiv, col. 336, 367, 369. The people believed he was forming a treasure.

[4] Corio, fol. 448. The after-effects of this state of things are clearly recognizable in those of the novels and introductions of Bandello which relate to Milan. [Malaguzzi Valeri (*La Corte di Lodovico il Moro, La Vita Privata e l'Arte*, pp. 126 *sqq.*, Milan, 1913) contests the view that crimes were especially numerous at the Milanese Court.—L. G.]

[5] Amoretti, *Memorie Storiche sulla Vita Ecc. di Lionardo da Vinci*, pp. 35 *sqq.*, 83 *sqq.* [Actually this academy never existed. Cf. *Giorn. Stor.*, xxix, 534; xxxvii, 414.—L. G.] Here we may also mention the Moor's efforts for the improvement of the University of Pavia.

[6] See his sonnets in Trucchi, *Poesie Ital. Ined.*

changed its rulers so often, and suffered so unspeakably in the change, endeavoured to secure itself against a reaction. In 1512 the French, retreating before the arms of Maximilian and the Spaniards,[1] were induced to make a declaration that the Milanese had taken no part in their expulsion, and, without being guilty of rebellion, might yield themselves to a new conqueror.[2] It is a fact of some political importance that in such moments of transition the

FIG. 21. FAMILY GROUP OF THE GONZAGA
By Mantegna
Mantua, Castello di Corte

unhappy city, like Naples at the flight of the Aragonese, was apt to fall a prey to gangs of (often highly aristocratic) scoundrels.

The house of Gonzaga at Mantua and that of Montefeltro of Urbino were among the best ordered and richest in men of ability during the second half of the fifteenth century. The Gonzaga were a tolerably harmonious family; for a long period no murder had been known among them, and their dead could be shown to the world without fear. The Marquis Francesco Gonzaga [3]

[1] It is a question rather of the armies of the Holy League and of Maximilian I.—W. G.]

[2] Prato, in the *Archiv. Stor.*, iii, 298. *Cf.* 302.

[3] Born 1466, betrothed to Isabella (herself six years of age) in 1480, suc. 1484, m. 1490, d. 1519. Isabella's death, 1539. Her sons, Federigo (1519-40), made Duke in 1530, and the famous Ferrante Gonzaga. What follows is taken from the correspondence of Isabella, with appendices, *Archiv. Stor.*, App., tom. ii, communicated by d'Arco. See the same writer, *Delle Arti e degli Artifici di Mantova* (2 vols., Mant., 1857-59). The catalogue of the collection has been repeatedly printed. Portrait and biography of Isabella in Didot, *Alde Manuce*, pp. lxi–lxviii (Paris, 1875). See also A. Luci o-R. Renier, *Mantova e Urbino, Isabella d'Este e Elisabetta*

and his wife, Isabella d'Este, in spite of some few irregularities, were a united and respectable couple, and brought up their sons to be successful and remark-

FIG. 22. ISABELLA D'ESTE
By Titian
Vienna, Art Gallery

able men at a time when their small but most important state was exposed to incessant danger. That Francesco, either as statesman or as soldier, should

Gonzaga nelle Relazioni Famigliari e nelle Vicende Politiche (Turin and Rome, 1893). A good summary may be found in an essay by F. v. Bezolds, *Aus dem Briefwechsel der Markgräfin Isabella von Este-Gonzaga*, in the *Archiv. für Kulturgeschichte*, 8 (1910).

adopt a policy of exceptional honesty was what neither the Emperor, nor Venice, nor the King of France could have expected or desired; but certainly since the battle at Taro (1495), so far as military honour was concerned, he felt and acted as an Italian patriot, and imparted the same spirit to his wife.[1] Every deed of loyalty and heroism, such as the defence of Faenza against Cesare Borgia, she felt as a vindication of the honour of Italy. Our judgment

FIG. 23. COURT OF SONG HELD BY ISABELLA D'ESTE
By Lorenzo Costa
Paris, Louvre

of her does not need to rest on the praises of the artists and writers who made the fair princess a rich return for her patronage; her own letters show her to us as a woman of unshaken firmness, full of kindliness and humorous observation. Bembo, Bandello, Ariosto, and Bernardo Tasso sent their works to this Court, small and powerless as it was, and empty as they found its treasury. A more polished and charming circle was not to be seen in Italy since the dissolution (1508) of the old Court of Urbino; and in one respect, in freedom of movement, the society of Ferrara was inferior to that of Mantua. In artistic

[1 The truth is that Francesco Gonzaga, in contrast to his wife, continued to waver between France and Milan.—W. G.]

matters Isabella had an accurate knowledge, and the catalogue of her small but choice collection can be read by no lover of art without emotion.

FIG. 24. BATTISTA SFORZA, WIFE OF DUKE FEDERIGO OF URBINO
By Piero della Francesca
Florence, Uffizi

In the great Federigo (1444–82), whether he were a genuine Montefeltro or not, Urbino possessed a brilliant representative of the princely order. As a *condottiere*—and in this capacity he served kings and Popes for thirty years after he became prince—he shared the political morality of soldiers of fortune,

FIG. 25. DUKE FEDERIGO DA MONTEFELTRE OF URBINO
By Piero della Francesca
Florence, Uffizi

a morality of which the fault does not rest with them alone; as ruler of his little territory he adopted the plan of spending at home the money he had earned abroad, and taxing his people as lightly as possible. Of him and his two

successors, Guidobaldo and Francesco Maria, we read: "They erected buildings, furthered the cultivation of the land, lived at home, and gave employment
to a large number of people: their subjects loved them." [1]   But not only the
State, but the Court too, was a work of art and organization, and this in every
sense of the word.   Federigo had five hundred persons in his service; the
arrangements of the Court were as complete as in the capitals of the greatest
monarchs, but nothing was wasted; all had its object, and all was carefully
watched and controlled.   The Court was no scene of vice and dissipation:
it served as a school of military education for the sons of other great houses,
the thoroughness of whose culture and instruction was made a point of honour
by the Duke.   The palace which he built, if not one of the most splendid, was
classical in the perfection of its plan; there was placed the greatest of his
treasures, the celebrated library. [2]   Feeling secure in a land where all gained
profit or employment from his rule, and where none were beggars, he habitually
went unarmed and almost unaccompanied; alone among the princes of his
time he ventured to walk in an open park, and to take his frugal meals in an
open chamber, while Livy, or in time of fasting some devotional work, was
read to him.   In the course of the same afternoon he would listen to a lecture
on some classical subject, and thence would go to the monastery of the Clarisse
and talk of sacred things through the grating with the abbess.   In the evening
he would overlook the martial exercises of the young people of his Court on
the meadow of S. Francesco, known for its magnificent view, and saw to it well
that all the feats were done in the most perfect manner.   He strove always to
be affable and accessible to the utmost degree, visiting the artisans who worked
for him in their shops, holding frequent audiences, and, if possible, attending
to the requests of each individual on the same day that they were presented.
No wonder that the people, as he walked along the street, knelt down and
cried: "*Dio ti mantenga, signore!*"   He was called by thinking people "the
light of Italy." [3]

His gifted son Guidobaldo, [4] visited by sickness and misfortune of every
kind, was able at the last (1508) to give his state into the safe hands of his
nephew Francesco Maria (nephew also of Pope Julius II), who, at least,
succeeded in preserving the territory from any permanent foreign occupation.   It is remarkable with what confidence Guidobaldo yielded and
fled before Cesare Borgia and Francesco before the troops of Leo X; each
knew that his restoration would be all the easier and the more popular the
less the country suffered through a fruitless defence.   When Lodovico made
the same calculation at Milan he forgot the many grounds of hatred which

---

[1] Franc. Vettori, in the *Archiv. Stor.*, App., tom. vi, p. 321.   For Federigo see Vespas. Fiorent., pp. 132 *sqq.*,
and Prendilacqua, *Vita di Vittorino da Feltre*, pp. 48–52.   Vespasiano endeavoured to calm the ambitious
youth Federigo, then his scholar, with the words "Tu quoque Cæsar eris."   There is much literary information
respecting him in, for example, Favre, *Mélanges d'Histoire Littéraire*, i, p. 125, note 1.

[2] See below, Part III, Chapter III.

[3] Castiglione, *Cortigiano*, lib. i.

[4] Petr. Bembus, *De Guido Ubaldo Feretrio deque Elizabetha Gonzaga Urbini Ducibus* (Venetis, 1530); also in
Bembo's *Works*, i, pp. 529–624 (Basel, 1566).   In the form of a dialogue; contains among other things the
letter of Frid. Fregosus and the speech of Odaxius on Guido's life and death.

existed against him. The Court of Guidobaldo has been made immortal as the high school of polished manners by Baldassare Castiglione, who represented his eclogue *Thyrsis* before, and in honour of, that society (1506), and who afterward (1518) laid the *scena* of the dialogue of his *Cortigiano* in the circle of the accomplished Duchess Elisabetta Gonzaga.

FIG. 26. THE DUCAL PALACE OF URBINO

The government of the family of Este at Ferrara, Modena, and Reggio displays curious contrasts of violence and popularity.[1] Within the palace frightful deeds were perpetrated; a princess was beheaded (1425) for alleged adultery with a stepson;[2] legitimate and illegitimate children fled from the Court, and even abroad their lives were threatened by assassins sent in pursuit of them (1471). Plots from without were incessant; the bastard of a bastard tried to wrest the crown from the lawful heir, Hercules I: this latter is said afterward (1493) to have poisoned his wife on discovering that she, at the instigation of her brother, Ferrante of Naples, was going to poison him. This list of tragedies is closed by the plot of two bastards against their brothers, the ruling Duke Alfonso I and Cardinal Ippolito (1506), which was discovered in time, and punished with imprisonment for life.

The financial system in this state was of the most perfect kind, and necessarily so, since none of the large or second-rate Powers of Italy were exposed to such danger and stood in such constant need of armaments and fortifications. It was the hope of the rulers that the increasing prosperity of the people would keep pace with the increasing weight of taxation, and the Marquis Niccolò (d. 1441) used to express the wish that his subjects might be richer than the people of other countries. If the rapid increase of the population be a measure of the prosperity actually attained,

[1] What follows is chiefly taken from the *Annales Estenses*, in Murat., xx, and the *Diario Ferrarese*, in Murat., xxiv.
[2] See Bandello, i, *Nov.* 32.

it is certainly a fact of importance that in 1497, notwithstanding the wonderful extension of the capital, no houses were to be let.[1]   Ferrara is the first really modern city in Europe; large and well-built quarters sprang up at the bidding of the ruler: here, by the concentration of the official classes and the active promotion of trade, was formed for the first time a true capital; wealthy fugitives from all parts of Italy, Florentines especially, settled and built their palaces at Ferrara.   But the indirect taxation, at all events, must have reached a point at which it could only just be borne.   The Government, it is true, took measures of alleviation which were also adopted by other Italian despots, such

FIG. 27. THE CITADEL, FERRARA

as Galeazzo Maria Sforza: in time of famine corn was brought from a distance, and seems to have been distributed gratuitously;[2] but in ordinary times it compensated itself by the monopoly, if not of corn, of many other of the necessaries of life—fish, salt meat, fruit, and vegetables, which last were carefully planted on and near the walls of the city.   The most considerable source of income, however, was the annual sale of public offices, a usage which was common throughout Italy, and about the working of which at Ferrara we have more precise information.   We read, for example, that at the new year 1502 the majority of the officials bought their places at *prezzi salati*; public servants of the most various kinds, custom-house officers, bailiffs (*massari*), notaries, *podestà*, judges, and even captains—*i.e.*, lieutenant-governors of provincial towns—are quoted by name.   As one of the "devourers of the people" who paid dearly for their places, and who were "hated worse than the devil," Tito

[1] *Diario Ferrarese, loc. cit.*, col. 347.
[2] Paul. Jovius, *Vita Alfonsi Ducis* (ed. Florence, 1550), also in Italian by Giovanbattista Gelli (Florence, 1553).

Strozzi—let us hope not the famous Latin poet—is mentioned.[1] About the same time every year the Dukes were accustomed to make a round of visits in Ferrara, the so-called *andar per ventura*, in which they took presents from, at any rate, the more wealthy citizens. The gifts, however, did not consist of money, but of natural products.

It was the pride of the Duke [2] for all Italy to know that at Ferrara the soldiers received their pay and the professors of the University their salary not

FIG. 28. BORSO D'ESTE AND RETINUE
Ferrara, Palazzo Schifanoja
Photo Alinari

a day later than it was due; that the soldiers never dared lay arbitrary hands on citizen or peasant; that the town was impregnable to assault; and that vast sums of coined money were stored up in the citadel. To keep two sets of accounts seemed unnecessary; the Minister of Finance was at the same time manager of the ducal household. The buildings erected by Borso (1430–71), by Hercules I (till 1505), and by Alfonso I (till 1534) were very numerous, but of small size: they are characteristic of a princely house which, with all its love of splendour—Borso never appeared but in embroidery and jewels—

---

[1] Tito Strozzi parried these attacks by saying: "Nulla magistratus gestos mihi sordida labes Foedavit, mundasque manus, dum munera cura Publica servavi." And Coel. Calcagninus has tried to prove that the popular hatred of the poet was undeserved.—L. G.]

[2] Paul. Jovius, *loc. cit.*

indulged in no ill-considered expense. Alfonso may perhaps have foreseen the fate which was in store for his charming little villas, the Belvedere, with its shady gardens, and Montana, with its fountains and beautiful frescoes.

It is undeniable that the dangers to which these princes were constantly exposed developed in them capacities of a remarkable kind. In so artificial

FIG. 29. ALFONSO I OF FERRARA
After Titian
Florence, Palazzo Pitti

a world only a man of consummate address could hope to succeed; each candidate for distinction was forced to make good his claims by personal merit and show himself worthy of the crown he sought. Their characters are not without dark sides; but in all of them lives something of those qualities which Italy then pursued as its ideal. What European monarch of the time so laboured for his own culture as, for instance, Alfonso I? His travels in France, England, and the Netherlands were undertaken for the purpose of study; by means of them he gained an accurate knowledge of the industry and commerce of these countries.[1]   It is ridiculous to reproach him with the turner's work which he practised in his leisure hours, connected as it was with his skill in the casting of cannon, and with the unprejudiced freedom with which he surrounded himself by masters of every art.   The Italian princes were not, like their contemporaries in the North, dependent on the society of an aristocracy which held itself to be the only class worth consideration, and which infected the monarch with the same conceit.   In Italy the prince was permitted and compelled to know and to use men of every grade in society; and the nobility, though by birth a caste, were forced in social intercourse to stand upon their personal qualifications alone.   But this is a point which we shall discuss more fully in the sequel.

The feeling of the Ferrarese toward the ruling house was a strange compound of silent dread, of the truly Italian sense of well-calculated interest, and of the loyalty of the modern subject: personal admiration was transformed into a new sentiment of duty.   The city of Ferrara raised in 1451 a bronze equestrian statue to their Prince Niccolò, who had died ten years earlier; Borso (1454) did not scruple to place his own statue, also of bronze, but in a sitting posture, hard by in the market; in addition to which the city, at the beginning of his reign, decreed to him a "marble triumphal pillar."   And when he was buried the whole people felt as if God Himself had died a second time.[2] A citizen who, when abroad from Venice, had spoken ill of Borso in public was denounced on his return home, and condemned to banishment and the confiscation of his goods; a loyal subject was with difficulty restrained from cutting him down before the tribunal itself, and with a rope round his neck the offender went to the Duke and begged for a full pardon.   The Government was well provided with spies, and the Duke inspected personally the daily list of travellers which the innkeepers were strictly ordered to present.   Under Borso,[3] who was anxious to leave no distinguished stranger unhonoured, this regulation served a hospitable purpose; Hercules I [4] used it simply as a measure of precaution.   In Bologna too it was then the rule, under Giovanni II Bentivoglio, that every passing traveller who entered at one gate must obtain a ticket in order to go out at another.[5]   An unfailing means of popularity was the sudden dismissal of oppressive officials.   When Borso arrested in person his chief and confidential counsellors, when Hercules I removed and disgraced a tax-gatherer who for years had been sucking the blood of the people, bonfires were lighted and the bells were pealed in their honour.   With one of his servants, however, Hercules let things go too far.   The director of the police, or by whatever name we should choose to call him (*capitano di giustizia*), was Gregorio Zampante of Lucca—a native being unsuited for an office of this kind.   Even the sons and brothers of the Duke trembled before this man; the fines he inflicted amounted to hundreds and thousands of ducats, and

---

[1] The journey of Leo X when cardinal may be also mentioned here. *Cf.* Paul. Jovius, *Vita Leonis X*, lib. i.   His purpose was less serious, and directed rather to amusement and knowledge of the world; but the spirit is wholly modern.   No Northerner then travelled with such objects.

[2] *Diario Ferrarese*, in Murat., xxiv, col. 232 and 240.   [3] Jov. Pontan., *De Liberalitate*, cap. 28.

[4] Giraldi, *Hecatommithi*, vi, *Nov.* 1 (ed. 1565, fol. 223*a*).   [5] Vasari, xii, 166, *Vita di Michelangelo*.

torture was applied even before the hearing of a case: bribes were accepted from wealthy criminals, and their pardon obtained from the Duke by false representations. Gladly would the people have paid any sum to this ruler for sending away the " enemy of God and man." But Hercules had knighted him and made him godfather to his children; and year by year Zampante laid

FIG. 30. ERCOLE I D'ESTE
By Dosso Dossi
Modena, Galleria Estense
Photo Anderson, Rome

by two thousand ducats. He dared only eat pigeons bred in his own house, and could not cross the street without a band of archers and bravoes. It was time to get rid of him; in 1490 two students and a converted Jew whom he had mortally offended killed him in his house while he was taking his *siesta*, and then rode through the town on horses held in waiting, raising the cry, " Come out! come out! we have slain Zampante!" The pursuers came too late, and found them already safe across the frontier. Of course it now rained satires—some of them in the form of sonnets, others of odes.

It was wholly in the spirit of this system that the sovereign imposed his own respect for useful servants on the Court and on the people. When in 1469 Borso's privy councillor Lodovico Casella died no court of law or place of business in the city, and no lecture-room at the University, was allowed to be open: all had to follow the body to S. Domenico, since the Duke intended to be present. And, in fact, "the first of the house of Este who attended the corpse of a subject" walked, clad in black, after the coffin, weeping, while behind him came the relatives of Casella, each conducted by one of the gentlemen of the Court; the body of the plain citizen was carried by nobles from the church into the cloister, where it was buried. Indeed this official sympathy with princely emotion first came up in the Italian states.[1] At the root of the practice may be a beautiful, humane sentiment; the utterance of it, especially in the poets, is, as a rule, of equivocal sincerity. One of the youthful poems of Ariosto,[2] on the death of Leonora of Aragon, wife of Hercules I, contains besides the inevitable graveyard flowers, which are scattered in the elegies of all ages, some thoroughly modern features.

> This death had given Ferrara a blow which it would not get over for years: its benefactress was now its advocate in heaven, since earth was not worthy of her; truly, the Angel of Death did not come to her, as to us common mortals, with bloodstained scythe, but fair to behold [onesta], and with so kind a face that every fear was allayed.

But we meet, also, with a sympathy of a different kind. Novelists, depending wholly on the favour of their patrons, tell us the love-stories of the prince, even before his death,[3] in a way which, to later times, would seem the height

---

[1] As early as 1446 the members of the house of Gonzaga followed the corpse of Vittorino da Feltre. For another early example see Bernabò Visconti, above, pp. 31 *sqq.*

[2] Capitolo 19, and in the *Opere Minore*, ed. Lemonnier, vol. i, p. 425, entitled *Elegia* 17. Doubtless the cause of this death (above, p. 66) was unknown to the young poet, then nineteen years old.

[3] The novels in the *Hecatommithi* of Giraldi relating to the house of Este are to be found, with one exception (i, *Nov.* 8), in the sixth book, dedicated to Francesco d'Este, Marchese della Massa, at the beginning of the second part of the whole work, which is inscribed to Alfonso II, "the fifth Duke of Ferrara." The tenth book too is specially dedicated to him, but none of the novels refer to him personally, and only one to his predecessor, Hercules I; the rest to Hercules I, "the second Duke," and Alfonso I, "the third Duke of Ferrara." But the stories told of these princes are for the most part not love-tales. One of them (i, *Nov.* 8) tells of the failure of an attempt made by the King of Naples to induce Hercules of Este to deprive Borso of the government of Ferrara; another (vi, *Nov.* 10) describes Hercules' high-spirited treatment of conspirators. The two novels that treat of Alfonso I (vi, *Nov.* 2, 4), in the latter of which he only plays a subordinate part, are also, as the title of the book shows and as the dedication to the above-named Francesco explains more fully, accounts of *atti di cortesia* toward knights and prisoners, but not toward women, and only the two remaining tales are love-stories. They are of such a kind as can be told during the lifetime of the Prince; they set forth his nobleness and generosity, his virtue and self-restraint. Only one of them (vi, *Nov.* 1) refers to Hercules I, who was dead long before the novels were compiled, and only one to the Hercules II then alive (b. 1508, d. 1568), son of Lucrezia Borgia, husband of Renata, of whom the poet says: "Il giovane, che non meno ha benigno l'animo, che cortese l' aspetto, come già il vedemmo in Roma, nel tempo, ch' egli, in vece del padre, venne a Papa Hadriano." The tale about him is briefly as follows. Lucilla, the beautiful daughter of a poor but noble widow, loves Nicandro, but cannot marry him, as the lover's father forbids him to wed a portionless maiden. Hercules, who sees the girl and is captivated by her beauty, finds his way, through the connivance of her mother, into her bedchamber, but is so touched by her beseeching appeal that he respects her innocence, and, giving her a dowry, enables her to marry Nicandro.

In Bandello, ii, *Nov.* 8 and 9 refer to Alessandro de' Medici, ii, 26, to Mary of Aragon, iii, 26, and iv, 13, to Galeazzo Sforza, iii, 36 and 37, to Henry VIII of England, and ii, 27, to the German Emperor Maximilian. The Emperor, "whose natural goodness and more than imperial generosity are praised by all writers," while chasing a stag is separated from his followers, loses his way, and at last, emerging from the wood, inquires the

of indiscretion, but which then passed simply as an innocent compliment. Lyrical poets even went so far as to sing the illicit flames of their lawfully married lords—*e.g.*, Angelo Poliziano those of Lorenzo the Magnificent, and Gioviano Pontano, with a singular gusto, those of Alfonso of Calabria. The poem in question [1] betrays unconsciously the odious disposition of the

FIG. 31. BORSO D'ESTE, HIS JESTER, AND COURTIERS
Fresco in the Palazzo Schifanoja, Ferrara
Photo Alinari

Aragonese ruler; in these things too he must needs be the most fortunate, else woe be to those who are more successful! That the greatest artists—for

way from a countryman. The latter, busied with lading wood, begs the Emperor, whom he does not know, to help him, and receives willing assistance. While still at work Maximilian is rejoined, and, in spite of his signs to the contrary, respectfully saluted by his followers, and thus recognized by the peasant, who implores forgiveness for the freedom he has unwittingly taken. The Emperor raises the kneeling suppliant, gives him presents, appoints him as his attendant, and confers upon him distinguished privileges. The narrator concludes: "Dimostrò Cesare nello amontar da cavallo e con allegra ciera aiutar il bisognoso contadino, una indicibile e degna d'ogni lode humanità, e in sollevarlo con danari e privilegii dalla sua faticosa vita, aperse il suo veramente animo Cesareo " (ii, 415). A story in the *Hecatommithi* (viii, *Nov.* 5) also treats of Maximilian. It is the same tale which has acquired a world-wide celebrity through Shakespeare's *Measure for Measure* (for its diffusion see Kirchhof's *Wendunmuth*, ed. Oesterley, Bd. v, pp. 152 *sqq.*), and the scene of which is transferred by Giraldi to Innsbruck. Maximilian is the hero, and here too receives the highest eulogies. After being first called "Massimiliano il Grande" he is designated as one "che fù raro esempio di cortesia, di magnanimità, e di singolare giustizia."

[1] In the *Deliciæ Poet. Italorum*, ii, pp. 455 *sqq.* (1608): "ad Alfonsum ducem Calabriæ." [Yet I do not believe that the above remark fairly applies to this poem, which clearly expresses the joys which Alfonso has with Drusula, and describes the sensations of the happy lover who, in his transports, thinks that the gods themselves must envy him.—L. G.]

example, Leonardo—should paint the mistresses of their patrons was no more than a matter of course.

But the house of Este was not satisfied with the praises of others; it undertook to celebrate them itself. In the Palazzo Schifanoja Borso caused himself to be painted in a series of historical representations, and Hercules kept the anniversary of his accession to the throne by a procession which was compared to the feast of Corpus Christi; shops were closed as on Sunday; in the centre of the line walked all the members of the princely house (bastards included), clad in embroidered robes. That the Crown was the fountain of honour and authority, that all personal distinction flowed from it alone, had been long [1] expressed at this Court by the Order of the Golden Spur—an order which had nothing in common with medieval chivalry. Hercules I added to the spur a sword, a gold-laced mantle, and a grant of money, in return for which there is no doubt that regular service was required.

The patronage of art and letters for which this Court has obtained a world-wide reputation was exercised through the University, which was one of the most perfect in Italy, and by the gift of places in the personal or official service of the prince; it involved consequently no additional expense. Bojardo, as a wealthy country gentleman and high official, belonged to this class. At the time when Ariosto began to distinguish himself there existed no Court, in the true sense of the word, either at Milan or Florence, and soon there was none either at Urbino or at Naples. He had to content himself with a place among the musicians and jugglers of Cardinal Ippolito till Alfonso took him into his service. It was otherwise at a later time with Torquato Tasso, whose presence at Court was jealously sought after.

[1] Mentioned as early as 1367, in the *Polistore*, in Murat., xxiv, col. 848, in reference to Niccolò the Elder, who makes twelve persons knights in honour of the twelve Apostles.

CHAPTER VI

The Opponents of Tyranny

N face of this centralized authority all legal opposition within the borders of the state was futile. The elements needed for the restoration of a republic had been for ever destroyed, and the field prepared for violence and despotism. The nobles, destitute of political rights, even where they held feudal possessions, might call themselves Guelphs or Ghibellines at will, might dress up their bravoes in padded hose and feathered caps,[1] or how else they pleased; thoughtful men like Machiavelli[2] knew well enough that Milan and Naples were too 'corrupt' for a republic. Strange judgments fall on these two so-called parties, which now served only to give an official sanction to personal and family disputes. An Italian prince, whom Agrippa of Nettesheim[3] advised to put them down, replied that their quarrels brought him in more than twelve thousand ducats a year in fines. And when in 1500, during the brief return of Lodovico il Moro to his states, the Guelphs of Tortona summoned a part of the neighbouring French army into the city, in order to make an end once for all of their opponents, the French certainly began by plundering and ruining the Ghibellines, but finished by doing the same to their hosts, till Tortona was utterly laid waste.[4] In Romagna, the hotbed of every ferocious passion, these two names had long lost all political meaning. It was a sign of the political delusion of the people that they not seldom believed the Guelphs to be the natural allies of the French and the Ghibellines of the Spaniards. It is hard to see that those who tried to profit by this error got much by doing so. France, after all her interventions, had to abandon the peninsula at last, and what became of Spain, after she had destroyed Italy, is known to every reader.

But to return to the despots of the Renaissance. A pure and simple mind, we might think, would perhaps have argued that, since all power is derived from God, these princes, if they were loyally and honestly supported by all their subjects, must in time themselves improve and lose all traces of their violent origin. But from characters and imaginations inflamed by passion and ambition reasoning of this kind could not be expected. Like bad physicians, they thought to cure the disease by removing the symptoms, and fancied that if the tyrant were put to death freedom would follow of itself. Or else,

---

[1] Burigozzo, in the *Archiv. Stor.*, iii, p. 432.
[2] *Discorsi*, i, 17, on Milan after the death of Filippo Visconti.
[3] *De Incert. et Vanitate Scientiar.*, cap. 55.
[4] Prato, *Archiv. Stor.*, iii, p. 241.

without reflecting even to this extent, they sought only to give a vent to the universal hatred, or to take vengeance for some family misfortune or personal affront. Since the Governments were absolute, and free from all legal restraints, the opposition chose its weapons with equal freedom. Boccaccio declares openly:[1]

> Shall I call the tyrant king or prince, and obey him loyally as my lord? No, for he is the enemy of the commonwealth. Against him I may use arms, conspiracies, spies, ambushes, and fraud; to do so is a sacred and necessary work. There is no more acceptable sacrifice than the blood of a tyrant.

FIG. 32. THE MURDER OF GALEAZZO MARIA SFORZA
Contemporary woodcut

We need not occupy ourselves with individual cases; Machiavelli,[2] in a famous chapter of his *Discorsi*, treats of the conspiracies of ancient and modern times from the days of the Greek tyrants downward, and classifies them with cold-blooded indifference according to their various plans and results. We need make but two observations, first on the murders committed in church, and next on the influence of classical antiquity. So well was the tyrant guarded that it was almost impossible to lay hands upon him elsewhere than at solemn religious services; and on no other occasion was the whole family to be found assembled together. It was thus that the Fabrianese[3] murdered (1435) the members of their ruling house; the Chiavistelli, during High Mass, the signal being given by the words of the Creed, "Et incarnatus est." At Milan the Duke Giovanni Maria Visconti (1412) was assassinated at the entrance of the church of S. Gottardo, Galeazzo Maria Sforza (1476) in the church of S. Stefano, and Lodovico il Moro only escaped (1484) the daggers of the adherents of the

[1] *De Casibus Virorum Illustrium*, lib. ii, cap. 15.
[2] *Discorsi*, iii, 6; cf. *Stor. Fiorent.*, lib. viii. The description of conspiracies has been a favourite theme of Italian writers from a very remote period. Luitprand (of Cremona, *Mon. Germ.*, iii, 264–363) gives us a few, which are more circumstantial than those of any other contemporary writer of the tenth century; in the eleventh the deliverance of Messina from the Saracens, accomplished by calling in Norman Roger (Baluz., *Miscell.*, i, p. 184), gives occasion to a characteristic narrative of this kind (1060); we need hardly speak of the dramatic colouring given to the stories of the Sicilian Vespers (1282). The same tendency is well known in the Greek writers.
[3] Corio, fol. 333. For what follows, *ibid.*, fol. 305, 422 *sqq.*, 440.

FIG. 33. THE DOWNFALL OF THE BONACOLSI

By Domenico Morone

Milan, Brera

Photo Propylaen-Verlag, Berlin

widowed Duchess Bona through entering the church of Sant' Ambrogio by another door than that by which he was expected. There was no intentional impiety in the act; the assassins of Galeazzo did not fail to pray before the murder to the patron saint of the church, and to listen devoutly to the first

FIG. 34. JUDITH
By Donatello
Florence, Loggia de' Lanzi

Mass. It was, however, one cause of the partial failure of the conspiracy of the Pazzi against Lorenzo and Giuliano de' Medici (1478) that the brigand Montesecco, who had bargained to commit the murder at a banquet, declined to undertake it in the cathedral of Florence. Certain of the clergy "who were familiar with the sacred place, and consequently had no fear," were induced to act in his stead.[1]

As to the imitation of antiquity, the influence of which on moral, and more especially on political, questions we shall often refer to, the example was set by the rulers themselves, who, both in their conception of the state and in their personal conduct, took the old Roman Empire avowedly as their model. In like manner their opponents, when they set to work with a deliberate theory, took pattern by the ancient tyrannicides. It may be hard to prove that in the main point—in forming the resolve itself—they consciously followed a classical example; but the appeal to antiquity was no mere phrase. The most striking disclosures have been left us with respect to the murderers of Galeazzo Sforza—Lampugnani, Olgiati, and Visconti.[2] Though all three had personal ends to serve, yet their enterprise may be partly ascribed to a more general reason. About this time Cola de' Montani, a humanist and professor of eloquence, had awakened among many of the young Milanese nobility a vague passion for glory and patriotic achievements, and had mentioned to Lampugnani and Olgiati his hope of delivering Milan. Suspicion was soon aroused against him: he was banished from the city, and his pupils were abandoned to the fanaticism he had excited. Some ten days before the deed they met together and took a solemn oath in the monastery of S. Ambrogio. "Then," says

[1] So in the quotations from Gallus, in Sismondi, xi, 93. For the whole subject see Reumont, *Lorenzo dei Medici*, pp. 387–397, especially 396.
[2] Corio, fol. 422. Allegretto, *Diari Sanesi*, in Murat., xxiii, col. 777. See above, p. 57.

Olgiati, "in a remote corner I raised my eyes before the picture of the patron saint, and implored his help for ourselves and for all *his* people." The heavenly protector of the city was called on to bless the undertaking, as was afterward St Stephen, in whose church it was fulfilled. Many of their comrades were now informed of the plot, nightly meetings were held in the house of Lampugnani, and the conspirators practised for the murder with the sheaths of their daggers. The attempt was successful, but Lampugnani was killed on the spot by the attendants of the Duke; the others were captured: Visconti was penitent, but Olgiati through all his tortures maintained that the deed was an acceptable offering to God, and exclaimed while the executioner was breaking his ribs, " Courage, Girolamo! thou wilt long be remembered; death is bitter, but glory is eternal." [1]

But however idealistic the object and purpose of such conspiracies may appear, the manner in which they were conducted betrays the influence of that worst of all conspirators, Catiline—a man in whose thoughts freedom had no place whatever. The annals of Siena tell us expressly that the conspirators were students of Sallust, and the fact is indirectly confirmed by the confession of Olgiati. [2] Elsewhere, too, we meet with the name of Catiline, and a more attractive pattern of the conspirator, apart from the end he followed, could hardly be discovered.

Among the Florentines, whenever they got rid of, or tried to get rid of, the Medici, tyrannicide was a practice universally accepted and approved. After the flight of the Medici in 1494 the bronze group of Donatello [3]—Judith with the dead Holofernes—was taken from their collection and placed before the Palazzo della Signoria, on the spot where the *David* of Michelangelo now stands, with the inscription, "Exemplum salutis publicæ cives posuere 1495." [4] No example was more popular than that of the younger Brutus, who, in Dante, [5] lies with Cassius and Judas Iscariot in the lowest pit of hell, because of

[1] The enthusiasm with which the Florentine Alamanno Rinuccini (b. 1419) speaks in his *Ricordi* (ed. by G. Aiazzi, Florence, 1840) of murderers and their deeds is very remarkable. For a contemporary, though not Italian, apology for tyrannicide see Kervyn de Lettenhove, *Jean sans Peur et l'Apologie du Tyrannicide*, in the *Bulletin de l'Académie de Bruxelles*, xi, pp. 558-571 (1861). A century later opinion in Italy had changed altogether. See the condemnation of Lampugnani's deed in Ignatius, *De Exemplis Ill. Vir.*, Ven., fol. 99b; *cf.* also 318b.

Petr. Crinitus also (*De Honesta Disciplina*, fol. 134b, Paris, 1510) writes a poem, *De Virtute Jo. Andr. Lamponiani Tyrannicidæ*, in which Lampugnani's deed is highly praised, and he himself is represented as a worthy companion of Brutus.

Cf. also the Latin poem *Bonini Mombritii Poetæ Mediol. Trenodia in Funere Illustrissimi D. Gal. Marie Sfor.* (two books, Milan, 1504), edited by Ascalon Vallis (*sic*), who in his dedication to the jurist Jac. Balsamus praises the poet and names other poems equally worthy to be printed. In this work, in which Megæra and Mars, Calliope and the poet, appear as interlocutors, the assassin—not Lampugnani, but a man from a humble family of artisans—is severely blamed, and he and his fellow-conspirators are treated as ordinary criminals; they are charged with high treason on account of a projected alliance with Charles of Burgundy. No fewer than ten prognostics of the death of Duke Galeazzo are enumerated. The murder of the Prince and the punishment of the assassin are vividly described; the close consists of pious consolations addressed to the widowed Princess and of religious meditations.

[2] "Con studiare el Catalinario," says Allegretto. *Cf.* (in Corio) a sentence like the following in the deposition of Olgiati: "Quisque nostrum magis socios potissime et infinitos alios sollicitare, infestare, alter alteri benevolos se facere cœpit. Aliquid aliquibus parum donare: simul magis noctu edere, bibere, vigilare, nostra omnia bona polliceri," etc.

[3] Vasari, iii, 251, note to *V. di Donatello.*

[4] It has now been removed to the Loggia de' Lanzi.   [5] *Inferno*, xxxiv, 64.

his treason to the Empire.   Pietro Paolo Boscoli, whose plot against Giuliano, Giovanni, and Giulio de' Medici failed (1513), was an enthusiastic admirer of Brutus, and in order to follow his steps only waited to find a Cassius.   Such a partner he met with in Agostino Capponi.   His last utterances in prison [1]— a striking evidence of the religious feeling of the time—show with what an effort he rid his mind of these classical imaginations in order to die like a

FIG. 35.   BUST OF BRUTUS
By Michelangelo
Florence, Bargello

Christian.   A friend and the confessor both had to assure him that St Thomas Aquinas condemned conspirators absolutely; but the confessor afterward admitted to the same friend that St Thomas drew a distinction and permitted conspiracies against a tyrant who had forced himself on a people against their will.   After Lorenzino de' Medici had murdered the Duke Alessandro (1537), and then escaped, an apology for the deed appeared, which is probably his

[1] Related by a hearer, Luca della Robbia, *Archiv. Stor.*, i, 273.   *Cf.* Paul. Jovius, *Vita Leonis X*, iii, in the *Viri Illustres*.

own work, and certainly composed in his interest,[1] and in which he praises tyrannicide as an act of the highest merit; on the supposition that Alessandro was a legitimate Medici, and therefore related to him, if only distantly, he boldly compares himself with Timoleon, who slew his brother for his country's sake. Others, on the same occasion, made use of the comparison with Brutus, and that Michelangelo himself, even late in life, was not unfriendly to ideas of this kind may be inferred from his bust of Brutus in the Uffizi. He left it unfinished, like nearly all his works, but certainly not because the murder of Cæsar was repugnant to his feeling, as the couplet beneath declares.

A popular radicalism in the form in which it is opposed to the monarchies of later times is not to be found in the despotic states of the Renaissance. Each individual protested inwardly against despotism, but was rather disposed to make tolerable or profitable terms with it than to combine with others for its destruction. Things must have been as bad as at Camerino, Fabriano, or Rimini (p. 45) before the citizens united to destroy or expel the ruling house. They knew in most cases only too well that this would but mean a change of masters. The star of the republics was certainly on the decline.

[1] First printed in 1723, as Appendix to Varchi's history, then in Roscoe, *Life of Lorenzo de' Medici*, vol. iv, App. 12, and often besides. *Cf.* Reumont, *Gesch. Toscana's seit dem Ende des Florent. Freistaates*, i, p. 67, note (Gotha, 1876). See also the report in the *Lettere dei Principi*, ed. Venez., 1577, iii, fol. 162 *sqq.*

CHAPTER VII

The Republics: Venice and Florence

THE Italian municipalities had, in earlier days, given signal proof of that force which transforms the city into the state. It remained only that these cities should combine in a great confederation; and this idea was constantly recurring to Italian statesmen, whatever differences of form it might from time to time display. In fact, during the struggles of the twelfth and thirteenth centuries great and formidable leagues actually were formed by the cities; and Sismondi (ii, 174) is of opinion that the time of the final armaments of the Lombard confederation against Barbarossa was the moment when a universal Italian league was possible. But the more powerful states had already developed characteristic features which made any such scheme impracticable. In their commercial dealings they shrank from no measures, however extreme, which might damage their competitors; they held their weaker neighbours in a condition of helpless dependence—in short, they all fancied they could get on by themselves without the assistance of the rest, and thus paved the way for future usurpation. The usurper was forthcoming when long conflicts between the nobility and the people, and between the different factions of the nobility, had awakened the desire for a strong government, and when bands of mercenaries ready and willing to sell their aid to the highest bidder had superseded the general levy of the citizens, which party leaders now found unsuited to their purposes.[1] The tyrants destroyed the freedom of most of the cities; here and there they were expelled, but not thoroughly, or only for a short time; and they were always restored, since the inward conditions were favourable to them, and the opposing forces were exhausted.

Among the cities which maintained their independence are two of deep significance for the history of the human race: Florence, the city of incessant movement, which has left us a record of the thoughts and aspirations of each and all who, for three centuries, took part in this movement, and Venice, the city of apparent stagnation and of political secrecy. No contrast can be imagined stronger than that which is offered us by these two, and neither can be compared to anything else which the world has hitherto produced.

Venice recognized itself from the first as a strange and mysterious creation—the fruits of a higher power than human ingenuity. The solemn foundation

---

[1] On the latter point see Jac. Nardi, *Vita di Ant. Giacomini*, Lucca, p. 18 (1818).

of the city was the subject of a legend. On March 25, 413, at midday the emigrants from Padua laid the first stone at the Rialto, that they might have a sacred, inviolable asylum amid the devastations of the barbarians. Later writers attributed to the founders the presentiment of the future greatness of the city; M. Antonio Sabellico, who has celebrated the event in the dignified

FIG. 36. THE BASILICA OF ST MARK, VENICE

flow of his hexameters, makes the priest, who completes the act of consecration, cry to heaven: "When we hereafter attempt great things grant us prosperity! Now we kneel before a poor altar; but if our vows are not made in vain, a hundred temples, O God, of gold and marble shall arise to Thee."[1] The island-city at the end of the fifteenth century was the jewel-casket of the world.

[1] "Genethliacum Venetæ Urbis," in the *Carmina* of Antonio Sabellicus. March 25 was chosen "essendo il cielo in singolar disposizione, si come da gli astronomi è stato calcolato più volte." *Cf.* Sansovino, *Venezia Città Nobilissima e Singolare, Descritta in 14 Libri*, fol. 203 (Venezia, 1581). For the whole chapter see *Johannis Baptistæ Egnatii Viri Doctissimi de Exemplis Illustrium Virorum Venetæ Civitatis atque Aliarum Gentium* (Paris, 1554). The oldest, or rather one of the oldest, Venetian chroniclers, Joh. Diaconi, *Chron. Venetum*, in Pertz, *Monum. SS.* vii, pp. 5, 6, places the occupation of the islands in the time of the Lombards and the foundation of the Rialto later.

It is so described by the same Sabellico,[1] with its ancient cupolas, its leaning towers, its inlaid marble façades, its compressed splendour, where the richest decoration did not hinder the practical employment of every corner of space. He takes us to the crowded *piazza* before S. Giacometto at the Rialto, where the business of the world is transacted, not amid shouting and confusion, but with the subdued hum of many voices; where in the porticos round the square [2] and in those of the adjoining streets sit hundreds of money-changers and gold-

FIG. 37. VENICE TOWARD THE END OF THE FIFTEENTH CENTURY
Part of the picture *The Miracle of the True Cross*, by Carpaccio
Venice, Accademia
Photo Anderson, Rome

smiths, with endless rows of shops and warehouses above their heads. He describes the great Fondaco of the Germans beyond the bridge, where their goods and their dwellings lay, and before which their ships are drawn up side by side in the canal; higher up is a whole fleet laden with wine and oil, and parallel with it, on the shore swarming with porters, are the vaults of the merchants; then from the Rialto to the Square of St Mark come the inns and the perfumers' cabinets. So he conducts the reader from one quarter of the city to another till he comes at last to the two hospitals which were among those institutions of public utility nowhere so numerous as at Venice. Care for the

[1] "De Venetæ urbis apparatu panegiricum carmen quod oraculum inscribitur."
[2] The whole quarter was altered in the reconstructions of the early sixteenth century.

84

SELF-PORTRAIT BY LEONARDO DA VINCI
Red-chalk drawing
Royal Library, Turin

RTION OF A VIEW OF VENICE AT THE END OF THE FIFTEENTH CENTURY
Woodcut after a drawing by Jacopo de' Barbari

people, in peace as well as in war, was characteristic of this Government, and its attention to the wounded, even to those of the enemy, excited the admiration of other states.[1] Public institutions of every kind found in Venice their pattern; the pensioning of retired servants was carried out systematically, and included a provision for widows and orphans. Wealth, political security, and acquaintance with other countries had matured the understanding of such questions. These slender fair-haired men,[2] with quiet, cautious steps and deliberate speech, differed but slightly in costume and bearing from one another; ornaments, especially pearls, were reserved for the women and girls. At that time the general prosperity, notwithstanding the losses sustained from the Turks, was still dazzling; the stores of energy which the city possessed, and the prejudice in its favour diffused throughout Europe, enabled it at a much later time to survive the heavy blows which were inflicted by the discovery of the sea route to the Indies, by the fall of the Mamelukes in Egypt, and by the war of the League of Cambray.

FIG. 38. VENETIAN FUNCTIONARY
Part of a picture belonging to the St Ursula Series,
by Carpaccio
Venice, Accademia

Sabellico, born in the neighbourhood of Tivoli, and accustomed to the frank loquacity of the scholars of his day, remarks elsewhere[3] with some astonishment that the young nobles who came of a morning to hear his lectures could not be prevailed on to enter into political discussions: "When I ask them what people think, say, and expect about this or that movement in Italy they all answer with one voice that they know nothing about the matter." Still, in spite of the strict inquisition of the state, much was to be learned from the more corrupt members of the aristocracy by those who were willing to pay enough for it. In the last quarter of the fifteenth century there were traitors among the highest officials; [4] the Popes, the Italian princes, and even second-

---

[1] Benedictus, *Carol. VIII*, in Eccard, *Scriptores*, ii, col. 1597, 1601, 1621. In the *Chron. Venetum*, in Murat., xxiv, col. 26, the political virtues of the Venetians are enumerated: "bontà, innocenza, zelo di carità, pietà, misericordia."

[2] Many of the nobles cropped their hair. See *Erasmi Colloquia*, ed. Tiguri, year 1553: "miles et carthusianus."

[3] *Epistolæ*, lib. v, fol. 28.

[4] Malipiero, *Ann. Venet.*, *Archiv. Stor.*, vii, i, pp. 377, 431, 481, 493, 530; ii, pp. 661, 668, 679. *Chron., Venetum*, in Murat., xxiv, col. 57. *Diario Ferrarese, ibid.*, col. 240. See also *Dispacci di Antonio Giustiniani* i, p. 392 (Florence, 1876).

rate *condottieri* in the service of the Government had informers in their pay, sometimes with regular salaries; things went so far that the Council of Ten found it prudent to conceal important political news from the Council of the Pregadi, and it was even supposed that Lodovico il Moro had control of a definite number of votes among the latter. Whether the hanging of single offenders and the high rewards—such as a life-pension of sixty ducats paid to those who informed against them—were of much avail, it is hard to decide;

FIG. 39. VENETIAN CITIZENS
Part of a picture belonging to the St Ursula Series, by Carpaccio
Venice, Accademia

one of the chief causes of this evil, the poverty of many of the nobility, could not be removed in a day. In 1492 a proposal was urged by two of that order that the State should annually spend seventy thousand ducats for the relief of those poorer nobles who held no public office; the matter was near coming before the Great Council, in which it might have had a majority, when the Council of Ten interfered in time and banished the two proposers for life to Nicosia, in Cyprus.[1] About this time a Soranzo was hung, though not at Venice itself, for sacrilege, and a Contarini put in chains for burglary; another of the same family came in 1499 before the Signoria, and complained that for many years he had been without an office, that he had only sixteen ducats a year

---

[1] Malipiero, in the *Archiv. Stor.*, vii, ii, p. 691. *Cf.* 694, 713, and i, 535.

and nine children, that his debts amounted to sixty ducats, that he knew no
trade and had lately been turned on to the streets. We can understand why
some of the wealthier nobles built houses, sometimes whole rows of them, to
provide free lodging for their needy comrades. Such works figure in wills
among deeds of charity.[1]

But if the enemies of Venice ever founded serious hopes upon abuses of
this kind they were greatly in error. It might be thought that the commercial
activity of the city, which put within reach of the humblest a rich reward for

FIG. 40. THE PALACE OF THE DOGES, VENICE
Photo Seemann, Leipzig

their labour, and the colonies on the Eastern shores of the Mediterranean would
have diverted from political affairs the dangerous elements of society. But had
not the political history of Genoa, notwithstanding similar advantages, been
of the stormiest? The cause of the stability of Venice lies rather in a combination of circumstances which were found in union nowhere else. Unassailable
from its position, it had been able from the beginning to treat of foreign
affairs with the fullest and calmest reflection, and ignore nearly altogether the
parties which divided the rest of Italy, to escape the entanglement of permanent
alliances, and to set the highest price on those which it thought fit to make.
The keynote of the Venetian character was, consequently, a spirit of proud
and contemptuous isolation, which, joined to the hatred felt for the city by the

[1] Marin Sanudo, *Vite dei Duchi*, in Murat., xxii, col. 1194.

other states of Italy, gave rise to a strong sense of solidarity within. The inhabitants meanwhile were united by the most powerful ties of interest in dealing both with the colonies and with the possessions on the mainland, forcing the population of the latter—that is, of all the towns up to Bergamo—to buy and sell in Venice alone. A power which rested on means so artificial could only be maintained by internal harmony and unity; and this conviction was so widely diffused among the citizens that the conspirator found few elements to work

FIG. 41. THE PALACE OF THE DOGES, VENICE : THE GREAT HALL

upon. And the discontented, if there were such, were held so far apart by the division between the noble and the burgher that a mutual understanding was not easy. On the other hand, within the ranks of the nobility itself travel, commercial enterprise, and the incessant wars with the Turks saved the wealthy and dangerous from that fruitful source of conspiracies—idleness. In these wars they were spared, often to a criminal extent, by the general in command, and the fall of the city was predicted by a Venetian Cato if this fear of the nobles "to give one another pain" should continue at the expense of justice.[1] Nevertheless this free movement in the open air gave the Venetian aristocracy, as a whole, a healthy bias.

And when envy and ambition called for satisfaction an official victim was forthcoming, and legal means and authorities were ready. The moral torture

[1] *Chron. Venetum*, in Murat., xxiv, col. 105.

which for years the Doge Francesco Foscari (d. 1457) suffered before the eyes of all Venice is a frightful example of a vengeance possible only in an aristocracy. The Council of Ten, which had a hand in everything, which disposed without appeal of life and death, of financial affairs and military appointments, which included the Inquisitors among its number, and which overthrew Foscari, as it had overthrown so many powerful men before—this council was yearly chosen afresh from the whole governing body, the *Gran Consilio*, and was consequently the most direct expression of its will. It is not probable that serious intrigues occurred at these elections, as the short duration of the office and the accountability which followed rendered it an object of no great desire. But violent and mysterious as the proceedings of this and other authorities might be, the genuine Venetian courted rather than fled their sentence, not only because the republic had long arms, and if it could not catch him might punish his family, but because in most cases it acted from rational motives and not from a thirst for blood.[1] No state, indeed, has ever exercised a greater moral influence over its subjects, whether abroad or at home. If traitors were to be found among the Pregadi, there was ample compensation for this in the fact that every Venetian away from home was a born spy for his Government. It was a matter of course that the Venetian cardinals at Rome sent home news of the transactions of the secret Papal consistories. Cardinal Domenico Grimani had the dispatches which Ascanio Sforza was sending to his brother Lodovico il Moro intercepted in the neighbourhood of Rome (1500), and forwarded them to Venice; his father, then exposed to a serious accusation, claimed public credit for this service of his son before the *Gran Consilio*—in other words, before all the world.[2]

The conduct of the Venetian Government to the *condottieri* in its pay has been spoken of already. The only further guarantee of their fidelity which could be obtained lay in their great number, by which treachery was made as difficult as its discovery was easy. In looking at the Venetian army list one is only surprised that among forces of such miscellaneous composition any common action was possible. In the catalogue for the campaign of 1495 we find 15,526 horsemen, broken up into a number of small divisions.[3] Gonzaga of Mantua alone had as many as 1200, and Gioffredo Borgia 740; then follow six officers with a contingent of 600 to 700, ten with 400, twelve with 200 to 400, fourteen or thereabouts with 100 to 200, nine with 80, six with 50 to 60, and so forth. These forces were partly composed of old Venetian troops, partly of veterans led by Venetian city or country nobles; the majority of the leaders were, however, princes and rulers of cities or their relatives. To these forces must be added 24,000 infantry—we are not told how they were raised

[1] *Chron. Venetum*, in Murat., xxiv, col. 123 *sqq.*, and Malipiero, *loc. cit.*, vii, i, pp. 175, 187 *sqq.*, relate the significant fall of Admiral Antonio Grimani, who, when accused on account of his refusal to surrender the command in chief to another, himself put irons on his feet before his arrival at Venice, and presented himself in this condition to the Senate. For him and his future lot see Egnatius, fol. 183*a sqq.*, 198*b sqq.*

[2] *Chron. Venetum, loc. cit.*, col. 166.

[3] Malipiero, *loc. cit.*, vii, i, 349. For other lists of the same kind see Marin Sanudo, *Vite dei Duchi*, in Murat., xxii, col. 990 (year 1426), col. 1088 (year 1440), in Corio, fol. 435-438 (year 1483), in Guazzo, *Historie*, fol. 151 *sqq.*

or commanded—with 3300 additional troops, who probably belonged to the special services. In time of peace the cities of the mainland were wholly unprotected or occupied by insignificant garrisons. Venice relied, if not exactly on the loyalty, at least on the good sense of its subjects; in the war of the League of Cambray (1509) it absolved them, as is well known, from their oath of allegiance, and let them compare the amenities of a foreign occupation with the mild government to which they had been accustomed. As there had been no treason in their desertion of St Mark, and consequently no punishment was to be feared, they returned to their old masters with the utmost eagerness.[1] This war, we may remark parenthetically, was the result of a century's outcry against the Venetian desire for aggrandizement. The Venetians, in fact, were not free from the mistake of those over-clever people who will credit their opponents with no irrational and inconsiderate conduct.[2] Misled by this optimism, which is, perhaps, a peculiar weakness of aristocracies, they had utterly ignored not only the preparations of Mohammed II for the capture of Constantinople, but even the armaments of Charles VIII, till the unexpected blow fell at last.[3] The League of Cambray was an event of the same character, in so far as it was clearly opposed to the interest of the two chief members, Louis XII and Julius II. The hatred of all Italy against the victorious city seemed to be concentrated in the mind of the Pope, and to have blinded him to the evils of foreign intervention; and as to the policy of Cardinal d'Amboise and his king, Venice ought long before to have recognized it as a piece of malicious imbecility, and to have been thoroughly on its guard. The other members of the League took part in it from that envy which may be a salutary corrective to great wealth and power, but which in itself is a beggarly sentiment. Venice came out of the conflict with honour, but not without lasting damage.

A Power whose foundations were so complicated, whose activity and interests filled so wide a stage, cannot be imagined without a systematic oversight of the whole, without a regular estimate of means and burdens, of profits and losses. Venice can fairly make good its claim to be the birthplace of statistical science, together, perhaps, with Florence, and followed by the more enlightened despotisms. The feudal state of the Middle Ages knew of nothing more than catalogues of signorial rights and possessions (*urbaria*); it looked on production as a fixed quantity, which it approximately is, so long as we have to do with landed property only. The towns, on the other hand, throughout the West must from very early times have treated production, which with them depended on industry and commerce, as exceedingly variable; but even in the most flourishing times of the Hanseatic League they never got beyond a simple commercial balance-sheet. Fleets, armies, political power, and influence fall under the debit and credit of a trader's ledger. In the Italian states a clear

[1 See Manfren, *Del Preteso Scioglimento di Sudditarza dopo la Battaglia di Agnadello*, *Arch. Veneto* (1872), in which this story is proved to be fictitious.—L. G.]

[2] Guicciardini (*Ricordi*, n. 150) is one of the first to remark that the passion for vengeance can drown the clearest voice of self-interest.

[3] Malipiero, *loc. cit.*, vii, i, p. 328.

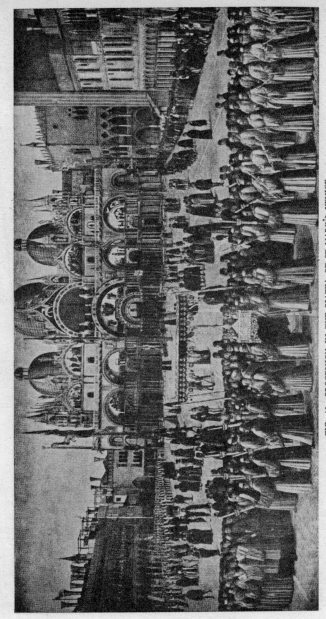

FIG. 42. PROCESSION IN THE PIAZZA OF ST MARK'S, VENICE

By Gentile Bellini

Venice, Accademia

political consciousness, the pattern of Mohammedan administration, and the long and active exercise of trade and commerce combined to produce for the first time a true science of statistics.[1]   The absolute monarchy of Frederick II in Lower Italy was organized with the sole object of securing a concentrated power for the death-struggle in which he was engaged.   In Venice, on the contrary, the supreme objects were the enjoyment of life and power, the

FIG. 43. THE APOTHEOSIS OF VENICE
Part of the ceiling-piece in the Palace of the Doges, by Paolo Veronese
Venice

increase of inherited advantages, the creation of the most lucrative forms of industry, and the opening of new channels for commerce.

The writers of the time speak of these things with the greatest freedom.[2] We learn that the population of the city amounted in 1422 to 190,000 souls; the Italians were, perhaps, the first to reckon, not according to hearths, or men able to bear arms, or people able to walk, and so forth, but according to *animæ*,

---

[1] The statistical view of Milan, in the *Manipulus Florum* (in Murat., xi, 711 *sqq.*) for 1288, is important, though not extensive.   It includes house-doors, population, men of military age, *loggie* of the nobles, trees, wells, bakeries, wine-shops, butchers' shops, fishmongers, the consumption of corn, dogs, birds of chase, the price of salt, wood, hay, and wines;   also the judges, notaries, doctors, schoolmasters, copying-clerks, armourers, smiths, hospitals, monasteries, endowments, and religious corporations.   A list perhaps still older is found in the *Liber de Magnalibus Mediolani*, in *Heinr. de Hervordia*, ed. Potthast, p. 165.   See also the statistical account of Asti about 1250 in Ogerius Alpherius (Alfieri), *De Gestis Astensium, Histor. Patr. Monumenta, Scriptorum*, tom. iii, col. 684 *sqq.*

[2] Especially Marin Sanudo, in the *Vite dei Duchi*, in Murat., xxii, *passim*.

and thus to get the most neutral basis for further calculation. About this time,[1] when the Florentines wished to form an alliance with Venice against Filippo Maria Visconti, they were for the moment refused, in the belief, resting on accurate commercial returns, that a war between Venice and Milan—that is, between seller and buyer—was foolish. Even if the Duke simply increased his army the Milanese, through the heavier taxation they must pay, would become worse customers.

> Better let the Florentines be defeated, and then, used as they are to the life of a free city, they will settle with us and bring their silk and woollen industry with them, as the Lucchese did in their distress.

The speech of the dying Doge Mocenigo (1423) to a few of the senators whom he had sent for to his bedside [2] is still more remarkable. It contains the chief elements of a statistical account of the whole resources of Venice. I cannot say whether or where a thorough elucidation of this perplexing document exists; by way of illustration, the following facts may be quoted. After repaying a war-loan of four million ducats the public debt (*il monte*) still amounted to six million ducats; the current trade reached (so it seems) ten millions, which yielded, the text informs us, a profit of four millions. The 3000 *navigli*, the 300 *navi*, and the 45 galleys were manned respectively by 17,000, 8000, and 11,000 seamen (more than 200 for each galley). To these must be added 16,000 shipwrights. The houses in Venice were valued at seven millions, and brought in a rent of half a million.[3] There were 1000 nobles whose income ranged from 70 to 4000 ducats. In another passage the ordinary income of the State in that same year is put at 1,100,000 ducats; through the disturbance of trade caused by the wars it sank about the middle of the century to 800,000 ducats.[4]

If Venice, by this spirit of calculation, and by the practical turn which she gave it, was the first fully to represent one important side of modern political life, in that culture, on the other hand, which Italy then prized most highly she did not stand in the front rank. The literary impulse in general was here wanting, and especially that enthusiasm for classical antiquity which prevailed elsewhere.[5] The aptitude of the Venetians, says Sabellico, for philosophy and eloquence was in itself not less remarkable than for commerce and politics;

---

[1] See for the marked difference between Venice and Florence an important pamphlet addressed 1472 to Lorenzo de' Medici by certain Venetians, and the answer to it by Benedetto Dei, in Paganini, *Della Decima*, iii, pp. 135 *sqq.* (Florence, 1763).

[2] In Sanudo, *loc. cit.*, col. 958. What relates to trade is extracted in Scherer, *Allgem. Gesch. des Welthandels*, i, 326, note.

[3] Here all the houses, not merely those owned by the State, are meant. The latter, however, sometimes yielded enormous rents. See Vasari, xiii, 83, *Vita d. Jac. Sansovino*. [In Cecchetti, *La Vita dei Veneziani nel 1300, Archiv. Ven.*, vol. xxvii, pp. 34 *sqq.*, the results of valuations in 1367 and 1425 are given differently. In 1367 the value of the houses amounted to about 2,900,000 ducats; in 1425 to 3,636,038 ducats. In 1582 there were 187 beggars in Venice.—L. G.]

[4] See Sanudo, col. 963. In the same place a list of the incomes of the other Italian and European Powers is given. An estimate for 1490 is to be found, col. 1245 *sqq.*

[5] This dislike seems to have amounted to positive hatred in Paul II, who called the humanists one and all heretics. Platina, *Vita Pauli II*, p. 323. See also for the subject in general Voigt, *Wiederbelebung des classischen Alterthums*, pp. 207-213 (Berlin, 1859). The neglect of the sciences is given as a reason for the flourishing condition of Venice by Lil. Greg. Giraldus, *Opera*, ii, p. 439.

but this aptitude was neither developed in themselves nor rewarded in strangers as it was rewarded elsewhere in Italy. Filelfo, summoned to Venice not by the State, but by private individuals, soon found his expectations deceived; and George of Trebizond, who in 1459 laid the Latin translation of Plato's laws at the feet of the Doge, and was appointed professor of philology with a yearly salary of a hundred and fifty ducats, and finally dedicated his *Rhetoric* to the Signoria,[1] soon left the city in dissatisfaction. Literature, in fact, like the rest at Venice, had mostly a practical end in view. If, accordingly, we look

FIG. 44. THE CATHEDRAL, FLORENCE

through the history of Venetian literature which Francesco Sansovino has appended to his well-known book [2] we shall find in the fourteenth century almost nothing but history and special works on theology, jurisprudence, and medicine; and in the fifteenth century, till we come to Ermolao Barbaro and Aldo Manucci, humanistic culture is, for a city of such importance, most scantily represented. Similarly we find comparatively few traces of the passion, elsewhere so strong, for collecting books and manuscripts; and the valuable texts which formed part of Petrarch's legacies were so badly preserved that soon all traces of them were lost. The library which Cardinal Bessarion bequeathed to the State (1468) narrowly escaped dispersion and destruction. Learning was certainly cultivated at the University of Padua, where, however, the physicians and the jurists—the latter as the authors of legal opinions— received by far the highest pay. The share of Venice in the poetical creations

---

[1] Sanudo, *loc. cit.*, col. 1167.

[2] Sansovino, *Venezia*, lib. xiii. It contains the biographies of the Doges in chronological order, and, following these lives one by one (regularly from 1312, under the heading *Scrittori Veneti*), short notices of contemporary writers.

94

of the country was long insignificant, till, at the beginning of the sixteenth century, her deficiencies were made good.[1] Even the art of the Renaissance was imported into the city from without, and it was not before the end of the fifteenth century that she learned to move in this field with independent freedom and strength. But we find more striking instances still of intellectual backwardness. This Government, which had the clergy so thoroughly in its control, which reserved to itself the appointment to all important ecclesiastical offices, and which, one time after another, dared to defy the Court of Rome, displayed an official piety of a most singular kind.[2] The bodies of saints and other relics imported from Greece after the Turkish conquest were bought at the greatest sacrifices and received by the Doge in solemn procession.[3] For the coat without a seam it was decided (1455) to offer 10,000 ducats, but it was not to be had. These measures were not the fruit of any popular excitement, but of the tranquil resolutions of the heads of the Government, and might have been omitted without attracting any comment, and at Florence, under similar circumstances, would certainly have been omitted. We shall say nothing of the piety of the masses, and of their firm belief in the indulgences of an Alexander VI. But the State itself, after absorbing the Church to a degree unknown elsewhere, had in truth a certain ecclesiastical element in its composition, and the Doge, the symbol of the State, appeared in twelve great processions (*andate*)[4] in a half-clerical character. They were almost all festivals in memory of political events, and competed in splendour with the great feasts of the Church; the most brilliant of all, the famous marriage with the sea, fell on Ascension Day.

The most elevated political thought and the most varied forms of human development are found united in the history of Florence, which in this sense deserves the name of the first modern state in the world. Here the whole people are busied with what in the despotic cities is the affair of a single family. That wondrous Florentine spirit, at once keenly critical and artistically creative, was incessantly transforming the social and political condition of the state, and as incessantly describing and judging the change. Florence thus became the home of political doctrines and theories, of experiments and sudden changes, but also, like Venice, the home of statistical science, and, alone and above all other states in the world, the home of historical representation in the modern sense of the phrase. The spectacle of ancient Rome and a familiarity with its leading writers were not without influence; Giovanni Villani[5] confesses that

[1] Venice was then one of the chief seats of the Petrarchists. See G. Crespan, *Del Petrarchismo*, in *Petrarca e Venezia*, pp. 187–253 (1874).

[2] See Heinric. de Hervordia, for the year 1293, p. 213, ed. Potthast, who says: "The Venetians wished to obtain the body of Jacob of Forlì from the inhabitants of that place, as many miracles were wrought by it. They promised many things in return, among others to bear all the expense of canonizing the defunct, but without obtaining their request."

[3] Sanudo, *loc. cit.*, col. 1158, 1171, 1177. When the body of St Luke was brought from Bosnia a dispute arose with the Benedictines of S. Giustina at Padua, who claimed to possess it already, and the Pope had to decide between the two parties. *Cf.* Guicciardini, *Ricordi*, n. 401.

[4] Sansovino, *Venezia*, lib. xii, "dell' andate publiche del principe"; Egnatius, fol. 50a. For the dread felt at the Papal interdict see Egnatius, fol. 12a *sqq.*

[5] G. Villani, viii, 36. The year 1300 is also a fixed date in the *Divine Comedy*.

he received the first impulse to his great work at the jubilee of 1300, and began it immediately on his return home. Yet how many among the 200,000 pilgrims of that year may have been like him in gifts and tendencies, and still did not write the history of their native cities! For not all of them could encourage themselves with the thought: "Rome is sinking; my native city is rising, and ready to achieve great things, and therefore I wish to relate its past history, and hope to continue the story to the present time, and as long as my life shall last." And besides the witness to its past, Florence obtained through its historians something further—a greater fame than fell to the lot of any other city of Italy.[1]

Our present task is not to write the history of this remarkable state, but merely to give a few indications of the intellectual freedom and independence for which the Florentines were indebted to this history.[2]

In no other city of Italy were the struggles of political parties so bitter, of such early origin, and so permanent. The descriptions of them, which belong, it is true, to a somewhat later period, give clear evidence of the superiority of Florentine criticism.

And what a politician is the great victim of these crises, Dante Alighieri, matured alike by home and by exile! He uttered his scorn of the incessant changes and experiments in the constitution of his native city in verses of adamant, which will remain proverbial so long as political events of the same kind recur;[3] he addressed his home in words of defiance and yearning which must have stirred the hearts of his countrymen. But his thoughts ranged over Italy and the whole world; and if his passion for the Empire, as he conceived it, was no more than an illusion, it must yet be admitted that the youthful dreams of a new-born political speculation are in his case not without a poetical grandeur. He is proud to be the first who had trod this path,[4] certainly in the footsteps of Aristotle, but in his own way independently. His ideal Emperor

---

[1] Stated about 1470 by Vespas. Fiorent., p. 554.

[2] The passage which followed in former editions referring to the *Chronicle of Dino Compagni* is here omitted, since the genuineness of the *Chronicle* has been disproved by Paul Scheffer-Boichhorst, *Florentiner Studien*, pp. 45–210, Leipzig, 1874, and the disproof maintained (*Die Chronik des D. C.*, Leipzig, 1875) against a distinguished authority (C. Hegel, *Die Chronik des D. C.*, *Versuch einer Rettung*, Leipzig, 1875). Scheffer's view is generally received in Germany (see W. Bernhardi, *Der Stand der Dino-Frage*, Hist. Ztschr. N.F., Bd. i, 1877), and even Hegel assumes that the text as we have it is a later manipulation of an unfinished work of Dino. Even in Italy, though the majority of scholars have wished to ignore this critical onslaught, as they have done other earlier ones of the same kind, some voices have been raised to recognize the spuriousness of the document. (See especially P. Fanfani in his periodical *Il Borghini*, and in the book *Dino Campagni Vendicato*, Milan, 1875.) On the earliest Florentine histories in general see Hartwig, *Forschungen* (Marburg, 1876), and C. Hegel in H. von Sybel's *Historischer Zeitschrift*, Bd. xxxv. Since then Isidoro del Lungo, who with remarkable decision asserts its genuineness, has completed his great edition of Dino, and furnished it with a detailed introduction: *Dino Campagni e la Sua Cronaca* (2 vols., Firenze, 1879–80). A manuscript of the history, dating back to the beginning of the fifteenth century, and consequently earlier than all the hitherto known references and editions, has been found lately. In consequence of the discovery of this manuscript and of the researches undertaken by C. Hegel, and especially of the evidence that the style of the work does not differ from that of the fourteenth century, the prevailing view of the subject is essentially this, that the chronicle contains an important kernel, which is genuine, which, however, perhaps even in the fourteenth century, was remodelled on the ground-plan of Villani's chronicle. *Cf.* Gaspary, *Geschichte der italienischen Literatur*, i, pp. 361–369, 531 *sqq.* (Berlin, 1885).

[3] *Purgatorio*, vi, at the end.

[4] *De Monarchia*, i, 1. (New critical edition by Witte, 71 (Halle, 1863); German translation by O. Hubatsch, Berlin, 1872.)

EQUESTRIAN STATUE OF THE CONDOTTIERE GATTAMELATA
By Donatello
Padua

is a just and humane judge, dependent on God only, the heir of the universal sway of Rome, to which belonged the sanction of nature, of right, and of the will of God. The conquest of the world was, according to this view, rightful, resting on a divine judgment between Rome and the other nations of the earth,

and God gave His approval to this empire since under it He became Man, submitting at His birth to the census of the Emperor Augustus, and at His death to the judgment of Pontius Pilate. We may find it hard to appreciate these and other arguments of the same kind, but Dante's passion never fails to carry us with him. In his letters he appears as one of the earliest publicists,[1] and is perhaps the first layman to publish political tracts in this form. He began early. Soon after the death of Beatrice he addressed a pamphlet on the state of Florence " to the great ones of the earth," and the public utterances of his later years, dating from the time of his banishment, are all directed to emperors, princes, and cardinals. In these letters and in his book *De Vulgari Eloquentia* the feeling, bought with such bitter

FIG. 45. THE PALAZZO VECCHIO (SEAT OF THE SIGNORIA), FLORENCE

pains, is constantly recurring that the exile may find elsewhere than in his native place an intellectual home in language and culture which cannot be taken from him. On this point we shall have more to say in the sequel.

To the two Villani, Giovanni as well as Matteo, we owe not so much

---

[1] *Dantis Alligherii Epistolæ, cum notis* C. Witte (Padua, 1827). Also in Fraticelli, *Opere Minori di Dante*, iii (1862), and Moore, *Opere di Dante* (1904). He wished to keep the Pope as well as the Emperor always in Italy. See his letter, p. 35, during the conclave of Carpentras, 1314. [The authenticity of this letter of Dante's has not yet been strictly established.—W. G.] On the first letter see *La Vita Nuova*, cap. 31, and *Epist.*, p. 9.

deep political reflection as fresh and practical observations, together with the elements of Florentine statistics and important notices of other states. Here too trade and commerce had given the impulse to economical as well as political science. Nowhere else in the world was such accurate information to be had on financial affairs. The wealth of the Papal Court at Avignon, which at the death of John XXII amounted to twenty-five millions of gold florins, would be incredible on any less trustworthy authority.[1] Here only, at Florence, do we meet with colossal loans like that which the King of England contracted from the Florentine houses of Bardi and Peruzzi, who lost to his Majesty the sum of 1,365,000 gold florins (1338)—their own money and that of their partners—and nevertheless recovered from the shock.[2] Most important facts are here recorded as to the condition of Florence at this time:[3] the public income (over 300,000 gold florins) and expenditure; the population of the city, here only roughly estimated, according to the consumption of bread in *bocche*—i.e., mouths—put at 90,000, and the population of the whole territory; the excess of 300 to 500 male children among the 5800 to 6000 annually baptized;[4] the school-children, of whom 8000 to 10,000 learned reading, 1000 to 1200 in six schools arithmetic; and besides these 600 scholars who were taught Latin grammar and logic in four schools. Then follow the statistics of the churches and monasteries; of the hospitals, which held more than a thousand beds; of the wool trade, with its most valuable details; of the mint, the provisioning of the city, the public officials, and so on.[5] Incidentally we learn many curious facts; how, for instance, when the public funds (*il monte*) were first established, in the year 1353, the Franciscans spoke from the pulpit in favour of the measure, the Dominicans and Augustinians against it.[6] The economical results of the Black Death were and could be observed and described nowhere else in all Europe as in this city.[7] Only a Florentine could have left it on record how it was expected that the scanty population would have made everything cheap, and how instead of that labour and commodities doubled in price; how the common people at first would do no work at all, but simply give themselves up to enjoyment; how in the city itself servants and maids were not to be had except at extravagant wages; how the peasants would only till the best lands, and left the rest uncultivated; and how the enormous legacies bequeathed to the poor at the time of the plague seemed afterward useless, since the poor had either died or had ceased to be poor. Lastly, on the

[1] Giov. Villani, xi, 20. *Cf.* Matteo Villani, ix, 93, who says that John XXII, "astuto in tutte sue cose e massime in fare il danaio," left behind him eighteen million florins in cash and six millions in jewels.

[2] See for this and similar facts Giov. Villani, xi, 87; xii, 54. He lost his own money in the crash, and was imprisoned for debt. See also Kervyn de Lettenhove, *L'Europe au Siècle de Philippe le Bel, Les Argentiers Florentins*, in *Le Bulletin de l'Académie de Bruxelles*, vol. xii, pp. 123 *sqq.* (1861).

[3] Giov. Villani, xi, 92, 93. In Machiavelli, *Stor. Fiorent.*, lib. ii, cap. 42, we read that 96,000 persons died of the plague in 1348.

[4] The priest put aside a black bean for every boy and a white one for every girl. This was the only means of registration.

[5] There was already a permanent fire brigade in Florence. Giov. Villani, xii, 35.

[6] Matteo Villani, iii, 106. –

[7] *Ibid.*, i, 2–7; *cf.* 58. The best authority for the plague itself is the famous description by Boccaccio at the beginning of the *Decamerone*.

occasion of a great bequest, by which a childless philanthropist left six *danari* to every beggar in the city, the attempt is made to give a comprehensive statistical account of Florentine mendicancy.[1]

This statistical view of things was at a later time still more highly cultivated at Florence. The noteworthy point about it is that, as a rule, we can perceive

FIG. 46. MACHIAVELLI
By Santi di Tito
London, Langton Douglas Collection
Photo Insel-Verlag, Leipzig

its connexion with the higher aspects of history, with art, and with culture in general. An inventory of 1422 [2] mentions, within the compass of the same document, the seventy-two exchange offices which surrounded the "Mercato Nuovo"; the amount of coined money in circulation (two million golden florins); the then new industry of gold-spinning; the silk wares; Filippo

[1] Giov. Villani, x, 164.
[2] *Ex Annalibus Ceretani*, in Fabroni, *Magni Cosmi Medicei Vita*, Adnot. 34, vol. ii, p. 63.

Brunellesco, then busy in digging classical architecture from its grave; and Leonardo Aretino, secretary of the republic, at work at the revival of ancient literature and eloquence; lastly it speaks of the general prosperity of the city, then free from political conflicts, and of the good fortune of Italy, which had rid itself of foreign mercenaries. The Venetian statistics quoted above (p. 93), which date from about the same year, certainly give evidence of larger property and profits and of a more extensive scene of action; Venice had long been mistress of the seas before Florence sent out its first galleys (1422) to Alexandria. But no reader can fail to recognize the higher spirit of the Florentine documents. These and similar lists recur at intervals of ten years, systematically arranged and tabulated, while elsewhere we find at best occasional notices. We can form an approximate estimate of the property and the business of the first Medici; they paid for charities, public buildings, and taxes from 1434 to 1471 no less than 633,755 gold florins, of which more than 400,000 fell to Cosimo alone, and Lorenzo the Magnificent was delighted that the money had been so well spent.[1] In 1472 we have again a most important and in its way complete view of the commerce and trades of this city,[2] some of which may be wholly or partly reckoned among the fine arts—such as those which had to do with damasks and gold or silver embroidery, with wood-carving and *intarsia*, with the sculpture of arabesques in marble and sandstone, with portraits in wax, and with jewellery and work in gold. The inborn talent of the Florentines for the systematization of outward life is shown by their books on agriculture, business, and domestic economy, which are markedly superior to those of other European people in the fifteenth century. It has been rightly decided to publish selections of these works,[3] although no little study will be needed to extract clear and definite results from them. At all events, we have no difficulty in recognizing the city, where dying parents begged the Government in their wills to fine their sons 1000 florins if they declined to practise a regular profession.[4]

For the first half of the sixteenth century probably no state in the world possesses a document like the magnificent description of Florence by Varchi.[5] In descriptive statistics, as in so many things besides, yet another model is left to us, before the freedom and greatness of the city sank into the grave.[6]

[1] *Ricordi* of Lorenzo, in Fabroni, *Laur. Med. Mag. Vita*, Adnot. 2 and 25. Paul. Jovius, *Elogia*, pp. 131 *sqq.*, on Cosmus.

[2] Given by Benedetto Dei, in the passage quoted above (p. 93, note 1). It must be remembered that the account was intended to serve as a warning to assailants. For the whole subject see Reumont, *Lorenzo de' Medici*, ii, p. 419. The financial project of a certain Lodovico Ghetti, with important facts, is given in Roscoe, *Life of Lorenzo de' Medici*, ii, App. I.

[3] For example, in the *Archiv. Stor.*, iv (?) See as a contrast the very simple ledger of Ott. Nuland, 1455-62 (Stuttgart, 1843), and for a rather later period the day-book of Lukas Rem, 1494-1541, edited by B. Greiff (Augsburg, 1861). A very remarkable publication is *Il Libro Segreto di Gregorio Dati*, edited by Carlo Ghargiolli (Bologna, 1869). The writer, a distinguished merchant, lived from 1362 till 1435. See also the account-books of the Rospigliosi of Pistoja, and that of the Cybò family, edited by L. Staffeti (1908). Also that of Bernabò Visconti, 1366, in *Arch. Stor. Lomb.*, xxxv.

[4] Libri, *Histoire des Sciences Mathématiques*, ii, 163 *sqq.*

[5] Varchi, *Stor. Fiorent.*, iii, pp. 56 *sqq.*, up to the end of the ninth book. Some obviously erroneous figures are probably no more than clerical or typographical blunders.

[6] In respect of prices and of wealth in Italy, I am only able, in default of further means of investigation, to bring together some scattered facts, which I have picked up here and there. Obvious exaggerations must be

This statistical estimate of outward life is, however, uniformly accompanied by the narrative of political events to which we have already referred.

Florence not only existed under political forms more varied than those of the free states of Italy and of Europe generally, but it reflected upon them far more deeply. It is a faithful mirror of the relations of individuals and classes to a variable whole. The pictures of the great civic democracies in France and in Flanders, as they are delineated in Froissart, and the narratives of the German chroniclers of the fourteenth century, are in truth of high importance; but in comprehensiveness of thought and in the rational development of the

put aside. The gold coins which are worth referring to are the ducat, the sequin, the *fiorino d'oro*, and the *scudo d'oro*. The value of all is nearly the same, fifty-five to sixty francs of the present French currency.

In Venice, for example, the Doge Andrea Vendramin (1475) with 170,000 ducats passed for an exceedingly rich man (Malipiero, *loc. cit.*, vii, ii, p. 666). The confiscated fortune of Colleoni amounted to 216,000 florins, *loc. cit.*, p. 244.

About 1460 the Patriarch of Aquileia, Lodovico Patavino, with 200,000 ducats, was called "perhaps the richest of all Italians" (Gasp. Veronens, *Vita Pauli II*, in Murat., iii, ii, col. 1027). Elsewhere fabulous statements.

Antonio Grimani paid 30,000 ducats for his son's election as cardinal. His ready money alone was put at 100,000 ducats (*Chron. Venetum*, in Murat., xxiv, col. 125).

For notices as to the grain in commerce and on the market at Venice see in particular Malipiero, *loc. cit.*, vii, ii, pp. 709 *sqq.* Date 1498.

In 1522 it is no longer Venice, but Genoa, next to Rome, which ranks as the richest city in Italy (only credible on the authority of Francesc. Vettori. See his history in the *Archiv. Stor.*, App., tom. vi, p. 343). Bandello, ii, *Nov.* 34 and 42, names as the richest Genoese merchant of his time Ansaldo Grimaldi.

Between 1400 and 1580 Franc. Sansovino assumes a depreciation of 50 per cent. in the value of money (*Venezia*, fol. 151 *bis*).

In Lombardy it is believed that the relation between the price of corn about the middle of the fifteenth and that at the middle of the nineteenth century is as three to eight. (Sacco di Piacenza, in *Archiv. Stor.*, App., tom. v. Note of editor Scarabelli.)

At Ferrara there were people at the time of Duke Borso with 50,000 to 60,000 ducats (*Diario Ferrarese*, in Murat., xxiv, col. 207, 214, 218; an extravagant statement, col. 187). In Florence the data are exceptional, and do not justify a conclusion as to averages. Of this kind are the loans to foreign princes, in which the names of one or two houses only appear, but which were, in fact, the work of great companies. So too the enormous fines levied on defeated parties; we read, for example, that from 1430 to 1453 seventy-seven families paid 4,875,000 gold florins (Varchi, iii, p. 115 *sqq.*), and that Giannozzo Mannetti alone, of whom we shall have occasion to speak hereafter, was forced to pay a sum of 135,000 gold florins, and was reduced thereby to beggary (Reumont, i, 157).

The fortune of Giovanni de' Medici amounted at his death (1428) to 179,221 gold florins, but the latter alone of his two sons Cosimo and Lorenzo left at his death (1440) as much as 235,137 (Fabroni, *Laur. Med.*, Adnot. 2). Cosimo's son Piero left (1469) 237,982 *scudi* (Reumont, *Lor. dei Medici*, i, 286).

It is a proof of the general activity of trade that the forty-four goldsmiths on the Ponte Vecchio paid in the fourteenth century a rent of 800 florins to the Government (Vasari, ii, 114, *Vita di Taddeo Gaddi*). The diary of Buonaccorso Pitti (in Délécluze, *Florence et ses Vicissitudes*, vol. ii) is full of figures, which, however, only prove in general the high price of commodities and the low value of money.

For Rome, the income of the Curia, which was derived from all Europe, gives us no criterion; nor are statements about Papal treasures and the fortunes of cardinals very trustworthy. The well-known banker Agostino Chigi left (1520) a fortune of in all 800,000 ducats (*Lettere Pittoriche*, i, App. 48).

During the high prices of the year 1505 the value of the *staro ferrarrese del grano*, which commonly weighed from sixty-eight to seventy pounds (German), rose to 1⅓ ducats. The *semola* or *remolo* was sold at *venti soldi lo staro*; in the following fruitful years the *staro* fetched six *soldi*. Bonaventura Pistofilo, p. 494. At Ferrara the rent of a house yearly in 1455 was twenty-five lire; cf. *Atti e Memorie*, Parma, vi, 250; see 265 *sqq.* for a documentary statement of the prices which were paid to artists and amanuenses.

From the inventory of the Medici (extracts in Muntz, *Précurseurs*, 158 *sqq.*) it appears that the jewels were valued at 12,205 ducats; the rings at 1792; the pearls (apparently distinguished from other jewels—S. G. C. M.) at 3512; the medallions, cameos, and mosaics at 2579; the vases at 4850; the reliquaries and the like at 3600; the library at 2700; the silver at 7000. Giov. Rucellai reckons that in 1473 (?) he has paid 60,000 gold florins in taxes, 10,000 for the dowries of his five daughters, 2000 for the improvement of the church of Santa Maria Novella. In 1474 he lost 20,000 gold florins through the intrigues of an enemy. (*Autografo dallo Tibaldone di G.R.*, Florence, 1872.) The marriage of Barnardo Rucellai with Nannina, the sister of Lorenzo de' Medici, cost 3686 florins (Muntz, *Précurseurs*, 244, i).

story, none will bear comparison with the Florentines. The rule of the nobility, the tyrannies, the struggles of the middle class with the proletariate, limited and unlimited democracy, pseudo-democracy, the primacy of a single house, the theocracy of Savonarola, and the mixed forms of government which prepared the way for the Medicean despotism—all are so described that the inmost motives of the actors are laid bare to the light.[1] At length Machiavelli in his Florentine history (down to 1492) represents his native city as a living organism and its development as a natural and individual process; he is the first of the moderns who has risen to such a conception. It lies without our province to determine whether and in what points Machiavelli may have done violence to history, as is notoriously the case in his life of Castruccio Castracane —a fancy picture of the typical despot. We might find something to say against every line of the *Istorie Fiorentine*, and yet the great and unique value of the whole would remain unaffected. And his contemporaries and successors, Jacopo Pitti,[2] Guicciardini, Segni, Varchi, Vettori, what a circle of illustrious names! And what a story it is which these masters tell us! The great and memorable drama of the last decades of the Florentine republic is here unfolded. The voluminous record of the collapse of the highest and most original life which the world could then show may appear to one but as a collection of curiosities, may awaken in another a devilish delight at the shipwreck of so much nobility and grandeur, to a third may seem like a great historical assize; for all it will be an object of thought and study to the end of time. The evil which was for ever troubling the peace of the city was its rule over once powerful and now conquered rivals like Pisa—a rule of which the necessary consequence was a chronic state of violence. The only remedy, certainly an extreme one and which none but Savonarola could have persuaded Florence to accept, and that only with the help of favourable chances, would have been the well-timed resolution of Tuscany into a federal union of free cities. At a later period this scheme, then no more than the dream of a past age, brought (1548) a patriotic citizen of Lucca to the scaffold.[3] From this

[1] So far as Cosimo (1433–65) and his grandson Lorenzo the Magnificent (d. 1492) are concerned, the author refrains from any criticism on their internal policy. For an accuser of importance see Giov. Cazzoni, in the *Archiv. Stor.*, i, pp. 315 *sqq.* The exaltation of both, particularly of Lorenzo, by William Roscoe (*Life of Lorenzo de' Medici, called the Magnificent*, 1st ed., Liverpool, 1795; 10th ed., London, 1851), seems to have been a principal cause of the reaction of feeling against them. This reaction appeared first in Sismondi (*Hist. des Rép. Italiennes*, xi), in reply to whose strictures, sometimes unreasonably severe, Roscoe again came forward (*Illustrations, Historical and Critical, of the Life of Lorenzo de' Medici*, London, 1822); later in Gino Capponi (*Arch. Stor. Ital.*, i (1842), pp. 315 *sqq.*), who afterward (*Storia della Rep. di Firenze*, 2 vols., Florence, 1875) gave further proofs and explanations of his judgment. See also the work of von Reumont (*Lor. dei Medici il Magn.*, 2 vols., Leipzig, 1874), distinguished no less by the judicial calmness of its views than by the mastery it displays of the extensive materials used. See also A. Castelman, *Les Médicis* (2 vols., Paris, 1879). The subject here is only casually touched upon. *Cf.* two works of B. Buser (Leipzig, 1879) devoted to the home and foreign policy of the Medici: (1) *Die Beziehungen der Medici zu Frankreich* (1434–94, etc.); (2) *Lorenzo de' Medici als italienischen Staatsman*, etc. (2nd ed., 1883). [It should be added that in the twelfth (German) edition, Bk. I, pp. 258 *sqq.*, Geiger expanded these notes of Burckhardt's with many notes of his own into a full discussion of the subject.—W. G.]

[2] Alc. Giorgetti, in the *Miscellanea Fiorentina*, i (1866), has proved that for the most part Pitti only copied down Bartolommeo Cerretani.

[3] Franc. Burlamacchi, father of the head of the Lucchese Protestants, Michele B. See *Arch. Stor. Ital.*, ser. i, tom. x, pp. 435–599; *Documenti*, pp. 146 *sqq.*; further Carlo Minutoli, *Storia di Fr. B.* (Lucca, 1844), and the important additions of Leone del Prete in the *Giornale Storico degli Archiv. Toscani*, iv, pp. 309 *sqq.* (1860). It

evil and from the ill-starred Guelph sympathies of Florence for a foreign prince, which familiarized it with foreign intervention, came all the disasters which followed. But who does not admire the people, which was wrought up by its venerated preacher to a mood of such sustained loftiness that for the first time in Italy it set the example of sparing a conquered foe, while the whole history of its past taught nothing but vengeance and extermination? The glow which melted patriotism into one with moral regeneration may seem, when looked at from a distance, to have soon passed away; but its best results shine forth again in the memorable siege of 1529-30. They were "fools," as Guicciardini then wrote, who drew down this storm upon Florence, but he confesses himself that they achieved things which seemed incredible; and when he declares that sensible people would have got out of the way of the danger he means no more than that Florence ought to have yielded itself silently and ingloriously into the hands of its enemies. It would no doubt have preserved its splendid suburbs and

FIG. 47. THE PALAZZO PUBBLICO (TOWN HALL), SIENA

gardens and the lives and prosperity of countless citizens; but it would have been the poorer by one of its greatest and most ennobling memories.

In many of their chief merits the Florentines are the pattern and the earliest type of Italians and modern Europeans generally; they are so also in many of their defects. When Dante compares the city which was always mending its constitution with the sick man who is continually changing his posture to escape from pain, he touches with the comparison a permanent feature of the

is well known how Milan, by its hard treatment of the neighbouring cities from the eleventh to the thirteenth century, prepared the way for the foundation of a great despotic state. Even at the time of the extinction of the Visconti in 1447 Milan frustrated the deliverance of Upper Italy, principally through not accepting the plan of a confederation of equal cities. *Cf.* Corio, fol. 358 *sqq.*

political life of Florence. The great modern fallacy that a constitution can be made, can be manufactured by a combination of existing forces and tendencies,[1] was constantly cropping up in stormy times; even Machiavelli is not wholly free from it. Constitutional artists were never wanting who by an ingenious distribution and division of political power, by indirect elections of the most complicated kind, by the establishment of nominal offices, sought to found a lasting order of things, and to satisfy or to deceive the rich and the poor alike. They naïvely fetch their examples from classical antiquity, and borrow the party names *ottimati, aristocrazia*,[2] as a matter of course. The world since then has become used to these expressions and given them a conventional European sense, whereas all former party names were purely national, and either characterized the cause at issue or sprang from the caprice of accident. But how a name colours or discolours a political cause!

But of all who thought it possible to construct a state the greatest beyond all comparison was Machiavelli.[3] He treats existing forces as living and active, takes a large and an accurate view of alternative possibilities, and seeks to mislead neither himself nor others. No man could be freer from vanity or ostentation; indeed, he does not write for the public, but either for princes and administrators or for personal friends. The danger for him does not lie in an affectation of genius or in a false order of ideas, but rather in a powerful imagination which he evidently controls with difficulty. The objectivity of his political judgment is sometimes appalling in its sincerity; but it is the sign of a time of no ordinary need and peril when it was a hard matter to believe in right, or to credit others with just dealing. Virtuous indignation at his expense is thrown away upon us who have seen in what sense political morality is understood by the statesmen of our own century. Machiavelli was at all events able to forget himself in his cause. In truth, although his writings, with the exception of very few words, are altogether destitute of enthusiasm, and although the Florentines themselves treated him at last as a criminal,[4] he was a patriot in the fullest meaning of the word. But free as he was, like most of his contemporaries, in speech and morals, the welfare of the State was yet his first and last thought.

His most complete programme for the construction of a new political system at Florence is set forth in the memorial to Leo X,[5] composed after the death of the younger Lorenzo de' Medici, Duke of Urbino (d. 1519), to whom he had dedicated his *Prince*. The State was by that time in extremities and utterly corrupt, and the remedies proposed are not always morally justifiable; but it is most interesting to see how he hopes to set up the republic in the form

---

[1] On the third Sunday in Advent 1494 Savonarola preached as follows on the method of bringing about a new constitution. The sixteen companies of the city were each to work out a plan, the Gonfalonieri to choose the four best of these, and the Signoria to name the best of all on the reduced list. Things, however, took a different turn, under the influence, indeed, of the preacher himself. See P. Villari, *Savonarola*. Besides this sermon, Savonarola had written a remarkable *Trattato circa il Regimento di Firenze* (reprinted at Lucca, 1817).

[2] The latter first in 1527, after the expulsion of the Medici. See Varchi, i, 121, etc.

[3] Machiavelli, *Stor. Fiorent.*, lib. iii, cap. 1: "Un savio dator di leggi" could save Florence.

[4] Varchi, *Stor. Fiorent.*, i, p. 210.

[5] *Discorso sopra il Riformar lo Stato di Firenze*, in the *Opere Minori*, p. 207.

of a moderate democracy, as heiress to the Medici. A more ingenious scheme of concessions to the Pope, to the Pope's various adherents, and to the different Florentine interests cannot be imagined; we might fancy ourselves looking into the works of a clock. Principles, observations, comparisons, political forecasts, and the like are to be found in numbers in the *Discorsi*, among them flashes of wonderful insight. He recognizes, for example, the law of a con-

tinuous though not uniform development in republican institutions, and requires the constitution to be flexible and capable of change, as the only means of dispensing with bloodshed and banishments. For a like reason, in order to guard against private violence and foreign interference—"the death of all freedom"—he wishes to see introduced a judicial procedure (*accusa*) against hated citizens, in place of which Florence had hitherto had nothing but the court of scandal. The tardy and involuntary decisions, which at critical moments play so important a part in republican states, are characterized with a masterly hand. Once, it is true, he is misled by his imagination and the pressure of events into unqualified praise of the people, which

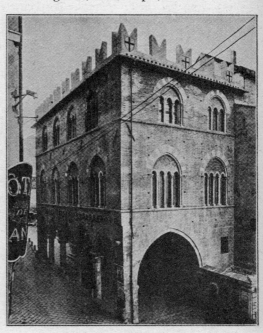

FIG. 48. THE PALAZZO DI S. GIORGIO
Formerly the headquarters of the Bank of Genoa

chooses its officers, he says, better than any prince, and which can be cured of its errors by "good advice."[1] With regard to the government of Tuscany, he has no doubt that it belongs to his native city, and maintains in a special *Discorso* that the reconquest of Pisa is a question of life or death; he deplores that Arezzo, after the rebellion of 1502, was not razed to the ground; he admits in general that Italian republics must be allowed to expand freely and add to their territory in order to enjoy peace at home, and not to be themselves attacked by others, but declares that Florence had always begun at the wrong end, and from the first made deadly enemies of Pisa, Lucca, and Siena, while Pistoja, "treated like a brother," had voluntarily submitted to her.[2]

[1] The same view, doubtless borrowed from here, occurs in Montesquieu.
[2] Belonging to a rather later period (1532?). Compare the opinion of Guicciardini, terrible in its frankness,

It would be unreasonable to draw a parallel between the few other republics which still existed in the fifteenth century and this unique city—the most important workshop of the Italian and, indeed, of the modern European spirit.   Siena suffered from the gravest organic maladies, and its relative prosperity in art and industry must not mislead us on this point.   Æneas Sylvius [1] looks with longing from his native town over to the "merry" German Imperial cities, where life is embittered by no confiscations of land and goods, by no arbitrary officials, and by no political factions. [2]   Genoa scarcely comes within range of our task, as before the time of Andrea Doria it took almost no part in the Renaissance.   Indeed, the inhabitant of the Riviera was proverbial among Italians for his contempt of all higher culture. [3] Party conflicts here assumed so fierce a character, and disturbed so violently the whole course of life, that we can hardly understand how, after so many revolutions and invasions, the Genoese ever contrived to return to an endurable condition.   Perhaps it was owing to the fact that nearly all who took part in public affairs were at the same time almost without exception active men of business. [4]   The example of Genoa shows in a striking manner with what insecurity wealth and vast commerce, and with what internal disorder the possession of distant colonies, are compatible.

Lucca is of small significance in the fifteenth century.

on the condition and inevitable organization of the Medicean party. *Lettere dei Principi*, iii, fol. 124 (ediz. Venez., 1577).

[1] Æneas Sylvius, *Apologia ad Martinum Mayer*, p. 701.   To the same effect Machiavelli, *Discorsi*, i, 55, and elsewhere.

[2] How strangely modern half-culture affected political life is shown by the party struggles of 1535.   Della Valle, *Lettere Sanesi*, iii, p. 317.   A number of small shopkeepers, excited by the study of Livy and of Machiavelli's *Discorsi*, call in all seriousness for tribunes of the people and other Roman magistrates against the misgovernment of the nobles and the official classes.

[3] Piero Valeriano, *De Infelicitate Literator.*, speaking of Bartolommeo della Rovere.   (The work of Piero Valeriano written 1527 is quoted according to the edition by Mencken, *Analecta de Calamitate Literatorum*, Leipzig, 1707.)   The passage here meant can only be that at p. 384, from which we cannot infer what is stated in the text, but in which we read that Bartolommeo della Rovere wished to make his son abandon a taste for study which he had conceived and put him into business.   [But Geiger holds that the exclusion of Genoa is unwarranted, as that city, at least in historical writings, can offer some brilliant performances.   *Cf.* also Braccio, *Giac. Bracelli e l'Umanesimo dei Liguri al suo Tempo* (Genoa, 1891).—W. G.]

[4] Senarega, *De Reb. Genuens.*, in Murat., xxiv, col. 548.   For the insecurity of the time see especially col. 519, 525, 528, etc.   For the frank language of the envoy on the occasion of the surrender of the state to Francesco Sforza (1464), when the envoy told him that Genoa surrendered in the hope of now living safely and comfortably, see Cagnola, *Archiv. Stor.*, iii, pp. 165 *sqq.*   The figures of the Archbishop, Doge, Corsair, and (later) Cardinal Paolo Fregoso form a notable contrast to the general picture of the condition of Italy.

CHAPTER VIII

The Foreign Policy of the Italian States

S the majority of the Italian states were in their internal constitution works of art—that is, the fruit of reflection and careful adaptation—so was their relation to one another and to foreign countries also a work of art. That nearly all of them were the result of recent usurpations was a fact which exercised as fatal an influence in their foreign as in their internal policy. Not one of them recognized another without reserve; the same play of chance which had helped to found and consolidate one dynasty might upset another. Nor was it always a matter of choice with the despot whether to keep quiet or not. The necessity of movement and aggrandizement is common to all illegitimate powers. Thus Italy became the scene of a 'foreign policy' which gradually, as in other countries also, acquired the position of a recognized system of public law. The purely objective treatment of international affairs, as free from prejudice as from moral scruples, attained a perfection which sometimes is not without a certain beauty and grandeur of its own. But as a whole it gives us the impression of a bottomless abyss.

Intrigues, armaments, leagues, corruption, and treason make up the outward history of Italy at this period. Venice in particular was long accused on all hands of seeking to conquer the whole peninsula, or gradually so to reduce its strength that one state after another must fall into her hands.[1] But on a closer view it is evident that this complaint did not come from the people, but rather from the courts and official classes, which were commonly abhorred by their subjects, while the mild government of Venice had secured for it general confidence.[2] Even Florence, with its restive subject cities, found itself in a false position with regard to Venice, apart from all commercial jealousy and from the progress of Venice in Romagna. At last the League of Cambray actually did strike a serious blow at the state (p. 91) which all Italy ought to have supported with united strength.

The other states also were animated by feelings no less unfriendly, and were at all times ready to use against one another any weapon which their evil

---

[1] So Varchi, at a much later time. *Stor. Fiorent.*, i, 57.

[2] Galeazzo Maria Sforza, indeed, declared the contrary (1467) to the Venetian agent—namely, that Venetian subjects had offered to join him in making war on Venice; but this is only vapouring. *Cf.* Malipiero, *Ann. Venet., Archiv. Stor.*, vii, i, pp. 216 *sqq.* On every occasion cities and villages voluntarily surrendered to Venice, chiefly, it is true, those that escaped from the hands of some despot, while Florence had to keep down the neighbouring republics, which were used to independence, by force of arms, as Guicciardini (*Ricordi*, n. 29) observes.

conscience might suggest.   Lodovico il Moro, the Aragonese Kings of Naples, and Sixtus IV—to say nothing of the smaller Powers—kept Italy in a state of constant and perilous agitation.   It would have been well if the atrocious game had been confined to Italy; but it lay in the nature of the case that intervention

FIG. 49. MOHAMMED II
By Gentile Bellini
London, National Gallery

and help should at last be sought from abroad—in particular from the French and the Turks.

The sympathies of the people at large were throughout on the side of France.   Florence had never ceased to confess with shocking *naïveté* its old Guelph preference for the French.[1]   And when Charles VIII actually appeared

[1] Most strongly, perhaps, in an instruction to the ambassadors going to Charles VII in 1452.   (See Fabroni, *Cosmus*, Adnot. 107, fol. ii, pp. 200 *sqq.*)   The Florentine envoys were instructed to remind the King of the centuries of friendly relations which had subsisted between France and their native city, and to recall to him that Charles the Great had delivered Florence and Italy from the barbarians (Lombards), and that Charles I and

on the south of the Alps all Italy accepted him with an enthusiasm which to himself and his followers seemed unaccountable.[1] In the imagination of the Italians, to take Savonarola for an example, the ideal picture of a wise, just, and powerful saviour and ruler was still living, with the difference that he was no longer the Emperor invoked by Dante, but the Capetian King of France. With his departure the illusion was broken; but it was long before all understood how completely Charles VIII, Louis XII, and Francis I had mistaken their true relation to Italy and by what inferior motives they were led. The princes, for their part, tried to make use of France in a wholly different way. When the Franco-English wars came to an end, when Louis XI began to cast about his diplomatic nets on all sides, and Charles of Burgundy to embark on his foolish adventures, the Italian Cabinets came to meet them at every point. It became clear that the intervention of France was only a question of time, even though the claims on Naples and Milan had never existed, and that the old interference with Genoa and Piedmont was only a type of what was to follow. The Venetians, in fact, expected it as early as 1642.[2] The mortal terror of the Duke Galeazzo Maria of Milan during the Burgundian war, in which he was apparently the ally of Charles as well as of Louis, and consequently had reason to dread an attack from both, is strikingly shown in his correspondence.[3] The plan of an equilibrium of the four chief Italian Powers, as understood by Lorenzo the Magnificent, was but the assumption of a cheerful, optimistic spirit, which had outgrown both the recklessness of an experimental policy and the superstitions of Florentine Guelphism, and persisted in hoping the best. When Louis XI offered him aid in the war against Ferrante of Naples and Sixtus IV he replied: "I cannot set my own advantage above the safety of all Italy; would to God it never came into the mind of the French kings to try their strength in this country! Should they ever do so, Italy is lost."[4] For the

the Romish Church were "fondatori della parte Guelfa. Il qual fondamento fa cagione della ruina della contraria parte e introdusse lo stato di felicità, in che noi siamo." When the young Lorenzo visited the Duke of Anjou, then staying at Florence, he put on a French dress. Fabroni, ii, p. 9.

[1] Comines, *Charles VIII*, chap. 10. The French were considered *comme saints*. *Cf.* chap. 17; *Chron. Venetum*, in Murat., xxiv, col. 5, 10, 14, 15; Matarazzo, *Chron. di Perugia, Archiv. Stor.*, xvi, ii, p. 23, not to speak of countless other proofs. See especially the documents in Desjardins, *op. cit.*, p. 127, note 1.

[2] *Pii II Comment.*, x, p. 492.

[3] Gingins, *Dépêches des Ambassadeurs Milanais*, etc., i, pp. 26, 153, 279, 283, 285, 327, 331, 345, 359; ii, pp. 29, 37, 101, 217, 306. Charles once spoke of giving Milan to the young Duke of Orleans.

[4] Niccolò Valori, *Vita di Lorenzo* (Florence, 1568). Italian translation of the Latin original, first printed in 1749 (later in Galletti, *Phil. Villani, Liber de Civit. Flor. Famosis Civibus*, pp. 161–183 (Florence, 1847); passage here referred to p. 171). It must not, however, be forgotten that this earliest biography, written soon after the death of Lorenzo, is a flattering rather than a faithful portrait, and that the words here attributed to Lorenzo are not mentioned by the French reporter, and can, in fact, hardly have been uttered. Comines, who was commissioned by Louis XI to go to Rome and Florence, says (*Mémoires*, lib. vi, chap. 5): "I could not offer him an army, and had nothing with me but my suite." (*Cf.* Reumont, *Lorenzo dei Medici*, i, pp. 197, 429; ii, 598.) In a letter from Florence to Louis XI we read (August 23, 1478): "Omnis spes nostra reposita est in favoribus suæ majestatis." A. Desjardins, *Négociations Diplomatiques de la France avec la Toscane*, i, p. 173 (Paris, 1859). Similarly Lorenzo himself in Kervyn de Lettenhove, *Lettres et Négociations de Philippe de Comines*, i, p. 190. Lorenzo, we see, is in fact the one who humbly begs for help, not who proudly declines it.

[Dr Geiger in his appendix maintains that Dr Burckhardt's view as to Lorenzo's national Italian policy is not borne out by evidence. Into this discussion the translator cannot enter. It would need strong proof to convince him that the masterly historical perception of Dr Burckhardt was in error as to a subject which he has studied with minute care. In an age when diplomatic lying and political treachery were matters of course documentary evidence loses much of its weight and cannot be taken without qualification as representing the

other princes, the King of France was alternately a bugbear to themselves and their enemies, and they threatened to call him in whenever they saw no more convenient way out of their difficulties. The Popes, in their turn, fancied that they could make use of France without any danger to themselves, and even Innocent VIII imagined that he could withdraw to sulk in the North and return as a conqueror to Italy at the head of a French army.[1]

Thoughtful men, indeed, foresaw the foreign conquest long before the expedition of Charles VIII.[2] And when Charles was back again on the other side of the Alps it was plain to every eye that an era of intervention had begun. Misfortune now followed on misfortune; it was understood too late that France and Spain, the two chief invaders, had become great European Powers, that they would be no longer satisfied with verbal homage, but would fight to the death for influence and territory in Italy. They had begun to resemble the centralized Italian states, and, indeed, to copy them, only on a gigantic scale. Schemes of annexation or exchange of territory were for a time indefinitely multiplied. The end, as is well known, was the complete victory of Spain, which, as sword and shield of the Counter-Reformation, long held the Papacy among its other subjects. The melancholy reflections of the philosophers could only show them how those who had called in the barbarians all came to a bad end.

Alliances were at the same time formed with the Turks too, with as little scruple or disguise; they were reckoned no worse than any other political expedients. The belief in the unity of Western Christendom had at various times in the course of the Crusades been seriously shaken, and Frederick II had probably outgrown it. But the fresh advance of the Oriental nations, the need and the ruin of the Greek Empire, had revived the old feeling, though not in its former strength, throughout Western Europe. Italy, however, was a striking exception to this rule. Great as was the terror felt for the Turks and the actual danger from them, there was yet scarcely a Government of any consequence which did not conspire against other Italian states with Mohammed II and his successors. And when they did not do so, they still had the credit of it; nor was it worse than the sending of emissaries to poison the cisterns of Venice, which was the charge brought against the heirs of Alfonso, King of Naples.[3] From a scoundrel like Sigismondo Malatesta nothing better

real feelings of the persons concerned, who fenced, turned about, and lied, first on one side and then on another, with an agility surprising to those accustomed to live among truth-telling people. Authorities quoted by Dr Geiger are Reumont, *Lorenzo dei Medici*, 2nd ed., i, 310; ii, 450. Desjardins, *Négociations Diplomatiques de la France avec la Toscane*, i, 173 (Paris, 1859). Kervyn de Lettenhove, *Lettres et Négociations de Philippe de Comines* i, 180.—S. G. C. M.]

[1] Fabroni, *Laurentius Magnificus*, Adnot. 205 *sqq.* In one of his Briefs it was said literally, "Flectere si nequeo superos, Acheronta movebo"; but it is to be hoped that he did not allude to the Turks. (Villari, *Storia di Savonarola*, ii, p. 48, of the *Documenti*.)

[2] For example, Jov. Pontan. in his *Charon*. In the dialogue between Æcus, Minos, and Mercurius (*Op.*, ed. Bas., ii, p. 1167) the first says: "Vel quod haud multis post sæculis futurum auguror, ut Italia, cujus intestina te odia male habent, Minos, in unius redacta ditionem resumat imperii majestatem." And in reply to Mercury's warning against the Turks Æcus answers: "Quamquam timenda hæc sunt, tamen si vetera respicimus, non ab Asia aut Græcia, verum a Gallis Germanisque timendum Italiæ semper fuit."

[3] Comines, *Charles VIII*, chap. 7. How Alfonso once tried in time of war to seize his opponents at a conference is told by Nantiporto, in Murat., iii, ii, col. 1073. He was a genuine predecessor of Cesare Borgia.

FIG. 50. PIUS II BLESSING THE CRUSADERS IN ANCONA
By Pinturicchio
Siena, Cathedral Library
Photo Alinari

could be expected than that he should call the Turks into Italy.[1] But the Aragonese monarchs of Naples, from whom Mohammed—at the instigation, we read, of other Italian Governments, especially of Venice[2]—had once wrested Otranto (1480), afterward hounded on the Sultan Bajazet II against the Venetians.[3] The same charge was brought against Lodovico il Moro. " The blood of the slain, and the misery of the prisoners in the hands of the Turks, cry to God for vengeance against him," says the State historian. In Venice, where the Government was informed of everything, it was known that Giovanni Sforza, ruler of Pesaro, the cousin of the Moor, had entertained the Turkish ambassadors on their way to Milan.[4] The two most respectable among the Popes of the fifteenth century, Nicholas V and Pius II, died in the deepest grief at the progress of the Turks, the latter, indeed, amid the preparations for a crusade which he was hoping to lead in person; their successors embezzled the contributions sent for this purpose from all parts of Christendom, and degraded the indulgences granted in return for them into a private commercial speculation.[5] Innocent VIII consented to be gaoler to the fugitive Prince Djem for a salary paid by the prisoner's brother, Bajazet II, and Alexander VI supported the steps taken by Lodovico il Moro in Constantinople to further a Turkish assault upon Venice (1498), whereupon the latter threatened him with a Council.[6] It is clear that the notorious alliance between Francis I and Soliman II was nothing new or unheard of.

Indeed, we find instances of whole populations to whom it seemed no particular crime to go over bodily to the Turks. Even if it were only held out as a threat to oppressive Governments, this is at least a proof that the idea had become familiar. As early as 1480 Battista Mantovano gives us clearly to understand that most of the inhabitants of the Adriatic coast foresaw something of this kind, and that Ancona in particular desired it.[7] When Romagna was suffering from the oppressive Government of Leo X a deputy from Ravenna said openly to the legate, Cardinal Giulio de' Medici: "Monsignore, the honourable Republic of Venice will not have us, for fear of a dispute with the Holy See; but if the Turk comes to Ragusa we will put ourselves into his hands."[8]

It was a poor but not wholly groundless consolation for the enslavement

---

[1] *Pii II Comment.*, x, p. 492. See a letter of Malatesta in which he recommends to Mohammed II a portrait-painter, Matteo de' Pasti of Verona, and announces the dispatch of a book on the art of war, probably in 1463, in Baluz., *Miscell.*, iii, 113. What Galeazzo Maria of Milan told in 1467 to a Venetian envoy—namely, that he and his allies would join with the Turks to destroy Venice—was said merely by way of threat. *Cf.* Malipiero, *Ann. Venet., Archiv. Stor.*, vii, i, p. 222. For Boccalino see page 44.

[2] Porzio, *Congiura dei Baroni*, lib. i, p. 5. That Lorenzo, as Porzio hints, really had a hand in it, is not credible. M. Brosch, *Julius II*, pp. 17-20, has proved conclusively that Venice prompted the Sultan to the deed. See Romanin, *Storia Documentata di Venezia*, lib. xi, cap. 3. After Otranto was taken Vespasiano Bisticci uttered his *Lamento d' Italia, Arch. Stor. Ital.*, iv, pp. 452 *sqq.*

[3] *Chron. Venetum*, in Murat., xxiv, col. 14 and 76.

[4] Malipiero, *loc. cit.*, pp. 565, 568.   [5] Trithem., *Annales Hirsaug.*, for the year 1490, tom. ii, pp. 535 *sqq.*

[6] Malipiero, *loc. cit.*, p. 161; *cf.* p. 152. For the surrender of Djem to Charles VIII see p. 145, from which it is clear that a connexion of the most shameful kind existed between Alexander and Bajazet, even if the documents in Burcardus be spurious. But for proof of their authenticity see *Zeitsch. f. Kirchengesch.*, v, pp. 511 *sqq.* See on the subject Ranke, *Zur Kritik neuerer Geschichtschreiber*, p. 99 (2 Auflage, Leipzig, 1874), and Gregorovius, Bd. vii, 353, note 1. *Ibid.*, p. 353, note 2, a declaration of the Pope that he was not allied with the Turks.

[7] Bapt. Mantuanus, *De Calamitatibus Temporum*, at the end of the second book, in the song of the Nereid Doris to the Turkish fleet.   [8] Tommaso Gar, *Relaz. della Corte di Roma*, i, p. 55.

of Italy then begun by the Spaniards that the country was at least secured from the relapse into barbarism, which would have awaited it under the Turkish rule.[1] By itself, divided as it was, it could hardly have escaped this fate.

If, with all these drawbacks, the Italian statesmanship of this period deserves our praise, it is only on the ground of its practical and unprejudiced treatment of those questions which were not affected by fear, passion, or malice. Here was no feudal system after the Northern fashion, with its artificial scheme of rights; but the power which each possessed he held in practice as in theory. Here was no attendant nobility to foster in the mind of the prince the medieval sense of honour, with all its strange consequences; but

FIG. 51. REVIEW OF THE FLEET AT NAPLES ON THE OCCASION OF THE VISIT
OF LORENZO THE MAGNIFICENT
Naples, Museo di S. Martino
Photo Diederich, Jena

princes and counsellors were agreed in acting according to the exigencies of the particular case and to the end they had in view. Toward the men whose services were used and toward allies, come from what quarter they might, no pride of caste was felt which could possibly estrange a supporter; and the class of the *condottieri*, in which birth was a matter of indifference, shows clearly enough in what sort of hands the real power lay; and lastly, the Government, in the hands of an enlightened despot, had an incomparably more accurate acquaintance with its own country and that of its neighbours than was possessed by Northern contemporaries, and estimated the economical and moral capacities of friend and foe down to the smallest particular. The rulers were, notwithstanding grave errors, born masters of statistical science. With such men negotiation was possible; it might be presumed that they would be convinced and their opinion modified when practical reasons were laid before them. When the great Alfonso of Naples was (1434) a prisoner of Filippo Maria Visconti he was able to satisfy his gaoler that the rule of the house of Anjou instead of his own at Naples would make the French masters of Italy; Filippo

---

[1] Ranke, *Geschichte der romanischen und germanischen Völker*. The opinion of Michelet (*Réforme*, p. 467), that the Turks would have adopted Western civilization in Italy, does not satisfy me. This mission of Spain is hinted at, perhaps for the first time, in the speech delivered by Fedra Inghirami in 1510 before Julius II, at the celebration of the capture of Bugia by the fleet of Ferdinand the Catholic. See *Anecdota Litteraria*, ii, p. 149.

Maria set him free without ransom and made an alliance with him.[1] A Northern prince would scarcely have acted in the same way, certainly not one whose morality in other respects was like that of Visconti. What confidence was felt in the power of self-interest is shown by the celebrated visit which Lorenzo the Magnificent, to the universal astonishment of the Florentines, paid the faithless Ferrante at Naples—a man who would be certainly tempted to keep him a prisoner, and was by no means too scrupulous to do so.[2] For to arrest a powerful monarch, and then to let him go alive, after extorting his signature and otherwise insulting him, as Charles the Bold did to Louis XI at Péronne (1468), seemed madness to the Italians;[3] so that Lorenzo was expected to come back covered with glory, or else not to come back at all. The art of political persuasion was at this time raised to a point—especially by the Venetian ambassadors—of which Northern nations first obtained a conception from the Italians, and of which the official addresses give a most imperfect idea. These are mere pieces of humanistic rhetoric. Nor, in spite of an otherwise ceremonious etiquette, was there in case of need any lack of rough and frank speaking in diplomatic intercourse.[4] A man like Machiavelli appears in his *legazioni* in an almost pathetic light. Furnished with scanty instructions, shabbily equipped, and treated as an agent of inferior rank, he never loses his gift of free and wide observation or his pleasure in picturesque description. From that time Italy was and remained the country of political *istruzioni* and *relazioni*. There was doubtless plenty of diplomatic ability in other states, but Italy alone at so early a period has preserved documentary evidence of it in considerable quantity. The long dispatch on the last period of the life of Ferrante of Naples (January 17, 1494), written by the hand of Pontano and addressed to the Cabinet of Alexander VI, gives us the highest opinion of this class of political writing, although it is only quoted incidentally and as one of many written. And how many other dispatches, as important and as vigorously written, in the diplomatic intercourse of this and later times still remain unknown or unedited![5]

A special division of this work will treat of the study of man individually and nationally, which among the Italians went hand in hand with the study of the outward conditions of human life.

[1] Among others Corio, fol. 333. Jov. Pontan., in his treatise *De Liberalitate*, cap. 28, considers the free dismissal of Alfonso as a proof of the *liberalitas* of Filippo Maria. (See above, p. 53, note.) *Cf.* the line of conduct adopted with regard to Sforza, fol. 329.

[2] Nic. Valori, *Vita di Lorenzo*; Paul. Jovius, *Vita Leonis X*, lib. i. The latter certainly upon good authority, though not without rhetorical embellishment. *Cf.* also Conti, i, 89: "Laurentius enim, sive prius fide a rege data, sive in necessaria consilium periculosum secutus, quod plerumque fides habita fidem obligat." See also Landucci, pp. 33 *sqq.* *Cf.* Reumont, i, 487, and the passage there quoted.

[3] If Comines on this and many other occasions observes and judges as objectively as any Italian, his intercourse with Italians, particularly with Angelo Catto, must be taken into account.

[4] *Cf.*, for example, Malipiero, pp. 216, 221, 236, 237, 468, etc., and above, pp. 107, note 2, and 112, note1. *Cf.* Egnatius, fol. 321a. The Pope curses an ambassador; a Venetian envoy insults the Pope; another, to win over his hearers, tells a fable.

[5] In Villari, *Storia di Savonarola*, vol. ii, p. xliii, of the *Documenti*, among which are to be found other important political letters. Other documents, particularly of the end of the fifteenth century, in Baluzius, *Miscellanea*, ed. Mansi, vol. i. See especially the collected dispatches of Florentine and Venetian ambassadors at the end of the fifteenth and beginning of sixteenth centuries in Desjardins, *Négociations Diplomatiques de la France avec la Toscane*, vols. i and ii (Paris, 1859, 1861).

CHAPTER IX

WAR AS A WORK OF ART

IT must here be briefly indicated by what steps the art of war assumed the character of a product of reflection.[1] Throughout the countries of the West the education of the individual soldier in the Middle Ages was perfect within the limits of the then prevalent system of defence and attack: nor was there any want of ingenious inventors in the arts of besieging and of fortification. But the development both of strategy and of tactics was hindered by the character and duration of military service, and

FIG. 52. BATTLE SCENE
By Paolo Uccello
Florence, Uffizi

by the ambition of the nobles, who disputed questions of precedence in the face of the enemy, and through simple want of discipline caused the loss of great battles like Crécy and Maupertuis. Italy, on the contrary, was the first country to adopt the system of mercenary troops, which demanded a wholly different organization; and the early introduction of firearms did its part in making war a democratic pursuit not only because the strongest castles were

[1] The subject has been treated more fully by Max Jähns, *Die Kriegskunst als Kunst* (Leipzig, 1874).

unable to withstand a bombardment, but because the skill of the engineer, of the gun-founder, and of the artillerist—men belonging to another class than the nobility—was now of the first importance in a campaign. It was felt, with regret, that the value of the individual, which had been the soul of

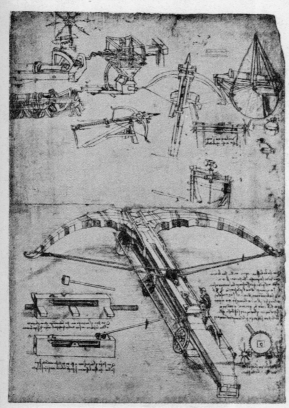

FIG. 53. SKETCHES OF WAR-WEAPONS
By Leonardo da Vinci
Codex Atlanticus

the small and admirably organized bands of mercenaries, would suffer from these novel means of destruction, which did their work at a distance; and there were *condottieri* who opposed to the utmost the introduction at least of the musket, which had been lately invented in Germany.[1] We read that Paolo Vitelli,[2] while recognizing and himself adopting the cannon, put out the eyes and cut off the hands of the captured *schioppettieri* of the enemy, because he held it unworthy that a gallant, and it might be noble, knight should be wounded and laid low by a common, despised foot-soldier. On the whole, however, the new discoveries were accepted and turned to useful account, till the Italians became the teachers of all Europe, both in the building of fortifications and in the means of attacking them.[3] Princes like Federigo of Urbino and Alfonso of Ferrara acquired a mastery of the subject

---

[1] *Pii II Comment.*, iv, p. 190, for the year 1459.

[2] The Cremonese prided themselves on their skill in this department. See *Cronaca di Cremona* in the *Bibliotheca Historica Italica*, vol. i, p. 214, and note (Milan, 1876). The Venetians did the same (Egnatius, fol. 300 *sqq.*).

[3] To this effect Paul Jovius (*Elogia*, p. 184), who adds: "Nondum enim invecto externarum gentium cruento more, Italiæ milites sanguinarii et multæ cædis avidi esse didicerant." We are reminded of Federigo of Urbino, who would have been "ashamed" to tolerate a printed book in his library. See Vespas. Fiorent.

compared to which the knowledge even of Maximilian I appears superficial. In Italy, earlier than elsewhere, there existed a comprehensive science and art of military affairs; here, for the first time, that impartial delight is taken in able generalship for its own sake, which might, indeed, be expected from the frequent change of party and from the wholly unsentimental mode of action of

FIG. 54. THE BATTLE BEFORE THE PORTA CAMOLLIA, SIENA (1526)
By Giovanni Cini
Siena, State Archives
Photo Alinari

the *condottieri.* During the Milano-Venetian war of 1451 and 1452, between Francesco Sforza and Jacopo Piccinino, the headquarters of the latter were attended by the scholar Gian Antonio Porcello dei Pandoni, commissioned by Alfonso of Naples to write a report of the campaign.[1] It is written, not in the purest, but in a fluent Latin, a little too much in the style of the humanistic

---

[1] *Porcellii Commentaria Jac. Piccinini,* in Murat., xx. A continuation for the war of 1453, *ibid.,* xxv. Paul Cortesius (*De Hominibus Doctis,* p. 33, Florence, 1734) criticizes the book severely on account of the wretched hexameters.

bombast of the day, is modelled on Cæsar's *Commentaries*, and interspersed with speeches, prodigies, and the like. Since for the past hundred years it had been seriously disputed whether Scipio Africanus or Hannibal was the greater,[1] Piccinino through the whole book must needs be called Scipio and Sforza Hannibal. But something positive had to be reported too respecting the Milanese army; the sophist presented himself to Sforza, was led along the ranks, praised highly all that he saw, and promised to hand it down to posterity.[2]

FIG. 55. THE BATTLE OF CADORE
By Titian. After the engraving by Fontana

Apart from him the Italian literature of the day is rich in descriptions of wars and strategic devices, written for the use of educated men in general as well as of specialists, while the contemporary narratives of Northerners, such as the *Burgundian Wars* by Diebold Schilling, still retain the shapelessness and matter-of-fact dryness of a mere chronicle. The greatest *dilettante* who has ever treated in that character[3] of military affairs was then busy writing his *Arte della Guerra*. But the development of the individual soldier found its most complete expression in those public and solemn conflicts between one or more pairs of combatants which were practised long before the famous *Challenge of*

---

[1] Porcello calls Scipio "Æmilianus" by mistake, meaning Africanus Major.
[2] Simonetta, *Hist. Fr. Sfortiæ*, in Murat., xxi, col. 630.
[3] So he was considered. *Cf.* Bandello, i, *Nov.* 40.

Barletta [1] (1503).   The victor was assured of the praises of poets and scholars, which were denied to the Northern warrior.   The result of these combats was no longer regarded as a divine judgment, but as a triumph of personal merit, and to the minds of the spectators seemed to be both the decision of an exciting competition and a satisfaction for the honour of the army or the nation.[2]

It is obvious that this purely rational treatment of warlike affairs allowed, under certain circumstances, of the worst atrocities, even in the absence of a strong political hatred, as, for instance, when the plunder of a city had been promised to the troops.   After the four days' devastation of Piacenza, which Sforza was compelled to permit to his soldiers (1447), the town long stood empty, and at last had to be peopled by force.[3]   Yet outrages like these were nothing compared with the misery which was afterward brought upon Italy by foreign troops, and most of all by the Spaniards, in whom perhaps a touch of Oriental blood, perhaps familiarity with the spectacles of the Inquisition, had unloosed the devilish element of human nature.   After seeing them at work at Prato, Rome, and elsewhere it is not easy to take any interest of the higher sort in Ferdinand the Catholic and Charles V, who knew what these hordes were, and yet unchained them.   The mass of documents which are gradually brought to light from the cabinets of these rulers will always remain an important source of historical information; but from such men no fruitful political conception can be looked for.

[1] *Cf.*, for example, *De Obsidione Tiphernatium*, in vol. 2 of the *Rer. Italic. Scriptores ex Codd. Florent.*, col. 690. The duel of Marshal Boucicault with Galeazzo Gonzaga (1406) in Cagnola, *Archiv. Stor.*, iii, p. 25.   Infessura tells us of the honour paid by Sixtus IV to the duellists among his guards.   His successors issued Bulls against duelling.   *Sept. Decret.*, v, Tit. 17.

[2] We may here notice parenthetically (see Jähns, pp. 26 *sqq.*) the less favourable side of the tactics of the *condottieri*.   The combat was often a mere sham-fight, in which the enemy was forced to withdraw by harmless manœuvres.   The object of the combatants was to avoid bloodshed, at the worst to make prisoners with a view to the ransom.   According to Machiavelli the Florentines lost in a great battle in 1440 one man only.

[3] For details see *Archiv. Stor.*, App., tom. v.

CHAPTER X

The Papacy and its Dangers

THE Papacy and the dominions of the Church [1] are creations of so peculiar a kind that we have hitherto, in determining the general characteristics of Italian states, referred to them only occasionally. The deliberate choice and adaptation of political expedients, which gives so great an interest to the other states, is what we find least of all at Rome, since here the spiritual power could constantly conceal or supply the defects of the temporal. And what fiery trials did this state undergo in the fourteenth and the beginning of the fifteenth century, when the Papacy was led captive to Avignon! All, at first, was thrown into confusion; but the Pope had money, troops, and a great statesman and general, the Spaniard Albornoz, who again brought the ecclesiastical state into complete subjection. The danger of a final dissolution was still greater at the time of the schism, when neither the Roman nor the French Pope was rich enough to reconquer the newly lost state; but this was done under Martin V, after the unity of the Church was restored, and done again under Eugenius IV, when the same danger was renewed. But the ecclesiastical state was and remained a thorough anomaly among the Powers of Italy; in and near Rome itself the Papacy was defied by the great families of the Colonna, Orsini, Savelli, and Anguillara; in Umbria, in the Marches, and in Romagna those civic republics for whose devotion the Papacy had showed so little gratitude had almost ceased to exist; their place had been taken by a crowd of princely dynasties, great or small, whose loyalty and obedience signified little. As self-dependent Powers, standing on their own merits, they have an interest of their own; and from this point of view the most important of them have been already discussed (pp. 45 *sqq.*, 60 *sqq.*).

Nevertheless a few general remarks on the Papacy can hardly be dispensed with. New and strange perils and trials came upon it in the course of the fifteenth century, as the political spirit of the nation began to lay hold upon it on various sides and to draw it within the sphere of its action. The least of these dangers came from the populace or from abroad; the most serious had their ground in the characters of the Popes themselves.

Let us, for this moment, leave out of consideration the countries beyond

---

[1] Here once for all we refer our readers to Ranke's *Päpste*, vol. i, and to Sugenheim, *Geschichte der Entstehung und Ausbildung des Kirchenstaates*. The still later works of Gregorovius and Reumont have also been made use of, and when they offer new facts or views are quoted. See also W. Wattenbach, *Geschichte des römischen Papstthums* (Berlin, 1876), and Pastor, *Geschichte der Päpste*, especially vols. i–iii.

the Alps. At the time when the Papacy was exposed to mortal danger in Italy it neither received nor could receive the slightest assistance either from France, then under Louis XI, or from England, distracted by the Wars of the Roses, or from the then disorganized Spanish monarchy, or from Germany, but lately betrayed at the Council of Basel. In Italy itself there were a certain number of instructed and even uninstructed people whose national vanity was flattered by the Italian character of the Papacy; the personal interests of very many depended on its having and retaining this character; and vast masses of

FIG. 56. THE CASTLE OF S. ANGELO AND ST PETER'S, ROME

the people still believed in the virtue of the Papal blessing and consecration; [1] among them notorious transgressors like that Vitellozzo Vitelli who still prayed to be absolved by Alexander VI when the Pope's son had him slaughtered.[2] But all these grounds of sympathy put together would not have

[1] For the impression made by the blessing of Eugenius IV in Florence see Vespas. Fiorent., p. 18. See also the passage quoted in Reumont, *Lorenzo dei Medici*, i, 171. For the impressive offices of Nicholas V see Infessura, in Eccard, ii, col. 1883 *sqq.*, and J. Manetti, *Vita Nicolai V*, in Murat., iii, ii, col. 923. For the homage given to Pius II see *Diario Ferrarese*, in Murat., xxiv, col. 205, and *Pii II Comment., passim*, especially iv, 201, 204, and xi, 562. For Florence see *Delizie degli Eruditi*, xx, 368. Even professional murderers respect the person of the Pope.

The great offices in church were treated as matters of much importance by the pomp-loving Paul II (Platina, *loc. cit.*, 321) and by Sixtus IV, who, in spite of gout, conducted Mass at Easter in a sitting posture. (*Jac. Volaterran. Diarium*, in Murat., xxiii, col. 131.) It is curious to notice how the people distinguished between the magical efficacy of the blessing and the unworthiness of the man who gave it; when he was unable to give the benediction on Ascension Day 1481 the populace murmured and cursed him. (*Ibid.*, col. 133.)

[2] Machiavelli, *Scritti Minori*, p. 142, in the well-known essay on the catastrophe of Sinigaglia. It is true that the French and Spanish soldiers were still more zealous than the Italians. *Cf.* in Paul. Jovius, *Vita Leonis X*, lib. ii, the scene before the battle of Ravenna, in which the legate, weeping for joy, was surrounded by the Spanish troops and besought for absolution. See further (*ibid.*) the statements respecting the French in Milan.

121

sufficed to save the Papacy from its enemies had the latter been really in earnest, and had they known how to take advantage of the envy and hatred with which the institution was regarded.

And at the very time when the prospect of help from without was so small the most dangerous symptoms appeared within the Papacy itself. Living, as it now did, and acting in the spirit of the secular Italian principalities, it was compelled to go through the same dark experiences as they; but its own exceptional nature gave a peculiar colour to the shadows.

As far as the city of Rome itself is concerned, small account was taken of its internal agitations, so many were the Popes who had returned after being expelled by popular tumult, and so greatly did the presence of the Curia minister to the interests of the Roman people. But Rome not only displayed at times a specific anti-Papal radicalism,[1] but in the most serious plots which were then contrived gave proof of the working of unseen hands from without. It was so in the case of the conspiracy of Stefano Porcaro against Nicholas V (1453), the very Pope who had done most for the prosperity of the city, but who, by enriching the cardinals and transforming Rome into a Papal fortress had aroused the discontent of the people.[2] Porcaro aimed at the complete overthrow of the Papal authority, and had distinguished accomplices, who, though their names are not handed down to us,[3] are certainly to be looked for among the Italian Governments of the time.[4] Under the pontificate of the same man, Lorenzo Valla concluded his famous declamation against the gift of Constantine, with the wish for the speedy secularization of the States of the Church.[5]

The Catilinarian gang, with which Pius II had to contend [6] (1460), avowed with equal frankness its resolution to overthrow the government of the priests, and its leader, Tiburzio, threw the blame on the soothsayers, who had fixed the accomplishment of his wishes for this very year. Several of the chief men of Rome, the Prince of Tarentum, and the *condottiere* Jacopo Piccinino, were accomplices and supporters of Tiburzio. Indeed, when we think of the booty which was accumulated in the palaces of wealthy prelates—the conspirators had the Cardinal of Aquileia especially in view—we are surprised that

[1] In the case of the heretics of Poli, in the Campagna, who held the doctrine that a genuine Pope must show the poverty of Christ as the mark of his calling, we have simply a kind of Waldensian doctrine. Their imprisonment under Paul II is related by Infessura (in Eccard, ii, col. 1893), Platina, p. 317, etc.

[2] As an illustration of this feeling see the poem addressed to the Pope, quoted in Gregorovius, vii, 136.

[3] *Dialogus de Conjuratione Stephani de Porcariis*, by his contemporary, Petrus Godes de Vicenza, quoted and used by Gregorovius, viii, 130. L. B. Alberti, *De Porcaria Conjuratione*, in Murat., xxv, col. 309. Porcari was desirous "omnem pontificiam turbam funditus exstinguere." The author concludes: "Video sane, quo stent loco res Italiæ; intelligo qui sint, quibus hic perturbata esse omnia conducat. . . ." He names them "Extrinsecus impulsores," and is of opinion that Porcari will find successors in his misdeeds. The dreams of Porcari certainly bore some resemblance to those of Cola di Rienzi. He also referred to himself the poem *Spirito Gentil*, addressed by Petrarch to Rienzi.

[4] A contemporary suspects Alfonso of Naples, and recently discovered documents show that he was probably right.

[5] "Ut Papa tantum vicarius Christi sit et non etiam Cæsaris. . . . Tunc Papa et dicetur et erit pater sanctus, pater omnium, pater ecclesiæ," etc. Valla's work was written rather earlier, and was aimed at Eugenius IV. See Vahlen, *Lor. Valla*, pp. 25 *sqq.*, especially 32 (Berlin, 1870). Nicholas V, on the other hand, is praised by Valla, Gregorovius, vii, 136.

[6] *Pii II Comment.*, iv, pp. 208 *sqq.* Voigt, *Enea Silvio*, iii, pp. 151 *sqq.*

in an almost unguarded city such attempts were not more frequent and more successful. It was not without reason that Pius II preferred to reside anywhere rather than in Rome; and even Paul II [1] was exposed to no small anxiety through a plot formed by some discharged abbreviators, who, under the command of Platina, besieged the Vatican for twenty days. The Papacy must sooner or later have fallen a victim to such enterprises, if it had not stamped out

FIG. 57. ST FRANCIS PREACHING BEFORE HONORIUS III
School of Giotto
Part of a fresco in the Upper Church of S. Francesco, Assisi
Photo Alinari

the aristocratic factions under whose protection these bands of robbers grew to a head.

This task was undertaken by the terrible Sixtus IV. He was the first Pope who had Rome and the neighbourhood thoroughly under his control, especially after his successful attack on the house of Colonna, and consequently, both in his Italian policy and in the internal affairs of the Church, he could venture to act with a defiant audacity, and to set at nought the complaints and threats to summon a council which arose from all parts of Europe. He supplied himself with the necessary funds by simony, which suddenly grew to unheard-of

---

[1] Platina, *Vita Pauli II. Cf.* Pastor, ii, pp. 310 *sqq.*, where, after an exhaustive inquiry, the conspiracy remains open to question.

proportions, and which extended from the appointment of cardinals down to the granting of the smallest favours.[1] Sixtus himself had not obtained the Papal dignity without recourse to the same means.

A corruption so universal might sooner or later bring disastrous consequences on the Holy See, but they lay in the uncertain future. It was otherwise with nepotism, which threatened at one time to destroy the Papacy altogether. Of all the *nipoti*, Cardinal Pietro Riario enjoyed at first the chief and almost exclusive favour of Sixtus. He soon drew upon him the eyes of all Italy,[2] partly by the fabulous luxury of his life, partly through the reports which were current of his irreligion and his political plans. He bargained with Duke Galeazzo Maria of Milan (1473) that the latter should become King of Lombardy and then aid him with money and troops to return to Rome and ascend the Papal throne; Sixtus, it appears, would have voluntarily yielded it to him.[3] This plan, which, by making the Papacy hereditary, would have ended in the secularization of the Papal State, failed through the sudden death of Pietro. The second *nipote*, Girolamo Riario, remained a layman, and did not seek the Pontificate. From this time the *nipoti*, by their endeavours to found principalities for themselves, became a new source of confusion to Italy. It had already happened that the Popes tried to make good their feudal claims on Naples in favour of their relatives;[4] but since the failure of Calixtus III such a scheme was no longer practicable, and Girolamo Riario, after the attempt to conquer Florence (and who knows how many other places?) had failed, was forced to content himself with founding a state within the limits of the Papal dominions themselves. This was justifiable in so far as Romagna, with its princes and civic despots, threatened to shake off the Papal supremacy altogether, and ran the risk of shortly falling a prey to Sforza or the Venetians, when Rome interfered to prevent it. But who, at times and in circumstances like these, could guarantee the continued obedience of *nipoti* and their descendants, now turned into sovereign rulers, to Popes with whom they had no further concern? Even in his lifetime the Pope was not always sure of his own son or nephew, and the temptation was strong to expel the *nipote* of a predecessor and replace him by one of his own. The reaction of the whole system on the Papacy itself was of the most serious character; all means of compulsion, whether temporal or spiritual, were used without scruple for the most questionable ends, and to these all the other objects of the Apostolic See were made subordinate. And when they were attained, at

[1] Battista Mantovano, *De Calamitatibus Temporum*, lib. iii. The Arabian sells incense, the Tyrian purple, the Indian ivory: "Venalia nobis templa, sacerdotes, altaria sacra, coronæ, ignes, thura, preces, cælum est venale Deusque." *Opera*, fol. 302b (ed. Paris, 1507). Then follows an exhortation to Pope Sixtus, whose previous efforts are praised, to put an end to these evils.

[2] See, for example, the *Annales Placentini*, in Murat., xx, col. 943.

[3] Corio, *Storia di Milano*, fol. 416–420. Pietro had already helped at the election of Sixtus. See Infessura, in Eccard, *Scriptores*, ii, col. 1895. It is curious that in 1469 it had been prophesied that deliverance would come from Savona (home of Sixtus, elected in 1471) within three years. See the letter and date in Baluz., *Miscell.*, iii, p. 181. According to Machiavelli, *Stor. Fiorent.*, lib. vii, the Venetians poisoned the cardinal. Certainly they were not without motives to do so. [Machiavelli's conjecture is most probably wrong. Even the agreement mentioned above, between Pietro and the Duke of Milan, was only a rumour!—W. G.]

[4] Honorius II wished, after the death of William I (1127), to annex Apulia, as a feoff reverted to St Peter.

whatever cost of revolutions and proscriptions, a dynasty was founded which had no stronger interest than the destruction of the Papacy.

FIG. 58. ALEXANDER VI
Part of the fresco of *The Resurrection of Christ*, by Pinturicchio
Rome, Vatican
Photo Anderson, Rome

At the death of Sixtus Girolamo was able to maintain himself in his usurped principality of Forlì and Imola only by the utmost exertions of his own, and by the aid of the house of Sforza. He was murdered in 1488. In the conclave (1484) which followed the death of Sixtus—that in which Innocent VIII was elected—an incident occurred which seemed to furnish the Papacy with a new external guarantee. Two cardinals, who, at the same time, were princes of ruling houses, Giovanni d'Aragona, son of King Ferrante, and Ascanio Sforza, brother of the Moor, sold their votes with the most shameless effrontery; [1] so that, at any rate, the ruling houses of Naples and Milan became interested, by their participation in the booty, in the continuance of the Papal system. Once again, in the following conclave, when all the cardinals but five sold themselves, Ascanio received enormous sums in bribes, not without cherishing the hope that at the next election he would himself be the favoured candidate. [2]

Lorenzo the Magnificent, on his part, was anxious that the house of Medici should not be sent away with empty hands. He married his daughter Maddalena to the son of the new Pope—the first who publicly acknowledged his children—Franceschetto Cybò, and expected not only favours of all kinds for his own son, Cardinal Giovanni, afterward Leo X, but also the rapid promotion of his son-in-law. [3] But with respect to the latter he demanded impossibilities. Under Innocent VIII there was no opportunity for the audacious nepotism by which states had been founded, since Franceschetto himself was a poor creature who, like his father the Pope, sought power only for the lowest purpose of all—the acquisition and accumulation of money. [4] The manner, however, in which father and son practised this occupation must have led sooner or later to a final catastrophe—the dissolution of the State. If Sixtus had filled his treasury by the rule of spiritual dignities and favours, Innocent and his son, for their part, established an office for the sale of secular favours, in which pardons for murder and manslaughter were sold for large sums of money. Out of every fine a hundred and fifty ducats were paid into the Papal exchequer, and what was over to Franceschetto. Rome, during the latter part of this pontificate, swarmed with licensed and unlicensed assassins; the factions, which Sixtus had begun to put down, were again as active as ever; the Pope, well guarded in the Vatican, was satisfied with now and then laying a trap, in which a wealthy misdoer was occasionally caught. For Franceschetto the chief point was to know by what means, when the Pope died, he could escape with well-filled coffers. He betrayed himself at last, on the occasion of a false report (1490) of his father's death; he endeavoured to carry off all the money in the Papal treasury, and when this proved impossible insisted that, at all events, the Turkish prince Djem should go with him, and serve as a living capital, to be advantageously disposed of, perhaps to Ferrante of Naples. [5] It is hard to estimate the political possibilities of remote periods,

---

[1] Fabroni, *Laurentius Magn.*, Adnot. 130, pp. 256 *sqq.* An informer, Vespucci, sends word of both: "Hanno in ogni elezione a mettere a sacco questa corte, e sono i maggior ribaldi del mondo."

[2] Corio, fol. 450. Details, partly from unpublished documents, of these acts of bribery in Gregorovius, vii, 310 *sqq.*

[3] A most characteristic letter of exhortation by Lorenzo, in Fabroni, *Laurentius Magn.*, Adnot. 217, and extracts in Ranke, *Päpste*, i, p. 45, and in Reumont, *Lorenzo dei Medici*, ii, pp. 482 *sqq.*

[4] And perhaps of certain Neapolitan feoffs, for the sake of which Innocent called in the Angevins afresh against the immovable Ferrante. The conduct of the Pope in this affair and his participation in the second conspiracy of the barons were equally foolish and dishonest.

[5] *Cf.* in particular Infessura, in Eccard, *Scriptores*, ii, *passim.*

but we cannot help asking ourselves the question whether Rome could have survived two or three pontificates of this kind. Even with reference to the believing countries of Europe, it was imprudent to let matters go so far that not only travellers and pilgrims, but a whole embassy of Maximilian, King of the Romans, were stripped to their shirts in the neighbourhood of Rome, and that envoys had constantly to turn back without setting foot within the city.

Such a condition of things was incompatible with the conception of power and its pleasures which inspired the gifted Alexander VI (1492–1503), and the first event that happened was the restoration, at least provisionally, of public order and the punctual payment of every salary.

Strictly speaking, as we are now discussing phases of Italian civilization, this pontificate might be passed over, since the Borgias are no more Italian than the house of Naples.[1] Alexander spoke Spanish in public with Cesare; Lucrezia, at her entrance to Ferrara, where she wore a Spanish costume, was sung to by Spanish buffoons; their confidential servants consisted of Spaniards, as did also the most ill-famed company of the troops of Cesare in the

FIG. 59. CESARE BORGIA
Woodcut from the *Elogia Virorum Bellica Virtute Illustrium*,
by Paolo Giovio (Basel, 1577)
Photo Insel-Verlag, Leipzig

war of 1500; and even his hangman, Don Micheletto, and his poisoner, Sebastian Pinzon,[2] seem to have been of the same nation. Among his other achievements, Cesare, in true Spanish fashion, killed, according to the rules of the craft, six wild bulls in an enclosed court. But the Roman corruption, which seemed to culminate in this family, was already far advanced when they came to the city.

[1] It should, however, be emphasized that the family of Borgia boasted of its Roman origin, that Cesare studied in Italian universities, and that Alexander VI and Lucrezia zealously fostered Italian literature and culture.
[2] According to the *Dispacci di Antonio Giustiniani*, i, p. 60, and ii, p. 309, Sebastian Pinzon was a native of Cremona. Micheletto was a Spaniard (Villari, *Machiavelli*, i, 390, note 1).

What they were and what they did has been often and fully described.[1] Their immediate purpose, which, in fact, they attained, was the complete subjugation of the Pontifical State. All the petty despots,[2] who were mostly more or less refractory vassals of the Church, were expelled or destroyed; and in Rome itself the two great factions were annihilated, the so-called Guelph Orsini as well as the so-called Ghibelline Colonna. But the means employed were of so frightful a character that they must certainly have ended in the ruin of the Papacy had not the contemporaneous death of both father and son by poison suddenly intervened to alter the whole aspect of the situation. The moral indignation of Christendom was certainly no great source of danger to Alexander; at home he was strong enough to extort terror and obedience; foreign rulers were won over to his side, and Louis XII even aided him to the utmost of his power. The mass of the people throughout Europe had hardly a conception of what was passing in Central Italy. The only moment which was really fraught with danger—when Charles VIII was in Italy—went by with unexpected fortune, and even then it was not the Papacy as such that was in peril, but Alexander, who risked being supplanted by a more respectable Pope.[3] The great, permanent, and increasing danger for the Papacy lay in Alexander himself, and, above all, in his son Cesare Borgia.

In the nature of the father ambition, avarice, and sensuality were combined with strong and brilliant qualities. All the pleasures of power and luxury he granted himself in the fullest measure from the first day of his pontificate. In the choice of means to this end he was wholly without scruple; it was known at once that he would more than compensate himself for the sacrifices which his election had involved,[4] and that the simony of the seller would far exceed the simony of the buyer. It must be remembered that the vice-chancellorship and other offices which Alexander had formerly held had taught him to know better and turn to more practical account than any other member of the Curia the various sources of revenue. As early as 1494 a Carmelite, Adam of Genoa, who had preached at Rome against simony, was found murdered in his bed with twenty wounds. Hardly a single cardinal was appointed without the payment of enormous sums of money.

[1] Recently by Gregorovius, *Lucrezia Borgia* (2 Bd., 3 Auflage, Stuttgart, 1875).

[2] Except the Bentivoglio at Bologna, and the house of Este at Ferrara. The latter was compelled to form a family relationship, Lucrezia marrying Prince Alfonso.

[3] According to Corio (fol. 479) Charles had thoughts of a council, of deposing the Pope, and even of carrying him away to France, this upon his return from Naples. According to Benedictus, *Carolus VIII* (in Eccard, *Scriptores*, ii, col. 1584), Charles, while in Naples, when Pope and cardinals refused to recognize his new crown, had certainly entertained the thought "de Italiæ imperio deque pontificis statu mutando," but soon after made up his mind to be satisfied with the personal humiliation of Alexander. The Pope, nevertheless, escaped him. Particulars in Pilorgerie, *Campagne et Bulletins de la Grande Armée d'Italie*, 1494, 1495 (Paris, 1866, 8vo), where the degree of Alexander's danger at different moments is discussed (pp. 111, 117, etc.). In a letter, there printed, of the Archbishop of Saint-Malo to Queen Anne, it is expressly stated: " Si nostre roy eust voulu obtemperer à la plupart des Messeigneurs les Cardinaulx, ilz eussent fait ung autre pappe en intention de refformer l'église ainsi qu'ilz disaient. Le roy désire bien la reformacion, mais il ne veult point entreprandre de sa depposicion."

[4] Corio, fol. 450. Malipiero, *Ann. Venet., Archiv. Stor.*, vii, i, p. 318. The rapacity of the whole family can be seen in Malipiero, among other authorities, *loc. cit.*, p. 565. A *nipote* was splendidly entertained in Venice as Papal legate, and made an enormous sum of money by selling dispensations; his servants, when they went away, stole whatever they could lay their hands on, including a piece of embroidered cloth from the high altar of a church at Murano.

But when the Pope in course of time fell under the influence of his son, Cesare Borgia, his violent measures assumed that character of devilish wickedness which necessarily reacts upon the ends pursued. What was done in the struggle with the Roman nobles and with the tyrants of Romagna exceeded in faithlessness and barbarity even that measure to which the Aragonese rulers of Naples had already accustomed the world; and the genius for deception was also greater. The manner in which Cesare isolated his father, murdering brother, brother-in-law, and other relations or courtiers whenever their favour with the Pope or their position in any other respect became inconvenient to him, is literally appalling. Alexander was forced to acquiesce in the murder of his best-loved son, the Duke of Gandia, since he himself lived in hourly dread of Cesare.[1]

What were the final aims of the latter? Even in the last months of his tyranny, when he had murdered the *condottieri* at Sinigaglia, and was to all intents and purposes master of the ecclesiastical state (1503), those who stood near him gave the modest reply that the Duke merely wished to put down the factions and the despots, and all for the good of the Church only; that for himself he desired nothing more than the lordship of the Romagna, and that he had earned the gratitude of all the following Popes by ridding them of the Orsini and Colonna.[2] But no one will accept this as his ultimate design. The Pope Alexander himself, in his discussions with the Venetian ambassador, went farther than this when committing his son to the protection of Venice. " I will see to it," he said, " that one day the Papacy shall belong either to him or to you." [3] Cesare certainly added that no one could become Pope without

[1] This in Panvinio alone among contemporary historians (*Contin. Platinæ*, p. 339): "insidiis Cæsaris fratris interfectus . . . connivente . . . ad scelus patre." An authentic statement certainly, with which may be contrasted the affirmations of Malipiero and Matarazzo (who lay the blame on Giovanni Sforza); see, to the same effect, Paul. Jovius, *Elog. Vir. Ill.*, p. 302. The profound emotion of Alexander looks like a sign of complicity. After the corpse was drawn out of the Tiber Sannazaro wrote (*Opera Omnia Latine Scripta*, fol. 41*a*, 1535):

" Piscatorem hominum ne te non, Sexte, putemus
Piscaris natum retibus, ecce, tuum."

Besides the epigram quoted there are others (fol. 36*b*, 42*b*, 47*b*, 51*a*, *b*—in the last passage five) in Sannazaro on—that is, against—Alexander. Among them is a famous one, referred to in Gregorovius, i, 314, on Lucrezia Borgia:

" Ergo te semper cupiet Lucretia Sextus?
O fatum diri nominis: hic pater est? "

Others execrate his cruelty and celebrate his death as the beginning of an era of peace. On the Jubilee there is another epigram, fol. 43*b*. There are others no less severe (fol. 34*b*, 35*a*, *b*, 42*b*, 43*a*) against Cesare Borgia, among which we find in one of the strongest:

" Aut nihil aut Cæsar vult dici Borgia; quidni?
Cum simul et Cæsar possit, et esse nihil."

(Made use of by Bandello, iv, *Nov.* 11.) On the murder of the Duke of Gandia see especially the admirable collection of the most original sources of evidence in Gregorovius, vii, 399–407, according to which Cesare's guilt is clear. [According to recent investigation, however, the assent of the Pope to the murder is more than doubtful. That he instigated it is, at any rate, unproven.—W. G.]

[2] Machiavelli, *Opere*, ed. Milan, vol. v, pp. 387, 393, 395, in the *Legazione al Duca Valentino*.

[3] Tommaso Gar, *Relazioni della Corte di Roma*, i, p. 12, in the *Rel. dei P. Capello*. Literally: " The Pope has more respect for Venice than for any other Power in the world." " E però desidera, che ella [Signoria di Venezia] protegga il figliuolo, e dice voler fare tale ordine, che il papato o sia suo, ovvero della signoria nostra." The word *suo* can refer only to Cesare. An instance of the uncertainty caused by this usage is found in the still lively controversy respecting the words used by Vasari in the *Vita di Raffaello*: " A Bindo Altoviti fece il ritratto suo," etc.

the consent of Venice, and for this end the Venetian cardinals had only to keep well together. Whether he referred to himself or not we are unable to say; at all events, the declaration of his father is sufficient to prove his designs on the Pontifical throne. We further obtain from Lucrezia Borgia a certain amount of indirect evidence, in so far as certain passages in the poems of Ercole Strozzi may be the echo of expressions which she as Duchess of Ferrara may easily have permitted herself to use. Here too Cesare's hopes of the Papacy are chiefly spoken of; [1] but now and then a supremacy over all Italy is hinted at,[2] and finally we are given to understand that as temporal ruler Cesare's projects were of the greatest, and that for their sake he had formerly surrendered his cardinalate.[3] In fact, there can be no doubt whatever that Cesare, whether chosen Pope or not after the death of Alexander, meant to

keep possession of the Pontifical state at any cost, and that this, after all the enormities he had committed, he could not as Pope have succeeded in doing permanently. He, if anybody, could have secularized the States of the Church, and he would have been forced to do so in order to keep them.[4] Unless we are much deceived, this is the real reason of the secret sympathy with which Machiavelli treats the great criminal; from Cesare, or from nobody, could it be hoped that he "would draw the steel from the wound"; in other words, annihilate the Papacy—the source of all foreign intervention and of all the divisions of Italy.

The intriguers who thought to divine Cesare's aims, when holding out to him hopes of the kingdom of Tuscany, seem to have been dismissed with contempt.[5]

But all logical conclusions from his premises are idle, not because of the unaccountable genius which in fact characterized him as little as it did the Duke of Friedland, but because the means which he employed were not compatible with any large and consistent course of action. Perhaps, indeed, in the very excess of his wickedness some prospect of salvation for the

---

[1] *Strozzii Poetæ*, p. 19, in the *Venatio* of Ercole Strozzi: ". . . cui triplicem fata invidere coronam"; and in the elegy on Cesare's death, pp. 31 *sqq.*: "Speraretque olim solii decora alta paterni."

[2] *Ibid.* Jupiter had once promised:
> "Affore Alexandri sobolem, quæ poneret olim
> Italiæ leges, atque aurea sæcla referret," etc.

[3] *Ibid.* "Sacrumque decus majora parantem deposuisse."

[4] He was married, as is well known, to a French princess of the family of Albret, and had a daughter by her; in some way or other he would have attempted to found a dynasty. It is not known that he took steps to regain the cardinal's hat, although (according to Machiavelli, *loc. cit.*, p. 285) he must have counted on the speedy death of his father.

[5] Machiavelli, *loc. cit.*, p. 334. Designs on Siena and eventually on all Tuscany certainly existed, but were not yet ripe; the consent of France was indispensable.

Papacy may have existed even without the accident which put an end to his rule.

Even if we assume that the destruction of the petty despots in the Pontifical State had gained for him nothing but sympathy, even if we take as proof of his great projects the army, composed of the best soldiers and officers in Italy, with Leonardo da Vinci as chief engineer, which followed his fortunes in 1503, other facts nevertheless wear such a character of unreason that our judgment,

FIG. 61. JULIUS II
Part of Raphael's *Mass of Bolsena*
Rome, Vatican

like that of contemporary observers, is wholly at a loss to explain them. One fact of this kind is the devastation and maltreatment of the newly won state, which Cesare still intended to keep and to rule over.[1] Another is the condition of Rome and of the Curia in the last decades of the pontificate. Whether it was that father and son had drawn up a formal list of proscribed persons,[2] or that the murders were resolved upon one by one, in either case the Borgias were bent on the secret destruction of all who stood in their way or whose

---

[1] Machiavelli, *loc. cit.*, pp. 326, 351, 414; Matarazzo, *Cronaca di Perugia, Archiv. Stor.*, xvi, ii, pp. 157 and 221. He wished his soldiers to quarter themselves where they pleased, so that they gained more in time of peace than of war. Petrus Alcyonius, *De Exilio* (1522), ed. Mencken, p. 19, says of the style of conducting war: " Ea scelera et flagitia a nostris militibus patrata sunt quae ne Scythae quidem aut Turcae aut Poeni in Italia commisissent." The same writer (p. 65) blames Alexander as a Spaniard: " Hispani generis hominem, cujus proprium est, rationibus et commodis Hispanorum consultum velle, non Italorum." See above, p. 127.

[2] To this effect Pierio Valeriano, *De Infelicitate Literat.*, ed. Mencken, p. 282, in speaking of Giovanni Regio: " In arcano proscriptorum albo positus."

inheritance they coveted. Of this money and movable goods formed the smallest part; it was a much greater source of profit for the Pope that the incomes of the clerical dignitaries in question were suspended by their death, and that he received the revenues of their offices while vacant, and the price of these offices when they were filled by the successors of the murdered men. The Venetian ambassador, Paolo Capello,[1] announces in the year 1500: " Every night four or five murdered men are discovered—bishops, prelates, and others—so that all Rome is trembling for fear of being destroyed by the Duke [Cesare]." He himself used to wander about Rome in the night-time with his guards,[2] and there is every reason to believe that he did so not only because, like Tiberius, he shrank from showing his now repulsive features by daylight, but also to gratify his insane thirst for blood, perhaps even on the persons of those unknown to him.

As early as the year 1499 the despair was so great and so general that many of the Papal guards were waylaid and put to death.[3] But those whom the Borgias could not assail with open violence fell victims to their poison. For the cases in which a certain amount of discretion seemed requisite a white powder [4] of an agreeable taste was made use of, which did not work on the spot, but slowly and gradually, and which could be mixed without notice in any dish or goblet. Prince Djem had taken some of it in a sweet draught before Alexander surrendered him to Charles VIII (1495),[5] and at the end of their career father and son poisoned themselves with the same powder by accidentally tasting a sweetmeat intended for a wealthy cardinal, probably Adrian of Corneto.[6] The official epitomizer of the history of the Popes, Onufrio Panvinio,[7] mentions three cardinals, Orsini, Ferrerio, and Michiel, whom Alexander caused to be poisoned, and hints at a fourth, Giovanni Borgia, whom Cesare took into his own charge—though probably wealthy prelates seldom died in Rome at that time without giving rise to suspicions of this sort. Even tranquil students who had withdrawn to some provincial town were not out of reach of the merciless poison. A secret horror seemed to hang about the Pope; storms and thunderbolts, crushing in walls and chambers, had in earlier times often visited and alarmed him; in the year 1500,[8] when these

---

[1] Tommaso Gar, *loc. cit.*, p. 11. From May 22, 1502, onward, the *Dispacci* of Giustiniani, edited by Pasquale Villari (3 vols., Florence, 1876), offer valuable information.

[2] Paul. Jovius, *Elogia*, p. 202, Cesare Borgia. In the *Commentarii Urbani* of Raph. Volaterranus, lib. xxii, there is a description of Alexander VI, composed under Julius II, and still written very guardedly. We here read: " Roma . . . nobilis jam carnificina facta erat."

[3] *Diario Ferrarese*, in Murat., xxiv, col. 362.

[4] Paul. Jovius, *Histor.*, ii, fol. 47.

[[5] This conjecture, expressed by contemporaries, remains uncertain.—W. G.]

[6] See the passages in Ranke, *Röm. Päpste*; Sämmtl. Werke, Bd. xxxvii, 35, and xxxix, Anh. Abschn. 1, Nro. 4, and Gregorovius, vii, 497 *sqq.* Giustiniani does not believe in the Pope's being poisoned. See his *Dispacci*, vol. ii, pp. 107 *sqq.*; Villari's note, pp. 120 *sqq.*, and App., pp. 458 *sqq.* [This view of Burckhardt's can hardly, however, be maintained. See Pastor, iii, pp. 495 *sqq.*—W. G.]

[7] Panvinius, *Epitome Pontificum*, p. 359. For the attempt to poison Alexander's successor, Julius II, see p. 363. According to Sismondi, xiii, p. 246, it was in this way that Lopez, Cardinal of Capua, for years the partner of all the Pope's secrets, came by his end; according to Sanudo (in Ranke, *Päpste*, i, p. 52, note), the Cardinal of Verona also. When Cardinal Orsini died the Pope obtained a certificate of natural death from a college of physicians.

[8] Prato, *Archiv. Stor.*, iii, p. 254; *cf.* Attilio Alessio, in Baluz., *Miscell.*, iv, pp. 518 *sqq.*

phenomena were repeated, they were held to be *cosa diabolica*. The report of these events seems at last, through the well-attended jubilee [1] of 1500, to have been carried far and wide throughout the countries of Europe, and the infamous traffic in indulgences did what else was needed to draw all eyes upon Rome.[2] Besides the returning pilgrims, strange white-robed penitents came from Italy to the North, among them disguised fugitives from the Papal state, who are not likely to have been silent. Yet none can calculate how far the scandal and indignation of Christendom might have gone before they became a source

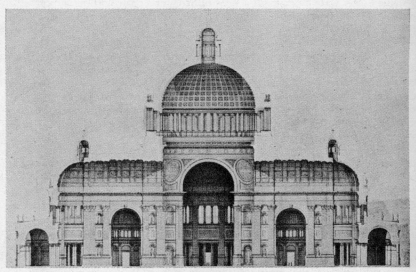

FIG. 62. ST PETER'S, ROME
Attempt at a reconstruction of the final cross-section according to Bramante's design
After Geymüller

of pressing danger to Alexander. "He would," says Panvinio elsewhere,[3] "have put all the other rich cardinals and prelates out of the way, to get their property, had he not, in the midst of his great plans for his son, been struck down by death." And what might not Cesare have achieved if, at the moment when his father died, he had not himself been laid upon a sick-bed! What a conclave would that have been, in which, armed with all his weapons, he had extorted his election from a college whose numbers he had judiciously reduced by poison—and this at a time when there was no French army at hand! In pursuing such an hypothesis the imagination loses itself in an abyss.

---

[1] And turned to the most profitable account by the Pope. Cf. *Chron. Venetum*, in Murat., xxiv, col. 133, given only as a report: "E si giudiceva, che il Pontefice dovesse cavare assai danari di questo Giubileo, che gli tornerà molto a proposito."

[2] Anshelm, *Berner Chronik*, iii, pp. 146–156. Trithem., *Annales Hirsaug.*, tom. ii, pp. 579, 584, 586.

[3] Panvin., *Contin. Platinæ*, p. 341.

Instead of this followed the conclave in which Pius III was elected, and, after his speedy death, that which chose Julius II—both elections the fruits of a general reaction.

Whatever may have been the private morals of Julius II, in all essential respects he was the saviour of the Papacy. His familiarity with the course of events since the pontificate of his uncle Sixtus had given him a profound insight into the grounds and conditions of the Papal authority. On these he founded his own policy, and devoted to it the whole force and passion of his unshaken soul. He ascended the steps of St Peter's chair without simony and amid general applause, and with him ceased, at all events, the undisguised traffic in the highest offices of the Church. Julius had favourites, and among them were some the reverse of worthy, but a special fortune put him above the temptation to nepotism. His brother, Giovanni della Rovere, was the husband of the heiress of Urbino, sister of the last Montefeltro, Guidobaldo, and from this marriage was born, in 1491, a son, Francesco Maria della Rovere, who was at the same time Papal *nipote* and lawful heir to the duchy of Urbino. What Julius elsewhere acquired, either on the field of battle or by diplomatic means, he proudly bestowed on the Church, not on his family; the ecclesiastical territory, which he found in a state of dissolution, he bequeathed to his successor completely subdued, and increased by Parma and Piacenza. It was not his fault that Ferrara too was not added to the dominions of the Church. The 700,000 ducats which were stored up in the Castle of S. Angelo were to be delivered by the Governor to none but the future Pope. He made himself heir of the cardinals, and, indeed, of all the clergy who died in Rome, and this by the most despotic means; but he murdered or poisoned none of them.[1] That he should himself lead his forces to battle was for him an unavoidable necessity, and certainly did him nothing but good at a time when a man in Italy was forced to be either hammer or anvil, and when personality was a greater power than the most indisputable right. If despite all his high-sounding "Away with the barbarians!" he nevertheless contributed more than any man to the firm settlement of the Spaniards in Italy, he may have thought it a matter of indifference to the Papacy, or even, as things stood, a relative advantage. And to whom, sooner than to Spain, could the Church look for a sincere and lasting respect,[2] in an age when the princes of Italy cherished none but sacrilegious projects against her? Be this as it may, the powerful, original nature, which could swallow no anger and conceal no genuine goodwill, made on the whole the impression most desirable in his situation—that of the *Pontefice terribile*. He could even, with a comparatively clear conscience, venture to summon a council to Rome, and so bid defiance to that outcry for a council which was raised by the opposition all over Europe. A ruler of this stamp needed some great outward symbol of his conceptions; Julius found it in the

---

[1] Hence the splendour of the tombs of the prelates erected during their lifetime. A part of the plunder was in this way saved from the hands of the Popes.

[2] Whether Julius really hoped that Ferdinand the Catholic would be induced to restore to the throne of Naples the expelled Aragonese dynasty remains, in spite of Giovio's declaration (*Vita Alfonsi Ducis*), very doubtful.

reconstruction of St Peter's.   The plan of it as Bramante wished to have it is
perhaps the grandest expression of power in unity which can be imagined.   In

FIG. 63.   LEO X WITH TWO CARDINALS
By Raphael
Florence, Palazzo Pitti

other arts besides architecture the face and the memory of the Pope live on in
their most ideal form, and it is not without significance that even the Latin

135

poetry of those days gives proof of a wholly different enthusiasm for Julius than that shown for his predecessors. The entrance into Bologna at the end of the *Iter Julii Secundi* by the Cardinal Adriano da Corneto has a splendour of its own, and Giovan Antonio Flaminio,[1] in one of the finest elegies, appealed to the patriot in the Pope to grant his protection to Italy.

In a constitution of his Lateran Council Julius had solemnly denounced the simony of the Papal elections.[2] After his death in 1513 the money-loving cardinals tried to evade the prohibition by proposing that the endowments and offices hitherto held by the chosen candidate should be equally divided among themselves, in which case they would have elected the best-endowed cardinal, the incompetent Rafael Riario.[3] But a reaction, chiefly arising from the younger members of the Sacred College, who, above all things, desired a liberal Pope, rendered the miserable combination futile; Giovanni de' Medici was elected—the famous Leo X.

We shall often meet with him in treating of the noonday of the Renaissance; here we wish only to point out that under him the Papacy was again exposed to great inward and outward dangers. Among these we do not reckon the conspiracy of the Cardinals Petrucci, de Saulis, Riario, and Corneto (1517), which at most could have occasioned a change of persons, and to which Leo found the true antidote in the unheard-of creation of thirty-nine new cardinals, a measure which had the additional advantage of rewarding, in some cases at least, real merit.[4]

But some of the paths which Leo allowed himself to tread during the first two years of his office were perilous to the last degree. He seriously endeavoured to secure by negotiation the kingdom of Naples for his brother Giuliano, and for his nephew Lorenzo a powerful North Italian state, to comprise Milan, Tuscany, Urbino, and Ferrara.[5] It is clear that the Pontifical state, thus hemmed in on all sides, would have become a mere Medicean appanage, and that, in fact, there would have been no further need to secularize it.[6]

The plan found an insuperable obstacle in the political conditions of the time. Giuliano died early. To provide for Lorenzo, Leo undertook to expel the Duke Francesco Maria della Rovere from Urbino, but reaped from the war nothing but hatred and poverty, and was forced, when in 1519 Lorenzo

---

[1] Both poems in Roscoe, *Leo X*, ed. Bossi, iv, pp. 257 and 297. Of his death the *Cronaca di Cremona* says: " Quale fu grande danno per la Italia, perchè era homo che non voleva tramontani in Italia, ed haveva cazato Francesi, e l' animo era de cazar le altri." *Bibl. Hist. Ital.*, i, 217 (1876). It is true that when Julius, in August 1511, lay one day for hours in a fainting fit, and was thought to be dead, the more restless members of the noblest families—Pompeo Colonna and Antimo Savelli—ventured to call "the people" to the Capitol, and to urge them to throw off the Papal yoke—"a vendicarsi in libertà . . . a pubblica ribellione," as Guicciardini tells us in his tenth book. See, too, Paul. Jovius in the *Vita Pompeii Columnæ*, and Gregorovius, viii, 71-75.

[2] *Septima Decretal.*, lib. i, tit. 3, cap. 1-3.

[3] Franc. Vettori, in the *Archiv. Stor.*, vi, 297.

[4] Besides which it is said (Paul. Lang., *Chronicon Cilicense*) to have produced not less than 500,000 gold florins; the Order of the Franciscans alone, whose general was made a cardinal, paid 30,000. For a notice of the various sums paid see Sanudo, xxiv, fol. 227; for the whole subject see Gregorovius, viii, 214 *sqq.*

[5] Franc. Vettori, *loc. cit.*, p. 301; *Archiv. Stor.*, App. I, pp. 293 *sqq.*; Roscoe, *Leo X*, ed. Bossi, vi, pp. 232 *sqq.*; Tommaso Gar, *loc. cit.*, p. 42.

[6] That Leo X pursued such a purely family policy was contested by F. Nitti (1892). Pastor, *Päpste*, iv, i, p. 60, believes in a policy uniting his family interests with his Papal and national aims.—W. G.]

followed his uncle to the grave, to hand over the hardly won conquests to the Church.[1]   He did on compulsion and without credit what, if it had been done voluntarily, would have been to his lasting honour.   What, partly alone, and partly in alternate negotiations with Francis I and Charles V, he attempted against Alfonso of Ferrara, and actually achieved against a few petty despots and *condottieri*, was assuredly not of a kind to raise his reputation.   And this was at a time when the monarchs of the West were yearly growing more and more accustomed to political gambling on a colossal scale, of which the stakes were this or that province of Italy.[2] Who could guarantee that, since the last decades had seen so great an increase of their power at home, their ambition could stop short of the States of the Church? Leo himself witnessed the prelude of what was fulfilled in the year 1527; a few bands of Spanish infantry appeared—of their own accord, it seems—at the end of 1520 on the borders of the Pontifical territory, with a view of laying the Pope under contribution,[3] but were driven back by the

FIG. 64.   CLEMENT VII
By Angelo Bronzino
Florence, Uffizi

Papal forces.   The public feeling, too, against the corruptions of the hierarchy had of late years been drawing rapidly to a head, and men with an eye for the future, like the younger Pico della Mirandola, called urgently for reform.[4] Meantime Luther had already appeared upon the scene.

[1] Ariosto, *Sat.*, vii, v, 106.   " Tutti morrete, ed è fatal che muoja Leone appresso."   Sat. 3 and 7 ridicule the hangers-on at Leo's Court.

[2] One of several instances of such combinations is given in the *Lettere dei Principi*, i, 65, in a dispatch of Cardinal Bibbiena from Paris of the year 1518 (December 21).

[3] Franc. Vettori, *loc. cit.*, p. 333.

[4] At the time of the Lateran Council in 1512 Pico wrote an address, *J. E. P. Oratio ad Leonem X et Concilium Lateranense de Reformandis Ecclesiæ Moribus* (ed. Hagenau, 1512, frequently printed in editions of his

Under Adrian VI (1522–23) the few and timid improvements carried out in the face of the great German Reformation came too late. He could do little more than proclaim his horror of the course which things had taken hitherto, of simony, nepotism, prodigality, brigandage, and profligacy. The danger from the side of the Lutherans was by no means the greatest; an acute observer from Venice, Girolamo Negro, uttered his fears that a speedy and terrible disaster would befall the city of Rome itself.[1]

Under Clement VII the whole horizon of Rome was filled with vapours, like that leaden veil which the sirocco draws over the Campagna, and which makes the last months of summer so deadly. The Pope was no less detested at home than abroad. Thoughtful people were filled with anxiety,[2] hermits appeared upon the streets and squares of Rome, foretelling the fate of Italy and of the world, and calling the Pope by the name of Antichrist;[3] the faction of the Colonna raised its head defiantly; the indomitable Cardinal Pompeo Colonna, whose mere existence[4] was a permanent menace to the Papacy, ventured to surprise the city in 1526, hoping with the help of Charles V to become Pope then and there, as soon as Clement was killed or captured. It was no piece of good fortune for Rome that the latter was able to escape to the Castle of S. Angelo, and the fate for which himself was reserved may well be called worse than death.

By a series of those falsehoods which only the powerful can venture on, but which bring ruin upon the weak, Clement brought about the advance of the Germano-Spanish army under Bourbon and Frundsberg (1527). It is certain[5] that the Cabinet of Charles V intended to inflict on him a severe castigation, and that it could not calculate beforehand how far the zeal of its unpaid hordes would carry them. It would have been vain to attempt to enlist men in Germany without paying any bounty, if it had not been well known that Rome was the object of the expedition. It may be that the written orders to Bourbon will be found some day or other, and it is not improbable that they will prove to be worded mildly. But historical criticism will not allow itself to be led astray. The Catholic King and Emperor owed it to his luck and nothing else that Pope and cardinals were not murdered by his troops. Had this happened no sophistry in the world could clear him of his share in the guilt. The massacre of countless people of less consequence, the plunder of

works). The address was dedicated to Pirckheimer, and was again sent to him in 1517. See Roscoe, *Leo X*, ed. Bossi, viii, pp. 105 *sqq.* Cf. *Vir. Doct. Epist. ad Pirck.*, p. 8 (ed. Freytag, Leipzig, 1838). Pico fears that under Leo evil may definitely triumph over good, " et in te bellum a nostræ religionis hostibus ante audias geri quam parari."

[1] *Lettere dei Principi*, i (Rome, March 17, 1523): "This city stands on a needle's point, and God grant that we are not soon driven to Avignon or to the end of the ocean. I foresee the early fall of this spiritual monarchy. . . . Unless God helps us we are lost." Whether Adrian were really poisoned or not cannot be gathered with certainty from Blas Ortiz, *Itinerar. Hadriani* (Baluz., *Miscell.*, ed. Mansi, i, pp. 386 *sqq.*); the worst of it was that everybody believed it.

[2] Negro, *loc. cit.*, on October 24 (should be September) and November 9, 1526, April 11, 1527. It is true that he found admirers and flatterers. The dialogue of Petrus Alcyonius' *De Exilio* was written in his praise shortly before he became Pope.

[3] Varchi, *Stor. Fiorent.*, i, 43, 46 *sqq.*

[4] Paul. Jovius, *Vita Pomp. Columnæ*. Cf. also Pastor, iv, ii, pp. 222 *sqq.*

[5] Ranke, *Deutsche Geschichte*, ii, 262 *sqq.* (4 Auflage). Also Pastor, iv, ii, pp. 241 *sqq.*

FIG. 65. CROWNING OF CHARLES V BY CLEMENT VII
By Vasari
Florence, Palazzo Vecchio
Photo Alinari

the rest, and all the horrors of torture and traffic in human life show clearly enough what was possible in the *Sacco di Roma*.

Charles seems to have wished to bring the Pope, who had fled a second time to the Castle of S. Angelo, to Naples, after extorting from him vast sums of money, and Clement's flight to Orvieto must have happened without any connivance on the part of Spain.[1] Whether the Emperor ever thought seriously of the secularization of the States of the Church,[2] for which everybody was quite prepared, and whether he was really dissuaded from it by the representations of Henry VIII of England, will probably never be made clear.

But if such projects really existed they cannot have lasted long: from the devastated city arose a new spirit of reform both in Church and State. It made itself felt in a moment. Cardinal Sadoleto, one witness of many, thus writes:

> If through our suffering a satisfaction is made to the wrath and justice of God, if these fearful punishments again open the way to better laws and morals, then is our misfortune perhaps not of the greatest. . . . What belongs to God He will take care of; before us lies a life of reformation, which no violence can take from us. Let us so rule our deeds and thoughts as to seek in God only the true glory of the priesthood and our own true greatness and power.[3]

In point of fact, this critical year, 1527, so far bore fruit that the voices of serious men could again make themselves heard. Rome had suffered too much to return, even under a Paul III, to the gay corruption of Leo X.

The Papacy too, when its sufferings became so great, began to excite a sympathy half religious and half political. The kings could not tolerate that one of their number should arrogate to himself the rights of Papal gaoler, and concluded (August 18, 1527) the Treaty of Amiens, one of the objects of which was the deliverance of Clement. They thus, at all events, turned to their own account the unpopularity which the deeds of the Imperial troops had excited. At the same time the Emperor became seriously embarrassed, even in Spain, where the prelates and grandees never saw him without making the most urgent remonstrances. When a general deputation of the clergy and laity, all clothed in mourning, was projected Charles, fearing that troubles might arise out of it, like those of the insurrection quelled a few years before, forbade the scheme.[4] Not only did he not dare to prolong the maltreatment of the Pope, but he was absolutely compelled, even apart from all considerations of foreign politics, to be reconciled with the Papacy, which he had so grievously wounded. For the temper of the German people, which certainly pointed to a different course, seemed to him, like German affairs generally, to afford no foundation for a policy. It is possible, too, as a Venetian maintains,[5] that the memory of the sack of Rome lay heavy on his conscience, and tended to hasten that expiation

---

[1] Varchi, *Stor. Fiorent.*, ii, 43 *sqq.*

[2] *Ibid.*, and Ranke, *Deutsche Geschichte*, ii, 278, note, and iii, 6 *sqq.* It was thought that Charles would transfer his seat of government to Rome. See Pastor, iv, ii, pp. 307 *sqq.*

[3] See his letter to the Pope, dated Carpentras, September 1, 1527, in the *Anecdota Litt.*, iv, p. 335.

[4] *Lettere dei Principi*, i, 72. Castiglione to the Pope, Burgos, December 10, 1527.

[5] Tommaso Gar, *Relaz. della Corte di Roma*, i, 299.

which was sealed by the permanent subjection of the Florentines to the Medicean family, of which the Pope was a member. The *nipote* and new Duke, Alessandro de' Medici, was married to the natural daughter of the Emperor.

In the following years the plan of a council enabled Charles to keep the Papacy in all essential points under his control, and at one and the same time to protect and to oppress it. The greatest danger of all—secularization—the danger which came from within, from the Popes themselves and their *nipoti*, was adjourned for centuries by the German Reformation. Just as this alone had made the expedition against Rome (1527) possible and successful, so did it compel the Papacy to become once more the expression of a world-wide spiritual power, to raise itself from the soulless debasement in which it lay, and to place itself at the head of all the enemies of this reformation. The institution thus developed during the latter years of Clement VII, and under Paul III, Paul IV, and their successors, in the face of the defection of half Europe, was a new, regenerated hierarchy, which avoided all the great and dangerous scandals of former times, particularly nepotism, with its attempts at territorial aggrandizement,[1] and which, in alliance with the Catholic princes, and impelled by a new-born spiritual force, found its chief work in the recovery of what had been lost. It only existed and is only intelli-gible in opposition to the seceders.

FIG. 66. CHARLES V
By Titian
Munich, Old Pinakothek
Photo Bruckmann, Munich

In this sense it can be said with perfect truth that the moral salvation of the Papacy was due to its mortal enemies. And now its political position too, though certainly under the permanent tutelage of Spain, became impregnable; almost without effort it inherited on the extinction of its vassals, the legitimate line of Este and the house of della Rovere, the duchies of Ferrara and Urbino. But without the Reformation—if, indeed, it is possible to think it away—the whole ecclesiastical state would long ago have passed into secular hands.

[1] The Farnese succeeded in something of the kind, the Caraffa were ruined.

141

In conclusion, let us consider briefly the effect of these political circumstances on the spirit of the nation at large.

It is evident that the general political uncertainty in Italy during the fourteenth and fifteenth centuries was of a kind to excite in the better spirits of the time a patriotic disgust and opposition. Dante and Petrarch [1] in their day proclaimed loudly a common Italy, the object of the highest efforts of all her children. It may be objected that this was only the enthusiasm of a few highly instructed men, in which the mass of the people had no share; but it can hardly have been otherwise even in Germany, although in name at least that country was united, and recognized in the Emperor one supreme head. The first patriotic utterances of German literature, if we except some verses of the *Minnesänger*, belong to the humanists of the time of Maximilian I [2] and after, and read like an echo of Italian declamations, or like a reply to Italian criticism on the intellectual immaturity of Germany. And yet, as a matter of fact, Germany had been long a nation in a truer sense than Italy ever was since the Roman days. France owes the consciousness of its national unity mainly to its conflicts with the English, and Spain has never permanently succeeded in absorbing Portugal, closely related as the two countries are. For Italy, the existence of the ecclesiastical state, and the conditions under which alone it could continue, were a permanent obstacle to national unity, an obstacle whose removal seemed hopeless. When, therefore, in the political intercourse of the fifteenth century the common fatherland is sometimes emphatically named it is done in most cases to annoy some other Italian state. [3] The first decades of the sixteenth century, the years when the Renaissance attained its fullest bloom, were not favourable to a revival of patriotism; the enjoyment of intellectual and artistic pleasures, the comforts and elegancies of life, and the supreme interests of self-development, destroyed or hampered the love of country. But those deeply serious and sorrowful appeals to national sentiment were not heard again till later, when the time for unity had gone by, when the country was inundated with Frenchmen and Spaniards, and when a German army had conquered Rome. The sense of local patriotism may be said in some measure to have taken the place of this feeling, though it was but a poor equivalent for it.

---

[1] Petrarch, *Epist. Fam.*, i, 3, p. 574, when he thanks God that he was born an Italian. And again in the *Apologia contra cujusdam Anonymi Galli Calumnias* of the year 1367 (*Opp.*, ed. Bas., 1581), pp. 1068 *sqq.* See L. Geiger, *Petrarca*, pp. 129–145.

[2] Particularly those in vol. i of Schardius, *Scriptores Rerum Germanicarum* (Basel, 1574). For an earlier period, Felix Faber, *Historia Suevorum*, libri duo (in Goldast, *Script. Rer. Suev.*, 1605); for a later, Irenicus, *Exegesis Germaniæ* (Hagenau, 1518). On the latter work and the patriotic histories of that time see various studies of A. Horawitz, *Hist. Ztschr.*, Bd. xxxiii, 118, note 1.

[3] One instance out of many, *The Answers of the Doge of Venice to a Florentine Agent respecting Pisa*, 1496, in Malipiero, *Ann. Venet., Archiv. Stor.*, vii, i, p. 427.

PART II
THE DEVELOPMENT OF THE INDIVIDUAL

CHAPTER I

The Italian State and the Individual

IN the character of these states, whether republics or despotisms, lies not the only but the chief reason for the early development of the Italian. To this it is due that he was the first-born among the sons of modern Europe.

In the Middle Ages both sides of human consciousness —that which was turned within as that which was turned without—lay dreaming or half awake beneath a common veil. The veil was woven of faith, illusion, and childish prepossession, through which the world and history were seen clad in strange hues. Man was conscious of himself only as member of a race, people, party, family, or corporation—only through some general category. In Italy this veil first melted into air; an *objective* treatment and consideration of the State and of all the things of this world became possible. The *subjective* side at the same time asserted itself with corresponding emphasis; man became a spiritual *individual*,[1] and recognized himself as such. In the same way the Greek had once distinguished himself from the barbarian, and the Arabian had felt himself an individual at a time when other Asiatics knew themselves only as members of a race. It will not be difficult to show that this result was owing, above all, to the political circumstances of Italy.

In far earlier times we can here and there detect a development of free personality which in Northern Europe either did not occur at all or could not display itself in the same manner. The band of audacious wrongdoers in the sixteenth century described to us by Luidprand, some of the contemporaries of Gregory VII, and a few of the opponents of the first Hohenstaufen, show us characters of this kind. But at the close of the thirteenth century Italy began to swarm with individuality; the charm laid upon human personality was dissolved, and a thousand figures meet us each in its own special shape and dress. Dante's great poem would have been impossible in any other country of Europe, if only for the reason that they all still lay under the spell of race. For Italy the august poet, through the wealth of individuality which he set forth, was the most national herald of his time. But this unfolding of the

[1] Observe the expressions *uomo singolare* and *uomo unico* for the higher and highest stages of individual development.

treasures of human nature in literature and art—this many-sided representation and criticism—will be discussed in separate chapters; here we have to deal only with the psychological fact itself. This fact appears in the most decisive and unmistakable form. The Italians of the fourteenth century knew little of false modesty or of hypocrisy in any shape; not one of them was afraid of singularity, of being and seeming [1] unlike his neighbours.[2]

Despotism, as we have already seen, fostered in the highest degree the individuality not only of the tyrant or *condottiere* himself,[3] but also of the men whom he protected or used as his tools—the secretary, minister, poet, and companion. These people were forced to know all the inward resources of their own nature, passing or permanent; and their enjoyment of life was enhanced and concentrated by the desire to obtain the greatest satisfaction from a possibly very brief period of power and influence.

But even the subjects whom they ruled over were not free from the same impulse. Leaving out of account those who wasted their lives in secret opposition and conspiracies, we speak of the majority who were content with a strictly private station, like most of the urban population of the Byzantine Empire and the Mohammedan states. No doubt it was often hard for the subjects of a Visconti to maintain the dignity of their persons and families, and multitudes must have lost in moral character through the servitude they lived under. But this was not the case with regard to individuality; for political impotence does not hinder the different tendencies and manifestations of private life from thriving in the fullest vigour and variety. Wealth and culture, so far as display and rivalry were not forbidden to them, a municipal freedom which did not cease to be considerable, and a Church which, unlike that of the Byzantine or of the Mohammedan world, was not identical with the State—all these conditions undoubtedly favoured the growth of individual thought, for which the necessary leisure was furnished by the cessation of party conflicts. The private man, indifferent to politics, and busied partly with serious pursuits, partly with the interests of a *dilettante*, seems to have been first fully formed in these despotisms of the fourteenth century. Documentary evidence cannot, of course, be required on such a point. The novelists, from whom we might expect information, describe to us oddities in plenty, but only from one point of view and in so far as the needs of the story demand. Their scene, too, lies chiefly in the republican cities.

[1] By the year 1390 there was no longer any prevailing fashion of dress for men at Florence, each preferring to clothe himself in his own way. See the *canzone* of Franco Sacchetti, "Contro alle nuove foggie," in the *Rime*, publ. dal Poggiali, p. 52.

[2] At the close of the sixteenth century Montaigne draws the following parallel (*Essais*, lib. iii, chap. 5, vol. iii, p. 367, of the Paris ed., 1816): " Ils [les Italiens] ont plus communement des belles femmes et moins de laides que nous; mais des rares et excellentes beautés j'estime que nous allons à pair. Et j'en juge autant des esprits; de ceux de la commune façon, ils en ont beaucoup plus et evidemment; la brutalité y est sans comparaison plus rare; d'âmes singulières et du plus hault estage, nous ne leur en debvons rien."

[3] And also of their wives, as is seen in the family of Sforza and among other North Italian rulers. *Cf.* in the work of Jacobus Phil. Bergomensis, *De Plurimis Claris Selectisque Mulieribus* (Ferrara, 1497), the lives of Battista Malatesta, Paola Gonzaga, Bona Lombarda, Riccarda d'Este, and the chief women of the house of Sforza, Beatrice and others. Among them are more than one genuine virago, and in several cases natural gifts are supplemented by great humanistic culture. (See below, Part V, Chapter III.)

In the latter circumstances were also, but in another way, favourable to the growth of individual character. The more frequently the governing party was changed, the more the individual was led to make the utmost of the exercise and enjoyment of power. The statesmen and popular leaders, especially in Florentine history,[1] acquired so marked a personal character that we can scarcely find, even exceptionally, a parallel to them in contemporary history, hardly even in Jacob van Artevelde.

The members of the defeated parties, on the other hand, often came into a position like that of the subjects of the despotic states, with the difference that the freedom or power already enjoyed, and in some cases the hope of recovering them, gave a higher energy to their individuality. Among these men of involuntary leisure we find, for instance, an Agnolo Pandolfini (d. 1446), whose work on domestic economy [2] is the first complete programme of a developed private life. His estimate of the duties of the individual as against the dangers and thanklessness of public life [3] is in its way a true monument of the age.

Banishment too has this effect above all, that it either wears the exile out or develops whatever is greatest in him. " In all our more populous cities," says Gioviano Pontano,[4] " we see a crowd of people who have left their homes of their own free-will; but a man takes his virtues with him wherever he goes." And, in fact, they were by no means only men who had been actually exiled, but thousands left their native place voluntarily, because they found its political or economical condition intolerable. The Florentine emigrants at Ferrara and the Lucchese in Venice formed whole colonies by themselves.

The cosmopolitanism which grew up in the most gifted circles is in itself a high stage of individualism. Dante, as we have already said, finds a new home in the language and culture of Italy, but goes beyond even this in the words " My country is the whole world! " [5] And when his recall to Florence was offered him on unworthy conditions he wrote back: " Can I not everywhere behold the light of the sun and the stars; everywhere meditate on the noblest truths, without appearing ingloriously and shamefully before the city and the people? Even my bread will not fail me! " [6] The artists exult no less defiantly in their freedom from the constraints of fixed residence. " Only he

[1] Franco Sacchetti, in his *Capitolo* (*Rime*, publ. dal Poggiali, p. 56), enumerates about 1390 the names of over a hundred distinguished people in the ruling parties who had died within his memory. However many mediocrities there may have been among them, the list is still remarkable as evidence of the awakening of individuality. On the *Vite* of Filippo Villani see below.

[2] *Trattato del Governo della Famiglia* forms a part of the work *La Cura della Famiglia* (*Opere Volgari di L. B. Alberti*, publ. da Anicio Bonucci, vol. ii, Florence, 1884). See there vol. i, pp. xxx–xl, vol. ii, pp. xxxv *sqq.*, and vol. v, pp. 1–127. Formerly the work was generally, as in the text, attributed to Agnolo Pandolfini (see on him Vespas. Fiorent., pp. 291 and 379); the recent investigations of Fr. Palermo (Florence, 1871) have shown Alberti to be the author. The work is quoted from the ed. Torino (Pomba, 1828).

[3] *Trattato*, pp. 65 *sqq.*

[4] Jov. Pontan., *De Fortitudine*, lib. ii, cap. 4, *De Tolerando Exilio*. Seventy years later Cardanus (*De Vita Propria*, cap. 32) could ask bitterly: " Quid est patria, nisi consensus tyrannorum minutorum ad opprimendos imbelles timidos, et qui plerumque sunt innoxii? "

[5] *De Vulgari Eloquentia*, lib. i, cap. 6. On the ideal Italian language, cap. 17. The spiritual unity of cultured men, cap. 18. On home-sickness *cf.* the famous passages in *Purgatorio*, viii, 1 *sqq.*, and *Paradiso*, xxv, 1 *sqq.*

[6] *Dantis Alligherii Epistolæ*, ed. Carolus Witte, p. 65. [It is doubtful whether this letter refers to the offer in question.—W. G.]

who has learned everything," says Ghiberti,[1] " is nowhere a stranger; robbed of his fortune and without friends, he is yet the citizen of every country, and can fearlessly despise the changes of fortune." In the same strain an exiled humanist writes: " Wherever a learned man fixes his seat there is home." [2]

[1] Ghiberti, *Secondo Commentario*, cap. xv (Vasari, ed. Lemonnier, i, p. xxix).

[2] *Codri Urcei Vita*, at the end of his works, first pub. Bologna, 1592. This certainly comes near the old saying, *Ubi bene, ibi patria*. Codrus Urceus was not called after the place of his birth, but after Forlì, where he lived long; see Malagola, *Codro Urceo*, cap. v, and App. XI (Bologna, 1877). The abundance of neutral intellectual pleasure, which is independent of local circumstances, and of which the educated Italians became more and more capable, rendered exile more tolerable to them. Cosmopolitanism is, further, a sign of an epoch in which new worlds are discovered, and men no longer feel at home in the old. We see it among the Greeks after the Peloponnesian War; Plato, as Niebuhr says, was not a good citizen, and Xenophon was a bad one; Diogenes went so far as to proclaim homelessness a pleasure, and calls himself, Laertius tells us, ἄπολις. Here another remarkable work may be mentioned. Petrus Alcyonius in his book *Medices Legatus de Exilio Lib. Duo*, Venice, 1522 (printed in Mencken, *Analecta de Calam. Literatorum*, pp. 1–250, Leipzig, 1707), devotes to the subject of exile a long and prolix discussion. He tries logically and historically to refute the three reasons for which banishment is held to be an evil—viz., (1) Because the exile must live away from his fatherland, (2) because he loses the honours given him at home, (3) because he must do without his friends and relatives ; and comes finally to the conclusion that banishment is not an evil. His dissertation culminates in the words: " Sapientissimus quisque omnem orbem terrarum unam urbem esse ducit. Atque etiam illam veram sibi esse patriam arbitratur quæ se perigrinantem exciperit, quæ pudorem, probitatem, virtutem colit, quæ optima studia, liberales disciplinas amplectitur, quæ etiam facit ut peregrini omnes honesto otio teneant statum et famam dignitatis suæ."

CHAPTER II

The Perfecting of the Individual

A N acute and practised eye might be able to trace, step by step, the increase in the number of complete men during the fifteenth century. Whether they had before them as a conscious object the harmonious development of their spiritual and material existence is hard to say; but several of them attained it, so far as is consistent with the imperfection of all that is earthly. It may be better to renounce the attempt at an estimate of the share which fortune, character, and talent had in the life of Lorenzo the Magnificent. But look at a personality like that of Ariosto, especially as shown in his satires. In what harmony are there expressed the pride of the man and the poet, the irony with which he treats his own enjoyments, the most delicate satire, and the deepest goodwill!

When this impulse to the highest individual development [1] was combined with a powerful and varied nature, which had mastered all the elements of the culture of the age, then arose the " all-sided man "—*l' uomo universale*—who belonged to Italy alone. Men there were of encyclopædic knowledge in many countries during the Middle Ages, for this knowledge was confined within narrow limits; and even in the twelfth century there were universal artists, but the problems of architecture were comparatively simple and uniform, and in sculpture and painting the matter was of more importance than the form. But in Italy at the time of the Renaissance we find artists who in every branch created new and perfect works, and who also made the greatest impression as men. Others, outside the arts they practised, were masters of a vast circle of spiritual interests.

Dante, who even in his lifetime was called by some a poet, by others a philosopher, by others a theologian,[2] pours forth in all his writings a stream of personal force, by which the reader, apart from the interest of the subject, feels himself carried away. What power of will must the steady, unbroken elaboration of the *Divine Comedy* have required! And if we look at the matter of the poem we find that in the whole spiritual or physical world there is hardly an important subject which the poet has not fathomed, and on which his utterances —often only a few words—are not the most weighty of his time. For the

---

[1] This awakening of personality is also shown in the great stress laid on the independent growth of character, in the claim to shape the spiritual life for oneself, apart from parents and ancestors. Boccaccio (*De Cas. Vir. Ill.*, Paris, *s.a.*, fol. xxix*b*) points out that Socrates came of uneducated, Euripides and Demosthenes of unknown, parents, and exclaims " Quasi animos a gignentibus habeamus!"

[2] Boccaccio, *Vita di Dante*, p. 16.

plastic arts he is of the first importance, and this for better reasons than the few references to contemporary artists—he soon became himself the source of inspiration.[1]

The fifteenth century is, above all, that of the many-sided men. There is no biography which does not, besides the chief work of its hero, speak of other pursuits all passing beyond the limits of dilettantism. The Florentine merchant and statesman was often learned in both the classical languages; the most famous humanists read the ethics and politics of Aristotle to him and his sons;[2] even the daughters of the house were highly educated. It is in these circles that private education was first treated seriously. The humanist, on his side, was compelled to the most varied attainments, since his philological learning was not limited, as it now is, to the theoretical knowledge of classical antiquity, but had to serve the practical needs of daily life. While studying Pliny,[3] he made collections of natural history; the geography of the ancients was his guide in treating of modern geography, their history was his pattern in writing contemporary chronicles, even when composed in Italian; he not only translated the comedies of Plautus, but acted as manager when they were put on the stage; every effective form of ancient literature down to the dialogues of Lucian he did his best to imitate; and besides all this he acted as magistrate, secretary, and diplomatist—not always to his own advantage.

But among these many-sided men some who may truly be called 'all-sided'

FIG. 67. ANDREA MANTEGNA
Mantua, S. Andrea
Photo Anderson, Rome

---

[1] The angels which he drew on tablets at the anniversary of the death of Beatrice (*La Vita Nuova*, p. 61) may have been more than the work of a *dilettante*. Leon. Aretino says he drew *egregiamente*, and was a great lover of music.

[2] For this and what follows see especially Vespasiano Fiorentino, an authority of the first order for Florentine culture in the fifteenth century. *Cf.* pp. 359, 379, 401, etc. See also the charming and instructive *Vita Jannoctii Manetti* (b. 1396), by Naldus Naldius, in Murat., xx, pp. 529–608.

[3] What follows is taken, for example, from Perticari's account of Pandolfo Collenuccio, in Roscoe, *Leo X*, ed. Bossi, iii, pp. 197 *sqq.*, and from the *Opere del Conte Perticari*, vol. ii (Milan, 1823).

tower above the rest. Before analysing the general phases of life and culture of this period we may here, on the threshold of the fifteenth century, consider for a moment the figure of one of these giants—Leon Battista Alberti (b. ? 1404, d. 1472).[1] His biography,[2] which is only a fragment, speaks of him but little as an artist, and makes no mention at all of his great significance in the history of architecture. We shall now see what he was apart from these special claims to distinction.

In all by which praise is won Leon Battista from his childhood excelled. Of his various gymnastic feats and exercises we read with astonishment how, with his feet together, he could spring over a man's head; how in the cathedral he threw a coin in the air till it was heard to ring against the distant roof; how the wildest horses trembled under him. In three things he desired to appear faultless to others, in walking, in riding, and in speaking. He learned music without a master, and yet his compositions were admired by professional judges. Under the pressure of poverty he studied both civil and canonical law for many years, till exhaustion brought on a severe illness. In his twenty-fourth year, finding his memory for words weakened, but his sense of facts unimpaired, he set to work at physics and mathematics. And all the while he acquired every sort of accomplishment and dexterity, cross-examining artists, scholars, and artisans of all descriptions, down to the cobblers, about the secrets

FIG. 68. LEON BATTISTA ALBERTI
Paris, Dreyfus Collection

and peculiarities of their craft. Painting and modelling he practised by the way, and especially excelled in admirable likenesses from memory. Great admiration was excited by his mysterious *camera obscura*,[3] in which he showed at one time the stars and the moon rising over rocky hills, at another wide landscapes with mountains and gulfs receding into dim perspective, and with fleets advancing on the waters in shade or sunshine. And that which others created he welcomed joyfully, and held every human achievement which followed the laws of beauty for something almost divine.[4] To all this must be added his literary works, first of all those on art, which are landmarks and authorities of the first order for the Renaissance of Form, especially in

---

[1] For what follows *cf.* Burckhardt, *Geschichte der Renaissance in Italien*, especially pp. 41 *sqq.* (Stuttgart, 1868), and A. Springer, *Abhandlungen zur neueren Kunstgeschichte*, pp. 69–102 (Bonn, 1867).

[2] In Murat., xxv, col. 295 *sqq.*, with the Italian translation in the *Opere Volgari di L. B. Alberti*, vol. i, pp. lxxxix–cix, where the conjecture is made and shown to be probable that this *Vita* is by Alberti himself. See, further, Vasari, iv, 52 *sqq.* Mariano Sozzini, if we can believe what we read of him in Æneas Sylvius (*Opera*, p. 622, *Epist.* 112), was a universal *dilettante*, and at the same time a master in several subjects.

[3] Similar attempts, especially an attempt at a flying-machine, had been made about 880 by the Andalusian Abul Abbas Kasim ibn Firnas. *Cf.* Gyangos, *The History of the Muhammedan Dynasties in Spain*, i, 148 *sqq.*, and 425–427 (London, 1840); extracts in Hammer, *Literaturgesch. der Araber*, i, Introd., p. li.

[4] "Quidquid ingenio esset hominum cum quadam effectum elegantia, id prope divinum ducebat."

architecture; then his Latin prose writings—novels and other works—of which some have been taken for productions of antiquity; his elegies, eclogues, and humorous dinner-speeches. He also wrote an Italian treatise on domestic life [1] in four books; various moral, philosophical, and historical works; and many speeches and poems, including a funeral oration on his dog. Notwithstanding his admiration for the Latin language, he wrote in Italian, and encouraged others to do the same; himself a disciple of Greek science, he maintained the doctrine that without Christianity the world would wander in a labyrinth of error. His serious and witty sayings were thought worth collecting, and specimens of them, many columns long, are quoted in his biography. And all that he had and knew he imparted, as rich natures always do, without the least reserve, giving away his chief discoveries for nothing. But the deepest spring of his nature has yet to be spoken of—the sympathetic intensity with which he entered into the whole life around him. At the sight of noble trees and waving cornfields he shed tears; handsome and dignified old men he honoured as a "delight of nature," and could never look at them enough. Perfectly formed animals won his goodwill as being specially favoured by nature; and more than once, when he was ill, the sight of a beautiful landscape cured him.[2] No wonder that those who saw him in this close and mysterious communion with the world ascribed to him the gift of prophecy. He was said to have foretold a bloody catastrophe in the family of Este, the fate of Florence, and the death of the Popes years before they happened, and to be able to read into the countenances and the hearts of men. It need not be added that an iron will pervaded and sustained his whole personality; like all the great men of the Renaissance, he said, "Men can do all things if they will."

And Leonardo da Vinci was to Alberti as the finisher to the beginner, as the master to the *dilettante*. Would only that Vasari's work were here supplemented by a description like that of Alberti! The colossal outlines of Leonardo's nature can never be more than dimly and distantly conceived.

---

[1] This is the book (*cf.* p. 145, note 2) of which one part, often printed alone, long passed for a work of Pandolfini.

[2] In his work *De Re Ædificatoria*, lib. viii, cap. i, there is a definition of a beautiful road: "Si modo mare, modo montes, modo lacum fluentem fontesve, modo aridam rupem aut planitiem, modo nemus vallemque exhibebit."

CHAPTER III

THE MODERN IDEA OF FAME

TO this inward development of the individual corresponds a new sort of outward distinction—the modern form of glory.[1] In the other countries of Europe the different classes of society lived apart, each with its own medieval caste sense of honour. The poetical fame of the troubadours and *Minnesänger* was peculiar to the knightly order. But in Italy social equality had appeared before the time of the tyrannies or the democracies. We there find early traces of a general society, having, as will be shown more fully later on, a common ground in Latin and Italian literature; and such a ground was needed for this new element in life to grow in. To this must be added that the Roman authors, who were now zealously studied, and especially Cicero, the most read and admired of all, are filled and saturated with the conception of fame, and that their subject itself—the universal empire of Rome—stood as a permanent ideal before the minds of Italians. From henceforth all the aspirations and achievements of the people were governed by a moral postulate, which was still unknown elsewhere in Europe.

Here, again, as in all essential points, the first witness to be called is Dante. He strove for the poet's garland [2] with all the power of his soul. As publicist and man of letters, he laid stress on the fact that what he did was new, and that he wished not only to be, but to be esteemed the first in his own walks.[3] But even in his prose writings he touches on the inconveniences of fame; he knows how often personal acquaintance with famous men is disappointing, and explains how this is due partly to the childish fancy of men, partly to envy, and partly to the imperfections of the hero himself.[4] And in his great poem he firmly maintains the emptiness of fame, although in a manner which betrays that his heart was not set free from the longing for it. In Paradise the sphere of Mercury is the seat of such blessed ones [5] as on earth strove after glory and

---

[1] One writer among many, Blondus, *Roma Triumphans*, lib. v, pp. 117 *sqq.*, where the definitions of glory are collected from the ancients, and the desire of it is expressly allowed to the Christian. Cicero's work *De Gloria*, which Petrarch claimed (probably erroneously) to own, was stolen from him by his teacher Convenevole, and has never since been seen. Alberti, in a youthful composition when he was only twenty years of age, praises the desire of fame (*Opere*, vol. i, pp. cxxvii–clxvi).

[2] *Paradiso*, xxv, at the beginning: " Se mai continga," etc. *Cf.* Boccaccio, *Vita di Dante*, p. 49. " Vaghissimo fu e d' onore e di pompa, e per avventura più che alla sua inclita virtù non si sarebbe richiesto."

[3] *De Vulgari Eloquentia*, lib. i, cap. i, and especially *De Monarchia*, lib. i, cap. i, where he wishes to set forth the idea of monarchy not only in order to be useful to the world, but also "ut palmam tanti bravii primus in meam gloriam adipiscar."

[4] *Convivio*, ed. Venezia, 1592, fol. 5 and 6. Ed. by Moore, pp. 240 *sqq.* (Oxford, 1894).
    Paradiso, vi, 112 *sqq.*

thereby dimmed "the beams of true love." It is characteristic that the lost souls in Hell beg of Dante to keep alive for them their memory and fame on earth,[1] while those in Purgatory entreat his prayers and those of others only for their deliverance.[2] And in a famous passage [3] the passion for fame—"lo gran desio dell' eccellenza"—is reproved for the reason that intellectual glory is not absolute, but relative to the times, and may be surpassed and eclipsed by greater successors.

The new race of poet-scholars which arose soon after Dante quickly made themselves masters of this fresh tendency. They did so in a double sense, being themselves the most acknowledged celebrities of Italy, and at the same time, as poets and historians, consciously disposing of the reputation of others. An outward symbol of this sort of fame was the coronation of the poets, of which we shall speak later on.

A contemporary of Dante, Albertinus Musattus, or Mussatus, crowned poet at Padua by the bishop and rector, enjoyed a fame which fell little short of deification. Every Christmas Day the doctors and students of both colleges at the university came in solemn procession before his house with trumpets and, as it seems, with burning tapers, to salute him [4] and bring him presents. His reputation lasted till, in 1318, he fell into disgrace with the ruling tyrant of the house of Carrara.[5]

This new incense, which once was offered only to saints and heroes, was given in clouds to Petrarch, who persuaded himself in his later years that it was but a foolish and troublesome thing. His letter To Posterity [6] is the confession of an old and famous man who is forced to gratify the public curiosity. He admits that he wishes for fame in the times to come, but would rather be without it in his own day.[7] In his dialogue on fortune and misfortune [8] the interlocutor, who maintains the futility of glory, has the best of the contest. But at the same time Petrarch is pleased that the autocrat of Byzantium [9] knows

---

[1] For example, *Inferno*, vi, 89; xiii, 53; xvi, 85; xxxi, 127.

[2] *Purgatorio*, v, 70, 87, 133; vi, 26; viii, 71; xi, 31; xiii, 147.

[3] *Purgatorio*, xi, 85–117. Besides *gloria* we here find close together *grido, fama, rumore, nominanza, onore*, all different names for the same thing. Boccaccio wrote, as he admits in his letter to Joh. Pizinga (*Op. Volg.*, xvi, 30 *sqq.*), "perpetuandi nominis desiderio."

[4] Scardeonius, *De Urb. Patav. Antiqu.* (Græv., *Thesaur.*, vi, iii, col. 260). Whether *cereis* or *certis muneribus* should be the reading cannot be said. Musattus himself says in *Ep.* I: "Præpositus binæ portans hastilia ceræ." The somewhat solemn nature of Musattus can be recognized in the tone of his history of Henry VII.

[[5] For a slightly different explanation see Cloëtta, *Beitr.*, ii, 18, 1.—W. G.]

[6] Petrarch, *Posteritati*, or *Ad Posteros*, at the beginning of the editions of his works, or the only letter of Book XVIII of the *Epp. Seniles*; also in Fracassetti, *Petr. Epistolæ Familiares*, i, 1–11 (1859). Some modern critics of Petrarch's vanity would hardly have shown as much kindness and frankness had they been in his place.

[7] *Opera*, ed. 1581, p. 177: "De celebritate nominis importuna." Fame among the mass of people was specially offensive to him. *Epp. Fam.*, i, 337, 340. In Petrarch, as in many humanists of the older generation, we can observe the conflict between the desire for glory and the claims of Christian humility.

[8] *De Remediis Utriusque Fortunæ* in the editions of the works. Often printed separately—for example, Bern, 1600. *Cf.* Petrarch's famous dialogue *De Contemptu Mundi*, or *De Conflictu Curarum Suarum*, in which the interlocutor Augustinus blames the love of fame as a damnable fault.

[9] *Epist. Fam.*, ed. Fracassetti, lib. xviii, 2. A measure of Petrarch's fame is given a hundred years later by the assertion of Blondus (*Italia Illustrata*, p. 416) that hardly even a learned man would know anything of Robert the Good if Petrarch had not spoken of him so often and so kindly.

FIG. 69. SEPULCHRAL MONUMENT OF THE DOGE VENDRAMINI
By Alessandro Leopardi
Venice, SS. Giovanni e Paolo

him as well by his writings as Charles IV [1] knows him. And, in fact, even in his lifetime his fame extended far beyond Italy. And the emotion which he felt was natural when his friends, on the occasion of a visit to his native Arezzo (1350), took him to the house where he was born and told him how the city had provided that no change should be made in it.[2] In former times the dwellings of certain great saints were preserved and revered in this way, like the cell of St Thomas Aquinas in the Dominican convent at Naples, and the

FIG. 70. TOMBS OF THE SCALIGERI, VERONA
Photo Alinari

Portiuncula of St Francis, near Assisi; and one or two great jurists also enjoyed the half-mythical reputation which led to this honour. Toward the close of the fourteenth century the people at Bagnolo, near Florence, called an old building the *studio* of Accursius (b. about 1150), but, nevertheless, suffered it to be destroyed.[3] It is probable that the great incomes and the political influence which some jurists obtained as consulting lawyers made a lasting impression on the popular imagination.

To the cultus of the birthplaces of famous men must be added that of their graves,[4] and, in the case of Petrarch, of the spot where he died. In memory of

---

[1] It is to be noted that even Charles IV, perhaps influenced by Petrarch, speaks in a letter to the historian Marignola of fame as the object of every striving man. H. Friedjung, *Kaiser Karl IV und sein Antheil am geistigen Leben seiner Zeit*, p. 221 (Vienna, 1876).

[2] *Epist. Seniles*, xiii, 3, to Giovanni Aretino, September 9, 1370.

[3] Filippo Villani, *Vite*, p. 19.

[4] Both together in the epitaph on Boccaccio: " Nacqui in Firenze al Pozzo Toscanelli; Di fuor sepolto a Certaldo giaccio," etc. Cf. *Op. Volg. di Boccaccio*, xvi, 44.

him Arquà became a favourite resort of the Paduans, and was dotted with graceful little villas.[1]   At this time there were no 'classic spots' in Northern Europe, and pilgrimages were made only to pictures and relics.   It was a point of honour for the different cities to possess the bones of their own and foreign celebrities; and it is most remarkable how seriously the Florentines, even in the fourteenth century—long before the building of S. Croce—laboured to make their cathedral a Pantheon.   Accorso, Dante, Petrarch, Boccaccio, and the jurist Zanobi della Strada were to have had magnificent tombs there erected to them.[2]   Late in the fifteenth century Lorenzo the Magnificent applied in person to the Spoletans, asking them to give up the corpse of the painter Fra Filippo Lippi for the cathedral, and received the answer that they had none too many ornaments to the city, especially in the shape of distinguished people, for which reason they begged him to spare them; and, in fact, he had to be contented with erecting a cenotaph.[3]   And even Dante, in spite of all the applications to which Boccaccio urged the Florentines with bitter emphasis,[4] remained sleeping tranquilly in the church of S. Francesco at Ravenna, "among ancient tombs of emperors and vaults of saints, in more honourable company than thou, O Home, couldst offer him." It even happened that a man once took away unpunished the lights from the altar on which the crucifix stood, and set them by the grave, with the words, "Take them; thou art more worthy of them than He, the Crucified One!"[5]

And now the Italian cities began again to remember their ancient citizens and inhabitants.   Naples, perhaps, had never forgotten its tomb of Virgil, since a kind of mythical halo had become attached to the name, and the memory of it had been revived by Petrarch and Boccaccio, who both stayed in the city.

The Paduans, even in the sixteenth century, firmly believed that they possessed not only the genuine bones of their founder Antenor, but also those of the historian Livy.[6]   "Sulmona," says Boccaccio,[7] "bewails that Ovid lies buried far away in exile; and Parma rejoices that Cassius sleeps within its walls." The Mantuans coined a medal in 1257 with the bust of Virgil, and raised a statue to represent him.   In a fit of aristocratic insolence,[8] the guardian of the

<hr/>

[1] Michele Savonarola, *De Laudibus Patavii*, in Murat., xxiv, col. 1157.   Arquà remained from thenceforth the object of special veneration (*cf.* Ettore Conte Macola, *I Codici di Arquà*, Padua, 1874), and was the scene of great solemnities at the fifth centenary of Petrarch's death.   His dwelling is said to have been given to the city of Padua by the last owner, Cardinal Silvestri.

[2] The decree of 1396 and its grounds in Gaye, *Carteggio*, i, 123.

[3] Reumont, *Lorenzo dei Medici*, ii, 180.

[4] Boccaccio, *Vita di Dante*, p. 39.   [5] Franco Sacchetti, *Nov.* 121.

[6] The former in the well-known sarcophagus near S. Lorenzo, the latter over a door in the Palazzo della Ragione.   For details as to their discovery in 1413 see Misson, *Voyage en Italie*, vol. i, and Michele Savonarola, col. 1157.

[7] *Vita di Dante, loc. cit.*   How came the body of Cassius from Philippi back to Parma?

[8] " Nobilitatis fastu " and " sub obtentu religionis," says Pius II (*Comment.*, x, p. 473).   The new sort of fame must have been inconvenient to those who were accustomed to the old.

That Carlo Malatesta caused the statue of Virgil to be pulled down and thrown into the Mincio, and this, as he alleged, from anger at the veneration paid to it by the people of Mantua, is a well-authenticated fact, specially attested by an invective written in 1397 by P. P. Vergerio against Carlo Malatesta, *De Diruta Statua Virgilii P. P. V. Eloquentissimi Oratoris Epistola ex Tugurio Blondi sub Apolline*, ed. by Marco Mantova Benavides (pub. certainly before 1560 at Padua).   From this work it is clear that till then the statue had not been set up again.   Did this happen in consequence of the invective?   Bartholomæus Facius (*De Vir. Ill.*,

FIG. 71. MONUMENT OF PLINY THE YOUNGER
By Tommaso and Bernardino Rodari
Como Cathedral. Photo Alinari

young Gonzaga, Carlo Malatesta, caused it to be pulled down in 1392, and was afterward forced, when he found the fame of the old poet too strong for him, to set it up again.[1] Even then, perhaps, the grotto, a couple of miles from the town, where Virgil was said to have meditated [2] was shown to strangers, like the " Scuola di Virgilio " at Naples. Como claimed both the Plinys for its own, and at the end

pp. 9 *sqq.*, in the life of P. P. V., 1456) says it did: "Carolum Malatestam invectus Virgilii statua, quam ille Mantuæ in foro everterat, quoniam gentilis fuerat, ut ibidem restitueretur, effecit "; but his evidence stands alone. It is true that, so far as we know, there are no contemporary chronicles for the history of Mantua at that period (Platina, *Hist. Mant.*, in Murat., xx, contains nothing about the matter), but later historians are agreed that the statue was not restored. See for evidence Prendilacqua, *Vita di Vitt. da Feltre*, written soon after 1446 (ed. 1871, p. 78), where the destruction, but not the restoration, of the statue is spoken of, and the work of Ant. Possevini, jun. (*Gonzaga*, Mantua, 1628), where (p. 486) the pulling down of the statue, the murmurings and violent opposition of the people, and the promise given in consequence by the Prince that he *would* restore it are all mentioned, with the addition " Nec tamen restitutus est Virgilius." Further, on March 17, 1499, Jacopo d'Hatry writes to Isabella d'Este that he has spoken with Pontano about a plan of the Princess to raise a statue to Virgil at Mantua, and that Pontano cried out with delight that Vergerio, if he were alive, would be even more pleased " che non se attristò quando el Conte Carola Malatesta persuase abuttare la statua di Virgilio nel fiume." The writer then goes on to speak of the manner of setting it up, of the inscription " P. Virgilius Mantuanus " and " Isabella Marchionissa Mantuæ restituit," and suggests that Andrea Mantegna would be the right man to be charged with the work. Mantegna did, in fact, make the drawings for it. (The drawing and the letter in question are given in Baschet, *Recherches de Documents d'Art et d'Histoire dans les Archives de Mantoue*; *Documents Inédits concernant la Personne et les Œuvres d'Andrea Mantegna*, in the *Gazette des Beaux-Arts*, xx (1866), 478–492, especially 486 *sqq.*) It is clear from this letter that Carlo Malatesta did not have the statue restored. In Comparetti's work on Virgil in the Middle Ages the story is told after Burckhardt, but without authorities. [1 As a matter of fact, this was only done by Isabella d'Este.—L. G.]
² *Cf.* Keyssler's *Neueste Reisen*, p. 1016.

of the fifteenth century erected statues in their honour, sitting under graceful baldachins on the façade of the cathedral.[1]

History and the new topography were now careful to leave no local celebrity unnoticed. At the same period the Northern chronicles only here and there among the list of Popes, emperors, earthquakes, and comets put in the remark that at such a time this or that famous man "flourished." We shall elsewhere have to show how, mainly under the influence of this idea of fame, an admirable biographical literature was developed. We must here limit ourselves to the local patriotism of the topographers who recorded the claims of their native cities to distinction.

In the Middle Ages the cities were proud of their saints and of the bones and relics in their churches.[2] With these the panegyrist of Padua in 1440, Michele Savonarola,[3] begins his list; from them he passes to "the famous men who were no saints, but who, by their great intellect and force [virtus] deserve to be added [adnecti] to the saints"—just as in classical antiquity the distinguished man came close upon the hero.[4] The further enumeration is most characteristic of the time. First comes Antenor, the brother of Priam, who founded Padua with a band of Trojan fugitives; King Dardanus, who defeated Attila in the Euganean hills, followed him in pursuit, and struck him dead at Rimini with a chessboard; the Emperor Henry IV, who built the cathedral; a King Marcus, whose head was preserved in Monselice (monte silicis arce); then a couple of cardinals and prelates as founders of colleges, churches, and so forth; the famous Augustinian theologian Fra Alberto; a string of philosophers beginning with Paolo Veneto and the celebrated Pietro of Albano; the jurist Paolo Padovano; then Livy and the poets Petrarch, Mussato, Lovato. If there is any want of military celebrities in the list the poet consoles himself for it by the abundance of learned men whom he has to show, and by the more durable character of intellectual glory; while the fame of the soldier is buried with his body, or, if it lasts, owes its permanence only to the scholar.[5] It is nevertheless honourable to the city that foreign warriors lie buried here by their own wish, like Pietro de Rossi of Parma, Filippo Arcelli of Piacenza, and especially Gattamelata of Narni (d. 1443),[6] whose brazen equestrian statue, "like a Cæsar in triumph," already stood by the church of the Santo. The author then names a crowd of jurists and physicians, among the latter two friends of Petrarch, Johannes ab Horologio and Jacob de Dondis, nobles "who had not only, like so many

---

[1] The elder Pliny was notoriously a native of Verona.

[2] This is the tone of the remarkable work De Laudibus Papiæ, in Murat., xi, dating from the fourteenth century—much municipal pride, but no idea of personal fame.

[3] De Laudibus Patavii, in Murat., xxiv, col. 1138 sqq. Only three cities, in his opinion, could be compared with Padua—Florence, Venice, and Rome.

[4] "Nam et veteres nostri tales aut divos aut æterna memoria dignos non immerito prædicabant, quum virtus summa sanctitatis sit consocia et pari ematur pretio." What follows is most characteristic: "Hos itaque meo facili judicio æternos facio."

[5] Similar ideas occur in many contemporary writers. Codrus Urceus, Sermo xiii (Opp., 1506, fol. xxxviiib), speaking of Galeazzo Bentivoglio, who was both a scholar and a warrior, " cognoscens artem militarem esse quidem excellentem, sed literas multo certe excellentiores."

[6] What follows immediately is not, as the editor remarks (in Murat., xxiv, col. 1059, note), from the pen of Michele Savonarola.

others, received, but deserved, the honour of knighthood." Then follows a list of famous mechanicians, painters, and musicians, which is closed by the name of a fencing-master, Michele Rosso, who, as the most distinguished man in his profession, was to be seen painted in many places.

By the side of these local temples of fame, which myth, legend, popular admiration, and literary tradition combined to create, the poet-scholars built up a great Pantheon of world-wide celebrity. They made collections of

FIG. 72. WALL WITH PORTRAITS OF FAMOUS MEN
By Andrea del Castagno
Florence, S. Apollonia
Photo Alinari

famous men and famous women, often in direct imitation of Cornelius Nepos, the pseudo-Suetonius, Valerius Maximus, Plutarch (*Mulierum Virtutes*), Hieronymus (*De Viris Illustribus*), and others; or they wrote of imaginary triumphal processions and Olympian assemblies, as was done by Petrarch in his *Trionfo della Fama*, and Boccaccio in the *Amorosa Visione*, with hundreds of names, of which three-fourths at least belong to antiquity and the rest to the Middle Ages.[1] By and by this new and comparatively modern element was

[1] Petrarch, in the *Triumph* here quoted, dwells only on characters of antiquity, and in his collection *De Rebus Memorandis* has little to say of contemporaries. In the *Casus Virorum Illustrium* of Boccaccio (among the men a number of women, besides Philippa Catinensis treated of at the end, are included, and even the goddess Juno is described) only the close of the eighth book and the last book—the ninth—deal with non-classical times. Boccaccio's remarkable work *De Claris Mulieribus* treats also almost exclusively of antiquity. It begins with Eve, speaks then of ninety-seven women of antiquity, and seven of the Middle Ages, beginning with Pope Joan and ending with Queen Johanna of Naples. And so at a much later time in the *Commentarii Urbani* of Raphael Volaterranus. In the work *De Claris Mulieribus* of the Augustinian Jacobus Bergomensis (printed 1497, but probably published earlier) antiquity and legend hold the chief place, but there are still some valuable biographies of Italian women. There are one or two lives of contemporary women by Vespasiano da Bisticci

THE MODERN IDEA OF FAME

treated with greater emphasis; the historians began to insert descriptions of character, and collections arose of the biographies of distinguished contemporaries, like those of Filippo Villani, Vespasiano Fiorentino, Bartolommeo Facio, Paolo Cortese,[1] and lastly of Paolo Giovio.

(*Arch. Stor. Ital.*, iv, i, pp. 430 *sqq.*). In Scardeonius (*De Urb. Patav. Antiqu.*, Græv., *Thesaur.*, ii, iii, col. 405 *sqq.*) only famous Paduan women are mentioned. First comes a legend or tradition from the time of the fall of the Empire, then tragical stories of the party struggles of the thirteenth and fourteenth centuries; then notices of several heroic women; then the foundress of nunneries, the political woman, the female doctor, the mother of many and distinguished sons, the learned woman, the peasant girl who dies defending her chastity; then the cultivated beauty of the sixteenth century, on whom everybody writes sonnets; and lastly the female novelist and poet at Padua. A century later the woman-professor would have been added to these. For the famous women of the house of Este see Ariosto, *Orlando*, xiii.

[1] *Bartolommeo Facio and Paolo Cortese.* Bartolommeo Facio's *De Viris Illustribus Liber* was first published by L. Mehus (Florence, 1745). The book was begun by the author (known by other historical works, and resident at the Court of Alfonso of Naples) after he had finished the history of that king (1455), and ended, as references to the struggles of Hungary and the writer's ignorance of the elevation of Æneas Sylvius to the cardinalate show, in 1456. (See, nevertheless, Wahlen, *Laurentii Vallæ Opuscula Tria*, p. 67, note 1, Vienna, 1869.) It is never quoted by contemporaries, and seldom by later writers. The author wishes in this book to describe the famous men, "ætatis memoriæque nostræ," and consequently only mentions such as were born in the last quarter of the fourteenth century, and were still living in, or had died shortly before, the middle of the fifteenth. He chiefly limits himself to Italians, except in the case of artists or princes, among the latter of whom he includes the Emperor Sigismund and Albrecht Achilles of Brandenburg; and in arranging the various biographies he neither follows chronological order nor the distinction which the subject of each attained, but puts them down "ut quisque mihi occurrerit," intending to treat in a second part of those whom he might have left out in the first. He divides the famous men into nine classes, nearly all of them prefaced by remarks on their distinctive qualities: (1) poets; (2) orators; (3) jurists; (4) physicians (with a few philosophers and theologians, as an appendix); (5) painters; (6) sculptors; (7) eminent citizens; (8) generals; (9) princes and kings. Among the latter he treats with special fullness and care of Pope Nicholas V and King Alfonso of Naples. In general he gives only short and mostly eulogistic biographies, confined in the case of princes and soldiers to the list of their deeds, and of artists and writers to the enumeration of their works. No attempt is made at a detailed description or criticism of these; only with regard to a few works of art which he had himself seen he writes more fully. Nor is any attempt made at an estimate of individuals; his heroes either receive a few general words of praise, or must be satisfied with the mere mention of their names. Of himself the author says next to nothing. He states only that Guarino was his teacher, that Manetti wrote a book on a subject which he himself had treated, that Bracellius was his countryman, and that the painter Pisano of Verona was known to him (pp. 17, 18, 19, 48); but says nothing in speaking of Laurentius Valla of his own violent quarrels with this scholar. On the other hand, he does not fail to express his piety and his hatred to the Turks (p. 64), to relieve his Italian patriotism by calling the Swiss barbarians (p. 60), and to say of P. P. Vergerius "dignus qui totam in Italia vitam scribens exegisset" (p. 9).

Of all celebrities he evidently sets most store by the scholars, and among these by the *oratores*, to whom he devotes nearly a third of his book. He nevertheless has great respect for the jurists, and shows a special fondness for the physicians, among whom he well distinguishes the theoretical from the practical, relating the successful diagnoses and operations of the latter. That he treats of theologians and philosophers in connexion with the physicians is as curious as that he should put the painters immediately after the physicians, although, as he says, they are most allied to the poets. In spite of his reverence for learning, which shows itself in the praise given to the princes who patronized it, he is too much of a courtier not to register the tokens of princely favour received by the scholars he speaks of, and to characterize the princes in the introduction to the chapters devoted to them as those who "veluti corpus membra, ita omnia genera quæ supra memoravimus, regunt ac tuentur."

The style of the book is simple and unadorned, and the matter of it full of instruction, notwithstanding its brevity. It is a pity that Facius did not enter more fully into the personal relations and circumstances of the men whom he described, and did not add to the list of their writings some notice of the contents and the value of them.

The work of Paolo Cortese (b. 1445, d. 1510), *De Hominibus Doctis Dialogus* (first ed. Florence, 1734), is much more limited in its character. This work, written about 1490, since it mentions Antonius Geraldinus as dead, who died in 1488, and was dedicated to Lorenzo de' Medici, who died in 1492, is distinguished from that of Facius, written a generation earlier, not only by the exclusion of all who are not learned men, but by various inward and outward characteristics. First by the form, which is that of a dialogue between the author and his two companions, Alexander Farnese and Antonius, and by the digressions and unequal treatment of the various characters caused thereby; and secondly by the manner of the treatment itself. While Facius speaks only of the men of his own time, Cortese treats only of the dead, and in part of those long dead, by which he enlarges his circle more than he narrows it by exclusion of the living; while Facius merely chronicles works and deeds

The North of Europe, until Italian influence began to tell upon its writers
—for instance, on Trithemius, the first German who wrote the lives of famous
men—possessed only either legends of the saints, or descriptions of princes
and Churchmen partaking largely of the character of legends and showing no
traces of the idea of fame—that is, of distinction won by a man's personal efforts.
Poetical glory was still confined to certain classes of society, and the names of
Northern artists are known to us at this period only in so far as they were
members of certain guilds or corporations.

The poet-scholar in Italy had, as we have already said, the fullest consciousness that he was the giver of fame and immortality, or, if he chose, of oblivion.[1]
Petrarch, notwithstanding all the idealism of his love to Laura, gives utterance
to the feeling that his sonnets confer immortality on his beloved as well as on
himself.[2] Boccaccio complains of a fair one to whom he had done homage,
and who remained hard-hearted in order that he might go on praising her and

as if they were unknown, Cortese criticizes the literary activity of his heroes as if the reader were already familiar
with it. This criticism is shaped by the humanistic estimate of eloquence, according to which no man could be
considered of importance unless he had achieved something remarkable in eloquence—*i.e.*, in the classical,
Ciceronian treatment of the Latin language. On this principle Dante and Petrarch are only moderately praised,
and are blamed for having diverted so much of their powers from Latin to Italian; Guarino is described as one
who had beheld perfect eloquence at least through a cloud; Leonardo Aretino as one who had offered his contemporaries "aliquid splendidius"; and Æneas Sylvius as he "in quo primum apparuit mutati sæculi signum."
This point of view prevailed over all others; never perhaps was it held so one-sidedly as by Cortese. To get
a notion of his way of thinking we have only to hear his remarks on a predecessor, also the compiler of a great
biographical collection, Sicco Polentone: "Ejus sunt viginti ad filium libri scripti de claris scriptoribus, utiles
admodum qui jam fere ab omnibus legi sint desiti. Est enim in judicando parum acer, nec servit aurium
voluptati quum tractat res ab aliis ante tractatas; sed hoc ferendum. Illud certe molestum est, dum alienis
verbis sententiisque scripta infarcit et explet sua; ex quo nascitur maxime vitiosum scribendi genus, quum
modo lenis et candidus, modo durus et asper appareat, et sic in toto genere tanquam in unum agrum plura inter
se inimicissima sparsa semina."

All are not treated with so much detail; most are disposed of in a few brief sentences; some are merely
named without a word being added. Much is nevertheless to be learned from his judgments, though we may
not be able always to agree with them. We cannot here discuss him more fully, especially as many of his most
characteristic remarks have been already made use of; on the whole, they give us a clear picture of the way
in which a later time, outwardly more developed, looked down with critical scorn upon an earlier age, inwardly
perhaps richer, but externally less perfect.

Facius, the author of the first-mentioned biographical work, is spoken of, but not his book. Like Facius,
Cortese is the humble courtier, looking on Lorenzo de' Medici as Facius looked on Alfonso of Naples; like
him, he is a patriot who only praises foreign excellence unwillingly and because he must, adding the assurance
that he does not wish to oppose his own country (p. 48, speaking of Janus Pannonius).

Information as to Cortese has been collected by Bernardus Paperinius, the editor of his work; we may add
that his Latin translation of the novel of L. B. Alberti, *Hippolytus and Dejanira*, is printed for the first time in
the *Opere di L. B. Alberti*, vol. iii, pp. 439–463.

How great the fame of the humanists was is shown by the fact that impostors attempted to make capital
out of the use of their names. There thus appeared at Verona a man strangely clad and using strange gestures,
who, when brought before the mayor, recited with great energy passages of Latin verse and prose, taken from
the works of Panormita, answered in reply to the questions put to him that he was himself Panormita, and
was able to give so many small and commonly unknown details about the life of this scholar that his statement
obtained general credit. He was then treated with great honour by the authorities and the learned men of
the city, and played his assumed part successfully for a considerable time, until Guarino and others who knew
Panormita personally discovered the fraud. *Cf.* Rosmini, *Vita di Guarino*, ii, 44 *sqq.*, 171 *sqq.* Few of the
humanists were free from the habit of boasting. Codrus Urceus (*Vita*, at the end of the *Opera*, 1506, fol. lxx),
when asked for his opinion about this or that famous man, used to answer: "Sibi scire videntur."
Bartolommeo Facius, *De Vir. Ill.*, p. 31, tells of the jurist Antonius Butriensis: "Id unum in eo viro
notandum est, quod neminem unquam, adeo excellere homines in eo studio volebat, ut doctoratu dignum in
examine comprobavit."

[1] A Latin poet of the twelfth century, one of the wandering scholars who barters his song for a coat, uses
this as a threat. *Carmina Burana*, p. 76 (Stuttgart, 1847), *Bibl. des Lit. Vereins*, xvi.

[2] Sonnet cli, "Lasso ch' i ardo."

making her famous, and he gives her a hint that he will try the effect of a little blame.[1] Sannazaro, in two magnificent sonnets, threatens Alfonso of Naples with eternal obscurity on account of his cowardly flight before Charles VIII.[2] Angelo Poliziano seriously exhorts (1491) King John of Portugal[3] to think betimes of his immortality in reference to the new discoveries in Africa, and to send him materials to Florence, there to be put into shape (*operosius excolenda*), otherwise it would befall him as it had befallen all the others whose deeds, unsupported by the help of the learned, "lie hidden in the vast heap of human frailty." The King, or his humanistic Chancellor, agreed to this, and promised that at least the Portuguese chronicles of African affairs should be translated

FIG. 73. SKETCH FOR A MAUSOLEUM
By Leonardo da Vinci

into Italian, and sent to Florence to be done into Latin. Whether the promise was kept is not known. These pretensions are by no means so groundless as they may appear at first sight; for the form in which events, even the greatest, are told to the living and to posterity is anything but a matter of indifference. The Italian humanists, with their mode of exposition and their Latin style, had long the complete control of the reading world of Europe, and till the eighteenth century the Italian poets were more widely known and studied than those of any other nation. The baptismal name of the Florentine Amerigo Vespucci was given, on account of his book of travels—certainly at the proposal of its German translator into Latin, Martin Waldseemüller (Hylacomylus)[4]—to a new quarter of the globe, and if Paolo Giovio, with all his superficiality and graceful caprice, promised himself immortality[5] his expectation has not altogether been disappointed.

[1] Boccaccio, *Opere Volgari*, vol. xvi, in Sonnet 13: "Pallido, vinto," etc.
[2] Elsewhere, and in Roscoe, *Leo X*, ed. Bossi, iv, 203.
[3] *Angeli Politiani Epist.*, lib. x.
[4] *Quatuor Navigationes*, etc. Deodatum (Saint-Dié, 1507). *Cf.* O. Peschel, *Geschichte des Zeitalters der Entdeckungen*, 1859, ed. 2, 1876.
[5] Paul. Jovius, *De Romanis Piscibus*, Præfatio (1525). The first decade of his histories would soon be published, "non sine aliqua spe immortalitatis."

Amid all these preparations outwardly to win and secure fame the curtain is now and then drawn aside, and we see with frightful evidence a boundless ambition and thirst after greatness, independent of all means and consequences. Thus, in the preface to Machiavelli's Florentine history, in which he blames his predecessors Leonardo Aretino and Poggio for their too considerate reticence with regard to the political parties in the city:

> They erred greatly and showed that they understood little the ambition of men and the desire to perpetuate a name. How many who could distinguish themselves by nothing praiseworthy strove to do so by infamous deeds! Those writers did not consider that actions which are great in themselves, as is the case with the actions of rulers and of states, always seem to bring more glory than blame, of whatever kind they are and whatever the result of them may be.[1]

In more than one remarkable and dreadful undertaking the motive assigned by serious writers is the burning desire to achieve something great and memorable. This motive is not a mere extreme case of ordinary vanity, but something demonic, involving a surrender of the will, the use of any means, however atrocious, and even an indifference to success itself. In this sense, for example, Machiavelli conceives the character of Stefano Porcaro (p. 122);[2] of the murderers of Galeazzo Maria Sforza (pp. 77, 78), the documents tell us about the same; and the assassination of Duke Alessandro of Florence (1537) is ascribed by Varchi himself to the thirst for fame which tormented the murderer, Lorenzino de' Medici (p. 80). Still more stress is laid on this motive by Paolo Giovio.[3] Lorenzino, according to him, pilloried by a pamphlet of Molza on account of the mutilation of some ancient statues at Rome, broods over a deed whose novelty shall make his disgrace forgotten, and ends by murdering his kinsman and prince. These are characteristic features of this age of overstrained and despairing passions and forces, and remind us of the burning of the temple of Diana at Ephesus in the time of Philip of Macedon.

[1] Cf. *Discorsi*, i, 27. *Tristizia* (crime) can have *grandezza* and be *in alcuna parte generosa*; *grandezza* can take away *infamia* from a deed; a man can be *onorevolmente tristo* in contrast to one who is *perfettamente buono*.
[2] *Stor. Fiorent.*, lib. vi, p. 20.
[3] Paul. Jovius, *Elog. Vir. Lit. Ill.*, p. 192, speaking of Marius Molza.

CHAPTER IV

MODERN WIT AND SATIRE

THE corrective not only of this modern desire for fame, but of all highly developed individuality, is found in ridicule, especially when expressed in the victorious form of wit.[1] We read in the Middle Ages how hostile armies, princes, and nobles provoked one another with symbolical insult, and how the defeated party was loaded with symbolical outrage. Here and there, too, under the influence of classical literature wit began to be used as a weapon in theological disputes, and the poetry of Provence produced a whole class of satirical compositions. Even the *Minnesänger*, as their political poems show, could adopt this tone when necessary.[2] But wit could not be an independent element in life till its appropriate victim, the developed individual with personal pretentions, had appeared. Its weapons were then by no means limited to the tongue and the pen, but included tricks and practical jokes—the so-called *burle* and *beffe*—which form a chief subject of many collections of novels.

The *Hundred Old Tales*, which must have been composed about the end of the thirteenth century, have as yet neither wit, the fruit of contrast, nor the *burla*, for their subject;[3] their aim is merely to give simple and elegant expression to wise sayings and pretty stories or fables. But if anything proves the great antiquity of the collection it is precisely this absence of satire. For with the fourteenth century comes Dante, who, in the utterance of scorn, leaves all other poets in the world far behind, and who, if only on account of his great picture of the deceivers,[4] must be called the chief master of colossal comedy. With Petrarch[5] begin the collections of witty sayings after the pattern of Plutarch (*Apophthegmata*, etc.).

What stores of wit were concentrated in Florence during this century is

---

[1] Mere railing is found very early, in Benzo of Alba, in the eleventh century (*Mon. Germ.*, pp. xi, 591–681).

[2] The Middle Ages are further rich in so-called satirical poems; but the satire is not individual, but aimed at classes, categories, and whole populations, and easily passes into the didactic tone. The whole spirit of this literature is best represented by *Reineke Fuchs*, in all its forms among the different nations of the West. For this branch of French literature see an admirable work by Lenient, *La Satire en France au Moyen-âge* (Paris, 1860), and the equally excellent continuation, *La Satire en France, ou la Littérature Militante au XVIᵉ Siècle* (Paris, 1866).

[3] See above, p. 25, note 2. Occasionally we find an insolent joke: *Nov.* 37.

[4] *Inferno*, xxi, xxii. The only possible parallel is with Aristophanes.

[5] A modest beginning. *Opera*, pp. 421 *sqq.*, in *De Rerum Memorandarum*, lib. iv. Again, in *Epist. Seniles*, x, 2. Cf. *Epist. Fam.*, ed. Fracassetti, lib. i, 68 *sqq.*, 70, 240, 245. The puns have a flavour of their medieval home, the monasteries. Petrarch's invectives *contra Gallum, contra medicum objurgantem*, and his work *De Sui Ipsius et Multorum Ignorantia*, perhaps also his *Epistolæ sine Titulo*, may be quoted as early examples of satirical writing.

most characteristically shown in the novels of Franco Sacchetti. These are, for the most part, not stories but answers, given under certain circumstances— shocking pieces of *naïveté*, with which silly folks, Court jesters, rogues, and profligate women make their retort. The comedy of the tale lies in the startling contrast of this real or assumed *naïveté* with conventional morality and the ordinary relations of the world—things are made to stand on their heads. All means of picturesque representation are made use of, including the introduction of certain North Italian dialects. Often the place of wit is taken by mere insolence, clumsy trickery, blasphemy, and obscenity; one or two jokes

FIG. 74. GROTESQUE
Florentine copper engraving, 1470–80

told of *condottieri* [1] are among the most brutal and malicious which are recorded. Many of the *burle* are thoroughly comic, but many are only real or supposed evidence of personal superiority, of triumph over another. How much people were willing to put up with, how often the victim was satisfied with getting the laugh on his side by a retaliatory trick, cannot be said; there was much heartless and pointless malice mixed up with it all, and life in Florence was no doubt often made unpleasant enough from this cause. [2] The inventors and retailers of jokes soon became inevitable figures, [3] and among them there must have been some who were classical—far superior to all the mere Court jesters, to whom competition, a changing public, and the quick apprehension of the audience, all advantages of life in Florence, were wanting. Some Florentine wits went touring among the despotic Courts of Lombardy and Romagna, [4] and found themselves much better rewarded than at home, where their talent was cheap and plentiful. The better type of these people is the amusing man (*l'uomo piacevole*), the worse is the buffoon and the vulgar parasite who presents himself at weddings and banquets with the argument, "If I am not invited the fault is not mine." Now and then the latter combine to pluck a young spendthrift, [5] but in general they are treated and despised as parasites, while wits of higher position bear themselves like princes, and consider their talent as something sovereign. Dolcibene, whom Charles IV, "Imperator

---

[1] *Nov.* 40 and 41; Ridolfo da Camerino is the man.

[2] The well-known jest of Brunellesco and the fat wood-carver, Manetto Ammanatini, who is said to have fled into Hungary before the ridicule he encountered, is clever but cruel. [It is questioned whether this joke originated with Ant. Manetti.—W. G.]

[3] The "Araldo" of the Florentine Signoria. One instance among many, *Commissioni di Rinaldo degli Albizzi*, iii, 651, 669. The fool as necessary to enliven the company after dinner; Petrus Alcyonius, *De Exilio*, ed. Mencken, p. 129.

[4] Franco Sacchetti, *Nov.* 49. And yet, according to *Nov.* 67, there was an impression that a Romagnole was superior to the worst Florentine.

[5] L. B. Alberti, *Trattato del Governo della Famiglia, Opere*, ed. Bonucci, v, 171. *Cf.* above, p. 145, note 2.

di Buem," had pronounced to be the "king of Italian jesters," said to him at Ferrara: "You will conquer the world, since you are my friend and the Pope's; you fight with the sword, the Pope with his Bulls, and I with my tongue." [1] This is no mere jest, but a foreshadowing of Pietro Aretino.

The two most famous jesters about the middle of the fifteenth century were a priest near Florence, Arlotto (1483), for more refined wit (*facezie*), and the Court fool of Ferrara, Gonnella, for buffoonery. We can hardly compare their stories with those of the parson of Kalenberg and Till Eulenspiegel, since the latter arose in a different and half-mythical manner, as fruits of the imagination of a whole people, and touch rather on what is general and intelligible to all, while Arlotto and Gonnella were historical beings, coloured and shaped by local influences. But if the comparison be allowed, and extended to the jests of the non-Italian nations, we shall find in general that the joke in the French *fabliaux*,[2] as among the Germans, is chiefly directed to the attainment of some advantage or enjoyment; while the wit of Arlotto and the practical jokes of Gonnella are an end in themselves, and exist simply for the sake of the triumph of production. (Till Eulenspiegel again forms a class by himself, as the personified quiz, mostly pointless enough, of particular classes and professions.) The Court fool of

FIG. 75. PORTRAIT OF A JESTER
By Dosso Dossi
Modena, Art Gallery
Photo Anderson, Rome

the Este saved himself more than once by his keen satire and refined modes of vengeance.[3]

The type of the *uomo piacevole* and the *buffone* long survived the freedom of Florence. Under Duke Cosimo flourished Barlacchia, and at the beginning of the seventeenth century Francesco Ruspoli and Curzio Marignolli. In Pope Leo X the genuine Florentine love of jesters showed itself strikingly. This prince, whose taste for the most refined intellectual pleasures was insatiable, endured and desired at his table a number of witty buffoons and jack-puddings, among them two monks and a cripple;[4] at public feasts he treated them with deliberate scorn as parasites, setting before them monkeys and crows in the

---

[1] Franco Sacchetti, *Nov.* 156; *cf.* 24 for Dolcibene and the Jews. (For Charles IV and the fools, *Friedjung, loc. cit.*, p. 109.) The *Faceti* of Poggio resemble Sacchetti's in substance—practical jokes, impertinences, refined indecency misunderstood by simple folk; the philologist is betrayed by the large number of verbal jokes. On L. B. Alberti see pp. 149 *sqq.*

[2] And consequently in those novels of the Italians whose subject is taken from them.

[3] According to Bandello, iv, *Nov.* 2, Gonnella could twist his features into the likeness of other people and mimic all the dialects of Italy.   [4] Paul. Jovius, *Vita Leonis X.*

place of savoury meats. Leo, indeed, showed a peculiar fondness for the *burla*; it belonged to his nature sometimes to treat his own favourite pursuits—music and poetry—ironically, parodying them with his factotum, Cardinal Bibbiena.[1] Neither of them found it beneath him to fool an honest old secretary till he thought himself a master of the art of music. The *improvisatore* Baraballo of Gaeta was brought so far by Leo's flattery that he applied in all seriousness for the poet's coronation on the Capitol. On the anniversary of S. Cosmas and S. Damian, the patrons of the house of Medici, he was first compelled, adorned with laurel and purple, to amuse the Papal guests with his recitations, and at last, when all were ready to

FIG. 76. THE MONKEY LAOCOÖN
Woodcut by Boldrini, after Titian
Photo Deutsche Verlagsanstalt, Stuttgart

split with laughter, to mount a gold-harnessed elephant in the court of the Vatican, sent as a present to Rome by Emanuel the Great of Portugal, while the Pope looked down from above through his eyeglass.[2] The brute, however, was so terrified by the noise of the trumpets and kettle-drums, and the cheers of the crowd, that there was no getting him over the bridge of S. Angelo.

The parody of what is solemn or sublime, which here meets us in the case of a procession, had already taken an important place in poetry.[3] It was

[1] "Erat enim Bibbiena mirus artifex hominibus ætate vel professione gravibus ad insaniam impellendis." We are here reminded of the jests of Christine of Sweden with her philologists. *Cf.* the remarkable passage of Jov. Pontan., *De Sermone*, lib. ii, cap. 9: "Ferdinandus Alfonsi filius, Neapolitanorum rex magnus et ipse fuit artifex et vultus componendi et orationes in quem ipse usus vellet. Nam ætatis nostri Pontifices maximi fingendis vultibus ac verbis vel histriones ipsos anteveniunt."

[2] The eyeglass I not only infer from Raphael's portrait, where it can be explained as a magnifier for looking at the miniatures in the prayer-book, but from a statement of Pellicanus, according to which Leo views an advancing procession of monks through a *specillum* (cf. *Züricher Taschenbuch* for 1858, p. 177), and from the *cristallus concava*, which, according to Giovio, he used when hunting. (Cf. *Leonis X Vita Auctore Anon. Conscripta* in the appendix to Roscoe.) In Attilius Alessius (Baluz., *Miscell.*, iv, 518) we read: "Oculari ex gemina (gemma?) utebatur quam manu gestans, signando aliquid videndum esset, oculis admovebat." The shortsightedness in the family of the Medici was hereditary. Lorenzo was short-sighted, and replied to the Sienese Bartolommeo Soccini, who said that the air of Florence was bad for the eyes: " E quella di Siena al cervello." The bad sight of Leo X was proverbial. After his election the Roman wits explained the number MCCCCXL engraved in the Vatican as follows: " Multi cæci Cardinales creaverunt cæcum decimum Leonem." *Cf.* Shepherd-Tonelli, *Vita del Poggio*, ii, 23 *sqq.*, and the passages there quoted.

[3] We find it also in plastic art—for example, in the famous plate parodying the group of the Laocoön as three monkeys. But here parody seldom went beyond sketches and the like, though much, it is true, may have been destroyed. Caricature, again, is something different. Leonardo, in the grotesque faces in the Biblioteca Ambrosiana, represents what is hideous when and because it is comical, and exaggerates the ludicrous element at pleasure.

naturally compelled to choose victims of another kind than those of Aristophanes, who introduced the great tragedian into his plays. But the same maturity of culture which at a certain period produced parody among the Greeks did the same in Italy. By the close of the fourteenth century the love-lorn wailings of Petrarch's sonnets and others of the same kind were taken off by caricaturists; and the solemn air of this form of verse was parodied in lines of mystic twaddle. A constant invitation to parody was offered by the *Divine Comedy*, and Lorenzo the Magnificent wrote the most admirable travesty in the style of the *Inferno* (*Simposio* or *I Beoni*). Luigi Pulci obviously imitates the *improvisatori* in his *Morgante*, and both his poetry and Bojardo's are in part, at

least, a half-conscious parody of the chivalrous poetry of the Middle Ages. Such a caricature was deliberately undertaken by the great parodist Teofilo Folengo (about 1520). Under the name of Limerno Pitocco he composed the *Orlandino*, in which chivalry appears only as a ludicrous setting for a crowd of modern figures and ideas. Under the name of Merlinus Coccajus he described the journeys and exploits of his phantastic vagabonds (also in the same

FIG. 77. CARICATURES
Drawing by Leonardo da Vinci

spirit of parody) in half-Latin hexameters, with all the affected pomp of the learned epos of the day (*Opus Macaronicorum*). Since then caricature has been constantly, and often brilliantly, represented on the Italian Parnassus.

About the middle period of the Renaissance a theoretical analysis of wit was undertaken, and its practical application in good society was regulated more precisely. The theorist was Gioviano Pontano.[1] In his work on speaking, especially in the third and fourth books, he tries by means of the comparison of numerous jokes or *facetiæ* to arrive at a general principle. How wit should be used among people of position is taught by Baldassar Castiglione in his *Cortigiano*.[2] Its chief function is naturally to enliven those present by the repetition of comic or graceful stories and sayings; personal jokes, on the contrary, are discouraged on the ground that they wound unhappy people, show too much honour to wrong-doers, and make enemies of the powerful and the spoiled children of fortune;[3] and even in repetition a wide reserve in the use

---

[1] Jov. Pontan., *De Sermone*, lib. iv, 10. He attributes a special gift of wit to the Sienese and Peruginese, as well as to the Florentines, adding the Spanish Court as a matter of politeness.

[2] *Il Cortigiano*, lib. ii, cap. 4 *sqq.*, ed. Baude de Vesme, pp. 124 *sqq.* (Florence, 1854). For the explanation of wit as the effect of contrast, though not clearly put, see *ibid.*, cap. lxxiii, p. 136.

[3] Jov. Pontan., *De Sermone*, lib. iv, cap. 3, also advises people to abstain from using *ridicula* either against the miserable or the strong.

of dramatic gestures is recommended to the gentleman. Then follows, not only for purposes of quotation but as patterns for future jesters, a large collection of puns and witty sayings, methodically arranged according to their species, among them some that are admirable. The doctrine of Giovanni della Casa, some twenty years later, in his guide to good manners, is much stricter and more cautious; [1] with a view to the consequences, he wishes to see the desire of triumph banished altogether from jokes and burle. He is the herald of a reaction, which was certain sooner or later to appear.

Italy had, in fact, become a school for scandal, the like of which the world cannot show, not even in France at the time of Voltaire. In him and his comrades there was assuredly no lack of the spirit of negation; but where, in the eighteenth century, was to be found the crowd of suitable victims, that countless assembly of highly and characteristically developed human beings, celebrities of every kind, statesmen, Churchmen, inventors and discoverers, men of letters, poets and artists, all of whom then gave the fullest and freest play to their individuality? This host existed in the fifteenth and sixteenth centuries, and by its side the general culture of the time had educated a poisonous brood of impotent wits, of born critics and railers, whose envy called for hecatombs of victims; and to all this was added the envy of the famous men among themselves. In this the philologists notoriously led the way—Filelfo, Poggio, Lorenzo Valla, and others—while the artists of the fifteenth century lived in peaceful and friendly competition with one another. The history of art may take note of the fact.

Florence, the great market of fame, was in this point, as we have said, in advance of other cities. "Sharp eyes and bad tongues" is the description given of the inhabitants. [2] An easy-going contempt of everything and everybody was probably the prevailing tone of society. Machiavelli, in the remarkable prologue to his Mandragola, refers rightly or wrongly the visible decline of moral force to the general habit of evil speaking, and threatens his detractors with the news that he can say sharp things as well as they. Next to Florence comes the Papal Court, which had long been a rendezvous of the bitterest and wittiest tongues. Poggio's Facetiæ are dated from the Chamber of Lies (bugiale) of the apostolic notaries; and when we remember the number of disappointed place-hunters, of hopeless competitors and enemies of the favourites, of idle, profligate prelates there assembled, it is intelligible how Rome became the home of the savage pasquinade as well as of more philosophical satire. If we add to this the wide-spread hatred borne to the priests, and the well-known instinct of the mob to lay any horror to the charge of the great, there results an untold mass of infamy. [3] Those who were able protected themselves best by

[1] Galateo del Casa, ed. Venez., 1789, pp. 26 sqq., 48.

[2] Lettere Pittoriche, i, p. 71, in a letter of Vinc. Borghini, 1577. Machiavelli (Stor. Fiorent., vii, cap. 28) says of the young gentlemen in Florence soon after the middle of the fifteenth century: " Gli studî loro erano apparire col vestire splendidi, e col parlare sagaci ed astuti, e quello che più destramente mordeva gli altri, era più savio e da più stimato."

[3] Cf. Fedra Inghirami's funeral oration on Lodovico Podocataro (d. August 25, 1504) in the Anecd. Litt., i, 319. The scandalmonger Massaino is mentioned in Paul. Jovius, Dialogus de Viris Litt. Illustr. (Tiraboschi, tom. vii, Parte IV, p. 1631).

contempt both of the false and true accusations, and by brilliant and joyous display.[1] More sensitive natures sank into utter despair when they found themselves deeply involved in guilt, and still more deeply in slander.[2] In course of time calumny became universal, and the strictest virtue was most certain of all to challenge the attacks of malice. Of the great pulpit orator Fra Egidio of Viterbo, whom Leo made a cardinal on account of his merits, and who showed himself a man of the people and a brave monk in the calamity of 1527,[3] Giovio gives us to understand that he preserved his ascetic pallor by the smoke of wet straw and other means of the same kind. Giovio is a genuine Curial in these matters.[4] He generally begins by telling his story, then adds that he does not believe it, and then hints at the end that perhaps after all there may be something in it. But the true scapegoat of Roman scorn was the pious and moral Adrian VI. A general agreement seemed to be made to take him only on the comic side. Adrian had contemptuously referred to the Laocoön group as *idola antiquorum*, had shut up the entrance to the Belvedere, had left the works of Raphael unfinished, and had banished the poets and players from the Court; it was even feared that he would burn some ancient statues to lime for the new church of St Peter. He fell out from the first with the formidable Francesco Berni, threatening to have thrown into the Tiber not, as people said,[5] the statue of Pasquino, but the writers of the satires themselves. The vengeance for this was the famous *Capitolo* against Pope Adrian, inspired not exactly by hatred, but by contempt for the comical Dutch barbarian;[6] the more savage menaces were reserved for the cardinals who had elected him. The plague, which then was prevalent in Rome, was ascribed to him;[7] Berni and others [8] sketch the environment of the Pope—the Germans by whom he was governed [9]—with the same sparkling untruthfulness with which the modern *feuilletoniste* turns black into white, and everything into anything. The biography which Paolo Giovio was commissioned to write by the Cardinal of Tortosa, and which was to have been a eulogy, is for anyone who can read between the lines an unexampled piece of satire. It sounds ridiculous—at least, for the Italians of that time—to hear how Adrian applied to the Chapter of Saragossa for the jaw-bone of St Lambert; how the devout Spaniards decked

---

[1] This was the plan followed by Leo X, and his calculations were not disappointed. Fearfully as his reputation was mangled after his death by the satirists, they were unable to modify the general estimate formed of him.

[2] This was probably the case with Cardinal Ardicino della Porta, who in 1491 wished to resign his dignity and take refuge in a monastery. See Infessura, in Eccard, ii, col. 2000.

[3] See his funeral oration in the *Anecd. Litt.*, iv, p. 315. He assembled an army of peasants in the March of Ancona, which was only hindered from acting by the treason of the Duke of Urbino. For his graceful and hopeless love-poems see Trucchi, *Poesie Inedite*, iii, 123.

[4] How he used his tongue at the table of Clement VII is told in Giraldi, *Hecatommithi*, vii, *Nov.* 5.

[5] The charge of taking into consideration the proposal to drown Pasquino (in Paul. Jovius, *Vita Hadriani*) is transferred from Sixtus IV to Adrian, but is confirmed by Aretino, *Ragionamento per le Corti* (Venice, 1539). Cf. *Lettere dei Principi*, i, 114 *sqq.*, letter of Negro, dated April 7, 1523. On St Mark's Day Pasquino had a special celebration, which the Pope forbade.

[6] In the passages collected in Gregorovius, viii, 380, note, 381 *sqq.*, 393 *sqq.*

[7] *Cf.* Pier. Valeriano, *De Infel. Lit.*, ed. Mencken, p. 178: " Pestilentia quæ cum Adriano VI invecta Romam invasit."

[8] For example, Firenzuola, *Opera*, vol. i, p. 116 (Milan, 1802), in the *Discorsi degli Animali.*

[9] *Cf.* the names in Höfler, *Sitzungsberichte der Wiener Academie*, vol. 82, p. 435 (1876).

him out till he looked "like a right well-dressed Pope"; how he came in a confused and tasteless procession from Ostia to Rome, took counsel about burning or drowning Pasquino, would suddenly break off the most important business when dinner was announced; and lastly, at the end of an unhappy reign, how he died of drinking too much beer—whereupon the house of his physician was hung with garlands by midnight revellers, and adorned with the inscription "Liberatori Patriæ S. P. Q. R." It is true that Giovio had lost his money in the general confiscation of public funds, and had received only a benefice by way of compensation because he was "no poet"—that is to say, no pagan.[1] But it was decreed that Adrian should be the last great victim. After the disaster which befell Rome in 1527 slander visibly declined along with the unrestrained wickedness of private life.

But while it was still flourishing was developed, chiefly in Rome, the greatest railer of modern times, Pietro Aretino. A glance at his life and character will save us the trouble of noticing many less distinguished members of his class.

We know him chiefly in the last thirty years of his life (1527–57), which he passed in Venice, the only asylum possible for him. From hence he kept all that was famous in Italy in a kind of state of siege, and here were delivered the presents of the foreign princes who needed or dreaded his pen. Charles V and Francis I both pensioned him at the same time, each hoping that Aretino would do some mischief to the other. Aretino flattered both, but naturally attached himself more closely to Charles, because he remained master in Italy. After the Emperor's victory at Tunis in 1535 this tone of adulation passed into the most ludicrous worship, in observing which it must not be forgotten that Aretino constantly cherished the hope that Charles would help him to a cardinal's hat. It is probable that he enjoyed special protection as Spanish agent, as his speech or silence could have no small effect on the smaller Italian Courts and on public opinion in Italy. He affected utterly to despise the Papal Court because he knew it so well; the true reason was that Rome neither could nor would pay him any longer.[2] Venice, which sheltered him, he was wise enough to leave unassailed. The rest of his relations with the great is mere beggary and vulgar extortion.

Aretino affords the first great instance of the abuse of publicity to such ends. The polemical writings which a hundred years earlier Poggio and his opponents

---

[1] The words of Pier. Valeriano, *De Infel. Lit.*, ed Mencken, p. 382, are most characteristic of the public feeling at Rome: "Ecce adest Musarum et eloquentiæ totiusque nitoris hostis acerrimus, qui literatis omnibus inimicitias minitaretur, quoniam, ut ipse dictitabat, Terentiani essent, quos quum odisse atque etiam persequi cœpisset voluntarium alii exilium, alias atque alias alii latebras quærentes tam diu latuere quoad Deo beneficio altero imperii anno decessit, qui si aliquanto diutius vixisset, Gothica illa tempora adversus bonas literas videbatur suscitaturus." The general hatred of Adrian was also due partly to the fact that in the great pecuniary difficulties in which he found himself he adopted the expedient of a direct tax. Ranke, *Päpste*, i, 411. It may here be mentioned that there were, nevertheless, poets to be found who praised Adrian. *Cf.* various passages in the *Coryciana* (ed. Rome, 1524), especially J. J., 2*b sqq.*

[2] To the Duke of Ferrara, January 1, 1536 (*Lettere*, ed. 1539, fol. 39): "You will now journey from Rome to Naples," "ricreando la vista avvilita nel mirar le miserie pontificali con la contemplazione delle eccellenze imperiali."

interchanged are just as infamous in their tone and purpose, but they were not composed for the press, but for a sort of private circulation. Aretino made all his profit out of a complete publicity, and in a certain sense may be considered the father of modern journalism. His letters and miscellaneous articles were

FIG. 78. ARETINO
By Titian
Florence, Palazzo Pitti

printed periodically, after they had already been circulated among a tolerably extensive public.[1]

Compared with the sharp pens of the eighteenth century, Aretino had the advantage that he was not burdened with principles, neither with liberalism nor philanthropy nor any other virtue, nor even with science; his whole baggage consisted of the well-known motto " Veritas odium parit." He never,

[1] The fear which he caused to men of mark, especially artists, by these means cannot be here described. The publicistic weapon of the German Reformation was chiefly the pamphlet dealing with events as they occurred; Aretino is a journalist in the sense that he has within himself a perpetual occasion for writing.

consequently, found himself in the false position of Voltaire, who was forced to disown his *Pucelle* and conceal all his life the authorship of other works. Aretino put his name to all he wrote, and openly gloried in his notorious *Ragionamenti*. His literary talent, his clear and sparkling style, his varied observation of men and things, would have made him a considerable writer under any circumstances, destitute as he was of the power of conceiving a genuine work of art, such as a true dramatic comedy; and to the coarsest as well as the most refined malice he added a grotesque wit so brilliant that in some cases it does not fall short of that of Rabelais.[1]

In such circumstances, and with such objects and means, he set to work to attack or circumvent his prey. The tone in which he appealed to Clement VII not to complain or to think of vengeance,[2] but to forgive, at the moment when the wailings of the devastated city were ascending to the castle of S. Angelo, where the Pope himself was a prisoner, is the mockery of a devil or a monkey. Sometimes, when he is forced to give up all hope of presents, his fury breaks out into a savage howl, as in the *Capitolo* to the Prince of Salerno, who after paying him for some time refused to do so any longer. On the other hand, it seems that the terrible Pierluigi Farnese, Duke of Parma, never took any notice of him at all. As this gentleman had probably renounced altogether the pleasures of a good reputation, it was not easy to cause him any annoyance; Aretino tried to do so by comparing his personal appearance to that of a constable, a miller, and a baker.[3] Aretino is most comical of all in the expression of whining mendicancy, as in the *Capitolo* to Francis I; but the letters and poems made up of menaces and flattery cannot, notwithstanding all that is ludicrous in them, be read without the deepest disgust. A letter like that one of his written to Michelangelo in November 1545 [4] is alone of its kind; along with all the admiration he expresses for the *Last Judgment* he charges him with irreligion, indecency, and theft from the heirs of Julius II, and adds in a conciliating postscript, " I only want to show you that if you are *divino*, I am not *d'acqua*." Aretino laid great stress upon it—whether from the insanity of conceit or by way of caricaturing famous men—that he himself should be called divine, as one of his flatterers had already begun to do; and he certainly attained so much personal celebrity that his house at Arezzo passed for one of the sights of the place.[5] There were, indeed, whole months during which he never ventured to cross his threshold at Venice, lest he should fall in with some incensed Florentine like the younger Strozzi. Nor did he escape the cudgels and the daggers of his enemies,[6] although they failed to have the effect which

---

[1] For example, in the *Capitolo* on Albicante, a bad poet; unfortunately the passages are unfit for quotation.
[2] *Lettere*, ed. Venez., 1539, fol. 12, dated May 31, 1527.
[3] In the first *Capitolo* to Cosimo. The truth is that Aretino carried it off so well that the Duke recommended him for a cardinalate.
[4] Gaye, *Carteggio*, ii, 332.
[5] See the insolent letter of 1536 in the *Lettere Pittor.*, i, App. 34. See above, p. 154, for the house where Petrarch was born in Arezzo.
[6] " L' Aretin, per Dio grazia, è vivo e sano,
　　Ma'l mostaccio ha fregiato nobilmente,
　　E più colpi ha, che dita in una mano."
　　MAURO, *Capitolo in Lode delle Bugie*

Berni prophesied him in a famous sonnet. Aretino died in his house, of apoplexy.

The differences he made in his modes of flattery are remarkable: in dealing with non-Italians he was grossly fulsome;[1] people like Duke Cosimo of Florence he treated very differently. He praised the beauty of the then youthful Prince, who in fact did share this quality with Augustus in no ordinary degree; he praised his moral conduct, with an oblique reference to the financial pursuits of Cosimo's mother, Maria Salviati, and concluded with a mendicant whine about the bad times and so forth. When Cosimo pensioned him,[2] which he did liberally, considering his habitual parsimony —to the extent, at last, of a hundred and sixty ducats a year —he had doubtless an eye to Aretino's dangerous character as Spanish agent. Aretino could ridicule and revile Cosimo, and in the same breath threaten the Florentine agent that he would obtain from the Duke his immediate recall; and if the Medicean prince felt himself at last to be seen through by Charles V he would naturally not be anxious that Aretino's jokes and rhymes against him should circulate at the Imperial Court. A curiously qualified piece of flattery was that addressed to the notorious Marquis of Marignano, who as Castellan of Musso (p. 44) had attempted to found an independent state. Thanking him for the gift of a hundred crowns, Aretino writes:

FIG. 79. SATYR MASK
By Michelangelo (?)
Florence, Museo Nazionale

All the qualities which a prince should have are present in you, and all men would think so were it not that the acts of violence inevitable at the beginning of all undertakings cause you to appear a trifle rough [*aspro*].[3]

It has often been noticed as something singular that Aretino reviled only the world, and not God also. The religious belief of a man who lived as he did is a matter of perfect indifference, as are also the edifying writings which

---

[1] See, for example, the letter to the Cardinal of Lorraine, *Lettere*, ed. Venez., fol. 29, dated November 21, 1534, and the letters to Charles V, in which he says that no man stands nearer to God than Charles.

[2] For what follows see Gaye, *Carteggio*, ii, 336, 337, 345.

[3] *Lettere*, ed. Venez., 1539, fol. 15, dated June 16, 1529. *Cf.* another remarkable letter to M. A., dated April 15, 1528, fol. 212.

he composed for reasons of his own.[1] It is, in fact, hard to say why he should
have been a blasphemer.   He was no professor, or theoretical thinker or writer;
and he could extort no money from God by threats or flattery, and was consequently never goaded into blasphemy by a refusal.   A man like him does
not take trouble for nothing.

It is a good sign of the present spirit of Italy that such a character and such
a career have become a thousand times impossible.   But historical criticism
will always find in Aretino an important study.

[1] He may have done so either in the hope of obtaining the red hat or from fear of the new activity of the
Inquisition, which he had ventured to attack bitterly in 1535 (*loc. cit.*, fol. 37), but which, after the reorganization
of the institution in 1542 suddenly took a fresh start, and soon silenced every opposing voice.

PART III

THE REVIVAL OF ANTIQUITY

CHAPTER I

INTRODUCTORY REMARKS

N OW that this point in our historical view of Italian civilization has been reached it is time to speak of the influence of antiquity, the " new birth " of which has been one-sidedly chosen as the name to sum up the whole period. The conditions which have been hitherto described would have sufficed, apart from antiquity, to upturn and to mature the national mind; and most of the intellectual tendencies which yet remain to be noticed would be conceivable without it. But both what has gone before and what we have still to discuss are coloured in a thousand ways by the influence of the ancient world; and though the essence of the phenomena might still have been the same without the classical revival, it is only with and through this revival that they are actually manifested to us. The Renaissance would not have been the process of world-wide significance which it is if its elements could be so easily separated from one another. We must insist upon it, as one of the chief propositions of this book, that it was not the revival of antiquity alone, but its union with the genius of the Italian people, which achieved the conquest of the Western world. The amount of independence which the national spirit maintained in this union varied according to circumstances. In the modern Latin literature of the period it is very small, while in plastic art, as well as in other spheres, it is remarkably great; and hence the alliance between two distant epochs in the civilization of the same people, because concluded on equal terms, proved justifiable and fruitful.[1] The rest of Europe was free either to repel or else partly or wholly to accept the mighty impulse which came forth from Italy. Where the latter was the case we may as well be spared the complaints over the early decay of medieval faith and civilization. Had these been strong enough to hold their ground they would be alive to this day. If those elegiac natures which long to see them return could pass but one hour in the midst of them they would gasp to be back in modern air. That in a great historical process of this kind flowers

---

[1 Against this view of Burckhardt's have arisen manifold objectors; but we must reject those who, placing the beginning of the Renaissance ever farther back in the Middle Ages, would see in the development of individualism its distinguishing mark. Against Burckhardt it can only be objected that he has not sufficiently stressed the development of the Renaissance out of the Middle Ages, the steady growth of one period into another.—W. G.]

of exquisite beauty may perish without being made immortal in poetry or tradition is undoubtedly true; nevertheless, we cannot wish the process undone. The general result of it consists in this—that by the side of the Church, which had hitherto held the countries of the West together (though it was unable to do so much longer), there arose a new spiritual influence, which, spreading itself abroad from Italy, became the breath of life for all the more instructed minds in Europe. The worst that can be said of the movement is that it was anti-

FIG. 80. FAÇADE OF THE MONASTERY AT FIESOLE, NEAR FLORENCE
Dating from about 1090 ; restored in 1300

popular, that through it Europe became for the first time sharply divided into the cultivated and uncultivated classes. The reproach will appear groundless when we reflect that even now the fact, though clearly recognized, cannot be altered. The separation, too, is by no means as cruel and absolute in Italy as elsewhere. The most artistic of her poets, Tasso, is in the hands of even the poorest.

The civilization of Greece and Rome, which ever since the fourteenth century obtained so powerful a hold on Italian life, as the source and basis of culture, as the object and ideal of existence, partly also as an avowed reaction

FIG. 81. THE SCHOOL OF ATHENS
By Raphael
Rome, Vatican

against preceding tendencies—this civilization had long been exerting a partial influence on medieval Europe, even beyond the boundaries of Italy. The culture of which Charles the Great was a representative was, in face of the barbarism of the seventh and eighth centuries, essentially a Renaissance, and could appear under no other form. Just as in the Romanesque architecture

FIG. 82. INTERIOR OF S. MINIATO AL MONTE, NEAR FLORENCE
Photo Alinari

of the North, beside the general outlines inherited from antiquity, remarkable direct imitations of the antique also occur, so too monastic scholarship had not only gradually absorbed an immense mass of materials from Roman writers, but the style of it, from the days of Eginhard onward, shows traces of conscious imitations.

But the resuscitation of antiquity took a different form in Italy from that which it assumed in the North. The wave of barbarism had scarcely gone by

178

before the people, in whom the former life was but half effaced, showed a consciousness of its past and a wish to reproduce it. Elsewhere in Europe men deliberately and with reflection borrowed this or the other element of classical civilization; in Italy the sympathies both of the learned and of the people were naturally engaged on the side of antiquity as a whole, which stood to them as a symbol of past greatness. The Latin language, too, was easy to an Italian, and the numerous monuments and documents in which the country abounded facilitated a return to the past. With this tendency other elements—the popular character, which time had now greatly modified, the political institutions

FIG. 83. THE ADORATION OF THE MAGI
By Niccolò Pisani
Relief on the pulpit of the Baptistery, Pisa

imported by the Lombards from Germany, chivalry and other Northern forms of civilization, and the influence of religion and the Church—combined to produce the modern Italian spirit, which was destined to serve as the model and ideal for the whole Western world.

How antiquity began to work in plastic art, as soon as the flood of barbarism had subsided, is clearly shown in the Tuscan buildings of the twelfth and in the sculptures of the thirteenth centuries. In poetry too there will appear no want of similar analogies to those who hold that the greatest Latin poet of the twelfth century, the writer who struck the keynote of a whole class of Latin poems, was an Italian. We mean the author of the best pieces in the so-called *Carmina Burana*. A frank enjoyment of life and its pleasures, as whose patrons the gods of heathendom are invoked, while Catos and Scipios hold the place of the saints and heroes of Christianity, flows in full current through the rhymed verses. Reading them through at a stretch, we can scarcely help coming to the

179

conclusion that an Italian, probably a Lombard, is speaking; in fact, there are positive grounds for thinking so.[1]   To a certain degree these Latin poems of the *clerici vagantes* of the twelfth century, with all their remarkable frivolity, are, doubtless, a product in which the whole of Europe had a share; but the writer of the song *De Phyllide et Flora* [2] and the *Æstuans interius* can have been a Northerner as little as the polished Epicurean observer to whom we owe *Dum Dianæ vitrea sero lampas oritur*.   Here, in truth, is a reproduction of the whole ancient view of life, which is all the more striking from the medieval form of the verse in which it is set forth.   There are many works of this and the following centuries in which a careful imitation of the antique appears both in the hexameter and pentameter of the metre in the classical, often mythological, character of the subject, and which yet have not anything like the same spirit of antiquity about them.   In the hexameter chronicles and other works of Gulielmus Apuliensis and his successors (from about 1100) we find frequent traces of a diligent study of Virgil, Ovid, Lucan, Statius, and Claudian; but this classical form is after all here a mere matter of archæology, as is the classical subject in collectors like Vincent of Beauvais, or in the mythological and allegorical writer, Alanus ab Insulis.   The Renaissance is not a mere fragmentary imitation or compilation, but a new birth; and the signs of this are visible in the poems of the unknown " Clericus " of the twelfth century.

But the great and general enthusiasm of the Italians for classical antiquity did not display itself before the fourteenth century.   For this a development of civic life was required, which took place only in Italy, and there not till then. It was needful that noble and burgher should first learn to dwell together on

---

[1] *Carmina Burana*, in the *Bibliothek des literarischen Vereins in Stuttgart*, vol. xvi (Stuttgart, 1847).   Another edition by Österley (Breslau, 1883).   The stay in Pavia (p. 68 *bis*), the Italian local references in general, the scene with the *pastorella* under the olive-tree (p. 146), the mention of the *pinus* as a shady field tree (p. 156), the frequent use of the word *bravium* (pp. 137, 144), and particularly the form ' Madii ' for ' Maji ' (p. 141) all speak in favour of our assumption.

[The conjecture of Dr Burckhardt that the best pieces of the *Carmina Burana* were written by an Italian is not tenable.   The grounds brought forward in its support have little weight (for example, the mention of Pavia—"Quis Paviæ demorans castus habeantur?"—which can be explained as a proverbial expression, or referred to a short stay of the writer at Pavia), cannot, further, hold their own against the reasons on the other side, and finally lose all their force in view of the probable identification of the author.   The arguments of O. Hubatsch, *Die lateinischen Vagantenlieder des Mittelalters*, p. 87 (Görlitz, 1870), against the Italian origin of these poems are, among others, the attacks on the Italian and praise of the German clergy, the rebukes of the Southerners as a *gens proterva*, and the reference to the poet as *transmontanus*.   Who he actually was, however, is not clearly made out.   That he bore the name of Walther throws no light upon his origin.   He was formerly identified with Gualterus de Mapes, a canon of Salisbury and chaplain to the English kings at the end of the twelfth century; since, by Giesebrecht, *Die Vaganten oder Goliarden und ihre Lieder, Allgemeine Monatschrift* (1855), with Walther of Lille or Chatillon, who passed from France into England and Germany, and thence possibly with the Archbishop Reinhold of Köln (1164 and 1175) to Italy (Pavia, etc.).   If this hypothesis, against which Hubatsch (*loc. cit.*) has brought forward certain objections, must be abandoned, it remains beyond a doubt that the origin of nearly all these songs is to be looked for in France, from whence they were diffused through the regular school which here existed for them over Germany, and there expanded and mixed with German phrases; while Italy, as Giesebrecht has shown, remained almost unaffected by this class of poetry. The Italian translator of Dr Burckhardt's work, Professor D. Valbusa, in a note to this passage (i, 235) also contests the Italian origin of the poem.   See J. Süssmilch, *Die lat. Vagantenpoesie des 12 u. 13 Jahrb*. (Leipzig, 1918).—L. G.]

[2] *Carm. Bur.*, p. 155, only a fragment; the whole in Wright, *Walter Mapes*, p. 258 (1841).   *Cf.* Hubatsch, pp. 27 *sqq.*, who points to the fact that a story often treated of in France is at the foundation.   *Æst. Inter.*, *Carm. Bur.*, p. 67; *Dum Dianæ, Carm. Bur.*, p. 124.   Additional instances: *Cor patet Jovi*; classical names for the loved one; once, when he calls her Blanciflor, he adds, as if to make up for it, the name of Helena.

FIG. 84. PARNASSUS
By Raphael
Rome, Vatican
Photo Anderson, Rome

equal terms, and that a social world should arise (see p. 151) which felt the want of culture, and had the leisure and the means to obtain it. But culture, as soon as it freed itself from the fantastic bonds of the Middle Ages, could not at once and without help find its way to the understanding of the physical and intellectual world. It needed a guide, and found one in the ancient civilization, with its wealth of truth and knowledge in every spiritual interest. Both the form and the substance of this civilization were adopted with admiring, gratitude; it became the chief part of the culture of the age.[1] The general condition of the country was favourable to this transformation. The medieval Empire, since the fall of the Hohenstaufen, had either renounced, or was unable to make good, its claims on Italy. The Popes had migrated to Avignon. Most of the political Powers actually in existence owed their origin to violent and illegitimate means. The spirit of the people, now awakened to self-consciousness, sought for some new and stable ideal on which to rest. And thus the vision of the world-wide empire of Italy and Rome so possessed the popular mind that Cola di Rienzi could actually attempt to put it into practice. The conception he formed of his task, particularly when tribune for the first time, could end only in some extravagant comedy; nevertheless, the memory of ancient Rome was no slight support to the national sentiment. Armed afresh with its culture, the Italian soon felt himself in truth citizen of the most advanced nation in the world.

It is now our task to sketch this spiritual movement, not, indeed, in all its fullness, but in its most salient features, and especially in its first beginnings.[2]

[1] In what way antiquity could serve as guide and teacher in all the higher regions of life is briefly sketched by Æneas Sylvius (*Opera*, p. 603, in *Epist.* 105, to the Archduke Sigismund).

[2] For particulars we must refer the reader to Roscoe, *Lorenzo de' Medici* and *Leo X*, as well as to Voigt, *Enea Silvio* (Berlin, 1856-63); to the works of Reumont and to Gregorovius, *Geschichte der Stadt Rom im Mittelalter*.

To form a conception of the extent which studies at the beginning of the sixteenth century had reached we cannot do better than turn to the *Commentarii Urbani* of Raphael Volaterranus (ed. Basil., 1544, fol. 16, etc.). Here we see how antiquity formed the introduction and the chief matter of study in every branch of knowledge, from geography and local history, the lives of great and famous men, popular philosophy, morals, and the special sciences, down to the analysis of the whole of Aristotle with which the work closes. To understand its significance as an authority for the history of culture we must compare it with all the earlier encyclopædias. A complete and circumstantial account of the matter is given in Voigt's admirable work *Die Wiederbelebung des klassischen Altertums oder das erste Jahrhundert des Humanismus* (Berlin, 1859, 3rd ed. 1893, 2 vols., revised by M. Lehnerdt). See also M. Monnier, *Le Quattrocento* (2 vols., Paris, 1900); and V. Rossi, *Il Quattrocento* (Florence, 1898).

CHAPTER II

Rome, the City of Ruins

ROME itself, the city of ruins, now became the object of a wholly different sort of piety from that of the time when the *Mirabilia Romæ* and the collection of William of Malmesbury were composed. The imaginations of the devout pilgrim, or of the seeker after marvels [1] and treasures, are supplanted in contemporary records by the interests of the patriot and the historian. In this sense we must understand Dante's words [2] that the stones of the walls of Rome deserve reverence, and that the ground on which the city is built is more worthy than men say. The jubilees, incessant as they were, have scarcely left a single devout record in literature properly so called. The best thing that Giovanni Villani (pp. 95–96) brought back from the jubilee of the year 1300 was the resolution to write his history, which had been awakened in him by the sight of the ruins of Rome. Petrarch gives evidence of a taste divided between classical and Christian antiquity. He tells us how often with Giovanni Colonna he ascended the mighty vaults of the Baths of Diocletian,[3] and there in the transparent air, amid the wide silence, with the broad panorama stretching far around them, they spoke, not of business, or political affairs, but of the history which the ruins beneath their feet suggested, Petrarch appearing in their dialogues as the partisan of classical, Giovanni of Christian, antiquity; then they would discourse of philosophy and of the inventors of the arts. How often since that time, down to the days of Gibbon and Niebuhr, have the same ruins stirred men's minds to the same reflections!

This double current of feeling is also recognizable in the *Dittamondo* of Fazio degli Uberti, composed about 1360—a description of visionary travels, in which the author is accompanied by the old geographer Solinus, as Dante was by Virgil. They visit Bari in memory of St Nicholas, and Monte Gargano

---

[1] In William of Malmesbury, *Gesta Regum Anglor.*, lib. ii, §§ 169, 170, 205, 206 (ed. London, 1840, vol. i, pp. 277 *sqq.* and pp. 354 *sqq.*), we meet with the dreams of treasure-hunters, Venus as ghostly love, and the discovery of the gigantic body of Pallas, son of Evander, about the middle of the eleventh century. *Cf.* Jac. ab Aquis, *Imago Mundi* (*Hist. Patr. Monum. Script.*, t. iii, col. 1603), on the origin of the house of Colonna, with reference to the discovery of hidden treasure. Besides the tales of the treasure-seekers, William of Malmesbury mentions the elegy of Hildebert of Mans, Bishop of Tours, one of the most singular examples of humanistic enthusiasm in the first half of the twelfth century.

[2] Dante, *Convivio*, tratt. iv, cap. v.

[3] *Epist. Fam.*, vi, 2, ed. Fracassetti, vol. i, p. 125; references to Rome before he had seen it, and expressions of his longing for the city, *Epist. Fam.*, vol. i, p. 213; vol. ii, pp. 336 *sqq.* See also the collected references in L. Geiger, *Petrarca*, p. 272, note 3. In Petrarch we already find complaints of the many ruined and neglected buildings, which he enumerates one by one (*De Rem. utriusque Fort.*, lib. i, dial. 118), adding the remark that many statues were left from antiquity, but no paintings (*loc. cit.*, 41).

of the archangel Michael, and in Rome the legends of Araceli and of S. Maria in Trastevere are mentioned. Still, the pagan splendour of ancient Rome unmistakably exercises a greater charm upon them. A venerable matron in torn garments—Rome herself is meant—tells them of the glorious past, and gives them a minute description of the old triumphs; [1] she then leads the strangers through the city and points out to them the seven hills and many of the chief ruins—" che comprender potrai, quanto fui bella."

FIG. 85. THE ROMAN FORUM IN THE FIRST HALF OF THE SIXTEENTH CENTURY
Drawing by Marten van Heemskerck
Berlin, Collection of Copper Engravings

Unfortunately this Rome of the schismatic and Avignonese Popes was no longer, in respect of classical remains, what it had been some generations earlier. The destruction of a hundred and forty fortified houses of the Roman nobles by the senator Brancaleone in 1258 must have wholly altered the character of the most important buildings then standing; for the nobles had no doubt ensconced themselves in the loftiest and best-preserved of the ruins. [2] Nevertheless, far more was left than we now find, and probably many of the remains had still their marble incrustation, their pillared entrances, and other

[1] *Dittamondo*, ii, cap. 3. The procession reminds one at times of the Three Kings and their suite in the old pictures. The description of the city (ii, cap. 31) is not without archæological value (Gregorovius, vi, 697, note 1). According to Polistoro (in Murat., xxiv, col. 845), Niccolò and Ugo d'Este journeyed in 1366 to Rome, "per vedere quelle magnificenze antiche, che al presente si possono vedere in Roma."
[2] Gregorovius, v, 316 *sqq.* Parenthetically we may quote foreign evidence that Rome in the Middle Ages was looked upon as a quarry. The famous Abbot Sugerius, who about 1140 was in search of lofty pillars for the rebuilding of St Denis, thought at first of nothing less than getting hold of the granite monoliths of the Baths of Diocletian, but afterward changed his mind. See *Sugerii Libellus Alter*, in Duchesne, *Hist. Franc. Scriptores*, iv, p. 352.

FIG. 86. PLAN OF THE CITY OF ROME IN THE FIFTEENTH CENTURY

ornaments where we now see only the skeleton of brickwork. In this state of things the first beginnings of a topographical study of the old city were made.

In Poggio's walks through Rome [1] the study of the remains themselves is for the first time more intimately combined with that of the ancient authors and inscriptions—the latter he sought out from among all the vegetation in which they were imbedded [2]—the writer's imagination is severely restrained, and the memories of Christian Rome carefully excluded. The only pity is that Poggio's work was not fuller and was not illustrated with sketches. Far more was left in his time than was found by Raphael eighty years later. He saw the tomb of Cæcilia Metella and the columns in front of one of the temples on the slope of the Capitol first in full preservation, and then afterward half destroyed, owing to that unfortunate quality which marble possesses of being easily burnt into lime. A vast colonnade near the Minerva fell piecemeal a victim to the same fate. A witness in 1443 tells us that this manufacture of lime still went on, "which is a shame, for the new buildings are pitiful, and the beauty of Rome is in its ruins." [3] The inhabitants of that day, in their peasants' cloaks and boots, looked to foreigners like cowherds; and, in fact, the cattle were pastured in the city up to the Banchi. The only opportunities for social gatherings were the services at church, on which occasion it was possible to get a sight of the beautiful women.

In the last years of Eugenius IV (d. 1447) Blondus of Forlì wrote his *Roma Instaurata*, making use of Frontinus and of the old *Libri Regionali*, as well as, it seems, of Anastasius. His object is not only the description of what existed, but still more the recovery of what was lost. In accordance with the dedication to the Pope, he consoles himself for the general ruin by the thought of the precious relics of the saints in which Rome was so rich. [4]

With Nicholas V (1447–55) that new monumental spirit which was distinctive of the age of the Renaissance appeared on the Papal throne. The new passion for embellishing the city brought with it on the one hand a fresh danger for the ruins, on the other a respect for them, as forming one of Rome's claims to distinction. Pius II was wholly possessed by antiquarian enthusiasm, and if he speaks little of the antiquities of Rome [5] he closely studied those of all other parts of Italy, and was the first to know and describe accurately the remains which abounded in the districts for miles round the capital. [6] It is

[1] *Poggii Opera*, fol. 50 *sqq. Ruinarum Urbis Romæ Descriptio*, written about 1430. The Baths of Caracalla and Diocletian had then their pillars and coating of marble. See Gregorovius, vi, 700–705.

[2] Poggio appears as one of the earliest collectors of inscriptions in his letter in the *Vita Poggii*, in Murat., xx, col. 177, and as collector of busts (col. 183, and letter in Shepherd-Tonelli, i, 258). See also *Ambros. Traversarii Epistolæ*, xxv, 42. A little book which Poggio wrote on inscriptions seems to have been lost. Shepherd, *Life of Poggio*, trad. Tonelli, i, 154 *sqq.*

[3] Fabroni, *Cosmus*, Adnot. 86. From a letter of Alberto degli Alberti to Giovanni de' Medici. See also Gregorovius, vii, 557. For the condition of Rome under Martin V see Platina, p. 227; and during the absence of Eugenius IV see Vespas. Fiorent., i, p. 23.

[4] *Roma Instaurata*, written in 1447, and dedicated to the Pope; first printed Rome, 1474.

[5] See, nevertheless, his distichs in Voigt, *Wiederbelebung des Altertums*, p. 275, note 2. He was the first Pope who published a Bull for the protection of old monuments (4 Kal. Maj., 1462), with penalties in case of disobedience. But these measures were ineffective. *Cf.* Gregorovius, vii, pp. 558 *sqq.*

[6] What follows is from Jo. Ant. Campanus, *Vita Pii II*, in Murat., iii, ii, col. 980 *sqq. Pii II Comment.*, pp. 48, 72 *sqq.*, 206, 248 *sqq.*, 501, and elsewhere.

true that, both as priest and cosmographer, he is interested alike in classical and Christian monuments and in the marvels of nature. Or was he doing violence to himself when he wrote that Nola was more highly honoured by the memory of St Paulinus than by all its classical reminiscences and by the heroic struggle of Marcellus? Not, indeed, that his faith in relics was assumed; but his mind was evidently rather disposed to an inquiring interest in nature and antiquity, to a zeal for monumental works, to a keen and delicate observation of human life. In the last years of his papacy, afflicted with the gout and yet in the most cheerful mood, he was borne in his litter over hill and dale to

FIG. 87. SEPULCHRAL MONUMENT OF CÆCILIA METELLA
Photo Seemann, Leipzig

Tusculum, Alba, Tibur, Ostia, Falerii, and Ocriculum, and whatever he saw he noted down. He followed the line of the Roman roads and aqueducts, and tried to fix the boundaries of the old tribes who dwelt round the city. On an excursion to Tivoli with the great Federigo of Urbino the time was happily spent in talk on the military system of the ancients, and particularly on the Trojan War. Even on his journey to the Congress of Mantua (1459) he searched, though unsuccessfully, for the labyrinth of Clusium mentioned by Pliny, and visited the so-called villa of Virgil, on the Mincio. That such a Pope should demand a classical Latin style from his abbreviators is no more than might be expected. It was he who, in the war with Naples, granted an amnesty to the men of Arpinum, as countrymen of Cicero and Marius, after whom many of them were named. It was to him alone, as both judge and patron, that Blondus could dedicate his *Roma Triumphans*, the first great attempt at a complete exposition of Roman antiquity.[1]

[1] First dated edition Brixen, 1482.

Nor was the enthusiasm for the classical past of Italy confined at this period to the capital. Boccaccio [1] had already called the vast ruins of Baiæ " old walls, yet new for modern spirits "; and since this time they were held to be the most interesting sight near Naples. Collections of antiquities of all sorts now became common.[2] Ciriaco of Ancona (d. 1457), who explained (1433) the Roman monuments to the Emperor Sigismund, travelled not only through Italy, but through other countries of the Old World, Hellas, and the islands of the Archipelago, and even parts of Asia and Africa, and brought back with him countless inscriptions and sketches. When asked why he took all this

FIG. 88. THE APPIAN WAY

trouble he replied, " To wake the dead." [3] The histories of the various cities of Italy had from the earliest times laid claim to some true or imagined connexion with Rome, had alleged some settlement or colonization which started from the capital;[4] and the obliging manufacturers of pedigrees seem constantly to have derived various families from the oldest and most famous blood of Rome. So highly was the distinction valued that men clung to it even in the light of the dawning criticism of the fifteenth century. When Pius II was at Viterbo [5] he said frankly to the Roman deputies who begged him to return,

---

[1] Boccaccio, *Fiammetta*, cap. 5, *Opere*, ed. Moutier, vi, 91.

[2] Geiger has shown that about 1335 a citizen of Treviso went to Venice to found a collection for himself, the catalogue of which has survived. See Müntz, *Les Arts à la Cour des Papes*, ii, p. 164, note, pp. 163–180, for information about Italian collections in the fourteenth and fifteenth centuries.—W. G.]

[3] His work, *Cyriaci Anconitani Itinerarium*, ed. Mehus (Florence, 1742). *Cf.* Leandro Alberti, *Descriz. di Tutto l'Italia*, fol. 285.

[4] Two instances out of many: the fabulous origin of Milan in Manipulus (in Murat., xi, col. 552), and that of Florence in Gio. Villani (who here, as elsewhere, enlarges on the forged chronicle of Ricardo Malespini), according to which Florence, being loyally Roman in its sentiments, is always in the right against the anti-Roman rebellious Fiesole (i, 9, 38, 41; ii, 2). Dante, *Inferno*, xv, 76.

[5] *Commentarii*, p. 206, in the fourth book.

" Rome is as much at home as Siena, for my house, the Piccolomini, came in
early times from the capital to Siena, as is proved by the constant use of the

FIG. 89. ROMAN AQUEDUCT (AQUA CLAUDIA)

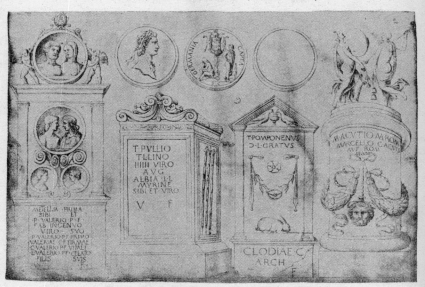

FIG. 90. ANCIENT MONUMENTS AND INSCRIPTIONS
From the sketch-book of Jacopo Bellini
Paris, Louvre

names Æneas and Sylvius in my family." He would probably have had no
objection to be held a descendant of the Julii. Paul II, a Barbo of Venice,

189

found his vanity flattered by deducing his house, notwithstanding an adverse pedigree, according to which it came from Germany, from the Roman Aheno-barbus, who led a colony to Parma, and whose successors were driven by party conflicts to migrate to Venice.[1] That the Massimi claimed descent from Q. Fabius Maximus, and the Cornaro from the Cornelii, cannot surprise us.

FIG. 91. APOLLO BELVEDERE
Rome, Vatican

On the other hand, it is a strikingly exceptional fact for the sixteenth century that the novelist Bandello tried to connect his blood with a noble family of Ostrogoths (i, *Nov.* 23).

To return to Rome. The inhabitants, "who then called themselves Romans," accepted greedily the homage which was offered them by the rest of Italy. Under Paul II, Sixtus IV, and Alexander VI magnificent processions formed part of the carnival, representing the scene most attractive to the imagination of the time—the triumph of the Roman Imperator. The sentiment of the people expressed itself naturally in this shape and others like it. In this mood of public feeling a report arose that on April 15, 1485, the corpse of a young Roman lady of the classical period—wonderfully beautiful and in perfect preservation— had been discovered.[2] Some Lombard masons digging out an ancient tomb on an estate of the convent of S. Maria Novella, on the Appian Way, beyond the Cæcilia Metella, were said to have found a marble sarcophagus with the inscription, " Julia, daughter of Claudius." On this basis the following

[1] Mich. Cannesius, *Vita Pauli II*, in Murat., iii, ii, col. 993. Toward even Nero, son of Domitius Ahenobarbus, the author will not be impolite, on account of his connexion with the Pope. He says of him only, "De quo verum Scriptores multa ac diversa commemorant." The family of Plato in Milan went still farther, and flattered itself on its descent from the great Athenian. Filelfo in a wedding speech, and in an encomium on the jurist Teodoro Plato, ventured to make this assertion; and a Giovanantonio Plato put the inscription on a portrait in relief carved by him in 1478 (in the court of the Pal. Magenta at Milan): " Platonem suum, a quo originem et ingenium refert."

[2] See on this point Nantiporto, in Murat., iii, ii, col. 1094; Infessura, in Eccard, *Scriptores*, ii, col. 1951; Matarazzo, in the *Archiv. Stor.*, xvi, ii, p. 180. Nantiporto, however, admits that it was no longer possible to decide whether the corpse was male or female. Cf. Pastor, *Päpste*, iii, pp. 253 *sqq.*

story was built. The Lombards disappeared with the jewels and treasure which were found with the corpse in the sarcophagus. The body had been coated with an antiseptic essence, and was as fresh and flexible as that of a girl of fifteen the hour after death. It was said that she still kept the colours of life, with eyes and mouth half open. She was taken to the palace of the " Conservatori," on the Capitol; and then a pilgrimage to see her

FIG. 92. ARIADNE
Formerly known as Cleopatra
Rome, Vatican

began. Among the crowd were many who came to paint her, " for she was more beautiful than can be said or written, and, were it said or written, it would not be believed by those who had not seen her." By the order of Innocent VIII she was secretly buried one night outside the Pincian Gate; the empty sarcophagus remained in the court of the " Conservatori." Probably a coloured mask of wax or some other material was modelled in the classical style on the face of the corpse, with which the gilded hair of which we read would harmonize admirably. The touching point in the story is not the fact itself, but the firm belief that an ancient body, which was now thought to be at last really before men's eyes, must of necessity be far more beautiful than anything of modern date.

Meanwhile the material knowledge of old Rome was increased by excavations. Under Alexander VI the so-called "Grotesques"—that is, the mural decorations of the ancients—were discovered, and the Apollo of the Belvedere was found at Porto d'Anzo. Under Julius II followed the memorable discoveries of the *Laocoön*, of the *Venus* of the Vatican, of the *Torso*, of the *Cleopatra*.[1] The palaces of the nobles and the cardinals began to be filled with ancient statues and fragments. Raphael undertook for Leo X that ideal restoration of the whole ancient city which his celebrated letter (1518 or 1519) speaks of.[2] After a bitter complaint over the devastations, which had not even

FIG. 93. COURTYARD WITH ANCIENT STATUES IN THE PALAZZO VALLE-CAPRANICA, ROME
Engraving after a drawing by Marten van Heemskerck

then ceased, and which had been particularly frequent under Julius II, he beseeches the Pope to protect the few relics which were left to testify to the power and greatness of that divine soul of antiquity whose memory was inspiration to all who were capable of higher things. He then goes on with penetrating judgment to lay the foundations of a comparative history of art, and concludes by giving the definition of an architectural survey which has been accepted since his time; he requires the ground plan, section, and elevation separately of every building that remained. How archæology devoted itself after his day to the study of the venerated city and grew into a special science,

---

[1] As early as Julius II excavations were made in the hope of finding statues. Vasari, xi, p. 302, *V. di Gio. da Udine*. *Cf.* Gregorovius, viii, 186.

[2] The letter was first attributed to Castiglione, *Lettere di Negozi del Conte Bald. Castiglione* (Padua, 1736 and 1769), but proved to be from the hand of Raphael by Daniele Francesconi in 1799. It is printed from a Munich manuscript in Passavant, *Leben Raphael's*, iii, p. 44. *Cf.* Gruyer, *Raphael et l'Antiquité*, i, 435–457 (1864). Quatremère, *Stor. d. Vita Ecc. di Rafaello*, ed. Longhena, p. 531. *Cf.* Pastor, iv, i, pp. 466 *sqq*.

and how the Vitruvian Academy at all events proposed to itself great aims,[1] cannot here be related. Let us rather pause at the days of Leo X, under whom the enjoyment of antiquity combined with all other pleasures to give to Roman life a unique stamp and consecration.[2] The Vatican resounded with song and music, and their echoes were heard through the city as a call to joy and gladness,

FIG. 94. RUINS
Woodcut from the *Poliphili Hypnerotomachia* (Aldus Manutius, Venice, 1499)

though Leo did not succeed thereby in banishing care and pain from his own life, and his deliberate calculation to prolong his days by cheerfulness was frustrated by an early death.[3] The Rome of Leo, as described by Paolo Giovio, forms a picture too splendid to turn away from, unmistakable as are also its

---

[1] *Lettere Pittoriche*, ii, 1, Tolomei to Landi, November 14, 1542.
[2] He tried "curis animique doloribus quacunque ratione aditum intercludere"; music and lively conversation charmed him, and he hoped by their means to live longer. *Leonis X Vita Anonyma*, in Roscoe, ed. Bossi, xii, p. 169.
[3] This point is referred to in the *Satires* of Ariosto. See the first ("Perc' ho molto," etc.) and the fourth ("Poiche, Annibale").

darker aspects—the slavery of those who were struggling to rise; the secret misery of the prelates, who, notwithstanding heavy debts, were forced to live in a style befitting their rank; the system of literary patronage which drove men to be parasites or adventurers; and, lastly, the scandalous maladministration of

FIG. 95. ADORATION OF THE SHEPHERDS
By Ghirlandaio
Florence, Accademia

the finances of the State.[1]   Yet the same Ariosto who knew and ridiculed all this so well gives in the sixth satire a longing picture of his expected intercourse with the accomplished poets who would conduct him through the city of ruins, of the learned counsel which he would there find for his own literary efforts, and of the treasures of the Vatican library.   These, he says, and not

---

[1] Ranke, *Päpste*, i, 408 *sqq.*; or better, Pastor, iv, 1, pp. 363 *sqq. Lettere dei Principi*, p. 107.   Letter of Negri, September 1, 1522: ". . . tutti questi cortigiani esausti da Papa Leone e falliti."   They avenged themselves after the death of Leo by satirical verses and inscriptions.

the long-abandoned hope of Medicean protection, were the real baits which attracted him when he was asked to go as Ferrarese ambassador to Rome.

But the ruins within and outside Rome awakened not only archæological zeal and patriotic enthusiasm, but an elegiac or sentimental melancholy. In Petrarch and Boccaccio we find touches of this feeling (pp. 183, 188). Poggio (p. 186) often visited the temple of Venus and Rome, in the belief that it was that of Castor and Pollux, where the Senate used so often to meet, and would lose himself in memories of the great orators Crassus, Hortensius, Cicero. The language of Pius II, especially in describing Tivoli, has a thoroughly sentimental ring,[1] and soon afterward (1467) appeared the first pictures of ruins, with a commentary by Polifilo.[2] Ruins of mighty arches and colonnades, half hid in plane-trees, laurels, cypresses, and brushwood figure in his pages. In the sacred legends it became the custom, we can hardly say how, to lay the scene of the birth of Christ in the ruins of a magnificent palace.[3] That artificial ruins became afterward a necessity of landscape-gardening is only a practical consequence of this feeling.

[1] *Pii II Comment.*, p. 251 in the fifth book. *Cf.* Sannazaro's elegy, *In Ruinas Cumarum Urbis Vetustissimæ* (*Opera*, fol. 236 *sqq.*, in Bk. II).

[2] Polifilo (that is, Franciscus Columna), *Hypnerotomachia, ubi humana omnia non nisi somnum esse docet atque obiter plurima scita sane quam digna commemorat* (Venice, Aldus Manutius, 1499). *Cf.* on this remarkable book and others A. Didot, *Alde Manuce*, pp. 132–142 (Paris, 1875), and Gruyer, *Raphael et l'Antiquité*, i, pp. 191 *sqq.*; J. Burckhardt, *Geschichte der Renaissance in Italien*, pp. 43 *sqq.*, and the work of A. Ilg (Vienna, 1872).

[3] While all the Fathers of the Church and all the pilgrims speak only of a cave. The poets too do without the palace. *Cf.* Sannazaro, *De Partu Virginis*, lib. ii, 284 *sqq.*

CHAPTER III

THE OLD AUTHORS

BUT the literary bequests of antiquity, Greek as well as Latin, were of far more importance than the architectural, and, indeed, than all the artistic remains which it had left. They were held in the most absolute sense to be the springs of all knowledge. The literary conditions of that age of great discoveries have been often set forth; no more can be attempted here than to point out a few less-known features of the picture.[1]

Great as was the influence of the old writers on the Italian mind in the fourteenth century and before, yet that influence was due rather to the wide diffusion of what had long been known than to the discovery of much that was new. The most popular Latin poets, historians, orators, and letter-writers, together with a number of Latin translations of single works of Aristotle, Plutarch, and a few other Greek authors, constituted the treasure from which a few favoured individuals in the time of Petrarch and Boccaccio drew their inspiration. The former, as is well known, owned and kept with religious care a Greek Homer, which he was unable to read. A complete Latin translation of the *Iliad* and *Odyssey*, though a very bad one, was made at Petrarch's suggestion and with Boccaccio's help by a Calabrian Greek, Leonzio Pilato.[2] But with the fifteenth century began the long list of new discoveries, the systematic creation of libraries by means of copies, and the rapid multiplication of translations from the Greek.[3]

Had it not been for the enthusiasm of a few collectors of that age, who shrank from no effort or privation in their researches, we should certainly possess only a small part of the literature, especially that of the Greeks, which is now in our hands. Pope Nicholas V, when only a simple monk, ran deeply into debt through buying manuscripts or having them copied. Even then he made no secret of his passion for the two great interests of the Renaissance, books and buildings.[4] As Pope he kept his word. Copyists wrote and spies

---

[1] Chiefly from Vespasiano Fiorentino, in the first volume of the *Spicileg. Romanum*, by Mai, from which edition the quotations in this book are made. More recent edition by Bartoli (Florence, 1859). The author was a Florentine bookseller and copying agent about and after the middle of the fifteenth century.

[2] *Cf.* Petrarch, *Epist. Fam.*, ed. Fracassetti, xviii, 2; xxiv, 12, var. 25, with the notes of Fracassetti in the Italian translation, vol. iv, pp. 92–101, line 196 *sqq.*, where the fragment of a translation of Homer before the time of Pilato is also given.

[3] Forgeries, by which the passion for antiquity was turned to the profit or amusement of rogues, are well known to have been not uncommon. See the articles in the literary histories on Annius of Viterbo.

[4] Vespas. Fiorent., p. 31. "Tommaso da Serezana usava dire, che dua cosa farebbe, se egli potesse mai spendere, ch' era in libri e murare. E l' una e l' altra fece nel suo pontificato." With respect to his translation see Æneas Sylvius, *De Europa*, cap. 59, p. 459, and Papencordt, *Ges. der Stadt Rom.*, p. 502. See especially Voigt, *op. cit.*, Book V.

searched for him through half the world. Perotto received 500 ducats for the Latin translation of Polybius; Guarino 1000 gold florins for that of Strabo, and he would have been paid 500 more but for the death of the Pope. Filelfo was to have received 10,000 gold florins for a metrical translation of Homer, and was only prevented by the Pope's death from coming from Milan to Rome. Nicholas left a collection of 5000 or, according to another way of calculating, 9000 volumes [1] for the use of the members of the Curia, which became the foundation of the library of the Vatican. It was to be preserved in the palace

FIG. 96. THE LIBRARY OF ST MARK'S, VENICE
Built by Jacopo Sansovino

itself, as its noblest ornament, like the library of Ptolemy Philadelphus at Alexandria. When the plague (1450) drove him and his Court to Fabriano, whence the best paper was procured, he took his translators and compilers with him, that he might run no risk of losing them.

The Florentine Niccolò Niccoli,[2] a member of that accomplished circle of friends which surrounded the elder Cosimo de' Medici, spent his whole fortune in buying books. At last, when his money was all gone, the Medici put their purse at his disposal for any sum which his purpose might require. We owe to him the completion of Ammianus Marcellinus, of the *De Oratore* of Cicero, the text of Lucretius which still has most authority, and other works; he

---

[1] Vespas. Fiorent., pp. 48 and 658, 665. *Cf.* J. Manetti, *Vita Nicolai V*, in Murat., iii, ii, col. 925 *sqq.* On the question whether and how Calixtus III partly dispersed the library again see Vespas. Fiorent., p. 284, with Mai's note. [That he did so Pastor says is untrue, while Rossi accepts it as a fact.—W. G.]

[2] Vespas. Fiorent., pp. 617 *sqq.*

197

persuaded Cosimo to buy the best manuscript of Pliny from a monastery at Lübeck. With noble confidence he lent his books to those who asked for them, allowed all comers to study them in his own house, and was ready to converse with the students on what they had read. His collection of eight hundred volumes, valued at 6000 gold florins, passed after his death, through Cosimo's intervention, to the monastery of S. Marco, on the condition that it should be accessible to the public, and is now one of the jewels of the Laurentian library.

FIG. 97. THE LIBRARY OF S. MARCO, FLORENCE
Built by Michelozzo
Photo Alinari

Of the two great book-finders, Guarino and Poggio, the latter,[1] on the occasion of the Council of Constance, and acting partly as the agent of Niccoli, searched industriously among the abbeys of South Germany. He there discovered six orations of Cicero and the first complete Quintilian, that of St Gall, now at Zürich; in thirty-two days he is said to have copied the whole of it in a beautiful handwriting. He was able to make important additions to Silius Italicus, Manilius, Lucretius, Valerius, Flaccus, Asconius Pedianus, Columella, Celsus, Aulus Gellius, Statius, and others; and with the help of Leonardo Aretino he unearthed the last twelve comedies of Plautus, as well as the Verrine orations, the *Brutus* and the *De Oratore* of Cicero.[2]

[1] Vespas. Fiorent., pp. 457 *sqq.*
[2] Poggio made his discoveries not only in South Germany, but in the monastery libraries of the Rhine and of Burgundy. Burckhardt also names Celsus and Gellius, but they were not discovered by Poggio, while he omits a commentary by Priscian on twelve lines of the *Æneid. Cf.* Walser, *Poggius Florentinus*, pp. 48 *sqq.* (Leipzig, 1914).—W. G.]

The famous Greek Cardinal Bessarion,[1] in whom patriotism was mingled with a zeal for letters, collected, at a great sacrifice (30,000 gold florins), five hundred manuscripts of pagan and Christian authors. He then looked round for some receptacle where they could safely lie until his unhappy country, if she ever regained her freedom, could reclaim her lost literature. The Venetian Government declared itself ready to erect a suitable building, and to this day the library of St Mark retains a part of these treasures.[2]

FIG. 98. THE BIBLIOTECA MEDICEO-LAURENZIANA
Sketch by Michelangelo
Florence
Photo Alinari

The formation of the celebrated Medicean library has a history of its own, into which we cannot here enter. The chief collector for Lorenzo the Magnificent was Johannes Lascaris. It is well known that the collection, after the plundering in the year 1494, had to be recovered piecemeal by Cardinal Giovanni de' Medici, afterward Leo X.[3]

The library of Urbino,[4] now in the Vatican, was wholly the work of the

[1] Vespas. Fiorent., p. 193. *Cf.* Marin Sanudo, in Murat., xxii, col. 1185 *sqq.*

[2] How the matter was provisionally treated is related in Malipiero, *Ann. Venet., Archiv. Stor.*, vii, ii, pp. 653, 655. Bessarion gave to the Venetian Republic 482 Greek and 264 Latin manuscripts; see H. Ormont in the *Revue des Bibliothèques*, iv, pp. 129–186 (1894).

[[3] See E. Rostagno, *Prefazione all' Eschilo Laurenziano*, pp. 6 *sqq.* (Florence, 1896), for slight corrections of the above information.—W. G.]

[4] Vespas. Fiorent., ed. Mai, pp. 124 *sqq.*, and *Inventario della Libreria Urbinata compilata nel Secolo XV da Federigo Veterano, Bibliotecario di Federigo I da Montefeltro Duca d'Urbino*, given by C. Guasti in the *Giornale Storico degli Archivi Toscani*, vi, 127–147 (1862), and vii, 46–55, 130–154 (1863). For contemporary opinions on the library see Favre, *Mélanges d'Hist. Lit.*, i, 127, note 6.

[The following is the substance of Dr Geiger's remarks on the subject of the old authors:

For the Medicean Library cf. *Delle Condicioni e delle Vicende della Libreria Medicea Privata dal 1494 al 1508*

great Federigo of Montefeltro (pp. 63 *sqq.*). As a boy he had begun to collect; in after-years he kept thirty or forty *scrittori* employed in various places, and spent in the course of time no less than 30,000 ducats on the collection. It was systematically extended and completed, chiefly by the help of Vespasiano, and his account of it forms an ideal picture of a library of the Renaissance. At Urbino there were catalogues of the libraries of the Vatican, of St Mark at Florence, of the Visconti at Pavia, and even of the library at Oxford. It was noted with pride that in richness and completeness none could rival Urbino. Theology and the Middle Ages were perhaps most fully represented. There was a complete Thomas Aquinas, a complete Albertus Magnus, a complete Buonaventura. The collection, however, was a many-sided one, and included every work on medicine which was then to be had. Among the 'moderns' the great writers of the fourteenth century—Dante and Boccaccio, with their complete works—occupied the first place. Then followed twenty-five select humanists, invariably with both their Latin and Italian writings and with all their translations. Among the Greek manuscripts the Fathers of the Church far outnumbered the rest; yet in the list of the classics we find all the works of Sophocles, all of Pindar, and all of Menander. The last must have quickly disappeared from Urbino,[1] else the philologists would have soon edited it. There were men, however, in this book-collecting age who raised a warning voice against the vagaries of the passion. These were not the enemies of learning, but its friends, who feared that harm would come from a pursuit which had become a mania. Petrarch himself protested against the fashionable folly of a useless heaping up of books ; and in the same century Giovanni Manzini ridiculed Andreolo de Ochis, a septuagenarian from Brescia, who was ready to sacrifice house and land, his wife and himself, to add to the stores of his library.

We have, further, a good deal of information as to the way in which

ricerche di Enea Piccolomini, Arch. Stor. Ital., pp. 265 *sqq.*, 3 serie, vol. xix, pp. 101–129, 254–281; xx, 51–94; xxi, 102–112, 282–296. Dr Geiger does not undertake an estimate of the relative values of the various rare and almost unknown works contained in the library, nor is he able to state where they are now to be found. He remarks that information as to Greece is much fuller than as to Italy, which is a characteristic mark of the time. The catalogue contains editions of the Bible, of single Books of it, with text and annotations, also Greek and Roman works in their then most complete forms, together with some Hebrew books—"tractatus quidam rabbinorum hebr."—with much modern work, chiefly in Latin, and with not a little in Italian.

Dr Geiger doubts the absolute accuracy of Vespasiano Fiorentino's catalogue of the library at Urbino. See the German edition, i, 313, 314.—S. G. C. M.]

[1] Perhaps at the capture of Urbino by the troops of Cesare Borgia. The existence of the manuscript has been doubted; but I cannot believe that Vespasiano would have spoken of the gnomic extracts from Menander, which do not amount to more than a couple of hundred lines, as "tutte le opere," nor have mentioned them in the list of comprehensive manuscripts, even though he had before him only our present Pindar and Sophocles. It is not inconceivable that this Menander may some day come to light.

[The catalogue of the library at Urbino (see foregoing note), which dates back to the fifteenth century, is not perfectly in accordance with Vespasiano's report, and with the remarks of Dr Burckhardt upon it. As an official document, it deserves greater credit than Vespasiano's description, which, like most of his descriptions, cannot be acquitted of a certain inaccuracy in detail and tendency to over-colouring. In this catalogue no mention is made of the manuscript of Menander. Mai's doubt as to its existence is therefore justified. Instead of "all the works of Pindar," we here find " Pindaris Olimpia et Pithia." The catalogue makes no distinction between ancient and modern books, contains the works of Dante (among others, *Comædiæ Thusco Carmine*) and Boccaccio in a very imperfect form; those of Petrarch, however, in all completeness. It may be added that this catalogue mentions many humanistic writings which have hitherto remained unknown and unprinted, that it contains collections of the privileges of the princes of Montefeltro, and carefully enumerates the dedications offered by translators or original writers to Federigo of Urbino.—L. G.]

manuscripts and libraries were multiplied.[1] The purchase of an ancient manuscript which contained a rare, or the only complete, or the only existing, text of an old writer was naturally a lucky accident of which we need take no further account. Among the professional copyists those who understood Greek took the highest place, and it was they especially who bore the honourable name of *scrittori*. Their number was always limited, and the pay they received very large.[2] The rest, simply called *copisti*, were partly mere clerks who made their living by such work, partly schoolmasters and needy men of learning, who desired an addition to their income, partly monks, or even nuns, who regarded the pursuit as a work pleasing to God. In the early stages of the Renaissance the professional copyists were few and untrustworthy; their ignorant and dilatory ways were bitterly complained of by Petrarch. In the fifteenth century they were more numerous, and brought more knowledge to their calling, but in accuracy of work they never attained the conscientious precision of the old monks. They seem to have done their work in a sulky and perfunctory fashion, seldom putting their signatures at the foot of the codices, and showed no traces of that cheerful humour, or of that proud consciousness of a beneficent activity, which often surprises us in the French and German manuscripts of the same period. This is more curious, as the copyists at Rome in the time of Nicholas V were mostly Germans or Frenchmen [3]— 'barbarians' as the Italian humanists called them, probably men who were in search of favours at the Papal Court, and who kept themselves alive meanwhile by this means. When Cosimo de' Medici was in a hurry to form a library for his favourite foundation, the Badia below Fiesole, he sent for Vespasiano, and received from him the advice to give up all thoughts of purchasing books, since those which were worth getting could not be had easily, but rather to make use of the copyists; whereupon Cosimo bargained to pay him so much a day, and Vespasiano, with forty-five writers under him, delivered two hundred volumes in twenty-two months.[4] The catalogue of the works to be copied was sent to Cosimo by Nicholas V,[5] who wrote it with his own hand. Ecclesiastical literature and the books needed for the choral services naturally held the chief place in the list.

---

[1] For what follows and in part for what has gone before see W. Wattenbach, *Das Schriftwesen im Mittelalter*, pp. 392 *sqq.*, 405 *sqq.*, 505 (2nd ed., Leipzig, 1875). *Cf.* also the poem, *De Officio Scribæ*, of Phil. Beroaldus, who however, is rather speaking of the public scrivener.

[2] When Piero de' Medici, at the death of Matthias Corvinus, the book-loving King of Hungary, declared that the *scrittori* must now lower their charges, since they would otherwise find no further employment (*sc.*, except in Italy), he can only have meant the Greek copyists, as the caligraphists, to whom one might be tempted to refer his words, continued to be numerous throughout all Italy. Fabroni, *Laurent. Magn.*, Adnot. 156. *Cf.* Adnot. 154.

[3] Gaye, *Carteggio*, i, p. 164. A letter of the year 1455 under Calixtus III. The famous miniature Bible of Urbino is written by a Frenchman, a workman of Vespasiano's. See D'Agincourt, *La Peinture*, tab. 78. On German copyists in Italy see further G. Campori, *Artisti Italiani e Stranieri negli Stati Estensi*, p. 277 (Modena, 1855), and *Giornale di Erudizione Artistica*, vol. ii, pp. 360 *sqq.* Wattenbach, *Schriftwesen*, p. 411, note 5. For German printers see below. [4] Vespas. Fiorent., p. 335.

[5] Ambr. Trav., *Epist.*, i, p. 63. The Pope was equally serviceable to the libraries of Urbino and Pesaro (that of Aless. Sforza, p. 45). *Cf.* *Arch. Stor. Ital.*, xxi, 103–106. The Bible and commentaries on it; the Fathers of the Church; Aristotle, with his commentators, including Averroes and Avicenna; Moses Maimonides; Latin translations of Greek philosophers; the Latin prose-writers; of the poets only Virgil, Statius, Ovid, and Lucan are mentioned.

FLAVII IOSEPHI PROLOGVS IN LIBRIS DE BELLO
IVDAICO INCIPIT. LEGE EVM FELICITER.

VONIAM BELLVM QVOD CV
ROMANIS GESSERE IVDEI OM
NIVM MAXIMVM QVE NOST
RA ETAS VIDIT QVEQ: AVDI

tu percepimus: ciuitates cum ciuitatibus gentes ue commisisse cum
gentibus quidam non quod rebus interfuerint sed uana & incong
rua narrantium sermones auribus colligentes oratorum more persci
bunt. Qui uero presto fuerunt aut romanorum obsequio aut odio
iudeorum contra fidem rerum falsa confirmant scriptis autem eorū
partim accusatio partim laudatio continetur nusquam uero exacta
fides reperitur historie Idcirco ego statui que retro barbaris antea
misi patria lingua digesta greca nunc his qui romano reguntur im
perio exponere Iosephus mathathie filius hebreus genere sacerdos ex
hierosolumis qui & initio cum romanis bello conflixi posteaq: gestis
que necessitas exegit interfui Nam cum hic ut dixi motus exortus
esset grauissimus romanorum quidem populum domesticus morbus
habebat Iudeorum autem qui etate ualidi & ingenio turbulenti
erant manu simul ac pecunia uigentes adeo temporibus insolen
ter abusi sunt ut pro tumultus magnitudine hos possidendarum
spei illos amittendarum partium orientis metus inuaderet Quo
niam iudei quidem cunctos qui transeufraten essent gentis nostre
etiam suos secum rebellatores esse crediderant Romanos autem
& finitimi galathe irritabant nec manus celtica quiescebat dissen
sionumq: erant plena omnia post neronem & multos quidem reges

FIG. 99. TITLE-PAGE FROM FLAVIUS JOSEPHUS' "DE BELLO JUDAICO"
Middle of the fifteenth century
Florence, Laurenziana

FIG. 100. VENETIAN PRINTING OF 1498, WITH A BORDER FROM AN ENGRAVED METAL PLATE

The handwriting was that beautiful modern Italian which was already in use in the preceding century, and which makes the sight of one of the books of that time a pleasure. Pope Nicholas V, Poggio, Giannozzo Manetti, Niccolò Niccoli, and other distinguished scholars themselves wrote a beautiful hand, and desired and tolerated none other. The decorative adjuncts, even when miniatures formed no part of them, were full of taste, as may be seen especially in the Laurentian manuscripts, with the light and graceful scrolls which begin and end the lines. The material used to write on, when the work was ordered by great or wealthy people, was always parchment; the binding, both in the Vatican and at Urbino, was a uniform crimson velvet with silver clasps. Where there was so much care to show honour to the contents of a book by the beauty of its outward form it is intelligible that the sudden appearance of printed books was greeted at first with anything but favour. The envoys of Cardinal Bessarion, when they saw for the first time a printed book in the house of Constantine Lascaris, laughed at the discovery "made among the barbarians in some German city," and Federigo of Urbino "would have been ashamed to own a printed book." [1]

But the weary copyists—not those who lived by the trade, but the many who were forced to copy a book in order to have it—rejoiced at the German invention,[2] " notwithstanding the praises and encouragements which the poets awarded to caligraphy." It was soon applied in Italy to the multiplication first of the Latin and then of the Greek authors, and for a long period nowhere but in Italy, yet it spread with by no means the rapidity which might have been expected from the general enthusiasm for these works. After a while the modern relation between author and publisher began to develop itself,[3] and under Alexander VI, when it was no longer easy to destroy a book, as Cosimo could make Filelfo promise to do,[4] the prohibitive censorship made its appearance.

The growth of textual criticism which accompanied the advancing study of languages and antiquity belongs as little to the subject of this book as the history of scholarship in general. We are here occupied not with the learning of the Italians in itself, but with the reproduction of antiquity in literature and life. One word more on the studies themselves may still be permissible.

Greek scholarship was chiefly confined to Florence and to the fifteenth and the beginning of the sixteenth centuries. It was never so general as Latin scholarship, partly because of the far greater difficulties which it involved,

---

[1] Vespas. Fiorent., p. 129.

[2] "Artes—Quis Labor est fessis demptus ab Articulis" in a poem by Robertus Ursus, about 1470, *Rerum Ital. Script. ex Codd. Fiorent.*, tom. ii, col. 693. He rejoices rather too hastily over the rapid spread of classical literature which was hoped for. Cf. Libri, *Hist. des Sciences Mathématiques*, ii, 278 *sqq.* (See also the eulogy of Lor. Valla, *Hist. Ztschr.*, xxxii, 62.) For the printers at Rome (the first were Germans: Hahn, Pannartz, Schweinheim) see Gaspar. Veron., *Vita Pauli II*, in Murat., iii, ii, col. 1046; Laire, *Spec. Hist. Typographiæ Romanæ, XV Sec.* (Rome, 1778); Gregorovius, vii, 525-33. For the first Privilegium in Venice see Marin Sanudo, in Murat., xxii, col. 1189.

[3] Something of the sort had already existed in the age of manuscripts. See Vespas. Fiorent., p. 656, on the *Cronaco del Mondo* of Zembino of Pistoja.

[4] Fabroni, *Laurent. Magn.*, Adnot. 212. It happened in the case of the libel *De Exilio*.

partly and still more because of the consciousness of Roman supremacy, and an instinctive hatred of the Greeks more than counterbalanced the attractions which Greek literature had for the Italians.[1]

The impulse which proceeded from Petrarch and Boccaccio,[2] superficial as was their own acquaintance with Greek, was powerful, but did not tell immediately on their contemporaries;[3] on the other hand, the study of Greek literature died out about the year 1520[4] with the last of the colony of learned Greek exiles, and it was a singular piece of fortune that Northerners like Agricola, Reuchlin, Erasmus, the Stephani, and Budæus had meanwhile made themselves masters of the language. That colony had begun with Manuel Chrysoloras and his relation John, and with George of Trebizond. Then followed, about and after the time of the conquest of Constantinople, Joh. Argyropulos, Theodore Gaza,[5] Demetrios Chalcondylas, who brought up his sons Theophilos and Basilios to be excellent Hellenists, Andronikos Kallistos, Marcos Musuros and the family of the Lascaris, not to mention others. But after the subjection of Greece by the Turks was completed the succession of scholars was maintained only by the sons of the fugitives and perhaps here and there by some Candian or Cyprian refugee. That the decay of Hellenistic studies began about the time of the death of Leo X was owing partly to a general change of intellectual attitude,[6] and to a certain satiety of classical influences which now made itself felt; but its coincidence with the death of the Greek fugitives was not wholly a matter of accident. The study of Greek among the Italians appears, if we take the year 1500 as our standard, to have been pursued with extraordinary zeal. The youths of that day learned to speak the language, and half a century later, like the Popes Paul III and Paul IV, they could still do so in their old age.[7] But this sort of mastery of the study presupposes intercourse with native Greeks.

Besides Florence, Rome and Padua nearly always maintained paid teachers of Greek, and Verona, Ferrara, Venice, Perugia, Pavia, and other cities occasional

[1] Even in Petrarch the consciousness of this superiority of Italians over Greeks is often to be noticed: *Epist. Fam.*, lib. i, *Ep.* 3; *Epist. Sen.*, lib. xii, *Ep.* 2; he praises the Greeks reluctantly: *Carmina*, lib. iii, 30, ed. Rossetti, vol. ii, p. 342. A century later Æneas Sylvius writes (Comm. to Panormita, *De Dictis et Factis Alfonsi*, App.): "Alfonsus tanto est Socrate major quanto gravior Romanus homo quam Græcus putatur." In accordance with this feeling the study of Greek was thought little of. From a document made use of below, written about 1460, it appears that Porcellio and Tommaso Seneca tried to resist the rising influence of Greek. Similarly Paolo Cortese (1490) was averse to Greek, lest the hitherto exclusive authority of Latin should be impaired, *De Hominibus Doctis*, p. 20. For Greek studies in Italy see especially the learned work of Favre, *Mélanges d'Hist. Littér.*, i, *passim*.

[2] See Geiger, *Exkurs* LIX in the twelfth German edition of *Die Kultur der Renaissance in Italien*.

[3] See above, p. 196, and *cf.* G. Voigt, *Wiederbelebung*, 323 *sqq.*

[4] The dying out of these Greeks is mentioned by Pierius Valerian, *De Infelicitate Literat.*, in speaking of Lascaris, ed. Mencken, p. 332. And Paul. Jovius, at the end of his *Elogia Literaria*, says of the Germans: "Quum literæ non latinæ modo cum pudore nostro, sed græcæ et hebraicæ in eorum terras fatali commigratione transierint" (about 1450). Similarly sixty years before (1482) Joh. Argyropulos had exclaimed, when he heard young Reuchlin translate Thucydides in his lecture-room at Rome, "Græcia nostra exilio transvolavit Alpes." Geiger, *Reuchlin*, pp. 26 *sqq.* (Leipzig, 1871). Burckhardt, 273. A remarkable passage is to be found in Jov. Pontan., *Antonius, Opp.*, iv, p. 203: "In Græcia magis nunc Turcaicum discas quam Græcum. Quicquid enim doctorum habent Græcæ disciplinæ, in Italia nobiscum victitat."

[5] Gaza came, as did Gemisthos Pletho and Bessarion, at the time of the Florentine council in 1438.

[6] Ranke, *Päpste*, i, 486 *sqq. Cf.* the end of this part of our work.

[7] Tommaso Gar, *Relazioni della Corte di Roma* i, pp. 338, 379.

teachers.[1] Hellenistic studies owed a priceless debt to the press of Aldo Manucci at Venice, where the most important and voluminous writers were for the first time printed in the original. Aldo ventured his all in the enterprise; he was an editor and publisher whose like the world has rarely seen.[2]

Along with this classical revival, Oriental studies now assumed considerable proportions.[3] Dante himself set a high value on Hebrew, though we cannot suppose that he understood it. From the fifteenth century onward scholars

ΆΡΙΣΤΟΤΈΛΟΥΣ ΉΘΙΚΩΝ ΕΎΔΗΜΊΩΝ. ΤΌ·Έ·

FIG. 101. SPECIMEN OF TYPE FROM THE PUBLISHED EDITION OF THE
WORKS OF ARISTOTLE AND THEOPHRASTUS
The edition referred to was printed by Aldus Manutius in Venice, 1495-98

were no longer content merely to speak of it with respect, but applied themselves to a thorough study of it. This scientific interest in the language was, however, from the beginning either furthered or hindered by religious considerations. Poggio, when resting from the labours of the Council of Constance, learnt Hebrew at that place and at Baden from a baptized Jew, whom he describes as

[1] George of Trebizond, teacher of rhetoric at Venice, with a salary of a hundred and fifty ducats a year (see Malipiero, *Archiv. Stor.*, vii, ii, p. 653). For the Greek chair at Perugia see *Archiv. Stor.*, xvi, ii, p. 19 of the Introduction. In the case of Rimini there is some doubt whether Greek was taught or not. Cf. *Aned. Litt.*, ii, p. 300. At Bologna, the centre of juristic studies, Aurispa had but little success. Details on the subject in Malagola.

[2] Exhaustive information on the subject in the admirable work of A. F. Didot, *Alde Manuce et l'Héllenisme à Venise* (Paris, 1875).

[3] For what follows see A. de Gubernatis, *Matériaux pour servir à l'Histoire des Études Orientales en Italie* (Paris, Florence, etc., 1876). Additions by Soave in the *Bolletino Italiano degli Studi Orientali*, i, 178 *sqq.* More precise details below.

"Stupid, peevish, and ignorant, like most converted Jews"; but he had to defend his conduct against Leonardo Bruni, who endeavoured to prove to him that Hebrew was useless, or even injurious. The controversial writings of the great Florentine statesman and scholar Giannozzo Manetti[1] (d. 1459) against the Jews afford an early instance of a complete mastery of their language and science.

His son Agnolo was from his childhood instructed in Latin, Greek, and Hebrew. The father, at the bidding of Nicholas V, translated the Psalms, but had to defend the principles of his translation in a work addressed to Alfonso. Commissioned by the same Pope, who had offered a reward of five thousand ducats for the discovery of the original Hebrew text of the Evangelist Matthew, he made a collection of Hebrew manuscripts, which is still preserved in the Vatican, and began a great apologetic work against the Jews.[2] The study of Hebrew was thus enlisted in the service of the Church. The Camaldolese monk Ambrogio Traversari learnt the language,[3] and Pope Sixtus IV, who erected the building for the Vatican library, and added to the collection extensive purchases of his own, took into his service *scrittori* (*librarios*)

FIG. 102. THE GRAMMAR LESSON
Relief by Luca della Robbia
Florence, Campanile

for Hebrew as well as for Greek and Latin.[4] The study of the language now became more general; Hebrew manuscripts were collected, and in some libraries, like that of Urbino, formed a specially valuable part of the rich treasure there stored up; the printing of Hebrew books began in Italy in 1475, and made the study easier both to the Italians themselves and to the other nations of Europe, who for many years drew their supply from Italy. Soon

[1] See below.
[2] See *Commentario della Vita di Messer Giannozzo Manetti, scritto da Vespasiano Bisticci*, especially pp. 11, 44, 91 *sqq.* (Torino, 1862).
[3] Vespas. Fiorent., ed. Mai, pp. 48, 476, 578, 614. Fra Ambrogio Camaldolese also knew Hebrew. *Ibid.*, p. 320. A. Trav., *Epist.*, lib. xi, 16.　　　　[4] Platina, *Vita Sixti IV*, p. 332.

there was no good-sized town where there were not individuals who were masters of the language and many anxious to learn it, and in 1488 a chair for Hebrew was founded at Bologna, and another in 1514 at Rome. The study became so popular that it was even preferred to Greek.[1]

Among all those who busied themselves with Hebrew[2] in the fifteenth century no one was of more importance than Pico della Mirandola. He was not satisfied with a knowledge of the Hebrew grammar and Scriptures, but penetrated into the Jewish Kabbalah and even made himself familiar with the literature of the Talmud. That such pursuits, though they may not have gone very far, were at all possible to him, he owed to his Jewish teachers. Most of the instruction in Hebrew was in fact given by Jews, some of whom, though generally not till after conversion to Christianity, became distinguished university professors and much-esteemed writers.[3]

[1] Benedictus Faleus, *De Origine Hebraicarum Græcarum Latinarumque Literarum* (Naples, 1520).

[2] For Dante see Wegele, *Dante*, 2nd ed., p. 268, and Lasinio, *Dante e le Lingue Semitiche*, in the *Rivista Orientale* (Florence, 1867–68). On Poggio, *Opera*, p. 297; Leon. Bruni, *Epist.*, lib. ix, 12; cf. Gregorovius, vii, 555, and Shepherd-Tonelli, *Vita di Poggio*, i, 65. The letter of Poggio to Niccoli, in which he treats of Hebrew, has been published in French and Latin under the title *Les Bains de Bade par Pogge*, by Antony Méray (Paris, 1876). Poggio desired to know on what principles Jerome translated the Bible, while Bruni maintained that now that Jerome's translation was in existence distrust was shown to it by learning Hebrew. For Manetti as a collector of Hebrew manuscripts see Steinschneider, in the work quoted below. In the library at Urbino there were in all sixty-one Hebrew manuscripts. Among them a Bible "opus mirabile et integrum, cum glossis mirabiliter scriptus in modo avium, arborum et animalium in maximo volumine, ut vix a tribus hominibus feratur." These, as appears from Assemanni's list, are now mostly in the Vatican. On the first printing in Hebrew see Steinschneider and Cassel, *Jud. Typographie in Esch. u. Gruber, Realencyclop.*, sect. ii, Bd. 28, p. 34, and *Catal. Bodl.*, by Steinschneider, pp. 2821–2866 (1852–60). It is characteristic that of the two first printers one belonged to Mantua, the other to Reggio, in Calabria, so that the printing of Hebrew books began almost contemporaneously at the two extremities of Italy. In Mantua the printer was a Jewish physician, who was helped by his wife. It may be mentioned as a curiosity that in the *Hypnerotomachia* of Polifilo, written 1467, printed 1499, fol. 68a, there is a short passage in Hebrew; otherwise no Hebrew occurs in the Aldine editions before 1501. The Hebrew scholars in Italy are given by De Gubernatis (p. 80), but authorities are not quoted for them singly. (Marco Lippomanno is omitted; cf. Steinschneider in the book given below.) Paolo de Canale is mentioned as a learned Hebraist by Pier. Valerian, *De Infel. Literat.*, ed. Mencken, p. 296; in 1488 professor in Bologna, Mag. *Vicentius*; cf. *Costituzione, Discipline e Riforme dell' Antico Studio Bolognese: Memoria del Prof. Luciano Scarabelli* (Piacenza, 1876); in 1514 professor in Rome, Agarius Guidacerius, according to Gregorovius, viii, 292, and the passages there quoted. On Guidacerius see Steinschneider, *Bibliogr. Handbuch*, pp. 56, 157–161 (Leipzig, 1859).

[3 The literary activity of the Jews in Italy is too great and of too wide an influence to be passed over altogether in silence. The following paragraphs, which, not to overload the text, I have relegated to the notes, are wholly the substance of communications made me by Dr M. Steinschneider, of Berlin,[1] to whom I here take the opportunity of expressing my thanks for his constant and friendly help. He has given exhaustive evidence on the subject in his profound and instructive treatise *Letteratura Italiana dei Giudei*, in the review *Il Buonarotti*, vols. vi, viii, xi, xii (Rome, 1871–77; also printed separately), to which, once for all, I refer the reader.

There were many Jews living in Rome at the time of the Second Temple. They had so thoroughly adopted the language and civilization prevailing in Italy that even on their tombs they used not Hebrew, but Latin and Greek inscriptions (communicated by Garucci; see Steinschneider, *Hebr. Bibliogr.*, vi, p. 102, 1863). In Lower Italy especially Greek learning survived during the Middle Ages among the inhabitants generally, and particularly among the Jews, of whom some are said to have taught at the University of Salerno, and to have rivalled the Christians in literary productiveness (cf. Steinschneider, *Donnolo*, in Virchow's *Archiv.*, Bd. 39, 40). This supremacy of Greek culture lasted till the Saracens conquered Lower Italy. But before this conquest the Jews of Middle Italy had been striving to equal or surpass their brethren of the South. Jewish learning centred in Rome, and from there spread, as early as the sixteenth century, to Cordova, Kairowan, and South Germany. By means of these emigrants Italian Judaism became the teacher of the whole race. Through its works, especially through the work *Aruch*, of Nathan ben Jechiel (1101), a great dictionary to the Talmud, the Midraschim, and the Thargum, " which, though not informed by a genuine scientific spirit, offers so rich a store of matter and rests on such early authorities that its treasures have even now not been wholly exhausted," it exercised indirectly a great influence (Abraham Geiger, *Das Judenthum und seine Geschichte*, Bd. ii, p. 170, Breslau,

Among the Oriental languages, Arabic was studied as well as Hebrew. The science of medicine, no longer satisfied with the older Latin translations of the great Arabian physicians, had constant recourse to the originals, to which an easy access was offered by the Venetian consulates in the East, where Italian doctors were regularly kept. But the Arabian scholarship of the Renaissance is only a feeble echo of the influence which Arabian civilization in the Middle Ages exercised over Italy and the whole cultivated world—an influence which not only preceded that of the Renaissance, but in some respects was hostile to it, and which did not surrender without a struggle the place which it had long and vigorously asserted. Hieronimo Ramusio, a Venetian physician, translated a great part of Avicenna from the Arabic, and died at Damascus in 1486. Andrea Mongajo of Belluno,[1] a disciple of the same Avicenna, lived long at Damascus, learnt Arabic, and improved on his master. The Venetian Government afterward appointed him as professor of this subject at Padua. The example set by Venice was followed by other Governments. Princes and wealthy men rivalled one another in collecting Arabic manuscripts. The first

1865; and the same author's *Nachgelassene Schriften*, Bd. II, pp. 129 and 154, Berlin, 1875). A little later, in the thirteenth century, the Jewish literature in Italy brought Jews and Christians into contact, and received through Frederick II, and still more perhaps through his son Manfred, a kind of official sanction. Of this contact we have evidence in the fact that an Italian, Niccolò di Giovinazzo, studied with a Jew, Moses ben Salomo, the Latin translation of the famous work of Maimonides, *More Nebuchim*; of this sanction in the fact that the Emperor, who was distinguished for his freethinking as much as for his fondness for Oriental studies, probably was the cause of this Latin translation being made, and summoned the famous Anatoli from Provence into Italy, to translate works of Averroes into Hebrew (*cf.* Steinschneider, *Hebr. Bibliogr.*, xv, 86, and Renan, *L'Averroes et l'Averroisme*, p. 290, 3rd ed., Paris, 1866). These measures prove the acquaintance of early Jews with Latin, which rendered intercourse possible between them and Christians—an intercourse which bore sometimes a friendly and sometimes a polemical character. Still more than Anatoli, Hillel ben Samuel, in the latter half of the thirteenth century, devoted himself to Latin literature; he studied in Spain, returned to Italy, and here made many translations from Latin into Hebrew; among them of writings of Hippocrates in a Latin version. (This was printed 1647 by Gaiotius, and passed for his own.) In this translation he introduced a few Italian words by way of explanation, and thus perhaps, or by his whole literary procedure, laid himself open to the reproach of despising Jewish doctrines.

But the Jews went farther than this. At the end of the thirteenth and in the fourteenth century they drew so near to Christian science and to the representatives of the culture of the Renaissance that one of them, Giuda Romano, in a series of hitherto unprinted writings, laboured zealously at the scholastic philosophy, and in one treatise used Italian words to explain Hebrew expressions. He is one of the first to do so (Steinschneider, *Giuda Romano*, Rome, 1870). Another, Giuda's cousin Manoella, a friend of Dante, wrote in imitation of him a sort of *Divine Comedy* in Hebrew, in which he extols Dante, whose death he also bewailed in an Italian sonnet (Abraham Geiger, *Jüd. Zeitsch.*, v, 286–331, Breslau, 1867). A third, Mose Riete, born toward the end of the century, wrote works in Italian (a specimen in the catalogue of Hebrew manuscripts, Leyden, 1858). In the fifteenth century we can clearly recognize the influence of the Renaissance in Messer Leon, a Jewish writer who, in his *Rhetoric*, uses Quintilian and Cicero as well as Jewish authorities. One of the most famous Jewish writers in Italy in the fifteenth century was Eliah del Medigo, a philosopher who taught publicly as a Jew in Padua and Florence, and was once chosen by the Venetian Senate as arbitrator in a philosophical dispute (Abraham Geiger, *Nachgelassene Schriften*, Bd. iii, 3, Berlin, 1876). Eliah del Medigo was the teacher of Pico della Mirandola; besides him, Jochanan Alemanno (*cf.* Steinschneider, *Polem. u. Apolog. Lit.*, Anh. 7, §25, Leipzig, 1877). The list of learned Jews in Italy may be closed by Kalonymos ben David and Abraham de Balmes (d. 1523), to whom the greater part of the translations of Averroes from Hebrew into Latin is due, which were still publicly read at Padua in the seventeenth century. To this scholar may be added the Jewish Aldus, Gerson Soncino, who not only made his press the centre of Jewish printing, but, by publishing Greek works, trespassed on the ground of the great Aldus himself (Steinschneider, *Gerson Soncino und Aldus Manutius*, Berlin, 1858).—L. G.]

[1] Pier. Valerian., *De Infel. Lit.*, ed. Mencken, 301, speaking of Mongajo. Gubernatis, p. 184, identifies him with Andrea Alpago of Bellemo, said to have also studied Arabian literature and to have travelled in the East. On Arabic studies generally, Gubernatis, pp. 173 *sqq.* For a translation made 1341 from Arabic into Italian *cf.* Narducci, *Intorno ad Una Tradizione Italiana di Una Composizione Astronomica di Alfonso X Rè di Castiglia* (Rome, 1865). On Ramusio see Sansovino, *Venezia*, fol. 250.

Arabian printing-press was begun at Fano under Julius II and consecrated in 1514 under Leo X.[1]

We must here linger for a moment over Pico della Mirandola before passing on to the general effects of humanism. He was the only man who loudly and vigorously defended the truth and science of all ages against the one-

IOAN·PICVS·MIRANDVLA~

sided worship of classical antiquity.[2] He knew how to value not only Averroes and the Jewish investigators, but also the scholastic writers of the Middle Ages, according to the matter of their writings. He seems to hear them say, " We shall live for ever, not in the schools of word-catchers, but in the circle of the wise, where they talk not of the mother of Andromache or of the sons of Niobe, but of the deeper causes of things human and divine; he who looks closely will see that even the barbarians had intelligence (*mercurium*) not on the tongue, but in the breast." Himself writing a vigorous and not inelegant Latin, and a master of clear exposition, he despised the purism of pedants

FIG. 103. PICO DELLA MIRANDOLA
Florence, Uffizi
Photo Alinari

and the current overestimate of borrowed forms, especially when joined, as they often are, with one-sidedness, and involving indifference to the wider truth of the things themselves. Looking at Pico, we can guess at the lofty flight which Italian philosophy would have taken had not the Counter-Reformation annihilated the higher spiritual life of the people.

[1] Gubernatis, p. 188. The first book contains Christian prayers in Arabic; the first Italian translations of the Koran appeared in 1547. In 1499 we meet with a few not very successful Arabic types in the work of Polifilo, b. 7*a*. For the beginnings of Egyptian studies see Gregorovius, viii, p. 304.

[2] Especially in the important letter of 1485 to Ermolao Barbaro, in *Ang. Politian. Epistolæ*, lib. ix. *Cf.* Jo. Pici, *Oratio de Hominis Dignitate*. For this discourse see the end of Part IV; on Pico himself more will be given in Part VI, Chapter IV.

CHAPTER IV

HUMANISM IN THE FOURTEENTH CENTURY

HO, now, were those who acted as mediators between their own age and a venerated antiquity, and made the latter a chief element in the culture of the former?

They were a crowd of the most miscellaneous sort, wearing one face to-day and another to-morrow; but they clearly felt themselves, and it was fully recognized by their time, that they formed a wholly new element in society. The *clerici vagantes* of the twelfth century, whose poetry we have already referred to (p. 180), may perhaps be taken as their forerunners—the same unstable existence, the same free and more than free views of life, and the germs at all events of the same pagan tendencies in their poetry. But now, as competitor with the whole culture of the Middle Ages, which was essentially clerical and was fostered by the Church, there appeared a new civilization, founding itself on that which lay on the other side of the Middle Ages. Its active representatives became influential[1] because they knew what the ancients knew, because they tried to write as the ancients wrote, because they began to think, and soon to feel, as the ancients thought and felt. The tradition to which they devoted themselves passed at a thousand points into genuine reproduction.

Some modern writers deplore the fact that the germs of a far more independent and essentially national culture, such as appeared in Florence about the year 1300, were afterward so completely swamped by the humanists.[2] There was then, we are told, nobody in Florence who could not read; even the donkey-men sang the verses of Dante; the best Italian manuscripts which we possess belonged originally to Florentine artisans; the publication of a popular encyclopædia, like the *Tesoro* of Brunetto Latini, was then possible; and all this was founded on a strength and soundness of character due to the universal participation in public affairs, to commerce and travel, and to the systematic reprobation of idleness. The Florentines, it is urged, were at that time respected and influential throughout the whole world, and were called in that year, not without reason, by Pope Boniface VIII, "the fifth element." The rapid progress of humanism after the year 1400 paralysed native impulses. Henceforth men looked to antiquity only for the solution of every problem, and consequently allowed literature to sink into mere quotation. Nay, the

---

[1] Their estimate of themselves is indicated by Poggio (*De Avaritia*, fol. 2), according to whom only such persons could say that they had lived (*se vixisse*) who had written learned and eloquent books in Latin or translated Greek into Latin.

[2] Especially Libri, *Histoires des Sciences Mathém.*, ii, 159 *sqq.*, 258 *sqq.*

very fall of civil freedom is partly to be ascribed to all this, since the New Learning rested on obedience to authority, sacrificed municipal rights to Roman law, and thereby both sought and found the favour of the despots.

These charges will occupy us now and then at a later stage of our inquiry, when we shall attempt to reduce them to their true value and to weigh the losses against the gains of this movement. For the present we must confine ourselves to showing how the civilization even of the vigorous fourteenth century necessarily prepared the way for the complete victory of humanism, and how precisely the greatest representatives of the national Italian spirit were themselves the men who opened wide the gate for the measureless devotion to antiquity in the fifteenth century.

To begin with Dante. If a succession of men of equal genius had presided over Italian culture, whatever elements their natures might have absorbed from the antique, they still could not fail to retain a characteristic and strongly marked national stamp. But neither Italy nor Western Europe produced another Dante, and he was and remained the man who first thrust antiquity into the foreground of national culture. In the *Divine Comedy* he treats the ancient and the Christian worlds not, indeed, as of equal authority, but as parallel to one another. Just as at an earlier period of the Middle Ages types and anti-types were sought in the history of the Old and New Testaments, so does Dante constantly bring together a Christian and a pagan illustration of the same fact.[1] It must be remembered that the Christian cycle of history and legend was familiar, while the ancient was relatively unknown, was full of promise and of interest, and must necessarily have gained the upper hand in the competition for public sympathy when there was no longer a Dante to hold the balance between the two.

Petrarch, who lives in the memory of most people nowadays chiefly as a great Italian poet, owed his fame among his contemporaries far rather to the fact that he was a kind of living representative of antiquity, that he imitated all styles of Latin poetry, endeavoured by his voluminous historical and philosophical writings not to supplant, but to make known, the works of the ancients, and wrote letters that, as treatises on matters of antiquarian interest, obtained a reputation which to us is unintelligible, but which was natural enough in an age without handbooks. Petrarch himself trusted and hoped that his Latin writings would bring him fame with his contemporaries and with posterity, and thought so little of his Italian poems that, as he often tells us, he would have destroyed them gladly if he could have succeeded thereby in blotting them out from the memory of men.

It was the same with Boccaccio. For two centuries, when but little was known of the *Decamerone* [2] north of the Alps, he was famous all over Europe

---

[1] *Purgatorio*, xviii, contains striking instances. Mary hastens over the mountains, Cæsar to Spain; Mary is poor and Fabricius disinterested. We may here remark on the chronological introduction of the Sibyls into the profane history of antiquity as attempted by Uberti in his *Dittamondo* (i, cap. 14, 15), about 1360.

[2] The first German translation of the *Decamerone*, by H. Steinhovel, was printed in 1472, and soon became popular. The translations of the whole *Decamerone* were almost everywhere preceded by those of the story of Griselda, written in Latin by Petrarch.

FIG. 104. THE CROWNING OF THE POETS BY ÆNEAS SYLVIUS
By Pinturicchio
Siena, Cathedral Library
Photo Alinari

simply on account of his Latin compilations on mythology, geography, and biography.[1]   One of these, *De Genealogia Deorum*, contains in the fourteenth and fifteenth books a remarkable appendix, in which he discusses the position of the then youthful humanism with regard to the age.   We must not be misled by his exclusive references to *poesia*, as closer observation shows that he means thereby the whole mental activity of the poet-scholars.[2]   This it is whose enemies he so vigorously combats—the frivolous ignoramuses who have no soul for anything but debauchery; the sophistical theologian, to whom Helicon, the Castalian fountain, and the grove of Apollo were foolishness; the greedy lawyers, to whom poetry was a superfluity, since no money was to be made by it; finally the mendicant friars, described periphrastically, but clearly enough, who made free with their charges of paganism and immorality.[3]   Then follows the defence of poetry, the proof that the poetry of the ancients and of their modern followers contains nothing mendacious, the praise of it, and especially of the deeper and allegorical meanings which we must always attribute to it, and of that calculated obscurity which is intended to repel the dull minds of the ignorant.

And finally, with a clear reference to his own scholarly work,[4] the writer justifies the new relation in which his age stood to paganism.   The case was wholly different, he pleads, when the Early Church had to fight its way among the heathen.   Now—praised be Jesus Christ!—true religion was strengthened, paganism destroyed, and the victorious Church in possession of the hostile camp.   It was now possible to touch and study paganism almost (*fere*) without danger.   Boccaccio, however, did not hold this liberal view consistently. The ground of his apostasy lay partly in the mobility of his character, partly in the still powerful and widespread prejudice that classical pursuits were unbecoming in a theologian.   To these reasons must be added the warning given him in the name of the dead Pietro Petroni by the monk Gioacchino Ciani to give up his pagan studies under pain of early death.   He accordingly determined to abandon them, and was brought back from this cowardly resolve only by the earnest exhortations of Petrarch, and by the latter's able demonstration that humanism was reconcilable with religion.[5]

There was thus a new cause in the world and a new class of men to maintain it.   It is idle to ask if this cause ought not to have stopped short in its career

---

[1] These Latin writings of Boccaccio have been admirably discussed by Schück, *Zur Characteristik des ital. Hum. im 14 und 15 Jahrh.* (Breslau, 1865); and in an article in Fleckeisen and Masius, *Jahrbücher für Phil. und Pädag.*, Bd. xx (1874).

[2] *Poeta*, even in Dante (*La Vita Nuova*, p. 47), means only the writer of Latin verses, while for Italian the expressions *Rimatore, Dicitore per rima*, are used.   It is true that the names and ideas became mixed in course of time.

[3] Petrarch too at the height of his fame complained in moments of melancholy that his evil star decreed him to pass his last years among scoundrels (*extremi fures*).   In the imaginary letter to Livy, *Epist. Fam.*, ed. Fracassetti, lib. xxiv, *Ep.* 8.   That Petrarch defended poetry, and how, is well known (*cf.* Geiger, *Petr.*, pp. 113–117).   Besides the enemies who beset him in common with Boccaccio, he had to face the doctors (cf. *Invectivæ in Medicum Objurgantem*, lib. i and ii).

[4] Boccaccio, in a later letter to Jacobus Pizinga (*Opere Volgari*, vol. xvi), confines himself more strictly to poetry properly so called.   And yet he recognizes as poetry only that which treats of antiquity, and ignores the Troubadours.

[5] Petrarch, *Epist. Senil.*, lib. i, *Ep.* 5.

FIG. 105. SEPULCHRAL MONUMENT OF CARLO ARETINO
By Desiderio da Settignano
Florence, S. Croce

of victory, to have restrained itself deliberately, and conceded the first place to purely national elements of culture. No conviction was more firmly rooted in the popular mind than that antiquity was the highest title to glory which Italy possessed.

There was a symbolical ceremony familiar to this generation of poet-scholars which lasted on into the fifteenth and sixteenth centuries, though losing the higher sentiment which inspired it—the coronation of the poets with the laurel wreath. The origin of this system in the Middle Ages is obscure, and the ritual of the ceremony never became fixed. It was a public demonstration, an outward and visible expression of literary enthusiasm,[1] and naturally its form was variable. Dante, for instance, seems to have understood it in the sense of a half-religious consecration; he desired to assume the wreath in the baptistery of S. Giovanni, where, like thousands of other Florentine children, he had received baptism.[2] He could, says his biographer, have any-where received the crown in virtue of his fame, but desired it nowhere but in his native city, and therefore died uncrowned. From the same source we learn that the usage was till then uncommon, and was held to be inherited by the ancient Romans from the Greeks. The most recent source to which the practices could be referred is to be found in the Capitoline contests of musicians, poets, and other artists, founded by Domitian in imitation of the Greeks, and celebrated every five years, which may possibly have survived for a time the fall of the Roman Empire; but as few other men would venture to crown themselves, as Dante desired to do, the question arises, to whom did this office belong? Albertino Mussato (p. 152) was crowned at Padua in 1310 by the bishop and the rector of the University. The University of Paris, the rector of which was then a Florentine (1341), and the municipal authorities of Rome competed for the honour of crowning Petrarch. His self-elected examiner, King Robert of Anjou, would gladly have performed the ceremony at Naples, but Petrarch preferred to be crowned on the Capitol by the Senator of Rome. This honour was long the highest object of ambition, and so it seemed to Jacobus Pizinga, an illustrious Sicilian magistrate.[3] Then came the Italian journey of Charles IV, whom it amused to flatter the vanity of ambitious men, and impress the ignorant multitude by means of gorgeous ceremonies. Starting from the fiction that the coronation of poets was a prerogative of the old Roman Emperors, and consequently was no less his own, he crowned (May 15, 1355) the Florentine scholar Zanobi della Strada at Pisa, to the annoyance of Petrarch, who complained that "the barbarian laurel had dared to adorn the man loved by the Ausonian Muses," and to the great disgust of Boccaccio, who declined to recognize this *laurea Pisana* as legitimate.[4] Indeed, it might

---

[1] Boccaccio (*Vita di Dante*, p. 50): "La quale (laurea) non scienza accresce ma è dell' acquistata certissimo testimonio e ornamento."

[2] *Paradiso*, xxv, 1 *sqq.* Boccaccio, *Vita di Dante*, p. 50. "Sopra le fonti di San Giovanni si era disposto di coronare." Cf. *Paradiso*, i, 25.

[3] See Boccaccio's letter to him in the *Opere Volgari*, vol. xvi, p. 36: "Si præstet Deus, concedente senatu Romuleo. . . ."

[4] Matt. Villani, v, 26. There was a solemn procession on horseback round the city, when the followers of the Emperor, his *baroni*, accompanied the poet. Boccaccio, *loc. cit.* Petrarch, *Invectiva contra Med. Præf.*

be fairly asked with what right this stranger, half Slavonic by birth, came to sit in judgment on the merits of Italian poets. But from henceforth the Emperors crowned poets wherever they went on their travels; and in the fifteenth century the Popes and other princes assumed the same right, till at last no regard whatever was paid to place or circumstances. In Rome, under Sixtus IV, the academy [1] of Pomponius Lætus gave the wreath on its own authority. The Florentines had the good taste not to crown their famous humanists till after death. Carlo Aretino and Leonardo Aretino were thus crowned; the eulogy of the first was pronounced by Matteo Palmieri, of the latter by Giannozzo Manetti, before the members of the Council and the whole people, the orator standing at the head of the bier, on which the corpse lay clad in a silken robe. [2] Carlo Aretino was further honoured by a tomb in S. Croce, which is among the most beautiful in the whole course of the Renaissance.

See also *Epist. Fam. Volgarizzate da Fracassetti*, iii, 128. For the speech of Zanobi at the coronation, Friedjung, *loc. cit.*, pp. 308 *sqq.* Fazio degli Uberti was also crowned, but it is not known where or by whom. [Renier doubts that he ever was crowned (*Liriche di Fazio degli Uberti*, pp. ccvi *sqq.*, Florence, 1883).—W. G.]

[1] Jac. Volaterranus, in Murat., xxiii, col. 185.

[2] Vespas. Fiorent., pp. 575, 589. *Vita Jan. Manetti*, in Murat., xx, col. 543. The celebrity of Leonardo Aretino was in his lifetime so great that people came from all parts merely to see him; a Spaniard fell on his knees before him (Vespas. Fiorent., p. 568). For the monument of Guarino the magistrate of Ferrara allowed, in 1461, the then considerable sum of a hundred ducats. On the coronation of poets in Italy there is a good summary of notices in Favre, *Mélanges d'Hist. Lit.*, i, 65 *sqq.* (1856).

CHAPTER V

THE UNIVERSITIES AND SCHOOLS

THE influence of antiquity on culture, of which we have now to speak, presupposes that the New Learning had gained possession of the universities. This was so, but by no means to the extent and with the results which might have been expected.

Few of the Italian universities [1] show themselves in their full vigour till the thirteenth and fourteenth centuries, when the increase of wealth rendered a more systematic care for education possible. At first there were generally three sorts of professorships—one for civil law, another for canonical law, the third for medicine; in course of time professorships of rhetoric, of philosophy, and of astronomy were added, the last commonly, though not always, identical with astrology. The salaries varied greatly in different cases. Sometimes a capital sum was paid down. With the spread of culture competition became so active that the different universities tried to entice away distinguished teachers from one another, under which circumstances Bologna is said to have sometimes devoted the half of its public income (20,000 ducats) to the university. The appointments were as a rule made only for a certain time,[2] sometimes for only half a year, so that the teachers were forced to lead a wandering life like actors. Appointments for life were, however, not unknown. Sometimes the promise was exacted not to teach elsewhere what had already been taught at one place. There were also voluntary, unpaid professors.

Of the chairs which have been mentioned that of rhetoric was especially sought by the humanist; yet it depended only on his familiarity with the matter of ancient learning whether or no he could aspire to those of law, medicine, philosophy, or astronomy. The inward conditions of the science of the day were as variable as the outward conditions of the teacher. Certain jurists and physicians received by far the largest salaries of all, the former chiefly as

---

[1] Cf. Libri, Histoire des Sciences Mathém., ii, pp. 92 sqq. Bologna, as is well known, was older. Pisa flourished in the fourteenth century, fell through the wars with Florence, and was afterward restored by Lorenzo the Magnificent, "ad solatium veteris amissæ libertatis," as Giovio says (Vita Leonis X, lib. i). The University of Florence (cf. Gaye, Carteggio, i, pp. 461–560 passim, and Matteo Villani, i, 8, vii, 90. See Gherardi, Statuti dell' Università e Studio Fiorentino (Florence, 1881); also Isid. del Lungo, Florentia, pp. 101 sqq.), which existed as early as 1321, with compulsory attendance for the natives of the city, was founded afresh after the Black Death in 1348, and, endowed with an income of 2500 gold florins, fell again into decay, and was refounded in 1357. The chair for the explanation of Dante, established in 1373 at the request of many citizens, was afterward commonly united with the professorship of philology and rhetoric, as when Filelfo held it.

[2] This should be noticed in the lists of professors, as in that of the University of Pavia in 1400 (Corio, Storia di Milano, fol. 290), where (among others) no fewer than twenty jurists appear.

consulting lawyers for the suits and claims of the state which employed them. In Padua a lawyer of the fifteenth century received a salary of 1000 ducats,[1] and it was proposed to appoint a celebrated physician with a yearly payment of 2000 ducats, and the right of private practice,[2] the same man having previously received 700 gold florins at Pisa. When the jurist Bartolommeo Socini, professor at Pisa, accepted a Venetian appointment at Padua, and was on the point of starting on his journey, he was arrested by the Florentine Government and only released on payment of bail to the amount of 18,000 gold florins.[3] The high estimation in which these branches of science were held makes it intelligible why distinguished philologists turned their attention to law and medicine, while

FIG. 106. THE LECTURER ON LAW
Relief from the tomb of the jurist Lorenzo Pini
Bologna, Cathedral

on the other hand specialists were more and more compelled to acquire something of a wide literary culture. We shall presently have occasion to speak of the work of the humanists in other departments of practical life.

Nevertheless, the position of the philologists, as such, even where the salary was large,[4] and did not exclude other sources of income, was on the whole uncertain and temporary, so that one and the same teacher could be connected with a great variety of institutions. It is evident that change was desired for its own sake, and something fresh expected from each new-comer, as was natural at a time when science was in the making, and consequently depended to no small degree on the personal influence of the teacher. Nor was it always the case that a lecturer on classical authors really belonged to the university of the town where he taught. Communication was so easy, and the supply of suitable accommodation in monasteries and elsewhere was so abundant, that a private undertaking was often practicable. In the first decades of the fifteenth century,[5]

---

[1] Marin Sanudo, in Murat., xxii, col. 990.
[2] Fabroni, *Laurent. Magn.*, Adnot. 52, in 1491.
[3] Allegretto, *Diario Sanesi*, in Murat., xiii, col. 824.
[4] Filelfo, when called to the newly founded University of Pisa, demanded at least five hundred gold florins. *Cf.* Fabroni, *Laurent. Magn.*, ii, 75 *sqq.* The negotiations were broken off not only on account of the high salary asked for.
[5] *Cf.* Vespas. Fiorent., pp. 271, 572, 582, 625. *Vita Jan. Manetti*, in Murat., xx, col. 531 *sqq.*

when the University of Florence was at its greatest brilliance, when the courtiers of Eugenius IV, and perhaps even of Martin V, thronged to the lecture-rooms, when Carlo Aretino and Filelfo were competing for the largest audience, there existed not only an almost complete university among the Augustinians of S. Spirito, not only an association of scholars among the Camaldolesi of the Angeli, but individuals of mark, either singly or in common, arranged to provide philosophical and philological teaching for themselves and others. Linguistic and antiquarian studies in Rome had next to no connexion with the university (Sapienza), and depended almost exclusively either on the favour of individual Popes and prelates, or on the appointments made in the Papal chancery. It was not till Leo X (1513) that the great reorganization of the Sapienza took place, with its eighty-eight lecturers, among whom there were able men, though none of the first rank, at the head of the archæological department. But this new brilliancy was of short duration. We have already spoken briefly of the Greek and Hebrew professorships in Italy (pp. 204 *sqq.*).

To form an accurate picture of the method of scientific instruction then pursued we must turn away our eyes as far as possible from our present academic system. Personal intercourse between the teachers and the taught, public disputations, the constant use of Latin and often of Greek, the frequent changes of lecturers, and the scarcity of books gave the studies of that time a colour which we cannot represent to ourselves without effort.

There were Latin schools in every town of the least importance, not by any means merely as preparatory to higher education, but because, next to reading, writing, and arithmetic, the knowledge of Latin was a necessity; and after Latin came logic. It is to be noted particularly that these schools did not depend on the Church, but on the municipality; some of them, too, were merely private enterprises.

This school system, directed by a few distinguished humanists, not only attained a remarkable perfection of organization, but became an instrument of higher education in the modern sense of the phrase. With the education of the children of two princely houses in North Italy institutions were connected which may be called unique of their kind.

At the Court of Giovan Francesco Gonzaga at Mantua (*reg.* 1407–44) appeared the illustrious Vittorino da Feltre [1] (b. 1379, d. 1446), otherwise Vittore dai Rambaldoni—he preferred to be called a Mantuan rather than a Feltrese—one of those men who devote their whole life to an object for which their natural gifts constitute a special vocation. He wrote almost nothing, and finally destroyed the few poems of his youth which he had long kept by him. He studied with unwearied industry; he never sought after titles, which, like all outward distinctions, he scorned; and he lived on terms of the closest friendship with teachers, companions, and pupils, whose goodwill he knew

[1] Vespas. Fiorent., p. 1460. Prendilacqua (a pupil of Vittorino), *Intorno alla Vita di V. da F.*, 1st ed. by Natale dalle Laste, 1774, translated by Giuseppe Brambilla (Como, 1871). C. Rosmini, *Idea dell' Ottimo Precettore nella Vita e Disciplina di Vittorino da Feltre e de' suoi Discepoli* (Bassano, 1801). Later works by Racheli (Milan, 1832) and Venoit (Paris, 1853).

how to preserve. He excelled in bodily no less than in mental exercises, was an admirable rider, dancer, and fencer, wore the same clothes in winter as in summer, walked in nothing but sandals even during the severest frost, and lived so that till his old age he was never ill. He so restrained his passions, his natural inclination to sensuality and anger, that he remained chaste his whole life through, and hardly ever hurt anyone by a hard word.

He directed the education of the sons and daughters of the princely house, and one of the latter became under his care a woman of learning. When his

FIG. 107. THE LATIN LESSON
Woodcut from Ferretus' *De Elegantia Linguæ Latinæ* (Forlì, 1495)
Photo Rosenthal, Munich

reputation extended far and wide over Italy, and members of great and wealthy families came from long distances, even from Germany, in search of his instructions, Gonzaga was not only willing that they should be received, but seems to have held it an honour for Mantua to be the chosen school of the aristocratic world. Here for the first time gymnastics and all noble bodily exercises were treated along with scientific instruction as indispensable to a liberal education. Besides these pupils came others, whose instruction Vittorino probably held to be his highest earthly aim, the gifted poor, often as many as seventy together, whom he supported in his house and educated, *per l'amore di Dio*, along with the high-born youths who here learned to live under the same roof with untitled genius. The greater the crowd of pupils who flocked to Mantua, the more teachers were needed to impart the instruction which Vittorino only directed—an instruction which aimed at giving each pupil that sort of learning which he was most fitted to receive. Gonzaga paid him a yearly salary of 240 gold florins, built him besides a splendid house, La Giocosa, in which the master lived with his scholars, and contributed to the expenses caused by the poorer pupils. What was still further needed Vittorino begged from princes and wealthy people, who did not always, it is true, give a ready ear to his entreaties, and forced him by their hardheartedness to run into debt. Yet in the end he found himself in comfortable circumstances, owned a small property in town and an estate in the country, where he stayed with his pupils during the holidays, and possessed a famous collection of books, which he gladly lent or gave away, though he was not a little angry when they were taken without leave. In the early morning he read religious books, then scourged himself and went to church; his pupils were also compelled to go to church, like him, to confess once a month, and to observe fast-days most strictly. His pupils respected him, but trembled before his glance. When they did anything wrong they were punished immediately after the offence. He was honoured by all

FIG. 108. THE EDUCATION OF MASSIMILIANO SFORZA
Miniature from the *Grammatica di Donato*
Milan, Trivulziana

contemporaries no less than by his pupils, and people took the journey to Mantua merely to see him.

More stress was laid on pure scholarship by Guarino of Verona [1] (1370–1460), who in 1429 was called to Ferrara by Niccolò d'Este to educate his son Lionello, and who, when his pupil was nearly grown up, in 1436, began to teach at the university as professor of eloquence and of the ancient languages. While still acting as tutor to Lionello, he had many other pupils from various parts of the country, and in his own house a select class of poor scholars, whom he partly or wholly supported. His evening hours till far into the night were devoted to hearing lessons or to instructive conversation. His house too was

[1] Vespas. Fiorent., p. 646, of which, however, C. Rosmini, *Vita e Disciplina di Guarino Veronese e de' suoi Discepoli* (3 vols., Brescia, 1856), says that it is (ii, 56) "formicolante di errori di fatto."

the home of a strict religion and morality. Guarino was a student of the Bible and lived in friendly intercourse with pious contemporaries, though he did not hesitate to write a defence of pagan literature against them. It signified little to him or to Vittorino that most of the humanists of their day deserved small praise in the matter of morals or religion. It is inconceivable how Guarino, with all the daily work which fell upon him, still found time to write translations from the Greek and voluminous original works.[1] He was wanting in that wise self-restraint and kindly sweetness which graced the character of Vittorino, and was easily betrayed into a violence of temper which led to frequent quarrels with his learned contemporaries.

Not only in these two Courts, but generally throughout Italy the education of the princely families was in part and for certain years in the hands of the humanists, who thereby mounted a step higher in the aristocratic world. The writing of treatises on the education of princes, formerly the business of theologians, fell now within their province.

From the time of Pier Paolo Vergerio the Italian princes were well taken care of in this respect, and the custom was transplanted into Germany by Æneas Sylvius, who addressed detailed exhortations to two young German princes of the house of Habsburg [2] on the subject of their further education, in which they are both urged, as might be expected, to cultivate and nurture humanism, but are chiefly bidden to make themselves able rulers and vigorous, hardy warriors. Perhaps Æneas was aware that in addressing these youths he was talking in the air, and therefore took measures to put his treatise into public circulation. But the relations of the humanists to the rulers will be discussed separately.

---

[1] For these and for Guarino generally see Facius, *De Vir. Ill.*, pp. 17 *sqq.*; and Cortesius, *De Hom. Doctis*, p. 13. Both agree that the scholars of the following generation prided themselves on having been pupils of Guarino; but while Fazio praises his works, Cortese thinks that he would have cared better for his fame if he had written nothing. Guarino and Vittorino were friends, and helped one another in their studies. Their contemporaries were fond of comparing them, and in this comparison Guarino commonly held the first place (Sabellico, *Dial. de Lingu. Lat. Reparata*, in Rosmini, ii, 112). Guarino's attitude with regard to the *Ermafrodito* is remarkable; see Rosmini, ii, 46 *sqq.* In both these teachers an unusual moderation in food and drink was observed; they never drank undiluted wine; in both the principles of education were alike; they neither used corporal punishment; the hardest penalty which Vittorino inflicted was to make the boy kneel and lie upon the ground in the presence of his fellow-pupils.

[2] To the Archduke Sigismond, *Epist.* 105, p. 600, and to King Ladislaus Postumus, p. 695; the latter as *Tractatus de Liberorum Educatione* (1450).

CHAPTER VI

THE FURTHERERS OF HUMANISM

E have here first to speak of those citizens, mostly Florentines, who made antiquarian interests one of the chief objects of their lives, and who were themselves either distinguished scholars, or else distinguished *dilettanti* who maintained the scholars. (*Cf.* pp. 201 *sqq.*) They were of peculiar significance during the period of transition at the beginning of the fifteenth century, since it was in them that humanism first showed itself practically as an indispensable element in daily life. It was not till after this time that the Popes and princes began seriously to occupy themselves with it.

Niccolò Niccoli and Giannozzo Manetti have been already spoken of more than once. Niccoli is described to us by Vespasiano [1] as a man who would tolerate nothing round him out of harmony with his own classical spirit. His handsome long-robed figure, his kindly speech, his house adorned with the noblest remains of antiquity, made a singular impression. He was scrupulously cleanly in everything, most of all at table, where ancient vases and crystal goblets stood before him on the whitest linen. [2] The way in which he won over a pleasure-loving young Florentine to intellectual interests is too charming not to be here described. [3] Fiero de' Pazzi, son of a distinguished merchant, and himself destined to the same calling, fair to behold, and much given to the pleasures of the world, thought about anything rather than literature. One day, as he was passing the Palazzo del Podestà, [4] Niccolò called the young man to him, and although they had never before exchanged a word the youth obeyed the call of one so respected. Niccolò asked him who his father was. He answered, "Messer Andrea de' Pazzi." When he was further asked what his pursuit was Piero replied, as young people are wont to do, "I enjoy myself" ("attendo a darmi buon tempo"). Niccolò said to him, "As son of such a father, and so fair to look upon, it is a shame thou knowest nothing of the Latin language, which would be so great an ornament to thee. If thou learnest it not, thou wilt be good for nothing, and as soon as the flower of youth is over, wilt be a man of no consequence" (*virtù*). When Piero heard this he

---

[1] P. 625.   On Niccoli see further a speech of Poggio, *Opera*, ed. 1513, fol. 102 *sqq.*; and a life by Manetti in his book *De Illustribus Longævis*.
[2] The following words of Vespasiano are untranslatable: "A vederlo in tavola cosi antico come era, era una gentilezza."
[3] *Ibid.*, p. 495.
[4] According to Vespasiano, p. 271, learned men were in the habit of meeting here for discussion.

ſtraightway perceived that it was true, and said that he would gladly take pains to learn, if only he had a teacher. Whereupon Niccolò answered that he would see to that. And he found him a learned man for Latin and Greek, named Pontano, whom Piero treated as one of his own house, and to whom he paid a hundred gold florins a year. Quitting all the pleasures in which he had hitherto lived, he ſtudied day and night, and became a friend of all learned men and a noble-minded ſtatesman. He learned by heart the whole Æneid and many speeches of Livy, chiefly on the way between Florence and his country house at Trebbio.[1] Antiquity was represented in another and higher sense by Giannozzo Manetti (1393–1459).[2] Precocious from his firſt years, he was hardly more than a child when he had finished his apprenticeship in commerce, and became book-keeper in a bank. But soon the life he led seemed to him empty and perishable, and he began to yearn after science, through which alone man can secure immortality. He then busied himself with books as few laymen had done before him, and became, as has been said (p. 217), one of the moſt profound scholars of his time. When appointed by the Government as its representative magiſtrate and tax-collector at Pescia and Piſtoja he fulfilled his duties in accordance with the lofty ideal with which his religious feeling and humaniſtic ſtudies combined to inspire him. He succeeded in collecting the moſt unpopular taxes which the Florentine State imposed, and declined payment for his services. As provincial governor he refused all presents, abhorred all bribes, checked gambling, kept the country well supplied with corn, required from his subordinates ſtrict obedience and thorough disintereſtedness, was indefatigable in settling law-suits amicably, and did wonders in calming inflamed passions by his goodness. The Piſtojese loved and reverenced him as a saint, and were never able to discover to which of the two political parties he leaned; when his term of office was over both sent ambassadors to Florence to beg that it might be prolonged. As if to symbolize the common rights and intereſts of all, he spent his leisure hours in writing the hiſtory of the city, which was preserved, bound in a purple cover, as a sacred relic in the town-hall.[3] When he took his leave the city presented him with a banner bearing the municipal arms and a splendid silver helmet. On diplomatic missions to Venice, Rome, and King Alfonso Manetti represented, as at

---

[1] Of Niccoli it may be further remarked that, like Vittorino, he wrote nothing, being convinced that he could not treat of anything in as perfect a form as he desired; that his senses were so delicately poised that he "neque rudentem asinum, neque secantem serram, neque muscipulam vagientem sentire audivere poterat." But the less favourable sides of Niccoli's character muſt not be forgotten. He robbed his brother of his sweetheart Benvenuta, roused the indignation of Leonardo Aretino by this act, and was embittered by the girl againſt many of his friends. He took ill the refusal to lend him books, and had a violent quarrel with Guarino on this account. He was not free from a petty jealousy, under the influence of which he tried to drive Chrysoloras, Poggio, and Filelfo away from Florence.

[2] See his *Vita*, by Naldus Naldi, in Murat., xx, col. 532 *sqq*. See further Vespasiano Biſticci, *Commentario della Vita di Messer Giannozzo Manetti*, firſt published by P. Fanfani in *Collezione di Opere Inedite o Rare*, vol. ii (Torino, 1862). This *Commentario* muſt be diſtinguished from the short *Vita* of Manetti by the same author, in which frequent reference is made to the former. Vespasiano was on intimate terms with Giannozzo Manetti, and in the biography tried to draw an ideal picture of a ſtatesman for the degenerate Florence. Vespasiano is Naldi's authority. *Cf.* also the fragment in Galetti, *Phil. Vill. Liber Flor.*, pp. 129–138 (1847). Half a century after his death Manetti was nearly forgotten. *Cf.* Paolo Cortese, p. 21.

[3] The title of the work, in Latin and Italian, is given in Biſticci, *Commentario*, pp. 109, 112.

Pistoja, the interests of his native city, watching vigilantly over its honour, but declining the distinctions which were offered to him, obtained great glory by

FIG. 109. MARSILIO FICINO
Part of the fresco *The Sacrifice of Zacharias*, by Ghirlandaio
Florence, S. Maria Novella
Photo Anderson, Rome

his speeches and negotiations, and acquired by his prudence and foresight the name of a prophet.

For further information as to the learned citizens of Florence at this period the reader must all the more be referred to Vespasiano, who knew them all personally, because the tone and atmosphere in which he writes, and the terms and conditions on which he mixed in their society, are of even more importance than the facts which he records. Even in a translation, and still more in the brief indications to which we are here compelled to limit ourselves, this chief merit of his book is lost. Without being a great writer he was thoroughly familiar with the subject he wrote on, and had a deep sense of its intellectual significance.

If we seek to analyse the charm which the Medici of the fifteenth century, especially Cosimo the Elder (d. 1464) and Lorenzo the Magnificent (d. 1492), exercised over Florence and over all their contemporaries we shall find it lay less in their political capacity than in their leadership in the culture of the age. A man in Cosimo's position—a great merchant and party leader, who also had on his side all the thinkers, writers, and investigators, a man who was the first of the Florentines by birth and the first of the Italians by culture—such a man was to all intents and purposes already a prince. To Cosimo belongs the special glory of recognizing in the Platonic philosophy the fairest flower of the ancient world of thought,[1] of inspiring his friends with the same belief, and thus of fostering within humanistic circles themselves another and a higher resuscitation of antiquity. The story is known to us minutely.[2] It all hangs on the calling of the learned Johannes Argyropulos, and on the personal enthusiasm of Cosimo himself in his last years, which was such that the great Marsilio Ficino could style himself, as far as Platonism was concerned, the spiritual son of Cosimo. Under Pietro de' Medici, Ficino was already at the head of a school; to him Pietro's son and Cosimo's grandson, the illustrious Lorenzo, came over from the Peripatetics. Among his most distinguished fellow-scholars were Bartolommeo Valori, Donato Acciajuoli, and Pierfilippo Pandolfini. The enthusiastic teacher declares in several passages of his writings that Lorenzo had sounded all the depths of the Platonic philosophy, and had uttered his conviction that without Plato it would be hard to be a good Christian or a good citizen. The famous band of scholars which surrounded Lorenzo was united together, and distinguished from all other circles of the kind, by this passion for a higher and idealistic philosophy. Only in such a world could a man like Pico della Mirandola feel happy. But perhaps the best thing of all that can be said about it is that, with all this worship of antiquity, Italian poetry found here a sacred refuge, and that of all the rays of light which streamed from the circle of which Lorenzo was the centre none was more powerful than this. As a statesman, let each man judge him as he pleases; a foreigner will hesitate to pronounce what was due to human guilt and what to circumstances in the

---

[1] What was known of Plato before can only have been fragmentary. A strange discussion on the antagonism of Plato and Aristotle took place at Ferrara in 1438, between Ugo of Siena and the Greeks who came to the Council. Cf. Æneas Sylvius, De Europa, cap. 52 (Opera, p. 450).

[2] In Niccolò Valori, Life of Lorenzo the Magnificent, ed. Gaietti, p. 167. Cf. Vespas. Fiorent., p. 426. The first supporters of Argyropulos were the Acciajuoli. Ibid., 192: Cardinal Bessarion and his parallels between Plato and Aristotle. Ibid., 223: Cusanus as Platonist; in fact, only the words grande platonista. Ibid., 308: the Catalonian Narciso and his disputes with Argyropulos. Ibid., 571: single dialogues of Plato, translated by Leonardo Aretino. Ibid., 298: the rising influence of Neoplatonism. On Marsilio Ficino see Reumont, Lorenzo dei Medici, ii, 27 sqq.

fate of Florence, but no more unjust charge was ever made than that in the field of culture Lorenzo was the protector of mediocrity, that through his fault Leonardo da Vinci and the mathematician Fra Luca Pacciolo lived abroad, and

FIG. 110. LORENZO DE' MEDICI
By Vasari
Florence, Uffizi

that Toscanella, Vespucci, and others at least remained unsupported. He was not, indeed, a man of universal mind; but of all the great men who have striven to favour and promote spiritual interests few certainly have been so many-sided, and in none probably was the inward need to do so equally deep.

The age in which we live is loud enough in proclaiming the worth of culture, and especially of the culture of antiquity. But the enthusiastic devotion to it, the recognition that the need of it is the first and greatest of all needs, is nowhere to be found but among the Florentines of the fifteenth and the early part of the sixteenth century. On this point we have indirect proof which precludes all doubt. It would not have been so common to give the daughters of the house a share in the same studies had they not been held to be the noblest of earthly pursuits; exile would not have been turned into a happy retreat, as was done by Palla Strozzi; nor would men who indulged in every conceivable excess have retained the strength and the spirit to write critical treatises on the *Natural History* of Pliny, like Filippo Strozzi.[1] Our business here is not to deal out either praise or blame, but to understand the spirit of the age in all its vigorous individuality.

Besides Florence, there were many cities of Italy where individuals and social circles devoted all their energies to the support of humanism and the protection of the scholars who lived among them. The correspondence of that period is full of references to personal relations of this kind.[2] The feeling of the instructed classes set strongly and almost exclusively in this direction.

But it is now time to speak of humanism at the Italian Courts. The natural alliance between the despot and the scholar, each relying solely on his personal talent, has already been touched upon (pp. 27-28); that the latter should avowedly prefer the princely Courts to the free cities was only to be expected from the higher pay which he there received. At a time when the great Alfonso of Aragon seemed likely to become master of all Italy Æneas Sylvius wrote to another citizen of Siena:[3] "I had rather that Italy attained peace under his rule than under that of the free cities, for kingly generosity rewards excellence of every kind."[4] Too much stress has latterly been laid on the unworthy side of this relation and the mercenary flattery to which it gave rise, just as formerly the eulogies of the humanists led to a too favourable judgment on their patrons. Taking all things together, it is greatly to the honour of the latter that they felt bound to place themselves at the head of the culture of their age and country, one-sided though this culture was. In some of the Popes[5] the fearlessness of the consequences to which the New Learning might lead strikes us as something truly but unconsciously imposing. Nicholas V was confident of the future of the Church, since thousands of learned men supported her. Pius II was far

---

[1] Varchi, *Stor. Fiorent.*, p. 321. An admirable sketch of character.

[2] The lives of Guarino and Vittorino by Rosmini mentioned above (pp. 220, note, and 222, note) as well as the life of Poggio by Shepherd, especially in the enlarged Italian translation of Tonelli (2 vols., Florence, 1825); the correspondence of Poggio, edited by the same writer (2 vols., Florence, 1832); and the letters of Poggio in Mai's *Spicilegium*, tom. x, pp. 221-272 (Rome, 1844), all contain much on this subject. Also a newly discovered letter of Poggio's in Walser, *Poggius Florentinus*, pp. 428 *sqq.* (Leipzig, 1914).

[3] *Epist.* 39 (*Opera*, p. 526) to Mariano Sozzino.

[4] We must not be misled by the fact that along with all this complaints were frequently heard of the inadequacy of princely patronage and of the indifference of many princes to their fame. See, for example, Bapt. Mantuan, *Eclog.* V, as early as the fifteenth century; and Ambrogio Traversari, *De Infelicitate Principum.* It was impossible to satisfy all.

[5] For the literary and scientific patronage of the Popes down to the end of the fifteenth century see Gregorovius, vols. vii and viii. For Pius II see Voigt, *En. Silvio als Papst Pius II*, Bd. iii, pp. 406-440 (Berlin, 1863). *Cf.* also Pastor.

from making such splendid sacrifices for humanism as were made by Nicholas, and the poets who frequented his Court were few in number; but he himself was much more the personal head of the republic of letters than his predecessor, and enjoyed his position without the least misgiving.   Paul II was the first to dread and mistrust the culture of his secretaries, and his three successors, Sixtus, Innocent, and Alexander, accepted dedications and allowed themselves to be sung to the heart's content of the poets—there even existed a *Borgiad*, probably in hexameters [1]—but were too busy elsewhere, and too occupied in seeking other foundations for their power, to trouble themselves much about the poet-scholars.   Julius II found poets to eulogize him because he himself was no mean subject for poetry (p. 134), but he does not seem to have troubled himself much about them.   He was followed by Leo X, "as Romulus by Numa"—in other words, after the war-like turmoil of the first pontificate a new one was hoped for, given wholly to the Muses.   The enjoyment of elegant Latin prose and melodious verse was part of the programme of Leo's life, and his patronage certainly had the result that his Latin poets have left us a living picture of that joyous and brilliant spirit of the Leonine days, with which the biography of Jovius is filled, in countless epigrams, elegies, odes, and orations.[2] Probably in all European history there is no prince who, in proportion to the few striking events of his life, has received such manifold homage.   The poets had access to him chiefly about noon, when the musicians had ceased playing; [3] but one of the best among them [4] tells us how they also pursued him when he walked in his garden or withdrew to the privacy of his chamber, and if they failed to catch him there would try to win him with a mendicant ode or elegy, filled, as usual, with the whole population of Olympus.[5]   For Leo, prodigal of his money, and disliking to be surrounded by any but cheerful faces, displayed a generosity in his gifts which was fabulously exaggerated in the hard times that followed.[6]   His reorganization of the Sapienza (p. 220) has been already spoken of.   In order not to underrate Leo's influence on humanism we must guard against being misled by the toy-work that was mixed up with it, and must not allow ourselves to be deceived by the apparent irony with which he himself sometimes treated these matters (p. 165).   Our judgment must rather dwell on the countless spiritual possibilities which are included in the word

---

[1] Lil. Greg. Gyraldus, *De Poetis nostri Temporis*, ed. Wotke, p. 38, speaking of the *Sphærulus* of Camerino. The worthy man did not finish it in time, and his work lay for forty years in his desk.   For the scanty payments made by Sixtus IV *cf.* Pier. Valeriano, *De Infel. Lit.*, on Theodoro Gaza.   He received for a translation and commentary of a work of Aristotle fifty gold florins, "ab eo a quo se totum inauratum iri speraverat."   On the deliberate exclusion of the humanists from the cardinalate by the Popes before Leo *cf.* Lor. Grana's funeral oration on Cardinal Egidio, *Aned. Lit.*, iv, p. 307.

[2] The best are to be found in the *Deliciæ Poetarum Italorum*, and in the Appendices to the various editions of Roscoe, *Leo X.*   Several poets and writers, like Alcyonius, *De Exilio*, ed. Mencken, p. 10, say frankly that they praise Leo in order themselves to become immortal.

[3] Paul. Jovius, *Elogia*, speaking of Guido Posthumus.

[4] Pier. Valeriano in his *Simia*.

[5] See the elegy of Joh. Aurelius Mutius in the *Deliciæ Poetarum Italorum*.

[6] The well-known story of the purple velvet purse filled with packets of gold of various sizes, in which Leo used to thrust his hand blindly, is in Giraldi, *Hecatommithi*, vi, *Nov.* 8.   On the other hand, the Latin *improvisatori*, when their verses were too faulty, were whipped.   Lil. Greg. Gyraldus, *De Poetis nostri Temp.*, *Opp.*, ii, 398 (Basel, 1580).

'Stimulus,' and which, though they cannot be measured as a whole, can still, on closer study, be actually followed out in particular cases. Whatever influence in Europe the Italian humanists have had since 1520 depends in some way or other on the impulse which was given by Leo. He was the Pope who in granting permission to print the newly found Tacitus [1] could say that the great writers were a rule of life and a consolation in misfortune; that helping learned men and obtaining excellent books had ever been one of his highest aims; and that he now thanked heaven that he could benefit the human race by furthering the publication of this book.

The sack of Rome in 1527 scattered the scholars no less than the artists in every direction, and spread the fame of the great departed Mæcenas to the farthest boundaries of Italy.

Among the secular princes of the fifteenth century none displayed such enthusiasm for antiquity as Alfonso the Great of Aragon, King of Naples (see p. 51). It appears that his zeal was thoroughly unaffected, and that the monuments and writings of the ancient world made upon him, from the time of his arrival in Italy, an impression deep and powerful enough to reshape his life. Possibly he was influenced by the example of his ancestor Robert, Petrarch's great patron, whom he may have wished to rival or surpass. With strange readiness he surrendered the stubborn Aragon to his brother, and devoted himself wholly to his new possessions. He had in his service,[2] either successively or together, George of Trebizond, the younger Chrysoloras, Lorenzo Valla, Bartolommeo Facio, and Antonio Panormita, of whom the two latter were his historians; Panormita daily instructed the King and his Court in Livy, even during military expeditions. These men cost him yearly 20,000 gold florins. He gave Panormita 1000 for his work; Facio received for the *Historia Alfonsi*, besides a yearly income of 500 ducats, a present of 1500 more when it was finished, with the words: " It is not given to pay you, for your work would not be paid for if I gave you the fairest of my cities; but in time I hope to satisfy you." [3] When he took Giannozzo Manetti as his secretary on the most brilliant conditions he said to him, " My last crust I will share with you." When Giannozzo first came to bring the congratulations of the Florentine Government on the marriage of Prince Ferrante the impression he made was so great that the King sat motionless on the throne, " like a brazen statue, and did not even brush away a fly, which had settled on his nose at the beginning of the oration." In restoring the castle he took Vitruvius as his guide; wherever he went he had the ancient classics with him; he looked on a day as lost in which he had read nothing; when he was reading he suffered no disturbance, not even the sound of music; and he despised all contemporary princes who

[1] Roscoe, *Leo X*, ed. Bossi, iv, 181.

[2] Vespas. Fiorent., pp. 68 *sqq.* For the translations from Greek made by Alfonso's orders see p. 51; *Vita Jan. Manetti*, in Murat., xx, col. 541 *sqq.*, 550 *sqq.*, 595. Panormita, *De Dictis et Factis Alphonsi, Regis Aragonum Libri Quatuor. Commentar. in eosdem Æneæ Sylvii*, ed. Jacob Spiegel (Basel, 1538).

[3] Even Alfonso was not able to please everybody—Poggio, for example. See Shepherd-Tonelli, *Poggio*, ii, 108 *sqq.*, and Poggio's letter to Facius in *Fac. de Vir. Ill.*, ed. Mehus, p. 88, where he writes of Alfonso: " Ad ostentationem quædam facit quibus videatur doctis viris favere"; and Poggio's letter in Mai, *Spicil.*, tom. x, p. 241.

were not either scholars or the patrons of learning. His favourite haunt seems to have been the library of the castle at Naples, which he opened himself if the librarian was absent, and where he would sit at a window overlooking the bay,

FIG. III. TRIUMPHAL ARCH OF ALFONSO I
Naples, Castel Nuovo

and listen to learned debates on the Trinity. For he was profoundly religious, and had the Bible, as well as Livy and Seneca, read to him, till after fourteen perusals he knew it almost by heart. He gave to those who wished to be nuns the money for their entrance to the monastery, was a zealous churchgoer, and listened with great attention to the sermon. Who can fully understand the feeling with which he regarded the supposititious remains (p. 155) of Livy at Padua? When, by dint of great entreaties, he obtained an arm-bone of the skeleton from the Venetians, and received it with solemn pomp at Naples, how strangely Christian and pagan sentiment must have been blended in his heart! During a campaign in the Abruzzi, when the distant Sulmona, the birthplace of Ovid, was pointed out to him, he saluted the spot and returned thanks to its tutelary genius. It gladdened him to make good the prophecy of the great poet as to his future fame.[1] Once, indeed, at his famous entry into the conquered city of Naples (1443), he himself chose to appear before the world in ancient style. Not far from the market a breach forty ells wide was made in the wall, and through this he drove in a gilded chariot, like a Roman triumphator.[2] The memory of the scene is preserved by a noble triumphal arch of marble in the Castello Nuovo. His Neapolitan successors (p. 52) inherited as little of this passion for antiquity as of his other good qualities.

[1] Ovid, *Amores*, iii, 11, vs. 11; Jov. Pontan., *De Principe.* [2] *Giorn. Napolet.*, in Murat., xxi, col. 1127.

FIG. 112. FEDERIGO DA MONTEFELTRE READING
By Joos van Gent
Rome, Palazzo Barberini
Photo Anderson, Rome

THE RENAISSANCE IN ITALY

Alfonso was far surpassed in learning by Federigo of Urbino [1]—the great pupil of the great teacher Vittorino da Feltre—who had but few courtiers around him, squandered nothing, and in his appropriation of antiquity, as in all other things, went to work considerately. It was for him and for Nicholas V that most of the translations from the Greek, and a number of the best commentaries and other such works, were written. He spent much on the scholars whose services he used, but spent it to good purpose. There were no traces of the official poet at Urbino, where the Duke himself was the most learned in the whole Court. Classical antiquity, indeed, formed only a part of his culture. An accomplished ruler, captain, and gentleman, he had mastered the greater part of the science of the day, and this with a view to its practical application. As a theologian, he was able to compare Scotus with Aquinas, and was familiar with the writings of the fathers of the Eastern and Western Churches, the former in Latin translations. In philosophy, he seems to have left Plato altogether to his contemporary, Cosimo, but he knew thoroughly not only the *Ethics* and *Politics* of Aristotle, but the *Physics* and some other works. The rest of his reading lay chiefly among the ancient historians, all of whom he possessed; these, and not the poets, " he was always reading and having read to him."

The Sforza [2] too were all of them men of more or less learning and patrons of literature; they have been already referred to in passing (pp. 54 *sqq.*). Duke Francesco probably looked on humanistic culture as a matter of course in the education of his children, if only for political reasons. It was felt universally to be an advantage if the Prince could mix with the most instructed men of his time on an equal footing. Lodovico il Moro, himself an excellent Latin scholar, showed an interest in intellectual matters which extended far beyond classical antiquity (pp. 58 *sqq.*).

Even the petty despots strove after similar distinctions, and we do them injustice by thinking that they supported the scholars at their Courts only as a means of diffusing their own fame. A ruler like Borso of Ferrara (p. 70), with all his vanity, seems by no means to have looked for immortality from the poets, eager as they were to propitiate him with a *Borseid* and the like. He had far too proud a sense of his own position as a ruler for that. But intercourse with learned men, interest in antiquarian matters, and the passion for elegant Latin correspondence were a necessity for the princes of that age. What bitter complaints are those of Duke Alfonso, competent as he was in practical matters, that his weakliness in youth had forced him to seek recreation in manual pursuits only! [3] Or was this merely an excuse to keep the humanists at a distance? A nature like his was not intelligible even to contemporaries.

Even the most insignificant despots of Romagna found it hard to do without one or two men of letters about them. The tutor and secretary were

[1] Vespas. Fiorent., pp. 3, 119 *sqq.* " Volle aver piena notizia d' ogni cosa, così sacra come gentile."
[2] The last Visconti divided his interest between Livy, the French chivalrous romances, Dante, and Petrarch. The humanists who presented themselves to him with the promise "to make him famous" were generally sent away after a few days. Cf. *Decembrio*, in Murat., xx, col. 1014.
[3] Paul. Jovius, *Vita Alfonsi Ducis.*

often one and the same person, who sometimes, indeed, acted as a kind of Court factotum.[1] We are apt to treat the small scale of these Courts as a reason for dismissing them with a too ready contempt, forgetting that the highest spiritual things are not precisely matters of measurement.

Life and manners at the Court of Rimini must have been a singular spectacle under the bold pagan *condottiere* Sigismondo Malatesta. He had a number of scholars round him, some of whom he provided for liberally, even giving them landed estates, while others earned at least a livelihood as officers in his army.[2] In his citadel—*arx Sismundea*—they used to hold discussions, often of a very venomous kind, in the presence of the *rex*, as they termed him. In their Latin poems they sing his praises and celebrate his *amour* with the fair Isotta, in whose honour and as whose monument the famous rebuilding of S. Francesco at Rimini took place—*Divæ Isottæ Sacrum*. When the humanists themselves came to die they were laid in or under the sarcophagi with which the niches of the outside walls of the church were adorned, with an inscription testifying that they were laid there at the time when Sigismundus, the son of Pandulfus, ruled.[3] It is hard for us nowadays to believe that a monster like this prince felt learning and the friendship of cultivated people to be a necessity of life; and yet the man who excommunicated him, made war upon him, and burnt him in effigy, Pope Pius II, says: "Sigismund knew history and had a great store of philosophy; he seemed born to all that he undertook."[4]

[1] On Collenuccio at the Court of Giovanni Sforza of Pesaro (son of Alessandro, see above, p. 45), who finally, in 1508, put him to death, see p. 148, note 3. At the time of the last Ordelaffi at Forlì the place was occupied by Codrus Urceus (1477–80); deathbed complaint of Codrus Urceus, *Opp.*, fol. liv (Ven. 1506); for his stay in Forlì, *Sermo* VI. *Cf.* Carlo Malagola, *Della Vita di C. U.*, App. IV (Bologna, 1877). Among the instructed despots we may mention Galeotto Manfreddi of Faenza, murdered in 1488 by his wife, and some of the Bentivoglio family at Bologna.

[2] *Anecd. Lit.*, ii, pp. 305 *sqq.*, 405. Basinius of Parma ridicules Porcellio and Tommaso Seneca; they are needy parasites, and must play the soldier in their old age, while he himself was enjoying an *ager* and a *villa*. It appears from a legal document of about 1460 that some humanists, like the last two, still sought to hinder the diffusion of Greek.

[3] For details respecting these graves see Keyssler, *Neueste Reisen*, p. 924.

[4] *Pii II Comment.*, ii, p. 92. By history he means all that has to do with antiquity. Cortesius also praises him highly, pp. 34 *sqq.*

CHAPTER VII

THE REPRODUCTION OF ANTIQUITY: LATIN CORRESPONDENCE AND ORATIONS

THERE were two purposes, however, for which the humanist was as indispensable to the republics as to princes or Popes —namely, the official correspondence of the State, and the making of speeches on public and solemn occasions.
Not only was the secretary required to be a competent Latinist, but conversely only a humanist was credited with the knowledge and ability necessary for the post of secretary. And thus the greatest men in the sphere of science during the fifteenth century mostly devoted a considerable part of their lives to serve the State in this capacity. No importance was attached to a man's home or origin. Of the four great Florentine secretaries who filled the office between 1427 and 1465 [1] three belonged to the subject city of Arezzo—namely, Leonardo (Bruni), Carlo (Marsuppini), and Benedetto Accolti; Poggio was from Terra Nuova, also in Florentine territory. For a long period, indeed, many of the highest offices of State were on principle given to foreigners. Leonardo, Poggio, and Giannozzo Manetti were at one time or another private secretaries to the Popes, and Carlo Aretino was to have been so. Blondus of Forlì, and, in spite of everything, at last even Lorenzo Valla, filled the same office. From the time of Nicholas V and Pius II onward [2] the Papal chancery continued more and more to attract the ablest men, and this was still the case even under the last Popes of the fifteenth century, little as they cared for letters. In Platina's *History of the Popes* the life of Paul II is a charming piece of vengeance taken by a humanist on the one Pope who did not know how to behave to his chancery —to that circle " of poets and orators who bestowed on the Papal Court as much glory as they received from it." It is delightful to see the indignation of these haughty and wealthy gentlemen, who knew as well as the Pope himself how to use their position to plunder foreigners;[3] when some squabble about precedence happened, when, for instance, the *advocati consistoriales* claimed equal or superior rank to theirs.[4] The Apostle John, to whom the *secreta cælestia*

---

[1] Fabroni, *Cosmus*, Adnot. 117; Vespas. Fiorent., *passim*. An important passage respecting the demands made by the Florentines on their secretaries (" quod honor apud Florentinos magnus habetur," says B. Facius, speaking of Poggio's appointment to the secretaryship, *De Vir. Ill.*, p. 17) is to be found in Æneas Sylvius, *De Europa*, cap. 54 (*Opera*, p. 454).

[2] See Voigt, *En. Silvio als Papst Pius II*, Bd. iii, 488 *sqq.*, for the often-discussed and often-misunderstood change which Pius II made with respect to the Abbreviators. *Cf.* also Pastor, *Papste*, ii, p. 304.

[3] *Cf.* the statement of Jacob Spiegel (1521) given in the reports of the Vienna Academy, lxxviii, 333.

[4] *Anecd. Lit.*, i, pp. 119 *sqq.* A plea (*Actio ad Cardinales Deputatos*) of Jacobus Volaterranus in the name of the secretaries, no doubt of the time of Sixtus IV (Voigt, *loc. cit.*, 552, note). The humanistic claims of the *advocati consistoriales* rested on their oratory, as that of the secretaries on their correspondence.

were revealed; the secretary of Porsenna, whom Mucius Scævola mistook for the king; Mæcenas, who was private secretary to Augustus; the archbishops, who in Germany were called chancellors, are all appealed to in turn.[1]

The Apostolic Secretaries have the most weighty business of the world in their hands. For who but they decide on matters of the Catholic faith, who else combat heresy, re-establish peace, and mediate between great monarchs? Who but they write the statistical accounts of Christendom? It is they who astonish kings, princes, and nations by what comes forth from the Pope. They write commands and instructions for the legates, and receive their orders only from the Pope, on whom they wait day and night.

But the highest summit of glory was attained only by the two famous secretaries and stylists of Leo X, Pietro Bembo and Jacopo Sadoleto.[2]

All the chanceries did not turn out equally elegant documents. A leathern official style, in the impurest of Latin, was very common. In the Milanese documents preserved by Corio there is a remarkable contrast between this sort of composition and the few letters written by members of the princely house, which must have been written, too, in moments of critical importance.[3]

FIG. 113. PLATINA
Part of the picture *The Reception of Platina by Sixtus IV*, by Melozzo da Forli. See frontispiece
Rome, Vatican

[1] The Imperial chancery under Frederick III was best known to Æneas Sylvius. Cf. *Epist.* 23 and 105 (*Opera*, pp. 516 and 607).

[2] The letters of Bembo and Sadoleto have been often printed; those of the former, for example, in the *Opera*, vol. ii (Basel, 1556), where the letters written in the name of Leo X are distinguished from private letters; those of the latter most fully (5 vols., Rome, 1760). Some additions to both have been given by Carlo Malagola in the review *Il Baretti* (Turin, 1875). Bembo's *Asolani* will be spoken of below; Sadoleto's significance for Latin style has been judged as follows by a contemporary, Petrus Alcyonius, *De Exilio*, ed. Mencken, p. 119: " Solus autem nostrorum temporum aut certe cum paucis animadvertit elocutionem emendatam et latinam esse fundamentum oratoris; ad eamque obtinendam necesse esse latinam linguam expurgate quam inquinarunt nonnulli exquisitarum literarum omnino rudes et nullius judicii homines, qui partim a circumpadanis municipiis partim ex transalpinis provinciis, in hanc urbem confluxerunt. Emendavit igitur eruditissmus hic vir corruptam et vitiosam linguæ latinæ consuetudinem, pura ac integra loquendi ratione."

[3] Corio, *Storia di Milano*, fol. 449, for the letter of Isabella of Aragon to her father, Alfonso of Naples; fols. 451, 464, two letters of the Moor to Charles VIII. *Cf.* the story in the *Lettere Pittoriche*, iii, 86 (Sebastiano

They are models of pure Latinity. To maintain a faultless style under all circumstances was a rule of good breeding and a result of habit. Besides these officials, private scholars of all kinds naturally had correspondence of their own. The object of letter-writing was seldom what it is nowadays, to give information as to the circumstances of the writer, or news of other people; it was rather treated as a literary work done to give evidence of scholar-

FIG. 114. PIETRO BEMBO
By Titian
Rome, Galleria Barberini

ship and to win the consideration of those to whom it was addressed. These letters began early to serve the purpose of learned disquisition; and Petrarch, who introduced this form of letter-writing, revived the forms of the old epistolary style, putting the classical 'thou' in place of the 'you' of medieval Latin. At a later period letters became collections of neatly turned phrases, by which subjects were encouraged or humiliated, colleagues flattered or insulted, and patrons eulogized or begged from.[1]

del Piombo to Aretino), how Clement VII during the sack of Rome called his learned men round him, and made each of them write separately a letter to Charles V.

[1] For the correspondence of the period in general see Voigt, *Wiederbelebung*, 414–427.

The letters of Cicero, Pliny, and others were at this time diligently studied as models. As early as the fifteenth century a mass of forms and instructions for Latin correspondence had appeared, as accessory to the great grammatical and lexicographic works, the mass of which is astounding to us even now when we look at them in the libraries. But just as the existence of these helps tempted many to undertake a task to which they had no vocation, so were the really capable men stimulated to a more faultless excellence, till at length the letters of Politian, and at the beginning of the sixteenth century those of Pietro Bembo, appeared, and took their place as unrivalled masterpieces not only of Latin style in general, but also of the more special art of letter-writing.

Together with these there appeared in the sixteenth century the classical style of Italian correspondence, at the head of which stands Bembo again.[1] Its form is wholly modern, and deliberately kept free from Latin influence, and yet its spirit is thoroughly penetrated and possessed by the ideas of antiquity. These letters, though partly of a confidential nature, are mostly written with a view to possible publication in the future, and always on the supposition that they might be worth showing on account of their elegance. After the year 1530 printed collections began to appear, either the letters of miscellaneous correspondents in irregular succession, or of single writers; and the same Bembo whose fame was so great as a Latin correspondent won as high a position in his own language.[2]

But at a time and among a people where 'listening' was among the chief pleasures of life, and where every imagination was filled with the memory of the Roman Senate and its great speakers, the orator occupied a far more brilliant place than the letter-writer.[3] Eloquence had shaken off the influence of the Church, in which it had found a refuge during the Middle Ages, and now became an indispensable element and ornament of all elevated lives. Many of the social hours which are now filled with music were then given to Latin or Italian oratory; and yet Bartolommeo Facio complained that the orators of his time were at a disadvantage compared with those of antiquity; of three kinds of oratory which were open to the latter one only was left to the former, since forensic oratory was abandoned to the jurists, and the speeches in the councils of the Government had to be delivered in Italian.[4]

The social position of the speaker was a matter of perfect indifference; what was desired was simply the most cultivated humanistic talent. At the Court of Borso of Ferrara the Duke's physician, Jeronimo da Castello, was chosen to deliver the congratulatory address on the visits of Frederick III and of Pius II.[5] Married laymen ascended the pulpits of the churches at any

---

[1] Bembo thought it necessary to excuse himself for writing in Italian, *Ad Sempronium, Bembi Opera*, vol. iii, 156 *sqq.* (Basel, 1556).

[2] On the collection of the letters of Aretino see above, pp. 170 *sqq.*, and note 2. Collections of Latin letters had been printed even in the fifteenth century.

[3] *Cf.* the speeches in the *Opera* of Philelphus, Sabellicus, Beroaldus, etc., and the writings and lives of Giannozzo Manetti, Æneas Sylvius, and others.

[4] B. F., *De Vir. Ill.*, ed. Mehus, p. 7. Manetti, as Vespas. Bisticci, *Comment.*, p. 51, states, delivered many speeches in Italian, and then afterward wrote them out in Latin. The scholars of the fifteenth century—for example, Paolo Cortese—judge the achievements of the past solely from the point of view of the *Eloquentia*.

[5] *Diario Ferrarese*, in Murat., xxiv, col. 198, 205.

occasion of festivity or mourning, and even on the feast-days of the saints. It struck the non-Italian members of the Council of Basel as something strange that the Archbishop of Milan should summon Æneas Sylvius, who was then unordained, to deliver a public discourse at the feast of St Ambrogius; but they suffered it in spite of the murmurs of the theologians, and listened to the speaker with the greatest curiosity.[1]

FIG. 115. ÆNEAS SYLVIUS MAKING A SPEECH WHEN PAPAL LEGATE
By Pinturicchio
Siena, Cathedral Library
Photo Alinari

Let us glance for a moment at the most frequent and important occasions of public speaking.

It was not for nothing, in the first place, that the ambassadors from one state to another received the title of orators. Whatever else might be done in the way of secret negotiation, the envoy never failed to make a public appearance and deliver a public speech, under circumstances of the greatest possible pomp and ceremony.[2] As a rule, however numerous the embassy might be, one individual spoke for all; but it happened to Pius II, a critic before whom all were glad to be heard, to be forced to sit and listen to a whole deputation, one

---

[1] *Pii II Comment.*, lib. i, p. 10.
[2] The success of the fortunate orator was great, and the humiliation of the speaker who broke down before distinguished audiences no less great. Examples of the latter in Petrus Crinitus, *De Honesta Disciplina*, v, cap. 3. *Cf.* Vespas. Fiorent., pp. 319, 431.

after another.[1] Learned princes who had the gift of speech were themselves fond of discoursing in Latin or Italian. The children of the house of Sforza were trained to this exercise. The boy Galeazzo Maria delivered in 1455 a fluent speech before the Great Council at Venice,[2] and his sister Ippolita saluted Pope Pius II with a graceful address at the Congress of Mantua.[3] Pius himself through all his life did much by his oratory to prepare the way for his final elevation to the Papal chair. Great as he was both as scholar and diplomatist, he would probably never have become Pope without the fame and the charm of his eloquence. "For nothing was more lofty than the dignity of his oratory."[4] Without doubt this was a reason why multitudes held him to be the fittest man for the office, even before his election.

Princes were also commonly received on public occasions with speeches which sometimes lasted for hours. This happened, of course, only when the prince was known as a lover of eloquence,[5] or wished to pass for such, and when a competent speaker was present, whether university professor, official, ecclesiastic, physician, or Court scholar.

Every other political opportunity was seized with the same eagerness, and according to the reputation of the speaker the concourse of the lovers of culture was great or small. At the yearly change of public officers, and even at the consecration of new bishops, a humanist was sure to come forward, and sometimes addressed his audience in hexameters or Sapphic verses.[6] Often a newly appointed official was himself forced to deliver a speech more or less relevant to his department, as, for instance, on justice; and lucky for him if he were well up in his part! At Florence even the *condottieri*, whatever their origin or education might be, were compelled to accommodate themselves to the popular sentiment, and on receiving the insignia of their office were harangued before the assembled people by the most learned Secretary of State.[7] It seems that beneath or close to the Loggia dei Lanzi—the porch where the Government was wont to appear solemnly before the people—a tribune or platform (*rostra*, *ringhiera*) was erected for such purposes.

Anniversaries, especially those of the death of princes, were commonly celebrated by memorial speeches. Even the funeral oration strictly so called

[1] *Pii II Comment.*, lib. iv, p. 205. There were some Romans too who awaited him at Viterbo. "Singuli per se verba fecere, ne alius alio melior videretur, cum essent eloquentia ferme pares." The fact that the Bishop of Arezzo was not allowed to speak in the name of the general embassy of the Italian states to the newly chosen Alexander VI is seriously placed by Guicciardini (at the beginning of Book I) among the causes which helped to produce the disaster of 1494. [2] Told by Marin Sanudo, in Murat., xxii, col. 1160.
[3] *Pii II Comment.*, lib. ii, p. 107. *Cf.* p. 87. Another oratorical princess, Madonna Battista Montefeltro, married to a Malatesta, harangued Sigismund and Martin. Cf. *Archiv. Stor.*, iv, i, p. 422, note.
[4] *De Expeditione in Turcas*, in Murat., xxiii, col. 68. "Nihil enim Pii concionantis majestate sublimius." Not to speak of the naïve pleasure with which Pius describes his own triumphs, see Campanus, *Vita Pii II*, in Murat., iii, ii, *passim*. At a later period these speeches were judged less admiringly. *Cf.* Voigt, *Enea Silvio*, ii, 275 *sqq.*
[5] Charles V, when unable on one occasion to follow the flourishes of a Latin orator at Genoa, sighed in the ear of Giovio: "Ah, my tutor Adrian was right when he told me I should be chastened for my childish idleness in learning Latin." Paul. Jovius, *Vita Hadriani VI.* Princes replied to these speeches through their official orators; Frederick III through Æneas Sylvius, in answer to Giannozzo Manetti. Vespas. Bisticci, *Comment.*, p. 64.
[6] Lil. Greg. Gyraldus, *De Poetis nostri Temp.*, ed. Wotke, p. 72, speaking of Collenuccio. Filelfo, a married layman, delivered an introductory speech in the Cathedral at Como for the Bishop Scarampi in 1460. Rosmini, *Filelfo*, ii, 122; iii, 147.   [7] Fabroni, *Cosmus*, Adnot. 52.

was generally entrusted to a humanist, who delivered it in church, clothed in a secular dress; nor was it only princes, but officials, or persons otherwise distinguished, to whom this honour was paid.[1] This was also the case with the speeches delivered at weddings or betrothals, with the difference that they seem to have been made in the palace, instead of in church, like that of Filelfo at the betrothal of Anna Sforza with Alfonso d'Este in the castle of Milan. It is still possible that the ceremony may have taken place in the chapel of the castle. Private families of distinction no doubt also employed such wedding orators as one of the luxuries of high life. At Ferrara Guarino was requested on these occasions to send some one or other of his pupils.[2] The church simply took charge of the religious ceremonies at weddings and funerals.

The academical speeches, both those made at the installation of a new teacher and at the opening of a new course of lectures,[3] were delivered by the professor himself, and treated as occasions of great rhetorical display. The ordinary university lectures also usually had an oratorical character.[4]

With regard to forensic eloquence, the quality of the audience determined the form of speech. In case of need it was enriched with all sorts of philosophical and antiquarian learning.

As a special class of speeches we may mention the addresses made in Italian on the battlefield, either before or after the combat. Federigo of Urbino[5] was esteemed a classic in this style; he used to pass among his squadrons as they stood drawn up in order of battle, inspiring them in turn with pride and enthusiasm. Many of the speeches in the military historians of the fifteenth century, as, for instance, in Porcellius (p. 117), may be, in fact at least, imaginary, but may be also in part faithful representations of words actually spoken. The addresses, again, which were delivered to the Florentine Militia,[6] organized in 1506 chiefly through the influence of Machiavelli, and which were spoken first at reviews, and afterward at special annual festivals, were of another kind. They were simply general appeals to the patriotism of the hearers, and were addressed to the assembled troops in the church of each quarter of the city by a citizen in armour, sword in hand.

---

[1] Which, nevertheless, gave some offence to Jac. Volaterranus (in Murat., xxiii, col. 171) at the service in memory of Platina.

[2] *Aneed. Lit.*, i, p. 299, in Fedra's funeral oration on Lod. Podacataro, whom Guarino commonly employed on these occasions. Guarino himself delivered over fifty speeches at festivals and funerals, which are enumerated in Rosmini, *Guarino*, ii, 139-146. [Burckhardt, 332. Dr Geiger here remarks that Venice also had its professional orators. *Cf.* C. Voigt, ii, 425.—S. G. C. M.]

[3] Many of these opening lectures have been preserved in the works of Sabellicus, Beroaldus Major, Codrus Urceus, etc. In the works of the latter there are also some poems which he recited " in principio studii."

[4] The fame of Pomponazzo's delivery is preserved in Paul. Jovius, *Elogia Vir. Doct.*, p. 134. In general it seems that the speeches, the form of which was required to be perfect, were learnt by heart. In the case of Giannozzo Manetti we know positively that it was so on one occasion (*Comment.*, 39). See, however, the account p. 64, with the concluding statement that Manetti spoke better *impromptu* than Aretino with preparation. We are told of Codrus Urceus, whose memory was weak, that he read his orations (*Vita*, at the end of his works, fol. lxx., Venice, 1506). The following passage will illustrate the exaggerated value set on oratory: "Ausim affirmare perfectum oratorem (si quisquam modo sit perfectus orator) ita facile posse nitorem, lætitiam, lumina et umbras rebus dare quas oratione exponendas suscipit, ut pictorem suis coloribus et pigmentis facere videmus" (Petr. Alcyonius, *De Exilio*, ed. Mencken, p. 136).

[5] Vespas. Fiorent., p. 103. *Cf.* p. 598, where he describes how Giannozzo Manetti came to him in the camp.

[6] *Archiv. Stor.*, xv, pp. 113, 121. Canestrini's Introduction, pp. 32 *sqq.* Reports of two such speeches to soldiers; the first, by Alamanni, is wonderfully fine and worthy of the occasion (1528).

Finally the oratory of the pulpit began in the fifteenth century to lose its distinctive peculiarities. Many of the clergy had entered into the circle of

FIG. 116. ST BERNARDINE PREACHING BEFORE THE CHURCH OF S. FRANCESCO, IN SIENA
By Sano di Pietro
Siena, Cathedral (chapter-house). Photo Alinari

classical culture, and were ambitious of success in it. The street-preacher Bernardino da Siena, who even in his lifetime passed for a saint, and who was worshipped by the populace, was not above taking lessons in rhetoric from the famous Guarino, although he had only to preach in Italian. Never, indeed, was more expected from preachers than at this time—especially from the Lenten preachers; and there were not a few audiences which could not only tolerate, but which demanded a strong dose of philosophy from the pulpit.[1] But we have here especially to speak of the distinguished occasional preachers in Latin. Many of their opportunities had been taken away from them, as has been observed, by learned laymen. Speeches on particular saints' days, at weddings and funerals, or at the installation of a bishop, and even the introductory speech at the first Mass of a clerical friend, or the address at the festival of some religious order, were all left to laymen.[2] But at all events at the Papal Court in the fifteenth century, whatever the occasion might be, the preachers were generally monks. Under Sixtus IV Giacomo da Volterra regularly enumerates these preachers, and criticizes them according to the rules of the art.[3] Fedra Inghirami, famous as an orator under Julius II, had at least received holy orders and was canon at St John Lateran; and besides him, elegant Latinists were now common enough among the prelates. In this matter, as in others, the exaggerated privileges of the profane humanists appear lessened in the sixteenth century—on which point we shall presently speak more fully.

What now was the subject and general character of these speeches? The national gift of eloquence was not wanting to the Italians of the Middle Ages, and a so-called ' rhetoric ' belonged from the first to the seven liberal arts; but so far as the revival of the ancient methods is concerned, this merit must be ascribed, according to Filippo Villani,[4] to the Florentine Bruno Casini, who died of the plague in 1348. With the practical purpose of fitting his country-men to speak with ease and effect in public, he treated, after the pattern of the ancients, invention, declamation, bearing, and gesticulation, each in its proper connexion. Elsewhere too we read of an oratorical training directed solely to practical application. No accomplishment was more highly esteemed than the power of elegant improvisation in Latin.[5] The growing study of Cicero's speeches and theoretical writings, of Quintilian, and of the Imperial panegyrists, the appearance of new and original treatises,[6] the general progress of anti-quarian learning, and the stores of ancient matter and thought which now could and must be drawn from—all combined to shape the character of the new eloquence.

This character, nevertheless, differed widely according to the individual.

---

[1] On this point see Faustinus Terdoceus, in his satire *De Triumpho Stultitiæ*, lib. ii.

[2] Both of these extraordinary cases occur in Sabellicus, *Opera*, fol. 61-82. *De Origine et Auctu Religionis*, delivered at Verona from the pulpit before the barefoot friars; and *De Sacerdotii Laudibus*, delivered at Venice.

[3] Jac. Volaterranus, *Diar. Roman.*, in Murat., xxiii, *passim*. In col. 173 a remarkable sermon before the Court, though in the absence of Sixtus IV, is mentioned. Pater Paolo Toscanella thundered against the Pope, his family, and the cardinals. When Sixtus heard of it he smiled.

[4] Fil. Villani, *Vitæ*, ed. Galetti, p. 30.

[5] See above, p. 242, note 4.

[6] Georg. Trapezunt, *Rhetorica*, the first complete system of instruction (1436). Æneas Sylvius, *Artis Rhetoricæ Præcepta* in the *Opera*, p. 992 (1456), treats purposely only of the construction of sentences and the position of words. It is characteristic as an instance of the routine which was followed. He names several other theoretical writers who are some of them no longer known. *Cf.* C. Voigt, ii, 262 *sqq.*

Many speeches breathe a spirit of true eloquence, especially those which keep to the matter treated of; of this kind is the mass of what is left to us of Pius II. The miraculous effects produced by Giannozzo Manetti [1] point to an orator the like of whom has not been often seen. His great audiences as envoy before Nicholas V and before the Doge and Council of Venice were events not to be soon forgotten. Many orators, on the contrary, would seize the opportunity not only to flatter the vanity of distinguished hearers, but to load their speeches with an enormous amount of antiquarian rubbish. How it was possible to endure this infliction for two and even three hours can only be understood when we take into account the intense interest then felt in everything connected with antiquity, and the rarity and defectiveness of treatises on the subject at a time when printing was but little diffused. Such orations had at least the value which we have claimed (p. 238) for many of Petrarch's letters. But some speakers went too far. Most of Filelfo's speeches are an atrocious patchwork of classical and Biblical quotations tacked on to a string of commonplaces, among which the great people he wishes to

FIG. 117. PRESENTATION OF A LAUDATORY ADDRESS BY CAPELLO TO THE DOGE BARBARIGO (1486)
Miniature from a manuscript in the British Museum

flatter are arranged under the head of the cardinal virtues, or some such category, and it is only with the greatest trouble, in his case and in that of many others, that we can extricate the few historical notices of value which they really contain. The speech, for instance, of a scholar and professor of Piacenza at the reception of the Duke Galeazzo Maria, in 1467, begins with Julius Cæsar, then proceeds to mix up a mass of classical quotations with a number from an allegorical work by the speaker himself, and concludes with some exceedingly indiscreet advice to the ruler. [2] Fortunately it was late at night,

---

[1] His life, in Murat., xx, is full of the triumphs of his eloquence. *Cf.* Vespas. Fiorent., pp. 592 *sqq.*, and *Comment.*, p. 30. On us these speeches make no great impression—for example, that at the coronation of Frederick III, in Freher-Struve, *Script. Rer. Germ.*, iii, 4–19. Of Manetti's oration at the burial of Leonardo Aretino Shepherd-Tonelli says (*Poggio*, ii, 67 *sqq.*): " L' orazione ch' ei compose, è ben la cosa la più meschina che potesse udirsi, piena di puerilità volgare nello stile, irrelevante negli argomenti e d' una prolissità insopportabile." [2] *Annales Placentini*, in Murat., xx, col. 918.

and the orator had to be satisfied with handing his written panegyric to the prince. Filelfo begins a speech at a betrothal with the words: "Aristotle, the peripatetic." Others start with P. Cornelius Scipio, and the like, as though neither they nor their hearers could wait a moment for a quotation. At the end of the fifteenth century public taste suddenly improved, chiefly through Florentine influence, and the practice of quotation was restricted within due limits. Many works of reference were now in existence, in which the first comer could find as much as he wanted of what had hitherto been the admiration of princes and people.

As most of the speeches were written out beforehand in the study the manuscripts served as a means of further publicity afterward. The great extemporaneous speakers, on the other hand, were attended by shorthand writers.[1] We must further remember that all the orations which have come down to us were not intended to be actually delivered. The panegyric, for example, of the elder Beroaldus on Lodovico il Moro was presented to him in manuscript.[2] In fact, just as letters were written addressed to all conceivable persons and parts of the world as exercises, as formularies, or even to serve a controversial end, so there were speeches for imaginary occasions [3] to be used as models for the reception of princes, bishops, and other dignitaries.

For oratory, as for the other arts, the death of Leo X (1521) and the sack of Rome (1527) mark the epoch of decadence. Giovio,[4] but just escaped from the desolation of the Eternal City, describes, not exhaustively, but on the whole truly, the causes of this decline.

The plays of Plautus and Terence, once a school of Latin style for the educated Romans, are banished to make room for Italian comedies. Graceful speakers no longer find the recognition and reward which they once did. The Consistorial Advocates no longer prepare anything but the introductions to their speeches, and deliver the rest—a confused muddle—on the inspiration of the moment. Sermons and occasional speeches have sunk to the same level. If a funeral oration is wanted for a cardinal or other great personage the executors do not apply to the best orators in the city, to whom they would have to pay a hundred pieces of gold, but they hire for a trifle the first impudent pedant whom they come across, and who only wants to be talked of, whether for good or ill. The dead, they say, is none the wiser if an ape stands in a black dress in the pulpit, and beginning with a hoarse, whimpering mumble, passes little by little into a loud howling. Even the sermons preached at great Papal ceremonies are no longer profitable, as they used to be. Monks of all Orders have again got them into their hands, and preach as if they were speaking to the mob. Only a few years ago a sermon at Mass before the Pope might easily lead the way to a bishopric.

---

[1] For example, Manetti. *Cf.* Vespasiano, *Comment.*, p. 30; so, too, Savonarola. *Cf.* Perrens, *Vie de Savonarole*, i, p. 163. The shorthand-writers, however, could not always follow him, or, indeed, any rapid *improvisatori*. Savonarola preached in Italian. See Pasq. Villari, *Vita di Savonarola*.

[2] It was by no means one of the best (*Opuscula Beroaldi*, fol. xviii-xxi, Basel, 1509). The most remarkable thing in it is the flourish at the end: "Esto tibi ipsi archetypon et exemplar, teipsum imitare," etc.

[3] Letters and speeches of this kind were written by Alberto da Rivalta; *cf.* the *Annales Placentini*, written by his father Antonius and continued by himself, in Murat., xx, col. 914 *sqq.*, where the pedant gives an instructive account of his own literary career.

[4] *Pauli Jovii Dialogus de Viris Litteris Illustribus*, in Tiraboschi, tom. vii, Parte IV. Yet he says some ten years later, at the close of the *Elogia Literaria*: "Tenemus adhuc [after the leadership in philology had passed to the Germans] sinceræ et constantis eloquentiæ munitam arcem," etc. The whole passage, given in German in Gregorovius, viii, 217 *sqq.*, is important, as showing the view taken of Germany by an Italian, and is again quoted below in this connexion.

CHAPTER VIII

LATIN TREATISES AND HISTORY

FROM the oratory and the epistolary writings of the humanists we shall here pass on to their other creations, which were all, to a greater or less extent, reproductions of antiquity.

Among these must be placed the treatise, which often took the shape of a dialogue.[1] In this case it was borrowed directly from Cicero. In order to do anything like justice to this class of literature—in order not to throw it aside at first sight as a bore—two things must be taken into consideration. The century which escaped from the influence of the Middle Ages felt the need of something to mediate between itself and antiquity in many questions of morals and philosophy; and this need was met by the writer of treatises and dialogues. Much which appears to us as mere commonplace in their writings was for them and their contemporaries a new and hardly won view of things upon which mankind had been silent since the days of antiquity. The language too, in this form of writing, whether Italian or Latin, moved more freely and flexibly than in historical narrative, in letters, or in oratory, and thus became in itself the source of a special pleasure. Several Italian compositions of this kind still hold their place as patterns of style. Many of these works have been, or will be, mentioned on account of their contents; we here refer to them as a class. From the time of Petrarch's letters and treatises down to near the end of the fifteenth century the heaping up of learned quotations, as in the case of the orators, is the main business of most of these writers. The whole style, especially in Italian, was then suddenly clarified, till in the *Asolani* of Bembo and the *Vita Sobria* of Luigi Cornaro[2] a classical perfection was reached. Here too the decisive fact was that antiquarian matter of every kind had meantime begun to be deposited in encyclopædic works (now printed), and no longer stood in the way of the essayist.

It was inevitable, too, that the humanistic spirit should control the writing of history. A superficial comparison of the histories of this period with the earlier chronicles, especially with works so full of life, colour, and brilliancy as those of the Villani, will lead us loudly to deplore the change. How insipid and conventional appear by their side the best of the humanists, and particularly their immediate and most famous successors among the historians of Florence,

---

[1] A special class is formed by the semi-satirical dialogues, which Collenuccio, and still more Pontano, copied from Lucian. Their example stimulated Erasmus and Hutten. For the treatises properly so called parts of the ethical writings of Plutarch may have served as models.

[2] See below, Part IV, Chapter V.

Leonardo Aretino and Poggio! [1] The enjoyment of the reader is incessantly marred by the sense that, in the classical phrases of Facius, Sabellicus, Folieta, Senarega, Platina in the chronicles of Mantua, Bembo in the annals of Venice, and even of Giovio in his histories, the best local and individual colouring and the full sincerity of interest in the truth of events have been lost. Our mistrust is increased when we hear that Livy, the pattern of this school of writers, was copied just where he is least worthy of imitation—on the ground, namely,[2] "that he turned a dry and naked tradition into grace and richness." In the

FIG. 118. WOODCUT FROM PLATINA'S "LIVES OF THE POPES" (VENICE, 1504)

Photo Rosenthal, Munich

same place we meet with the suspicious declaration that it is the function of the historian—just as if he were one with the poet—to excite, charm, or overwhelm the reader. We must further remember that many humanistic historians knew but little of what happened outside their own sphere, and this little they were often compelled to adapt to the taste of their patrons and employers. We ask ourselves finally whether the contempt for modern things which these same humanists sometimes avowed openly [3] must not necessarily have had an unfortunate influence on their treatment of them. Unconsciously the reader finds himself looking with more interest and confidence on the unpretending Latin and Italian annalists, like those of Bologna and Ferrara, who remained true to the old style, and still more grateful does he feel to the best of the genuine chroniclers who wrote in Italian—to Marino Sanudo, Corio, and Infessura—who were followed at the beginning of the sixteenth century by that new and illustrious band of great national historians who wrote in their mother tongue.

Contemporary history, no doubt, was written far better in the language of the day than when forced into Latin. Whether Italian was also more suitable

---

[1] *Cf.* the epigram of Sannazaro:

> "Dum patriam laudat, damnat dum Poggius hostem,
> Nec malus est civis, nec bonus historicus."

[2] Benedictus, *Caroli VIII Hist.*, in Eccard, *Scriptores*, ii, col. 1577.

[3] Petrus Crinitus deplores this contempt, *De Honesta Disciplina*, lib. xviii, cap. 9. The humanists here resemble the writers in the decline of antiquity, who also severed themselves from their own age. *Cf.* Burckhardt, *Die Zeit Constantins des Grossen*, 4th ed., pp. 272–275 (1924). See for the other side several declarations of Poggio in Voigt, *Wiederbelebung*, pp. 443 *sqq.*

for the narrative of events long past or for historical research is a question which admits, for that period, of more answers than one. Latin was, at that time, the *lingua franca* of instructed people not only in an international sense, as a means of intercourse between Englishmen, Frenchmen, and Italians, but also in an interprovincial sense. The Lombard, the Venetian, and the Neapolitan modes of writing, though long modelled on the Tuscan, and bearing but slight traces of the dialect, were still not recognized by the Florentines. This was of less consequence in local contemporary histories, which were sure of readers at the place where they were written, than in the narratives of the past, for which a larger public was desired. In these the local interests of the people had to be sacrificed to the general interests of the learned. How far would the influence of a man like Blondus of Forlì have reached if he had written his great monuments of learning in the dialect of the Romagna? They would have assuredly sunk into neglect, if only through the contempt of the Florentines, while written in Latin they exercised the profoundest influence on the whole European world of learning. And even the Florentines in the fifteenth century wrote Latin not only because their minds were imbued with humanism, but in order to be more widely read.

Finally there exist certain Latin essays in contemporary history which stand on a level with the best Italian works of the kind. When the continuous narrative after the manner of Livy—that Procrustean bed of so many writers—is abandoned the change is marvellous. The same Platina and Giovio, whose great histories we only read because and so far as we must, suddenly come forward as masters in the biographical style. We have already referred to Tristan Caracciolo, the biographical works of Facius, and the Venetian topography of Sabellico, and others will be mentioned in the sequel. Historical composition, like letters and oratory, soon had its theory. Following the example of Cicero, it proclaims with pride the worth and dignity of history, boldly claims Moses and the Evangelists as simple historians, and concludes with earnest exhortations to strict impartiality and love of truth.[1]

The Latin treatises on past history were naturally concerned, for the most part, with classical antiquity. What we are more surprised to find among these humanists are some considerable works on the history of the Middle Ages. The first of this kind was the chronicle of Matteo Palmieri (449-1449), beginning where Prosper Aquitanus ceases, the style of which was certainly an offence to later critics like Paolo Cortese. On opening the *Decades* of Blondus of Forlì we are surprised to find a universal history, "ab inclinatione Romanorum imperii," as in Gibbon, full of original studies on the authors of each century, and occupied, through the first three hundred folio pages, with early medieval history down to the death of Frederick II. And this when in Northern countries nothing more was wanted than chronicles of the Popes and Emperors, and the *fasciculus temporum*. We cannot here stay to show what writings Blondus made use of, and where he found his materials, though this justice will

[1] Lorenzo Valla, in the preface to the *Historia Ferdinandi Regis Arag.*; in opposition to him Giacomo Zeno in the *Vita Caroli Zeni*, in Murat., xix, 204. See too Guarino, in Rosmini, ii, 62 *sqq.*, 177 *sqq.*

some day be done to him by the historians of literature.[1] This book alone would entitle us to say that it was the study of antiquity which made the study of the Middle Ages possible, by first training the mind to habits of impartial historical criticism. To this must be added that the Middle Ages were now over for Italy, and that the Italian mind could the better appreciate them because it stood outside them. It cannot, nevertheless, be said that it at once judged them fairly, and still less that it judged them with piety. In art a fixed prejudice showed itself against all that those centuries had created, and the humanists date the new era from the time of their own appearance. Boccaccio says:[2]

> I begin to hope and believe that God has had mercy on the Italian name, since I see that His infinite goodness puts souls into the breasts of the Italians like those of the ancients—souls which seek fame by other means than robbery and violence, namely, on the path of poetry, which makes men immortal.

But this narrow and unjust temper did not preclude investigation in the minds of the more gifted men, at a time, too, when elsewhere in Europe any such investigation would have been out of the question. An historical criticism[3] of the Middle Ages was practicable just because the rational treatment of all subjects by the humanists had trained the historical spirit. In the fifteenth century this spirit had so far penetrated the history even of the individual cities of Italy that the stupid fairy-tales about the origin of Florence, Venice, and Milan vanished, while at the same time, and long after, the chronicles of the North were stuffed with this fantastic rubbish, destitute for the most part of all poetical value, and invented as late as the fourteenth century.

The close connexion between local history and the sentiment of glory has already been touched on in reference to Florence (Part I, Chapter VII). Venice would not be behindhand. Just as a great rhetorical triumph of the Florentines[4] would cause a Venetian embassy to write home post-haste for an orator to be sent after them, so too the Venetians felt the need of a history which would bear comparison with those of Leonardo Aretino and Poggio. And it was to satisfy this feeling that in the fifteenth century, after negotiations with Giovanni Maria Filelfo and others had failed, the *Decades* of Sabellico appeared, and in the sixteenth the *Historia Rerum Venetarum* of Pietro Bembo, both written at the express charge of the republic, the latter a continuation of the former.

The great Florentine historians at the beginning of the sixteenth century (pp. 102 *sqq.*) were men of a wholly different kind from the Latinists Bembo and Giovio. They wrote Italian not only because they could not vie with the Ciceronian elegance of the philologists, but because, like Machiavelli, they could

---

[1] It has since been done by Alfred Masius, *Flavio Biondo* (Leipzig, 1879), and Paul Buchholz, *Die Quellen der Historiarum Decades von Flavius Blondus* (Leipzig, 1881). See also G. Romano, *Degli Studi sul Medioevo nella Storici del Rinascimento* (Pavia, 1892).—W.G.]

[2] In the letter to Pizinga, *Opere Volgari*, vol. xvi, p. 38. With Raph. Volaterranus, lib. xxi, the intellectual world begins in the fourteenth century. He is the same writer whose early books contain so many notices—excellent for his time—of the history of all countries.

[3] Here, too, Petrarch cleared the way. See especially his critical investigation of the Austrian Charter, claiming to descend from Cæsar. *Epist. Sen.*, xvi, 1.

[4] Like that of Giannozzo Manetti in the presence of Nicholas V, of the whole Papal Court, and of a great concourse of strangers from all parts. *Cf.* Vespas. Fiorent., p. 591, and more fully in the *Comment.*, pp. 37-40.

record only in a living tongue the living results of their own immediate observations—and we may add in the case of Machiavelli of his observation of the past—and because, as in the case of Guicciardini, Varchi, and many others, what they most desired was that their view of the course of events should have as wide and deep a practical effect as possible. Even when they write only for a few friends, like Francesco Vettori, they feel an inward need to utter their testimony on men and events, and to explain and justify their share in the latter.

And yet, with all that is characteristic in their language and style, they were powerfully affected by antiquity, and without its influence would be inconceivable. They were not humanists, but they had passed through the school of humanism, and they have in them more of the spirit of the ancient historians than most of the imitators of Livy. Like the ancients, they were citizens who wrote for citizens.

CHAPTER IX

GENERAL LATINIZATION OF CULTURE

WE cannot attempt to trace the influence of humanism in the special sciences. Each has its own history, in which the Italian investigators of this period, chiefly through their rediscovery of the results attained by antiquity,[1] mark a new epoch, with which the modern period of the science in question begins with more or less distinctness. With regard to philosophy too we must refer the reader to the special historical works on the subject. The influence of the old philosophers on Italian culture will appear at times immense, at times inconsiderable; the former, when we consider how the doctrines of Aristotle, chiefly drawn from the *Ethics* [2] and *Politics*—both widely diffused at an early period—became the common property of educated Italians, and how the whole method of abstract thought was governed by him;[3] the latter, when we remember how slight was the dogmatic influence of the old philosophies, and even of the enthusiastic Florentine Platonists, on the spirit of the people at large. What looks like such an influence is generally no more than a consequence of the new culture in general, and of the special growth and development of the Italian mind. When we come to speak of religion we shall have more to say on this head. But in by far the greater number of cases we have to do not with the general culture of the people, but with the utterances of individuals or of learned circles; and here too a distinction must be drawn between the true assimilation of ancient doctrines and fashionable make-believe. For with many antiquity was only a fashion, even among very learned people.

Nevertheless, all that looks like affectation to our age need not then have been actually so. The giving of Greek and Latin names to children, for example, is better than the practice of taking them, especially the female names, from novels. When the enthusiasm for the ancient world was greater than for the saints it was simple and natural enough that noble families called

---

[1] In fact, it was already said that Homer alone contained the whole of the arts and sciences—that he was an encyclopædia. Cf. *Codri Urcei Opera, Sermo* XIII, at the end. It is true that we meet with a similar opinion in several ancient writers. The words of Codrus Urceus (*Sermo* XIII, "habitus in laudem liberalium artium"; *Opera*, fol. xxxviii*b*, ed. Ven., 1506) are as follows: "Eia ergo bono animo esto; ego græcas litteras tibi exponam; et præcipue divinum Homerum, a quo ceu fonte perenni, ut scribit Naso, vatum Pieriis ora rigantur aquis. Ab Homero grammaticam discere poteris, ab Homero rhetoricam, ab Homero medicinam, ab Homero astrologiam, ab Homero fabulas, ab Homero historias, ab Homero mores, ab Homero philosophorum dogmata, ab Homero artem militarem, ab Homero coquinariam, ab Homero architecturam, ab Homero regendarum urbium modum percipies; et in summa, quidquid boni quidquid honesti animus hominis discendi cupidus optare potest, in Homero facile poteris invenire." To the same effect *Sermo* VII and VIII, *Opera*, fol. xxvi *sqq.*, which treat of Homer only.

[2] A cardinal under Paul II had his cooks instructed in the *Ethics* of Aristotle. *Cf.* Gaspar. Veron., *Vita Pauli II*, in Murat., iii, ii, col. 1034.

[3] For the study of Aristotle in general a speech of Hermolaus Barbarus is specially instructiv

their sons Agamemnon, Tydeus, and Achilles,[1] and that a painter named his son Apelles and his daughter Minerva.[2] Nor will it appear unreasonable that instead of a family name, which people were often glad to get rid of, a well-sounding ancient name was chosen. A local name, shared by all residents in the place, and not yet transformed into a family name, was willingly given up, especially when its religious associations made it inconvenient; Filippo da S. Gemignano called himself Callimachus. The man, misunderstood and insulted by his family, who made his fortune as a scholar in foreign cities, could afford, even if he were a Sanseverino, to change his name to Julius Pomponius Lætus. Even the simple translation of a name into Latin or Greek, as was almost uniformly the custom in Germany, may be excused to a generation which spoke and wrote Latin, and which needed names

FIG. 119. ST JEROME: CORNER OF A STUDY OF THE
FIFTEENTH CENTURY
By Ghirlandaio
Florence, Ognissanti

[1] Bursellis, *Ann. Bonon.*, in Murat., xxiii, col. 898.

[2] Vasari, xi, pp. 189, 257. *Vite di Sodoma e di Garofalo.* It is not surprising that the profligate women at Rome took the most harmonious ancient names—Julia, Lucretia, Cassandra, Portia, Virginia, Penthesilea, under which they appear in Aretino. It was then, perhaps, that the Jews took the names of the great Semitic enemies of the Romans—Hannibal, Hamilcar, Hasdrubal, which even now they commonly bear in Rome. [This last assertion cannot be maintained. Neither Zunz, *Namen der Juden* (Leipzig, 1837), reprinted in Zunz, *Gesammelte Schriften* (Berlin, 1876), nor Steinschneider in his collection in *Il Buonarotti*, ser. ii, vol. vi, pp. 196–199 (1871), speaks of any Jew of that period who bore these names, and even now, according to the inquiries of Prince Buoncompagni from Signor Tagliacapo, in charge of the Jewish archives in Rome, there are only a few who are named Asdrubale, and none Amilcare or Annibale.—L. G.] A careful choice of names is recommended by L. B. Alberti, *Della Famiglia, Opp.*, ii, p. 171. Maffeo Vegio (*De Educatione Liberorum*, lib. i, c. x.) warns his readers against the use of "nomina indecora barbara aut nova, aut quæ gentilium deorum sunt." Names like 'Nero' disgrace the bearer; while others, such as Cicero, Brutus, Naso, Maro, can be used "qualiter per se parum venusta propter tamen eximiam illorum virtutem."

that could be not only declined, but used with facility in verse and prose. What was blameworthy and ridiculous was the change of half a name, baptismal or family, to give it a classical sound and a new sense. Thus Giovanni was turned into Jovianus or Janus, Pietro to Petreius or Pierius, Antonio to Aonius, Sannazaro to Syncerus, Luca Grasso to Lucius Crassus. Ariosto, who speaks with such derision of all this,[1] lived to see children called after his own heroes and heroines.[2]

Nor must we judge too severely the Latinization of many usages of social life, such as the titles of officials, of ceremonies, and the like, in the writers of the period. As long as people were satisfied with a simple, fluent Latin style, as was the case with most writers from Petrarch to Æneas Sylvius, this practice was not so frequent and striking; it became inevitable when a faultless, Ciceronian Latin was demanded. Modern names and things no longer harmonized with the style, unless they were first artificially changed. Pedants found a pleasure in addressing municipal counsellors as *Patres Conscripti*, nuns as *Virgines Vestales*, and entitling every saint *Divus* or *Deus*; but men of better taste, such as Paolo Giovio, did so only when and because they could not help it. But as Giovio does it naturally, and lays no stress upon it, we are not offended if in his melodious language the cardinals appear as *Senatores*, their dean as *Princeps Senatus*, excommunication as *Diræ*,[3] and the carnival as *Lupercalia*. This example of this author alone is enough to warn us against drawing a hasty inference from these peculiarities of style as to the writer's whole mode of thinking.

The history of Latin composition cannot here be traced in detail. For fully two centuries the humanists acted as if Latin were, and must remain, the only language worthy to be written. Poggio[4] deplores that Dante wrote his great poem in Italian; and Dante, as is well known, actually made the attempt in Latin, and wrote the beginning of the *Inferno* first in hexameters. The whole future of Italian poetry hung on his not continuing in the same style,[5] but even Petrarch relied more on his Latin poetry than on the *Sonnets* and *Canzoni*, and Ariosto himself was desired by some to write his poem in Latin. A stronger coercion never existed in literature;[6] but poetry shook it off for the most part,

---

[1] "Quasi che 'l nome i buon giudici inganni,
   E che quel meglio t' abbia a far poeta,
   Che non farà lo studio di molt' anni ?"

So jests Ariosto, to whom fortune had certainly given a harmonious name, in the seventh satire, vs. 64.

[2] Or after those of Bojardo, which are in part the same as his.

[3] The soldiers of the French army in 1512 were "omnibus diris ad inferos devocati !" The honest canon Tizio, who in all seriousness pronounced a curse from Macrobius against foreign troops, will be spoken of farther on.

[4] *De Infelicitate Principum*, in Poggio's *Opera*, fol. 152: " Cujus [Dantis] exstat poema præclarum, neque, si literis Latinis constaret, ulla ex parte poetis superioribus [the ancients] postponendum." According to Boccaccio, *Vita di Dante*, p. 74, " many wise men " even then discussed the question why Dante had not written in Latin. Cortesius (*De Hominibus Doctis*, p. 7) complains: " Utinam tam bene cogitationes suas Latinis litteris mandare potuisset, quam bene patrium sermonem illustravit !" He makes the same complaint in speaking of Petrarch and Boccaccio.

[5] His work *De Vulgari Eloquentia* was for long almost unknown, and, valuable as it is to us, could never have exercised the influence of the *Divina Commedia*.

[6] To know how far this fanaticism went we have only to refer to Lil. Greg. Gyraldus, *De Poetis nostri Temporis*, *passim*. Vespasiano Bisticci is one of the few Latin writers of that time who openly confessed that they knew

and it may be said without the risk of too great optimism that it was well for Italian poetry to have had both means of expressing itself. In both something

FIG. 120. CICERO AS ORATOR
Miniature from a manuscript in the Hofbibliothek, Vienna

little of Latin (*Commentario della Vita di G. Manetti*, p. 2), but he knew enough to introduce Latin sentences here and there in his writings, and to read Latin letters (*ibid.*, pp. 96, 165). In reference to this exclusive regard for Latin the following passage may be quoted from Petr. Alcyonius, *De Exilio*, ed. Mencken, p. 213. He says that if Cicero could rise up and behold Rome, "Omnium maxime illum credo perturbarent ineptiæ quorumdam qui, amisso studio veteris linguæ quæ eadem hujus urbis et universæ Italiæ propria erat, dies noctesque incumbunt in linguam Geticam aut Dacicam discendam eandemque omni ratione ampliendam, cum Gothi, Visigothi et Vandali [qui erant olim Getæ et Daci] eam in Italos invexerant, ut artes et linguam et nomen Romanum delerent."

great and characteristic was achieved, and in each we can see the reason why Latin or Italian was chosen. Perhaps the same may be said of prose. The position and influence of Italian culture throughout the world depended on the fact that certain subjects were treated in Latin [1]—*urbi et orbi*—while Italian prose was written best of all by those to whom it cost an inward struggle not to write in Latin.

FIG. 121. PAOLO GIOVIO
Florence, Uffizi
Photo Alinari

From the fourteenth century Cicero was recognized universally as the purest model of prose. This was by no means due solely to a dispassionate opinion in favour of his choice of language, of the structure of his sentences, and of his style of composition, but rather to the fact that the Italian spirit responded fully and instinctively to the amiability of the letter-writer, to the brilliancy of the orator, and to the lucid exposition of the philosophical thinker. Even Petrarch recognized clearly the weaknesses of Cicero as a man and a statesman,[2] though he respected him too much to rejoice over them. After Petrarch's time the epistolary style was formed entirely on the pattern of Cicero; and the rest, with the exception of the narrative style, followed the same influence. Yet the true Ciceronianism, which rejected every phrase which could not be justified out of the great authority, did not appear till the end of the fifteenth century, when the grammatical writings of Lorenzo Valla had begun to tell on all Italy, and when the opinions of the Roman historians of literature had been sifted and compared.[3] Then every shade of difference in the style of the

[1] There were regular stylistic exercises, as in the *Orationes* of the elder Beroaldus, where there are two tales of Boccaccio and even a *canzone* of Petrarch translated into Latin.

[2] *Cf.* Petrarch's letter from the earth to illustrious shades below, *Opera*, pp. 704 *sqq.* See also p. 372 in the work *De Rep. Optime Administranda*: "Sic esse doleo, sed sic est."

[3] A burlesque picture of the fanatical purism prevalent in Rome is given by Jovian. Pontanus in his *Antonius.*

256

ancients was studied with closer and closer attention, till the consoling conclusion was at last reached that in Cicero alone was the perfect model to be
found, or, if all forms of literature were to be embraced, in "that immortal
and almost heavenly age of Cicero." [1]   Men like Pietro Bembo and Pierio
Valeriano now turned all their energies to this one object.   Even those who
had long resisted the tendency and had formed for themselves an archaic style
from the earlier authors [2] yielded at last, and joined in the worship of Cicero.
Longolius, at Bembo's advice, determined to read nothing but Cicero for five
years, and finally took an oath to use no word which did not occur in this
author.   It was this temper which broke out at last in the great war among the
scholars, in which Erasmus and the elder Scaliger led the battle.

For all the admirers of Cicero were by no means so one-sided as to consider
him the only source of language.   In the fifteenth century Politian and Ermolao
Barbaro made a conscious and deliberate effort to form a style of their own,[3]
naturally on the basis of their 'overflowing' learning, though they failed to
inspire their pupils with a similar desire for independence; and our informant
of this fact, Paolo Giovio, pursued the same end.   He first attempted, not
always successfully, but often with remarkable power and elegance, and at no
small cost of effort, to reproduce in Latin a number of modern, particularly of
æsthetic, ideas.   His Latin characteristics of the great painters and sculptors of
his time contain a mixture of the most intelligent and of the most blundering
interpretation.[4]   Even Leo X, who placed his glory in the fact "ut lingua
latina nostra pontificatu dicatur factu auctior," [5] was inclined to a liberal and
not too exclusive Latinity, which, indeed, was in harmony with his pleasure-
loving nature.   He was satisfied when the Latin which he had to read and hear
was lively, elegant, and idiomatic.   Then, too, Cicero offered no model for
Latin conversation, so that here other gods had to be worshipped beside him.
The want was supplied by representations of the comedies of Plautus and
Terence, frequent both in and out of Rome, which for the actors were an
incomparable exercise in Latin as the language of daily life.   The impulse to
the study of the old Latin comedies and to modern imitations of them was
given by the discovery of plays by Plautus in the *Cod. Ursinianus*, which was
brought to Rome in 1428 or 1429.   A few years later, in the pontificate of

[1] *Hadriani (Cornetani) Card. S. Chrysogoni de Sermone Latino Liber*, especially the introduction.   He finds in
Cicero and his contemporaries Latinity in its absolute form (*an sich*).   The same Codrus Urceus, who found in
Homer the sum of all science (see above, p. 252, note 1) says (*Opp.*, ed. 1506, fol. lxv): " Quidquid temporibus
meis aut vidi aut studui libens omne illud Cicero mihi felici dedit omine," and goes so far as to say in another
poem (*ibid.*): " Non habet huic similem doctrinæ Græcia mater."

[2] Paul. Jovius, *Elogia Doct. Vir.*, pp. 187 *sqq.*, speaking of Bapt. Pius.

[3] Paul. Jovius, *Elogia*, on Naugerius, p. 145.   Their ideal, he says, was: " Aliquid in stylo proprium, quod
peculiarem ex certa nota mentis effigiem referret, ex naturæ genio effinxisse."   Politian when in a hurry objected
to writing his letters in Latin.   *Cf.* Raph. Volaterranus, *Comment. Urban.*, lib. xxi.   Politian to Cortesius
(*Epist.*, lib. viii, *Ep.* 16): " Mihi vero longe honestior tauri facies, aut item leonis, quam simiæ videtur "; to
which Cortesius replied: " Ego malo esse assecla et simia Ciceronis quam alumnus."   For Pico's opinion on
the Latin language see the letter quoted above, p. 210.

[4] Paul. Jovius, *Dialogus de Viris Literis Illustribus*, in Tiraboschi, ed. Venez., 1796, tom. vii, p. iv.   It is
well known that Giovio was long anxious to undertake the great work which Vasari accomplished.   In the
dialogue mentioned above it is foreseen and deplored that Latin would now altogether lose its supremacy.

[5] In the *breve* of 1517 to Franc. de' Rosi, composed by Sadoleto, in Roscoe, *Leo X*, ed. Bossi, vi, p. 172.

Paul II, the learned Cardinal of Teano [1] (probably Niccolò Forteguerra of Pistoja) became famous for his critical labours in this branch of scholarship. He set to work upon the most defective plays of Plautus, which were destitute even of the list of characters, and went carefully through the whole remains of this author, chiefly with an eye to the language. Possibly it was he who gave the first impulse for the public representations of these plays. Afterward Pomponius Lætus took up the same subject, and acted as manager when Plautus was put on the stage in the houses of great Churchmen. [2] That these representations became less common after 1520 is mentioned by Giovio, as we have seen (p. 246), among the causes of the decline of eloquence.

We may mention, in conclusion, the analogy between Ciceronianism in literature and the revival of Vitruvius by the architects in the sphere of art. [3] And here, too, the law holds good which prevails elsewhere in the history of the Renaissance, that each artistic movement is preceded by a corresponding movement in the general culture of the age. In this case the interval is not more than about twenty years, if we reckon from Cardinal Hadrian of Corneto (? 1505) to the first avowed Vitruvians.

[1] Gaspar. Veron., *Vita Pauli II*, in Murat., iii, ii, col. 1031. The plays of Seneca and Latin translations of Greek dramas were also performed.

[2] At Ferrara Plautus was played chiefly in the Italian adaptations of Collenuccio, the younger Guarino, and others, and principally for the sake of the plots. Isabella Gonzaga took the liberty of finding him dull. For Latin comedy in general see R. Peiper, in Fleckeisen and Masius, *Neue Jahrb. für Phil. u. Pädag.*, xx, 131–138 (Leipzig, 1874), and *Archiv. für Literaturgesch.*, v, 541 *sqq.* On Pomp. Lætus see *Sabellici Opera, Epist.*, lib. xi, fol. 56 *sqq.*, and below, at the close of Part III.

[3] *Cf.* Burckhardt, *Gesch. der Renaissance in Italien*, 38–41.

CHAPTER X

MODERN LATIN POETRY

THE chief pride of the humanists is, however, their modern Latin poetry. It lies within the limits of our task to treat of it, at least in so far as it serves to characterize the humanistic movement.

How favourable public opinion was to that form of poetry, and how nearly it supplanted all others, has been already shown (p. 254). We may be very sure that the most gifted and highly developed nation then existing in the world did not renounce the use of a language such as the Italian out of mere folly and without knowing what they were doing. It must have been a weighty reason which led them to do so.

This cause was the devotion to antiquity. Like all ardent and genuine devotion, it necessarily prompted men to imitation. At other times and among other nations we find many isolated attempts of the same kind. But only in Italy were the two chief conditions present which were needful for the continuance and development of neo-Latin poetry: a general interest in the subject among the instructed classes, and a partial reawakening of the old Italian genius among the poets themselves—the wondrous echo of a far-off strain. The best of what is produced under these conditions is not imitation, but free production. If we decline to tolerate any borrowed forms in art, if we either set no value on antiquity at all or attribute to it some magical and unapproachable virtue, or if we will pardon no slips in poets who were forced, for instance, to guess or to discover a multitude of syllabic quantities, then we had better let this class of literature alone. Its best works were not created in order to defy criticism, but to give pleasure to the poet and to thousands of his contemporaries.[1]

The least success of all was attained by the epic narratives drawn from the history or legends of antiquity. The essential conditions of a living epic poetry were denied not only to the Romans, who now served as models, but even to the Greeks after Homer. They could not be looked for among the Latins of the Renaissance. And yet the *Africa* of Petrarch[2] probably found as many and as enthusiastic readers and hearers as any epos of modern times. The purpose and origin of the poem are not without interest. The fourteenth

---

[1] For what follows see *Deliciæ Poetarum Italorum*; Paul. Jovius, *Elogia*; Lil. Greg. Gyraldus, *De Poetis nostri Temporis*; and the Appendices to Roscoe, *Leo X*, ed. Bossi.

[2] Two editions of the poem are that of Pingaud (Paris, 1872) and that of Corradini (Padua, 1874). In 1874 two Italian translations also appeared by G. B. Gaudo and A. Palesa. On the *Africa* compare L. Geiger, *Petrarca*, pp. 122 *sqq.*, and p. 270, note 7.

century recognized with sound historical tact the time of the Second Punic War as the noonday of Roman greatness; and Petrarch could not resist writing of this time. Had Silius Italicus been then discovered Petrarch would probably

FIG. 122. VENUS BEFORE JUPITER
From the fresco cycle on the legend of Cupid and Psyche, by Raphael
Rome, Villa Farnesina

have chosen another subject; but as it was, the glorification of Scipio Africanus the Elder was so much in accordance with the spirit of the fourteenth century that another poet, Zanobi di Strada, also proposed to himself the same task, and only from respect for Petrarch withdrew the poem, with which he had already made great progress.[1] If any justification were needed for the *Africa*

[1] Filippo Villani, *Vita*, ed. Galetti, p. 16.

it lies in the fact that in Petrarch's time and afterward Scipio was as much an object of public interest as if he had been alive, and that he was held by many to be a greater man than Alexander, Pompey, and Cæsar.[1] How many modern epics treat of a subject at once so popular, so historical in its basis, and so striking to the imagination? For us, it is true, the poem is unreadable. For other themes of the same kind the reader may be referred to the histories of literature.

A richer and more fruitful vein was discovered in expanding and completing the Græco-Roman mythology. In this too Italian poetry began early to take a part, beginning with the *Teseide* of Boccaccio, which passes for his best poetical work. Under Martin V Maffeo Vegio wrote in Latin a thirteenth book to the *Æneid*; besides which we meet with many less considerable attempts, especially in the style of Claudian—a *Meleagris*, a *Hesperis*, and so forth. Still more curious were the newly invented myths, which peopled the fairest regions of Italy with a primeval race of gods, nymphs, genii, and even shepherds, the epic and bucolic styles here passing into one another. In the narrative or conversational eclogue after the time of Petrarch pastoral life was treated in a purely conventional manner,[2] as a vehicle of all possible feelings and fancies; and this point will be touched on again in the sequel. For the moment we have only to do with the new myths. In them, more clearly than anywhere else, we see the double significance of the old gods to the men of the Renaissance. On the one hand, they replace abstract terms in poetry, and render allegorical figures superfluous; and on the other, they serve as free and independent elements in art, as forms of beauty which can be turned to some account in any and every poem. The example was boldly set by Boccaccio, with his fanciful world of gods and shepherds who people the country round Florence in his *Ninfale d'Ameto* and *Ninfale Fiesolano*. Both these poems were written in Italian. But the masterpiece in this style was the *Sarca* of Pietro Bembo,[3] which tells how the river-god of that name wooed the nymph Garda; of the brilliant marriage-feast in a cave of Monte Baldo; of the prophecies of Manto, daughter of Tiresias; of the birth of the child Mincius; of the founding of Mantua; and of the future glory of Virgil, son of Mincius and of Maia, nymph of Andes. This humanistic rococo is set forth by Bembo in verses of great beauty, concluding with an address to Virgil which any poet might envy him. Such works are often slighted as mere declamation. This is a matter of taste on which we are all free to form our own opinion.

Further, we find long epic poems in hexameters on Biblical or ecclesiastical

---

[1] *Franc. Aleardi Oratio in Laudem Franc. Sfortiæ*, in Murat., xxv, col. 384. In comparing Scipio with Cæsar, Guarino and Cyriacus Anconitanus held the latter, Poggio (*Opera, Epp.*, fol. 125, 134 *sqq.*) the former, to be the greater. For Scipio and Hannibal in the miniatures of Attavante see Vasari, iv, 41. *Vita di Giovanni di Fiesole.* The names of both used for Piccinino and Sforza. See p. 118. There were great disputes as to the relative greatness of the two. Shepherd-Tonelli, i, 262 *sqq.*, and Rosmini; Guarino, ii, 97–111.

[2] The brilliant exceptions, where rural life is treated realistically, will also be mentioned below.

[3] Printed in Mai, *Spicilegium Romanum*, vol. viii, pp. 488–504; about five hundred hexameter verses. [The authenticity of this poem, which Bembo never mentions, is doubtful.—W. G.] Pierio Valeriano followed out the myth in his poetry. See his *Carpio*, in the *Deliciæ Poetarum Italorum*, also in the poet's lesser works, pp. 42–46, published at Cologne, 1811. The frescoes of Brusasorci in the Palazzo Murari at Verona represent the subject of the *Sarca*.

subjects. The authors were by no means always in search of preferment or of Papal favour. With the best of them, and even with less gifted writers, like Battista Mantovano, the author of the *Parthenice*, there was probably an honest desire to serve religion by their Latin verses—a desire with which their half-pagan conception of Catholicism harmonized well enough. Gyraldus goes through a list of these poets, among whom Vida, with his *Christiad*, and Sannazaro, with his three books, *De Partu Virginis*,[1] hold the first place. Sannazaro (b. 1458, d. 1530) is impressive by the steady and powerful flow of his verse, in which Christian and pagan elements are mingled without scruple, by the plastic vigour of his description, and by the perfection of his workmanship. He could venture to introduce Virgil's fourth eclogue into his song of the shepherds at the manger (III, 200 *sqq.*) without fearing a comparison. In treating of the unseen world he sometimes gives proofs of a boldness worthy of Dante, as when King David in the Limbo of the Patriarchs rises up to sing and prophesy (I, 236 *sqq.*), or when the Eternal, sitting on the throne clad in a mantle shining with pictures of all the elements, addresses the heavenly host (III, 17 *sqq.*). At other times he does not hesitate to weave the whole classical mythology into his subject, yet without spoiling the harmony of the whole, since the pagan deities are only accessory figures, and play no important part in the story. To appreciate the artistic genius of that age in all its bearings we must not refuse to notice such works as these. The merit of Sannazaro will appear the greater when we consider that the mixture of Christian and pagan elements is apt to disturb us much more in poetry than in the plastic arts. The latter can still satisfy the eye by beauty of form and colour, and in general are much more independent of the significance of the subject than poetry. With them, the imagination is interested chiefly in the form, with poetry, in the matter. Honest Battista Mantovano in his calendar of the festivals [2] tried another expedient. Instead of making the gods and demigods serve the purposes of sacred history he puts them, as the fathers of the Church did, in active opposition to it. When the Angel Gabriel salutes the Virgin at Nazareth Mercury flies after him from Carmel, and listens at the door. He then announces the result of his eavesdropping to the assembled gods, and stimulates them thereby to desperate resolutions. Elsewhere in his writings,[3] it is true, Thetis, Ceres, Æolus, and other pagan deities pay willing homage to the glory of the Madonna.

The fame of Sannazaro, the number of his imitators, the enthusiastic homage which was paid to him by the greatest men—by Bembo, who wrote his epitaph, and by Titian, who painted his portrait—all show how dear and necessary he was to his age. On the threshold of the Reformation he solved for the Church the problem whether it were possible for a poet to be a Christian as well as a classic; and both Leo and Clement were loud in their thanks for his achievements.

---

[1] Edited and translated by Th. A. Fassnacht in *Drei Perlen der neulateinischen Poesie* (Leutkirch and Leipzig, 1875). See, further, Goethe's *Werke* (Hempel's ed.), vol. xxxii, pp. 157 and 411.

[2] *De Sacris Diebus.* [3] For example, in his eighth eclogue.

FIG. 123. ASSEMBLY OF THE GODS

From the fresco cycle on the legend of Cupid and Psyche, by Raphael

Rome, Villa Farnesina

And, finally, contemporary history was now treated in hexameters or distichs, sometimes in a narrative and sometimes in a panegyrical style, but most commonly to the honour of some prince or princely family. We thus meet with a *Sforziad*,[1] a *Borseid*, a *Laurentiad*, a *Borgiad* (see p. 230), a *Triulziad*, and the like. The object sought after was certainly not attained; for those who became famous and are now immortal owe it to anything rather than to this sort of poems, to which the world has always had an ineradicable dislike, even when they happen to be written by good poets. A wholly different effect is produced by smaller, simpler, and more unpretentious scenes from the lives of distinguished men, such as the beautiful poem on Leo X's *Hunt at Palo*,[2] or the

FIG. 124. MARS AND VENUS
By Piero di Cosimo
Berlin, Kaiser-Friedrich Museum

Journey of Julius II by Hadrian of Corneto (p. 136). Brilliant descriptions of hunting-parties are found in Ercole Strozzi, in the above-mentioned Hadrian, and in others; and it is a pity that the modern reader should allow himself to be irritated or repelled by the adulation with which they are doubtless filled. The masterly treatment and the considerable historical value of many of these most graceful poems guarantee to them a longer existence than many popular works of our own day are likely to attain.

In general, these poems are good in proportion to the sparing use of the sentimental and the general. Some of the smaller epic poems, even of recognized masters, unintentionally produce, by the ill-timed introduction of mythological elements, an impression that is indescribably ludicrous. Such, for instance, is the lament of Ercole Strozzi[3] on Cesare Borgia. We there listen to the complaint of Rome, who had set all her hopes on the Spanish Popes Calixtus III and Alexander VI, and who saw her promised deliverer in Cesare.

---

[1] There are two unfinished and unprinted *Sforziads*, one by the elder, the other by the younger Filelfo. On the latter see Favre, *Mélanges d'Hist. Lit.*, i, 156; on the former see Rosmini, *Filelfo*, ii, 157-175. It is said to be 12,800 lines long, and contains the passage: "The sun falls in love with Bianca."

[2] Roscoe, *Leo X*, ed. Bossi, viii, 184. A poem in a similar style, xii, 130. The poem of Angilbert on the Court of Charles the Great curiously reminds us of the Renaissance. *Cf.* Pertz, *Monum.*, ii.

[3] Strozzi, *Poetæ*, pp. 31 *sqq* : "Cæsaris Borgiæ ducis epicedium."

His history is related down to the catastrophe of 1503. The poet then asks the Muse what were the counsels of the gods at that moment,[1] and Erato tells how, upon Olympus, Pallas took the part of the Spaniards, Venus of the Italians, how both then embrace the knees of Jupiter, how thereupon he kisses them, soothes them, and explains to them that he can do nothing against the fate woven by the Parcæ, but that the divine promises will be fulfilled by the child of the house of Este-Borgia.[2] After relating the fabulous origin of both families he declares that he can confer immortality on Cesare as little as he could once, in spite of all entreaties, on Memnon or Achilles; and concludes with the consoling assurance that Cesare, before his own death, will destroy many people

FIG. 125. DEATH OF PROCRIS
By Piero di Cosimo
London, National Gallery

in war. Mars then hastens to Naples to stir up war and confusion, while Pallas goes to Nepi, and there appears to the dying Cesare under the form of Alexander VI. After giving him the good advice to submit to his fate and be satisfied with the glory of his name the Papal goddess vanishes " like a bird."

Yet we should needlessly deprive ourselves of an enjoyment, which is sometimes very great, if we threw aside everything in which classical mythology plays a more or less appropriate part. Here, as in painting and sculpture, art has often ennobled what is in itself purely conventional. The beginnings of parody are also to be found by lovers of that class of literature (pp. 167 *sqq.*)— *e.g.*, in the *Macaroneide*—to which the comic *Revels of the Gods*, by Giovanni Bellini, forms an early parallel.

Many, too, of the narrative poems in hexameters are merely exercises, or adaptations of histories in prose, which latter the reader will prefer, where he can find them. At last everything—every quarrel and every ceremony—came to be put into verse, and this even by the German humanists of the Reformation.[3]

[1] "Pontificem addiderat, flammis lustralibus omneis
Corporis ablutum labes, Dis Juppiter ipsis," etc.

[2] This was Hercules II of Ferrara, b. April 4, 1508, probably either shortly before or shortly after the composition of this poem. "Nascere, magne puer, matri expectate patrique," is said near the end.

[3] *Cf.* the collections of the *Scriptores* by Schardius, Freher, etc., and see above, p. 142, note 2.

And yet it would be unfair to attribute this to mere want of occupation, or to an excessive facility in stringing verses together. In Italy, at all events, it was rather due to an abundant sense of style, as is further proved by the mass of contemporary reports, histories, and even pamphlets in the *terza rima*. Just as Niccolò da Uzzano published his scheme for a new constitution, Machiavelli his view of the history of his own time, a third the life of Savonarola, and a fourth the siege of Piombino by Alfonso the Great,[1] in this difficult metre, in order to produce a stronger effect, so did many others feel the need of hexameters in order to win their special public. What was then tolerated and demanded in this shape is best shown by the didactic poetry of the time. Its popularity in the fifteenth century is something astounding. The most distinguished humanists were ready to celebrate in Latin hexameters the most commonplace, ridiculous, or disgusting themes, such as the making of gold, the game of chess, the management of silkworms, astrology, and venereal diseases (*morbus gallicus*), to say nothing of many long Italian poems of the same kind. Nowadays this class of poems is condemned unread, and how far, as a matter of fact, they are really worth the reading we are unable to say.[2] One thing is certain, that epochs far above our own in the sense of beauty—the Renaissance and the Græco-Roman world—could not dispense with this form of poetry. It may be urged in reply that it is not the lack of a sense of beauty but the greater seriousness and the altered method of scientific treatment which renders the poetical form inappropriate, on which point it is unnecessary to enter.

One of these didactic works has of late years been occasionally republished[3] —the *Zodiac of Life*, by Marcellus Palingenius (Pier Angello Manzolli), a secret adherent of Protestantism at Ferrara, written about 1528. With the loftiest speculations on God, virtue, and immortality, the writer connects the discussion of many questions of practical life, and is, on this account, an authority of some weight in the history of morals. On the whole, however, his work must be considered as lying outside the boundaries of the Renaissance, as is further indicated by the fact that, in harmony with the serious didactic purpose of the poem, allegory tends to supplant mythology.

But it was in lyric, and more particularly in elegiac poetry, that the poet-scholar came nearest to antiquity; and next to this in epigram.

In the lighter style, Catullus exercised a perfect fascination over the Italians. Not a few elegant Latin madrigals, not a few little satires and malicious epistles,

---

[1] Uzzano, see *Arch. Stor. Ital.*, iv, i. 296. Machiavelli, *I Decennali*. The life of Savonarola, under the title *Cedrus Libani*, by Fra Benedetto. *Assedio di Piombino*, in Murat., xxv. We may quote as a parallel the *Teuerdank* and other Northern works in rhyme (later ed. of that by Haltaus, Quedlinb. and Leipzig, 1836). The popular historical songs of the Germans, which were produced in great abundance in the fifteenth and sixteenth centuries, may be compared with these Italian poems.

[2] We may remark of the *Coltivazione* of L. Alamanni, written in Italian *versi sciolti*, that all the really poetical and enjoyable passages are directly or indirectly borrowed from the ancients (an old ed., Paris, 1540; ed. of the works of Alamanni, 2 vols., Florence, 1867).

[3] For example, by C. G. Weise (Leipzig, 1832). The work, divided into twelve books, named after the twelve constellations, is dedicated to Hercules II of Ferrara. In the dedication occur the remarkable words: "Nam quem alium patronum in tota Italia invenire possum, cui musæ cordi sunt, qui carmen sibi oblatum aut intelligat, aut examine recto expendere sciat?" Palingenius uses *Juppiter* and *Deus* indiscriminately.

are mere adaptations from him; and the death of parrots and lapdogs is bewailed, even where there is no verbal imitation, in precisely the tone and style of the verses on Lesbia's sparrow. There are short poems of this sort, the date of which even a critic would be unable to fix [1] in the absence of positive evidence that they are works of the fifteenth and sixteenth centuries.

On the other hand, we can find scarcely an ode in the Sapphic or Alcaic

FIG. 126. REVELS OF THE GODS
By Giovanni Bellini
Philadelphia, Widener Collection

metre which does not clearly betray its modern origin. This is shown mostly by a rhetorical verbosity, rare in antiquity before the time of Statius, and by a singular want of the lyrical concentration which is indispensable to this style of poetry. Single passages in an ode, sometimes two or three strophes together, may look like an ancient fragment; but a longer extract will seldom keep this character throughout. And where it does so, as, for instance, in the fine ode to Venus by Andrea Navagero, it is easy to detect a simple paraphrase of ancient masterpieces.[2] Some of the ode-writers take the saints for their subject, and

[1] L. B. Alberti's first comic poem, which purported to be by an author Lepidus, was long considered as a work of antiquity.

[2] In this case (see below, p. 268, note 3) of the introduction to Lucretius, and of Horace, *Od.*, iv, 1.

invoke them in verses tastefully modelled after the pattern of analogous odes of Horace and Catullus. This is the manner of Navagero, in the ode to the Archangel Gabriel, and particularly of Sannazaro (p. 262), who goes still farther in his appropriation of pagan sentiment. He celebrates above all his patron saint,[1] whose chapel was attached to his lovely villa on the shores of Posilippo, "there where the waves of the sea drink up the stream from the rocks, and surge against the walls of the little sanctuary." His delight is in the annual feast of S. Nazzaro, and the branches and garlands with which the chapel is hung on this day seem to him like sacrificial gifts. Full of sorrow, and far off in exile at St-Nazaire, on the banks of the Loire, with the banished Frederick of Aragon, he brings wreaths of box and oak-leaves to his patron saint on the same anniversary, thinking of former years, when all the youth of Posilippo used to come forth to greet him on flower-hung boats, and praying that he may return home.[2]

Perhaps the most deceptive likeness to the classical style is borne by a class of poems in elegiacs or hexameters whose subject ranges from elegy, strictly so called, to epigram. As the humanists dealt most freely of all with the text of the Roman elegiac poets, so they felt themselves most at home in imitating them. The elegy of Navagero addressed to the night, like other poems of the same age and kind, is full of points which remind us of his models; but it has the finest antique ring about it. Indeed, Navagero[3] always begins by choosing a truly poetical subject, which he then treats not with servile imitation, but with masterly freedom, in the style of the *Anthology*, of Ovid, of Catullus, or of the Virgilian eclogues. He makes a sparing use of mythology, only, for instance, to introduce a sketch of country life in a prayer to Ceres and other rural divinities. An address to his country on his return from an embassy to Spain, though left unfinished, might have been worthy of a place beside the *Bella Italia, Amate Sponde* of Vincenzo Monti if the rest had been equal to this beginning:

> Salve, cura Deum, mundi felicior ora,
> Formosæ Veneris dulces salvete recessus;
> Ut vos post tantos animi mentisque labores
> Aspicio lustroque libens, ut munere vestro
> Sollicitas toto depello e pectore curas![4]

The elegiac or hexametral form was that in which all higher sentiment found expression, both the noblest patriotic enthusiasm (see p. 136, the elegy on Julius II) and the most elaborate eulogies on the ruling houses,[5] as well as the

---

[1] The invocation of a patron saint is an essentially pagan undertaking,. On a more serious occasion, *cf.* Sannazaro's elegy *In Festo die Divi Nazarii Martyris* (Sann., *Elegia*, fol. 166 *sqq.*, 1535).

[2] "Sit satis ventos tolerasse et imbres
Ac minas fatorum hominumque fraudes
Da Pater tecto salientem avito.
Cernere fumum!"

[3] *Andr. Naugerii, Orationes duæ Carminaque Aliquot* (4to, Venice, 1530). The few *carmina* are to be found partly or wholly in the *Deliciæ*. On Navagero and his death see Pier. Valeriano, *De Inf. Lit.*, ed. Mencken, 326 *sqq.*

[4] *Cf.* Petrarch's greeting to Italy, written more than a century earlier (1353) in *Petr. Carmina Minora*, ed. Rossetti, ii, 266 *sqq.*

[5] To form a notion of what Leo X could swallow see the prayer of Guido Postumo Silvestri to Christ, the Virgin, and all the saints, that they would long spare this *numen* to earth, since heaven had enough of such already. Printed in Roscoe, *Leo X*, ed. Bossi, v, 237.

tender melancholy of a Tibullus.   Francesco Mario Molza, who rivals Statius and Martial in his flattery of Clement VII and the Farnesi, gives us in his elegy to his 'comrades,' written from a sick-bed, thoughts on death as beautiful and genuinely antique as can be found in any of the poets of antiquity, and this without borrowing anything worth speaking of from them.[1]   The spirit and range of the Roman elegy were best understood and reproduced by Sannazaro, and no other writer of his time offers us so varied a choice of good poems in this style as he.   We shall have occasion now and then to speak of some of these elegies in reference to the matter they treat of.

The Latin epigram finally became in those days an affair of serious importance, since a few clever lines, engraved on a monument or quoted with laughter in society, could lay the foundation of a scholar's celebrity.   This tendency showed itself early in Italy.   When it was known that Guido della Polenta wished to erect a monument at Dante's grave epitaphs poured in from all directions,[2] "written by such as wished to *show themselves*, or to honour the dead poet, or to win the favour of Polenta."   On the tomb of the Archbishop Giovanni Visconti (d. 1354) in the cathedral at Milan we read at the foot of thirty-six hexameters: "Master Gabrius di Zamoreis of Parma, Doctor of Laws, wrote these verses."   In course of time, chiefly under the influence of Martial, and partly of Catullus, an extensive literature of this sort was formed. It was held the greatest of all triumphs when an epigram was mistaken for a genuine copy from some old marble,[3] or when it was so good that all Italy learned it by heart, as happened in the case of some of Bembo's.   When the Venetian Government paid Sannazaro six hundred ducats for a eulogy in three distichs [4] no one thought it an act of generous prodigality.   The epigram was prized for what it was, in truth, to all the educated classes of that age—the concentrated essence of fame.   Nor, on the other hand, was any man then so powerful as to be above the reach of a satirical epigram, and even the most powerful needed, for every inscription which they set before the public eye, the aid of careful and learned scholars, lest some blunder or other should qualify it for a place in the collections of ludicrous epitaphs.[5]   The epigraph and the epigram were branches of the same pursuit; the reproduction of the former was based on a diligent study of ancient monuments.

The city of epigrams and inscriptions was, above all others, Rome.   In this state without hereditary honours each man had to look after his own immortality, and at the same time found the epigram an effective weapon against his

---

[1] Molza's *Poesie Volgari e Latine*, ed. by Pierantonio Serassi (Bergamo, 1747).

[2] Boccaccio, *Vita di Dante*, p. 36.

[3] Sannazaro ridicules a man who importuned him with such forgeries: "Sint vetera hæc aliis, mi nova semper erunt."   (*Ad Rufum, Opera*, fol. 41*a*, 1535).

[4] *De Mirabili Urbe Venetiis (Opera*, fol. 38*b*):

> " Viderat Adriacis Venetam Neptunus in undis
>   Stare urbem et toto ponere jura mari:
> Nunc mihi Tarpejas quantum vis Juppiter arces
>   Objice et illa tui mœnia Martis ait,
> Si pelago Tybrim præfers, urbem aspice utramque
>   Illam homines dices, hanc posuisse deos."

[5] *Lettere dei Principi*, i, 88, 91.

competitors. Pius II counts with satisfaction the distichs which his chief poet, Campanus, wrote on any event of his government which could be turned to poetical account. Under the following Popes satirical epigrams came into fashion, and reached, in the opposition to Alexander VI and his family, the highest pitch of defiant invective. Sannazaro, it is true, wrote his verses in a place of comparative safety, but others in the immediate neighbourhood of the Court ventured on the most reckless attacks (p. 129). On one occasion when eight threatening distichs were found fastened to the door of the library [1] Alexander strengthened his guard by eight hundred men; we can imagine what he would have done to the poet if he had caught him. Under Leo X Latin epigrams were like daily bread. For complimenting or for reviling the Pope, for punishing enemies and victims, named or unnamed, for real or imaginary subjects of wit, malice, grief, or contemplation, no form was held more suitable. On the famous group of the Virgin with Saint Anna and the Child, which Andrea Sansovino carved for S. Agostino, no fewer than a hundred and twenty persons wrote Latin verses, not so much, it is true, from devotion, as from regard for the patron who ordered the work. [2] This man, Johann Goritz of Luxemburg, Papal referendary of petitions, not only held a religious service on the feast of St Anna, but gave a great literary dinner in his garden on the slopes of the Capitol. It was then worth while to pass in review, in a long poem, *De Poetis Urbanis*, the whole crowd of singers who sought their fortune at the Court of Leo. This was done by Franciscus Arsillus [3]—a man who needed the patronage neither of Pope nor prince, and who dared to speak his mind, even against his colleagues. The epigram survived the pontificate of Paul III only in a few rare echoes, while the epigraph continued to flourish till the seventeenth century, when it perished finally of bombast.

In Venice also this form of poetry had a history of its own, which we are able to trace with the help of the *Venezia* of Francesco Sansovino. A standing task for the epigram-writers was offered by the mottoes (*brievi*) on the pictures of the Doges in the great hall of the ducal palace—two or four hexameters, setting forth the most noteworthy facts in the government of each. [4] In addition to this, the tombs of the Doges in the fourteenth century bore short inscriptions

---

[1] Malipiero, *Ann. Venet., Archiv. Stor.*, vii, i, p. 508. At the end we read, in reference to the bull as the arms of the Borgia:

"Merge, Tyber, vitulos animosas ultor in undas;
Bos cadat inferno victima magna Jovi!"

[2] On the whole affair see Roscoe, *Leo X*, ed. Bossi, vii, 211; viii, 214 *sqq.* The printed collection, now rare, of these *Coryciana* of 1524 contains only the Latin poems; Vasari saw another book in the possession of the Augustinians in which were sonnets. So contagious was the habit of affixing poems that the group had to be protected by a railing, and even hidden altogether. The change of Goritz into *Corycius senex* is suggested by Virgil, *Georg.*, iv, 127. For the miserable end of the man at the sack of Rome see Pier. Valeriano, *De Infel. Lit.*, ed. Mencken, p. 369.

[3] The work appeared first in the *Coryciana*, with introductions by Silvanus and Corycius himself; also reprinted in the Appendices to Roscoe, *Leo X*, ed. Bossi, and in the *Deliciæ*. *Cf.* Paul. Jovius, *Elogia*, speaking of Arsillus. Further, for the great number of the epigrammatists, see Lil. Greg. Gyraldus, *loc. cit.* One of the most biting pens was that of Marcantonio Casanova. Among the less known, Joh. Thomas Muscanius (see *Delicia*) deserves mention. On Casanova see Pier. Valer., *De Infel. Lit.*, ed. Mencken, pp. 376 *sqq.*, and Paul. Jovius, *Elogia*, pp. 142 *sqq.*, who says of him: " Nemo autem eo simplicitate ac innocentia vitæ melior " Arsillus, *loc. cit.*, speaks of his *placidos sales.* Some few of his poems are in the *Coryciana*, J 3*a sqq.*, L 1*a*, L 4*b*.

[4] Marin Sanudo, in the *Vite de' Duchi di Venezia*, in Murat., xxii, quotes them regularly.

in prose, recording merely facts, and beside them turgid hexameters or leonine verses. In the fifteenth century more care was taken with the style; in the sixteenth century it is seen at its best; and then soon after came pointless antithesis, prosopopœia, false pathos, praise of abstract qualities—in a word, affectation and bombast. A good many traces of satire can be detected, and veiled criticism of the living is implied in open praise of the dead. At a much later period we find a few instances of a deliberate recurrence to the old, simple style.

Architectural works and decorative works in general were constructed with a view to receiving inscriptions, often in frequent repetition; while the Northern Gothic seldom, and with difficulty, offered a suitable place for them, and in sepulchral monuments, for example, left free only the most exposed parts— namely, the edges.

By what has been said hitherto we have, perhaps, failed to convince the reader of the characteristic value of this Latin poetry of the Italians. Our task was rather to indicate its position and necessity in the history of civilization. In its own day a caricature of it appeared [1]—the so-called macaronic poetry. The masterpiece of this style, the *Opus Macaronicorum*, was written by Merlinus Coccaius (Teofilo Folengo of Mantua). We shall now and then have occasion to refer to the matter of this poem. As to the form—hexameter and other verses, made up of Latin words and Italian words with Latin endings—its comic effect lies chiefly in the fact that these combinations sound like so many slips of the tongue, or the effusions of an over-hasty Latin *improvisatore*. The German imitations do not give the smallest notion of this effect.

---

[1] Scardeonius, *De Urb. Patav. Antiq.* (Græv., *Thesaur.*, vi, III, col. 270), names as the inventor a certain Odaxius of Padua, living about the middle of the fifteenth century. Mixed verses of Latin and the language of the country are found much earlier in many parts of Europe.

CHAPTER XI

FALL OF THE HUMANISTS IN THE SIXTEENTH CENTURY

FTER a brilliant succession of poet-scholars had, since the beginning of the fourteenth century, filled Italy and the world with the worship of antiquity, had determined the forms of education and culture, had often taken the lead in political affairs, and had, to no small extent, reproduced ancient literature—at length in the sixteenth century, before their doctrines and scholarship had lost hold of the public mind, the whole class fell into deep and general disgrace. Though they still served as models to the poets, historians, and orators, personally no one would consent to be reckoned of their number. To the two chief accusations against them—that of malicious self-conceit and that of abominable profligacy—a third charge of irreligion was now loudly added by the rising powers of the Counter-Reformation.

Why, it may be asked, were not these reproaches, whether true or false, heard sooner? As a matter of fact, they were heard at a very early period, but the effect they produced was insignificant, for the plain reason that men were far too dependent on the scholars for their knowledge of antiquity—that the scholars were personally the possessors and diffusers of ancient culture. But the spread of printed editions of the classics,[1] and of large and well-arranged handbooks and dictionaries, went far to free the people from the necessity of personal intercourse with the humanists, and, as soon as they could be but partly dispensed with, the change in popular feeling became manifest. It was a change under which the good and bad suffered indiscriminately.

The first to make these charges were certainly the humanists themselves. Of all men who ever formed a class, they had the least sense of their common interests, and least respected what there was of this sense. All means were held lawful if one of them saw a chance of supplanting another. From literary discussion they passed with astonishing suddenness to the fiercest and the most groundless vituperation. Not satisfied with refuting, they sought to annihilate an opponent. Something of this must be put to the account of their position and circumstances; we have seen how fiercely the age, whose loudest spokesmen they were, was borne to and fro by the passion for glory and the passion for satire. In practical life too their position was one that they had continually to fight for. In such a temper they wrote and spoke and described one another. Poggio's works alone contain dirt enough to create a prejudice against the whole

---

[1] It must not be forgotten that they were very soon printed with both the old *scholia* and modern commentaries.

class—and these *Opera Poggii* were just those most often printed, on the north as well as on the south side of the Alps. We must take care not to rejoice too soon when we meet among these men a figure which seems immaculate; on further inquiry there is always a danger of meeting with some foul charge, which, even when it is incredible, still discolours the picture. The mass of indecent Latin poems in circulation, and such things as the ribaldry on the subject of his own family, in Pontano's dialogue *Antonius* did the rest to discredit the class. The sixteenth century was not only familiar with all these ugly symptoms, but had also grown tired of the type of the humanist. These men had to pay both for the misdeeds they had done, and for the excess of honour which had hitherto fallen to their lot. Their evil fate willed it that the greatest poet of the nation wrote of them in a tone of calm and sovereign contempt.[1]

Of the reproaches which combined to excite so much hatred many were only too well founded. Yet a clear and unmistakable tendency to strictness in matters of religion and morality was alive in many of the philologists, and it is a proof of small knowledge of the period if the whole class is condemned. Yet many, and among them the loudest speakers, were guilty.

Three facts explain, and perhaps diminish, their guilt: the overflowing excess of favour and fortune when the luck was on their side; the uncertainty of the future, in which luxury or misery depended on the caprice of a patron or the malice of an enemy: and, finally, the misleading influence of antiquity. This undermined their morality without giving them its own instead; and in religious matters, since they could never think of accepting the positive belief in the old gods, it affected them only on the negative and sceptical side. Just because they conceived of antiquity dogmatically—that is, took it as the model for all thought and action—its influence was here pernicious. But that an age existed which idolized the ancient world and its products with an exclusive devotion was not the fault of individuals. It was the work of an historical Providence, and all the culture of the ages which have followed, and of the ages to come, rests upon the fact that it was so, and that all the ends of life but this one were then deliberately put aside.

The career of the humanists was, as a rule, of such a kind that only the strongest characters could pass through it unscathed. The first danger came, in some cases, from the parents, who sought to turn a precocious child into a miracle of learning,[2] with an eye to his future position in that class which then was supreme. Youthful prodigies, however, seldom rise above a certain level; or, if they do, are forced to achieve their further progress and development at the cost of the bitterest trials. For an ambitious youth, the fame and the brilliant position of the humanists were a perilous temptation; it seemed to

---

[1] Ariosto, *Satira*, vii (date 1531).

[2] We meet with several such children, yet I cannot give an instance in which they were demonstrably so treated. The youthful prodigy Giulio Campagnola was not one of those who were forced with an ambitious object. *Cf.* Scardeonius, *De Urb. Patav. Antiq.*, in Græv., *Thesaur.*, vi, 3, col. 276. For the similar case of Cecchino Bracci (d. 1445, in his fifteenth year) *cf.* Trucchi, *Poesie Ital. Ined.*, iii, p. 229. The father of Cardano tried " memoriam artificialem instillare," and taught him when still a child the astrology of the Arabians. See Cardanus, *De Propria Vita*, cap. 34. Manoello may be added to the list, unless we are to take his expression, " At the age of six years I am as good as at eighty," as a meaningless phrase. *Cf. Litbl. des Orients*, p. 21 (1843).

him that he too "through inborn pride could no longer regard the low and common things of life." He was thus led to plunge into a life of excitement and vicissitude, in which exhausting studies, tutorships, secretaryships, professorships, offices in princely households, mortal enmities and perils, luxury and beggary, boundless admiration and boundless contempt, followed confusedly one upon the other, and in which the most solid worth and learning were often pushed aside by superficial impudence. But the worst of all was that the position of the humanist was almost incompatible with a fixed home, since it either made frequent changes of dwelling necessary for a livelihood, or so affected the mind of the individual that he could never be happy for long in one place. He grew tired of the people, and had no peace among the enmities which he excited, while the people themselves in their turn demanded something new (p. 219). Much as this life reminds us of the Greek sophists of the Empire, as described to us by Philostratus, yet the position of the sophists was more favourable. They often had money, or could more easily do without it than the humanists, and as professional teachers of rhetoric, rather than men of learning, their life was freer and simpler. But the scholar of the Renaissance was forced to combine great learning with the power of resisting the influence of ever-changing pursuits and situations. And to this the deadening effect of licentious excess and—since do what he might, the worst was believed of him—a total indifference to the moral laws recognized by others. Such men can hardly be conceived to exist without an inordinate pride. They needed it, if only to keep their heads above water, and were confirmed in it by the admiration which alternated with hatred in the treatment they received from the world. They are the most striking examples and victims of an unbridled subjectivity.

The attacks and the satirical pictures began, as we have said, at an early period. For all strongly marked individuality, for every kind of distinction, a corrective was at hand in the national taste for ridicule. And in this case the men themselves offered abundant and terrible materials which satire had but to make use of. In the fifteenth century Battista Mantovano, in discoursing of the seven monsters,[1] includes the humanists, with many others, under the head *Superbia*. He describes how, fancying themselves children of Apollo, they walk along with affected solemnity and with sullen, malicious looks, now gazing at their own shadow, now brooding over the popular praise they hunted after, like cranes in search of food. But in the sixteenth century the indictment was presented in full. Besides Ariosto, their own historian Gyraldus[2] gives evidence of this, whose treatise, written under Leo X, was probably revised about the year 1540. Warning examples from ancient and modern times of the moral disorder and the wretched existence of the scholars meet us in astonishing abundance, and along with these accusations of the most serious nature are brought formally against them. Among these are anger, vanity, obstinacy, self-adoration, a dissolute private life, immorality of all descriptions, heresy,

---

[1] Bapt. Mantuan., *De Calamitatibus Temporum*, lib. i.
[2] Lil. Greg. Gyraldus, *Progymnasma adversus Literas et Literatos* (*Opp.*, ii, 422–455, ed. Basil., 1580). Dedications 1540–41; the work itself addressed to Giov. Franc. Pico, and therefore finished before 1533.

FALL OF THE HUMANISTS

atheism; further, the habit of speaking without conviction, a sinister influence on government, pedantry of speech, thanklessness toward teachers, and abject flattery of the great, who first give the scholar a taste of their favours and then leave him to starve. The description is closed by a reference to the Golden Age, when no such thing as science existed on the earth. Of these charges that of heresy soon became the most dangerous, and Gyraldus himself, when he afterward republished a perfectly harmless youthful work,[1] was compelled to take refuge beneath the mantle of Duke Hercules II of Ferrara,[2] since men now had the upper hand who held that people had better spend their time on Christian themes than on mythological researches. He justifies himself on the ground that the latter, on the contrary, were at such a time almost the only harmless branches of study, as they deal with subjects of a perfectly neutral character.

But if it is the duty of the historian to seek for evidence in which moral judgment is tempered by human sympathy he will find no authority comparable in value to the work so often quoted of Pierio Valeriano,[3] *On the Infelicity of the Scholar*. It was written under the gloomy impressions left by the sack of Rome, which seems to the writer not only the direct cause of untold misery to the men of learning, but, as it were, the fulfilment of an evil destiny which had long pursued them. Pierio is here led by a simple and, on the whole, just feeling. He does not introduce a special power, which plagued the men of genius on account of their genius, but he states facts, in which an unlucky chance often wears the aspect of fatality. Not wishing to write a tragedy or to refer events to the conflict of higher powers, he is content to lay before us the scenes of everyday life. We are introduced to men who in times of trouble lose first their incomes and then their places; to others who in trying to get two appointments miss both; to unsociable misers who carry about their money sewn into their clothes, and die mad when they are robbed of it; to others who accept well-paid offices and then sicken with a melancholy, longing for their lost freedom. We read how some died young of a plague or fever, and how the writings which had cost them so much toil were burnt with their bed and clothes; how others lived in terror of the murderous threats of their colleagues; how one was slain by a covetous servant and another by highwaymen on a journey, and left to pine in a dungeon, because unable to pay his ransom. Many died of unspoken grief for the insults they received and the prizes of which they were defrauded. We are told of the death of a Venetian, because his son, a youthful prodigy, was dead; and the mother and brothers followed, as if the lost child drew them all after him. Many, especially Florentines, ended their lives by suicide;[4] others through the secret justice of a tyrant. Who, after all, is happy?—and by what means? By blunting all feeling for such misery? One of the speakers in the dialogue in which Pierio clothed his

---

[1] Lil. Greg. Gyraldus, *Hercules* (*Opp.*, i, pp. 544-570). The dedication is a striking evidence of the first threatening movements of the Inquisition.

[2] He passed, as we have seen, for the last protector of the scholars.

[3] *De Infel. Lit.* On the editions see above, p. 106, note 3. Pierio Valeriano after leaving Rome lived long in a good position as professor at Padua. At the end of his work he expresses the hope that Charles V and Clement VII would bring about a better time for the scholars.

[4] *Cf.* Dante, *Inferno*, xiii, 58 *sqq.*, especially 93 *sqq.*, where Petrus de Vineis speaks of his own suicide.

275

argument can give an answer to these questions—the illustrious Gasparo Contarini, at the mention of whose name we turn with the expectation to hear at least something of the truest and deepest which was then thought on such matters. As a type of the happy scholar, he mentions Fra Urbano Valeriano of Belluno,[1] who was for years teacher of Greek at Venice, who visited Greece and the East, and toward the close of his life travelled now through this country, now through that, without ever mounting a horse; who never had a penny of his own, rejected all honours and distinctions, and after a gay old age died in his eighty-fourth year, without, if we except a fall from a ladder, having ever known an hour of sickness. And what was the difference between such a man and the humanists? The latter had more free will, more subjectivity, than they could turn to purposes of happiness. The mendicant friar who had lived from his boyhood in the monastery, and had never eaten or slept except by rule, ceased to feel the compulsion under which he lived. Through the power of this habit he led, amid all outward hardships, a life of inward peace, by which he impressed his hearers far more than by his teaching. Looking at him, they could believe that it depends on ourselves whether we bear up against misfortune or surrender to it.

> Amid want and toil he was happy, because he willed to be so, because he had contracted no evil habits, was not capricious, inconstant, immoderate; but was always contented with little or nothing.

If we heard Contarini himself, religious motives would no doubt play a part in the argument—but the practical philosopher in sandals speaks plainly enough. An allied character, but placed in other circumstances, is that of Fabio Calvo of Ravenna, the commentator of Hippocrates.[2] He lived to a great age in Rome, eating only pulse "like the Pythagoreans," and dwelt in a hovel little better than the tub of Diogenes. Of the pension which Pope Leo gave him he spent enough to keep body and soul together, and gave the rest away. He was not a healthy man, like Fra Urbano, nor is it likely that, like him, he died with a smile on his lips. At the age of ninety, in the sack of Rome, he was dragged away by the Spaniards, who hoped for a ransom, and died of hunger in a hospital. But his name has passed into the kingdom of the immortals, for Raphael loved the old man like a father, and honoured him as a teacher, and came to him for advice in all things. Perhaps they discoursed chiefly of the projected restoration of ancient Rome (p. 192), perhaps of still higher matters. Who can tell what a share Fabio may have had in the conception of *The School of Athens*, and in other great works of the master?

We would gladly close this part of our essay with the picture of some pleasing and winning character. Pomponius Lætus, of whom we shall briefly speak, is known to us principally through the letter of his pupil Sabellicus,[3] in which an antique colouring is purposely given to his character. Yet many of

---

[1] Pier. Valeriano, pp. 397 *sqq.*, 402. He was the uncle of the writer.

[2] Cœlii Calcagnini, *Opera*, ed. Basil., 1544, p. 101, in the seventh book of the *Epistles*, No. 27, letter to Jacob Ziegler. *Cf.* Pier. Valeriano, *De Inf. Lit.*, ed. Mencken, pp. 369 *sqq.*

[3] M. Ant. Sabellici Opera, Epist., lib. xi, fol. 56. See also the biography in the *Elogia* of Paolo Giovio, pp. 76 *sqq.* The former appeared separately at Strasburg in 1510 under the title Sabellicus, *Vita Pomponii Læti.*

its features are clearly recognizable.   He was (p. 253) a bastard of the house of
the Neapolitan Sanseverini, princes of Salerno, whom he nevertheless refused
to recognize, writing in reply to an invitation to live with them the famous letter:

> Pomponius Lætus cognatis et propinquis suis, salutem.   Quod petitis fieri non
> potest.   Valete.

An insignificant little figure, with small, quick eyes and quaint dress, he lived
during the last decades of the fifteenth century, as professor in the University
of Rome, either in his cottage in a garden on the Esquiline Hill, or in his vine-
yard on the Quirinal.   In the one he bred his ducks and fowls; the other he
cultivated according to the strictest precepts of Cato, Varro, and Columella.
He spent his holidays in fishing or bird-catching in the Campagna, or in feasting
by some shady spring or on the banks of the Tiber.   Wealth and luxury he
despised.   Free himself from envy and uncharitable speech, he would not
suffer them in others.   It was only against the hierarchy that he gave his tongue
free play, and passed, till his latter years, for a scorner of religion altogether.
He was involved in the persecution of the humanists begun by Pope Paul II,
and was surrendered to this pontiff by the Venetians; but no means could be
found to wring unworthy confessions from him.   He was afterward befriended
and supported by Popes and prelates, and when his house was plundered in the
disturbances under Sixtus IV more was collected for him than he had lost.
No teacher was more conscientious.   Before daybreak he was to be seen
descending the Esquiline with his lantern, and on reaching his lecture-room
found it always filled to overflowing with pupils who had come at midnight to
secure a place.   A stutter compelled him to speak with care, but his delivery
was even and effective.   His few works give evidence of careful writing.   No
scholar treated the text of ancient authors more soberly and accurately.   The
remains of antiquity which surrounded him in Rome touched him so deeply
that he would stand before them as if entranced, or would suddenly burst into
tears at the sight of them.   As he was ready to lay aside his own studies in
order to help others, he was much loved and had many friends; and at his
death even Alexander VI sent his courtiers to follow the corpse, which was
carried by the most distinguished of his pupils.   The funeral service in the
Araceli was attended by forty bishops and by all the foreign ambassadors.

It was Lætus who introduced and conducted the representations of ancient,
chiefly Plautine, plays in Rome (p. 258).   Every year he celebrated the anniversary of the foundation of the city by a festival at which his friends and pupils
recited speeches and poems.   Such meetings were the origin of what acquired
and long retained the name of the Roman Academy.   It was simply a free
union of individuals, and was connected with no fixed institution.   Besides
the occasions mentioned, it met [1] at the invitation of a patron, or to celebrate
the memory of a deceased member, as of Platina.   At such times a prelate
belonging to the Academy would first say Mass; Pomponio would then ascend
the pulpit and deliver a speech; some one else would then follow him and
recite an elegy.   The customary banquet, with declamations and recitations,

---

[1] Jac. Volaterranus, *Diar. Rom.*, in Murat., xxiii, col. 161, 171, 185; *Anecd. Lit.*, ii, 168 *sqq.*

concluded the festival, whether joyous or serious, and the academicians, notably Platina himself, early acquired the reputation of epicures.[1] At other times the guests performed farces in the old Atellan style. As a free association of very varied elements, the Academy lasted in its original form down to the sack of Rome, and included among its guests Angelus Coloccius, Joh. Corycius (p. 270), and others. Its precise value as an element in the intellectual life of the people is as hard to estimate as that of any other social union of the same kind; yet a man like Sadoleto [2] reckoned it among the most precious memories of his youth.

FIG. 127. JOVIANUS PONTANUS (GIOVIANO PONTANO)

A large number of other academies appeared and passed away in many Italian cities, according to the number and significance of the humanists living in them and to the patronage bestowed by the great and wealthy. Of these we may mention the Academy of Naples, of which Jovianus Pontanus was the centre, and which sent out a colony to Lecce,[3] and that of Pordenone, which formed the Court of the *condottiere* Alviano.[4] The circle of Lodovico il Moro, and its peculiar importance for that prince, has been already spoken of (p. 58).

About the middle of the sixteenth century these associations seem to have undergone a complete change. The humanists, driven in other spheres from their commanding position, and viewed askance by the men of the Counter-Reformation, lost the control of the academies; and here, as elsewhere, Latin poetry was replaced by Italian. Before long every town of the least importance had its academy, with some strange, fantastic name,[5] and its endowment and subscriptions. Besides the recitation of verses, the new institutions inherited from their predecessors the regular banquets and the representation of plays, sometimes acted by the members themselves, sometimes under their direction by young amateurs, and sometimes by paid players. The fate of the Italian stage, and afterward of the opera, was long in the hands of these associations.

---

[1] Paul. Jovius, *De Romanis Piscibus*, cap. 17 and 34.   [2] Sadoleto, *Epist.* 106, of the year 1529.
[3] Anton. Galatei, *Epist.* 10 and 12, in Mai, *Spicileg. Rom.*, vol. viii.
[⁴ Though it is to be questioned whether this did not deserve the name rather of an occasional meeting of learned men than of an academy.—W. G.]
[5] This was the case even before the middle of the century. *Cf.* Lil. Greg. Gyraldus, *De Poetis nostri Temp.*, ii, ed. Wotke, p. 91.

NOTES TO THE INTRODUCTION

1. This work was first published in 1860 under the title *Die Cultur der Renaissance in Italien: Ein Versuch*. Subsequent editions and translations have been numerous. Most notable were the third and later editions expanded by Ludwig Geiger and the thirteenth and later editions restored by Walter Goetz. The present translation by S. G. C. Middlemore is based on the fifteenth German edition.

   Burckhardt was born in Basel in 1818 and died there in 1897. The following recent studies are especially helpful for an appreciation of his life, works, and significance: Werner Kaegi, *Jacob Burckhardt: Eine Biographie* (Basel and Stuttgart,1947ff); Alfred von Martin, *Die Religion Jacob Burckhardts*, 2d ed. (Munich, 1947); Karl Loewith, *Von Hegel zu Nietzsche*, 3d ed. (Zurich, 1950). James Hastings Nichols has provided a stimulating introduction to his translation of Burckhardt's *Weltgeschichtliche Betrachtungen*; see *Force and Freedom: Reflections on History* (New York, 1943; reprinted Meridian Books, 1955). See also Alexander Dru's introduction to his translation, *The Letters of Jacob Burckhardt* (New York, 1955).

2. See below, p. 21; also, pp. 426-27 for a striking statement.

3. Cf. Wallace K. Ferguson, *The Renaissance in Historical Thought* (Cambridge, Mass., 1948), for the most noteworthy recent study of the "Renaissance-idea". Cf. also Carlo Angelieri, *Il problema religioso del Rinascimento: Storia della critica e bibliografia* (Florence, 1952).

4. Lynn Thorndike, who has stoutly defended his denial of the originality and distinctiveness of the Renaissance in many of his writings, takes occasion in "Renaissance or Prenaissance? (*Journal of the History of Ideas*, January 1943, Vol. IV, No. 1, pp. 63-74), to recognize that Burckhardt was seeking to delineate the "spirit" of the Renaissance but objects that "his book hardly touches the domain of intellectual history and seems to possess a will-o'-the-wisp sort of character."

5. For example: Heinrich Thode, *Franz von Assisi und die Anfänge der Kunst der Renaissance* (Berlin, 1885) and Konrad Burdach, *Vom Mittelalter zur Reformation* (Halle, 1893). For criticism of such derivations of the Renaissance from Franciscan mysticism, see Walter Goetz, "Renaissance und Antike," *Historische Zeitschrift*, CXIII (1914), 237-59; "Franz von Assisi und die Entwicklung der mittelalterlichen Religiösitat," *Archiv fur Kulturgeschichte*, XVII (1927), 129-49. For more subtly inflected efforts to trace the connections of medieval, notably Franciscan, spirituality, with the "individualism" of Petrarch and the humanists' conception of Christian perfection, see two recent papers by Dayton Phillips:

"Petrarch's Doctrine of Meditation," *Vanderbilt Studies in the Humanities,* I (1951) 251-75; *idem,* "The Way to Religious Perfection according to St. Bonaventure's *De Triplice Via." Essays in Medieval Life and Thought,* ed. J. H. Mundy, R. W. Emery, and B. N. Nelson (New York, 1955), 31-58, esp. p. 58.

6. On this tendency to select isolated parts from the pattern of the whole, see Norman Nelson, "Individualism as a Criterion of the Renaissance," *The Journal of English and Germanic Philology,* XXXII (1933), 316-34.

7. *Kunstwerke der belgischen Städte* (1842) and *Conrad von Hochstaden* (1843) in Vol. I of *Gesamtausgabe* (Stuttgart, 1930-34). Ferguson, *op. cit.,* 183. In 1847 Burckhardt had revised and enlarged Franz Kugler, *Handbuch der Geschichte der Malerei von Constantin dem Grossen bis auf die neuere Zeit* (2 vols., Berlin 1837).

8. Cf. Part VI, "Morality and Religion," esp. ch. ii, "Religion in Daily Life."

9. See below, p. 179.

10. Cf. Charles Homer Haskins, *The Renaissance of the Twelfth Century* (Cambridge, Mass., 1927), reprinted New York: Meridian Books, 1957; Erwin Panofsky, "Renaissance and Renascences," *Kenyon Review,* VI (1944), 201-36. A provocative statement of this view will be found in Johan Nordström, *Moyen-Age et Renaissance* (Paris, 1933).

11. See below, pp. 176-78.

12. See G. Voigt, *Die Wiederbelebung des classischen Altertums, oder das erste Jahrhundert des Humanismus* (Berlin, 1859); Cf. the studies by R. R. Bolgar, E. Curtius, R. Sabbadini, G. Toffanin, R. Weiss and, above all, the summing up by P. O. Kristeller, *The Classics and Renaissance Thought* (Cambridge, Mass., 1955). For a valuable survey of research on one important aspect of this theme, see Kenneth M. Setton, "The Byzantine Background to the Italian Renaissance." *Proceedings of the American Philosophical Society,* Vol. 100, No. 1 (February 1956), 1-76.

13. Perhaps the most widely appreciated of the works in this genre since the days of Burckhardt is Johan Huizinga, *The Waning of the Middle Ages* (London, 1924), now available in inexpensive reprint in Anchor Books. De Tocqueville's *Democracy in America* (1835), though not intended as a cultural history, also deserves mention in this connection.

14. Thus, Professor Herschel Baker writes: ". . . throughout the *Civilization of the Renaissance in Italy* he (Burckhardt) conceives of *Kultur* as some transcendent spiritual reality finding expression in the works of magnificent artisans. His acute aesthetic judgments are everywhere interlarded with such phrases as *Entwicklung des Individuums* and *die Entdeckung-des-Menschen und der Welt." The Dignity of Man* (Cambridge, Mass., 1947). As it happens, the phrases here given in the original by Professor Baker appeared before Burckhardt in the less forbidding French prose of Michelet, who, to be sure, was greatly influenced by Hegel. The differences between Burckhardt's version of the Renaissance and that of Hegel and Michelet need to be emphasized at least as strongly as the similarities. The whole matter deserves a special study. See, now, Ferguson, *op. cit.,* 169-194; cf. K. Loewith, "Burckhardts Stellung zu Hegels Geschichtsphilosophie," *Deutsche Vierteljahrschrift für Litteraturwissenschaft und Geistesgeschichte,* VI (1928), 719 ff.

15. See E. B. Tylor, *Primitive Culture* (London, 1871; now available in the Harper Torchbook series, New York 1958), Part I, p. 1. It may be noted that Burckhardt precedes Tylor in his scientific use of the concept of "culture". For previous uses of the term, which already appears in several senses in the pages of Kant, see A. L. Kroeber, "The Concept of Culture in Science," (1949) in *The Nature of Culture* (Chicago, 1952), 118-35, esp. at 119.

16. Burckhardt's importance as an interpreter and theoretician of culture is gaining belated recognition, at least among anthropologists. A. L. Kroeber, for example, in an essay in 1950 on "The History and Present Orientation of Cultural Anthropology," *The Nature of Culture*, Chicago, 1952, 144-51, places Burckhardt among the founders of the science in the years between 1859 and 1871 when the works of Darwin and Tylor respectively appeared.

     For recent attempts to classify "configurations," "components," and "determinants" of culture and personality, see: C. Kluckhohn, "The Study of Culture", in *The Policy Sciences*, ed. D. Lerner and Harold Lasswell (Palo Alto, California: Stanford University Press, 1951), ch v; C. Kluckhohn and H. A. Murray, eds. *Personality in Nature, Society, and Culture* (New York, 1953), Hans Gerth and C. Wright Mills, *Character and Social Structure* (New York, 1953).

17. Stuttgart, 1867.

18. See below, p. 143. This sentence, along with a number of others scattered through the work, never fails to distress professional students of the Middle Ages. It must be said in Burckhardt's defense that he did not anticipate that he would be judged only on the basis of sentences of this sort. He counted on the willingness of his readers to be discriminating both in recognizing the context of his utterances and in modulating his meanings from chapter to chapter in this book and in his previous writings. As he says with exemplary candor in his introduction: ". . . we are content if a gracious hearing be granted us, and if this book be taken and judged as a whole. It is the most serious difficulty of the history of civilization that a great intellectual process must be broken up into single, and often into what seem arbitrary, categories in order to be in any way intelligible. It was formerly our intention to fill up the gaps in this book by a special work on the art of the Renaissance—an intention, however, which we have been able only to fulfill in part." See below, p. 21. G. P. Gooch's temperate pages on Burckhardt's purposes and achievements still have something to say to merely partisan and pedantic critics of his masterpiece; *History and Historians in the Nineteenth Century*, 2nd ed. (New York, 1952), 529-33.

19. See below, p. 144.

20. Cf. Ferguson's comments in his chapter on "The Traditional Interpretation of the Renaissance in the North," *op. cit.*, pp. 253-57; *idem*, "The Interpretation of the Renaissance: Suggestions for a Synthesis," *Journal of the History of Ideas*, XII (1951), p. 48. The outcomes of the broad construction of the term may be noted in Myron Gilmore, *The World of Humanism* (New York, 1952) and chapters on the Renaissance gathered and edited by G. R. Potter as the first volume of *The New Cambridge Modern History* (Cambridge, 1958).

21. See below, p. 143.

22. For an interesting sidelight on this problem of the nature of the state and orientations to it, see J. H. Hexter, *"Il principe* and *lo stato," Studies on the*

Renaissance, IV (1957), 113-38. There are helpful studies on political life and theory by R. von Albertini, H. Baron, E. Emerton, A. Gewirth, Allen H. Gilbert, Felix Gilbert, N. Rubenstein, N. Valeri and others.

23. See below, pp. 26, 27-28.

24. Expressions of this viewpoint may be found in the writings of F. Antal, Hans Baron, E. P. Cheyney, Alfred Doren, Arnold Hauser, Halvdan Koht, Gino Luzzatto, Y. Renouard, Armando Sapori, Ferdinand Schevill, W. Sombart, Edgar Zilsel, and others. An attempt to suggest certain shortcomings in the usual formulations of this issue and to connect the problem with the hypotheses of Max Weber concerning the Protestant ethic and the "spirit of capitalism" will be found in B. N. Nelson, "The Usurer and the Merchant Prince. Italian Businessmen and the Ecclesiastical Law of Restitution, 1100-1550," *The Journal of Economic History* (annual supplemental issue), VII (1947), 104-22; Cf. *idem, The Idea of Usury: From Tribal Brotherhood to Universal Otherhood* (Princeton, 1949), esp. pp. 18-28.

25. For especially helpful introductions to the sources and problems, see the recent writings of Raymond de Roover, Yves Renouard, and Armando Sapori. (The latter's collected papers and the essays recently published in his honor are mines of information.) Iris Origo has just published a lively documentary account of the life and far-flung business career of an outstanding fourteenth-century merchant, Francesco di Marco Datini of Prato; *A Merchant of Prato* (New York, 1957).

26. For example, see below, p. 361. Indispensable material on the cultural and economic setting of the production of art in the Renaissance will be found in M. Wackernagl, *Der Lebensraum des Künstlers in der florentinischen Renaissance* (Leipzig, 1938). R. S. Lopez has recently taken the extreme view that leading citizens invested in arts because of the shrinkage of alternative opportunities for gain in the domestic and foreign markets. This is an elaboration of a special thesis concerning the "crisis" or "stagnation" of the late medieval and Renaissance business scene adopted in recent years by a number of economic historians of Europe. See Lopez, "Hard Times and Investment in Culture," *Renaissance News,* Vol. V (1952), pp. 61-63.

27. See below, pp. 180-82.

28. Cf. Haskins, *op. cit.,* chs. iv., v., ix. On the other hand, as P. O. Kristeller has pointed out, while "the Middle Ages possessed a significant selection of classical literature," "Renaissance humanism extended its knowledge almost to the entire range of its extant remains . . ." and, "the entire range of Greek philosophical and scientific literature was made more completely available to the West than it had been in the Middle Ages or in Roman antiquity . . ." *The Classics and Renaissance Thought,* pp. 17, 23.

29. See below, p. 204.

30. Cf. on the one hand, the various writings of Giuseppe Toffanin, of which his *Storia dell'umanesimo* (Naples, 1933) has been recently translated into English by Elio Gianturco, *History of Humanism* (New York, 1954). On the other side may be mentioned Eugenio Garin, *L'umanesimo italiano* (Bari, 1952).

31. P. O. Kristeller, *op. cit.*, p. 12 and "Humanism and Scholasticism in the Italian Renaissance," *Studies in Renaissance Thought and Letters* (Rome, 1956), 553-83.

32. Kristeller, *The Classics and Renaissance Thought*, pp. 11-14.

33. Kristeller emphasizes that these five disciplines of grammar, rhetoric, poetry, history and moral philosophy comprise the *studia humanitatis* of the humanists; cf. works previously cited. Thorndike reserves his only words of praise for this part of Burckhardt's book. "Of its six parts, the third on the Revival of Antiquity seems to me scholarly and just, recognizing the defects as well as the merits of the Italian humanists and containing many bits of illuminating detail." *loc. cit.*, p. 69.

34. See below, p. 229.

35. See below, p. 272.

36. See below, p. 274.

37. Especially Thorndike, *op. cit.*, pp. 71-3; *Science and Thought in the Fifteenth Century* (New York, 1929), Introduction. George Sarton made perhaps the most violent statements about the humanists and the Renaissance on the grounds of their lack of contribution to the history of science in his lecture "Science in the Renaissance," in *The Civilization of the Renaissance* (Chicago, 1929). However, cf. his more recent books on science in the Renaissance: *The Appreciation of Ancient and Medieval Science during the Renaissance, 1450-1600* (Philadelphia, 1955); and *Six Wings: Men of Science in the Renaissance* (Bloomington, Ind., 1957) where he takes a more moderate view.

38. A. R. Hall has recently written: "Obviously . . . rigid adherence to the fruits of humanistic scholarship did not yield the renaissance of scientific activity beginning in the late fifteenth century. Rather it sprang from the fertile conjunction of elements in medieval science with others derived from rediscovered antiquity." *The Scientific Revolution, 1500-1800* (New York, 1954), p. 9. An impressive summary of medieval and early modern developments is found in A. C. Crombie, *From Augustine to Galileo: The History of Science, A.D. 400-1650* (London, 1952; Cambridge, Mass., 1953) esp. Chs. iv. and v. and bibliography. Cf. also Ernest Moody, "Galileo and Avempace," *Journal of the History of Ideas,* XII (1951), 163-93, 375-422.

39. Cf. Kristeller, "Humanism and Scholasticism," *Studies in Renaissance Thought and Letters.* Also Eugenio Garin, *La disputa delle arti nel Quattrocento* (Florence, 1948).

40. Cf. Marshall Clagett, *Giovanni Marliani and Late Medieval Physics* (New York, 1941); J. H. Randall, Jr., "Development of the Scientific Method in the School of Padua," *Journal of the History of Ideas,* I (1940), 177-206.

41. See below, p. 286.

42. See below, p. 292.

43. "On His Own Ignorance," Eng. trans., by Hans Nachod in Cassirer, Kristeller and Randall, eds. *The Renaissance Philosophy of Man* (Chicago, 1948), p. 105.

44. Most emphatic in urging this aspect of humanism is Hans Baron, *The Crisis of the Early Italian Renaissance* (Princeton, 1955). Cf. also Eugenio Garin, *Umanesimo e vita civile* (Florence, 1947).

NOTES TO THE INTRODUCTION

45. Charles Trinkaus, "Petrarch's Views of the Individual and His Society," *Osiris,* XI (1954), 169-198, as well as *Adversity's Noblemen: The Italian Humanists on Happiness* (New York, 1940).

46. In addition to the well-known influence on Bembo and as expressed through him on Castiglione in *Il Cortegiano*, Rudolf Wittkower, *Architectural Principles in the Age of Humanism* (London, 1949) and Charles de Tolnay, *Michelangelo*, II, *The Sistine Ceiling* (Princeton, 1945) may be mentioned for their exposition of the application of Christian-Neoplatonism in architecture and painting.

47. Cf. P. O. Kristeller, "The Scholastic Background of Marsilio Ficino," *Studies in Renaissance Thought and Letters*, p. 35-55, and his *The Philosophy of Marsilio Ficino* (New York, 1943); Eugenio Garin, *Giovanni Pico della Mirandola, Vita e dottrina* (Florence, 1937).

48. See below, p. 516.

49. See below, p. 479.

50. Translated as *Force and Freedom: Reflections on History* (New York, 1943), pp. 79-103.

51. See below, p. 427.

52. See below, p. 442.

53. See below, p. 273.

54. See below, pp. 442-43.

55. K. Loewith, *Von Hegel zu Nietzsche,* esp. 324-6; cf. A. von Martin's comparison of Burckhardt with Kierkegaard, *Die Religion Jacob Burckhardts*, 216-55, esp. at pp. 252-53.

INDEX TO VOLUME I & II

INDEX

xxii

INDEX

INDEX

INDEX

INDEX

INDEX

INDEX

Marcus, King, 157
Marcus Aurelius, 330
Margaret of Anjou, 390
Maria, Giovan, 386
Mariano da Genazzano, Fra, 458
Marignano, Marquis of, Castellan of Musso, 44, 173
Marignolli, Curzio, 165
Mariolatry, 467 sqq.
Marriages, morganatic, 40
Marsuppini, Carlo, 236
Martial, 269
Martin V, Pope, 120, 220, 261
Martius, Galeottus (Galleoto), 479, 480
Masks, 401, 413, 415, 419
Massimi family, the, 190
Massuccio, 446-447
Matteo da Siena, 407
Maupertius, battle of, 115
Maximilian I, Emperor, 37, 58, 60, 62, 117, 142
Maximilian, King of the Romans, 127
Mazzoni, Guido, 407
Medici, Alessandro de', 40, 80-81, 141, 162
Medici, Clarice de', 393
Medici, Cosimo de', 100, 165, 173, 197, 198, 201, 204, 227, 234, 355, 357, 360, 366, 440, 479, 485, 513
Medici, Giovanni de', Cardinal, 80, 126, 136, 199. See also Leo X, Pope
Medici, Giuliano de', 78, 80, 136, 456
Medici, Giulio de', Cardinal, 80, 112. See also Clement VII, Pope
Medici, Ippolito de', Cardinal, 38-40, 291
Medici, Lorenzino de', 80-81, 162
Medici, Lorenzo I de' (the Magnificent), 44, 73, 78, 100, 109, 114, 126, 136-137, 147, 155, 167, 199, 227-228, 319, 346, 349, 351, 355, 381, 425, 456, 491, 515
Medici, Lorenzo II de', 104, 136
Medici, Maddalena de', 126
Medici, Pietro I de', 227, 360, 459
Medici, Pietro II de', 360
Medici family, the, 78, 79, 80, 358, 381, 449, 459, 510
Medicine, 285-286
Meditations (Marcus Aurelius), 330

Meinwerk of Paderborn, 324
Meleager (pantomime), 411
Menageries, 286 sqq., 290
Menander, 200
Meneghino (mask), 317
Merlinus Coccaius, 271
Michelangelo, 79, 81, 172, 380, 468
Micheletto, Don, 127
Michiel, Cardinal, 132
Milan, 40, 43, 59-60, 317, 363, 373, 394, 411, 417, 437, 470, 505
Milan, Cathedral, 33, 455
Milan, Dukes of—see Sforza
Milano-Venetian war, 117-118
Minnesänger, the, 151, 163
Mirabilia Romæ, 183
Miracles, 407
Mirandola, Pico della (Giovanni), 50, 137, 208, 210, 227, 351-352, 460, 492, 512, 515
Mistresses of princes, 72-74, 395
Mocenigo, Doge, 93
Modena, 66
Mohammed, 475
Mohammed II, Sultan, 90, 110, 112
Mohammedans and Islam, 24, 473, 474 sqq.
Molza, Francesco Mario, 162, 269
Mongajo, Andrea, 209
Monica, 479
Monks and mendicant orders, 446 sqq.
Mont Ventoux, 296
Montani, Cola de', 78
Monte Amiata, 50, 299
Montefeltro, Federigo, of Urbino, 38, 43, 63 sqq., 116, 199, 200, 204, 234, 242, 321, 384
Montefeltro, Guidobaldo, 65, 66, 134, 379, 488, 506
Montefeltro family, the, 38, 60
Montesecco, 78
Montone, Braccio di, 441-442
Morality, 426 sqq.
Morgante Maggiore, the, 462, 476
Moses, 475
Mount Pilatus, 508
Mucius Scævola, 237

xxix

INDEX

Musattus (Mussatus, Mussato), Albertinus (Albertino), 152, 157, 216
Music and musical composition, 385 *sqq.*
Musuros, Marcos, 205
Mysteries, the, 401, 402, 405 *sqq.*
Mysticism, medieval, 516
Mythology, 261, 264, 315, 419

Naples, 34, 51 *sqq.*, 114, 155, 156, 232, 356, 362, 363, 373, 417, 437, 439-440, 446, 505
Naples, University of, 24
Napoleon I, 417
National unity, 142
Nations described, 334 *sqq.*
Natural History (Pliny), 229
Natural science, 283 *sqq.*
Navagero, Andrea, 267, 268
Negro, Girolamo, 138
Nencia da Barberino, 349, 351
Niccoli, Niccolò, 197-198, 204, 224-225, 355-356, 479
Niccolò da Uzzano, 266
Niccolò da Verona, 448
Nicholas V, Pope, 122, 196-197, 201, 204, 229, 234, 236, 245, 407, 479
Nieto, Fra Tommaso, 471
Ninfale d' Ameto, 261
Ninfale Fiesolano, 261
Nobility, 354 *sqq.*
Nola, 187
Norcia, witches of, 500, 501
Norman empire of Frederick II, 24
Normandy, 356
"Nove" and "Popolari" parties, 431
Novelists, morality of, 434 *sqq.*

"Oath of the Pheasant," 404
Oaths, 431
Observantines, the, 453, 459
Ochis, Andreolo de, 200
Oddi-Baglioni feud, the, 45 *sqq.*
Olgiati, Girolamo, 78, 79
Olivier de la Marche, 404
Omens, 494
On the Infelicity of the Scholar, 275-276
On the Sober Life, 332-333
Opus Macaronicorum, 167

Oratory in Latin, 239 *sqq.*
Orbetello, 43
Orchestra, the, 385 *sqq.*
Ordelaffo, 480
Order of the Golden Spur, the, 74
Order of St Stephen, the, 357
Orlandino, the, 167, 323, 450
Orlando Furioso, 322-323
Orsini, Cardinal, 132, 504
Orsini family, the, 120, 128, 129, 323
Otranto, 112
Ovid, 155, 232, 460

Pacciolo (Paccioli), Fra Luca, 228, 286
Padovano, Paolo, 157
Padua, 31, 83, 155, 157, 205, 209, 232, 465, 490
Pagan elements in Catholicism, 464, 468, 483, 505
Pagolo, Maestro, 485
Palazzo Schifanoja, 74, 418, 490
Palermo, 402
Palestrina, 385
Palmieri, Matteo, 217, 249
Pandolfini, Agnolo, 145, 397, 514-515
Pandolfini, Pierfilippo, 227
Pandoni, Gian Antonio Porcello dei, 117
Panormita, Antonio, 231, 328
Pantalone (Mask), 316
Pantomime, 401, 410-411
Papacy, the, 120 *sqq.*, 445-446, 450
Papal secretaries, 236
Paracelsus, 509
Parma, 155, 190, 438
Parody, 166-167
Parthenice, the, 262
Pasolini family, the, 42
Pasquino, and the pasquinades, 169, 170
Paul II, Pope, 123, 189-190, 230, 258, 277, 326, 419, 422, 431, 483, 506
Paul III, Pope, 49, 140, 141, 205, 270, 485
Paul IV, Pope, 141, 205
Paul of Bagdad, 484
Pavia, 205, 456; battle of, 44; Certosa of, 33
Pazzi, Andrea de', 224
Pazzi, Giacomo, 496

INDEX

INDEX

INDEX

INDEX

INDEX